Daring to Struggle

Daring to Struggle

China's Global Ambitions under Xi Jinping

BATES GILL

OXFORD
UNIVERSITY PRESS

Oxford University Press is a department of the University of Oxford. It furthers the University's objective of excellence in research, scholarship, and education by publishing worldwide. Oxford is a registered trade mark of Oxford University Press in the UK and certain other countries.

Published in the United States of America by Oxford University Press
198 Madison Avenue, New York, NY 10016, United States of America.

© Oxford University Press 2022

Library of Congress Cataloging-in-Publication Data
Names: Gill, Bates, author.
Title: Daring to struggle : China's global ambitions under Xi Jinping /
Bates Gill.
Description: New York, NY : Oxford University Press, 2022. |
Includes bibliographical references and index.
Identifiers: LCCN 2022001977 (print) | LCCN 2022001978 (ebook) |
ISBN 9780197545645 (hardback) | ISBN 9780197545669 (epub)
Subjects: LCSH: China—Foreign relations—21st century. | China—Foreign
economic relations. | China—Military policy. |
Geopolitics—Indo-Pacific Region. | Xi, Jinping
Classification: LCC JZ1734 .G559 2022 (print) | LCC JZ1734 (ebook) |
DDC 327.51—dc23/eng/20220218
LC record available at https://lccn.loc.gov/2022001977
LC ebook record available at https://lccn.loc.gov/2022001978

DOI: 10.1093/oso/9780197545645.001.0001

3 5 7 9 8 6 4 2
Printed by Integrated Books International, United States of America

To Chris and J.P.

"Where words fail, music speaks."

Hans Christian Andersen

Contents

Illustrations

Acknowledgments

Book writing affords many pleasures. Chief among them is thanking those who had a hand in the book's fruition. After all, while writing can be a solitary enterprise, the writer is never truly alone. Instead, in the long hours of transforming thoughts to page, I find myself surrounded by the ideas and insights of colleagues past and present, old and new, all engaged in profound and raucous debate. The global community of China-watchers has changed over the past 40 years, as has China itself. But I have always benefitted from a spirit of kinship among that community—whether in the Americas, Africa, Europe, the Indo-Pacific, or in China—drawn together by an abiding fascination with Chinese culture, language, history, and the country's current affairs. While this book's words are my own, they are enriched by the work of so many who endeavor to understand China's growing impact—for better and for worse—on our world.

Specifically, my profound thanks go to all those who took the time to comment on all or parts of the work's initial drafts, provide timely advice, or share valuable insights, information, and assistance over the course of the project, from conception to completion. These esteemed colleagues include Dennis Blasko, Chris Buckley, Mathieu Duchâtel, Elizabeth Economy, John Fitzgerald, Chas Freeman, Evelyn Goh, Eric Hagt, Peter Hamman, Kai He, Chin-hao Huang, Yun Jiang, Alastair Iain Johnston, Eunok Lee, Evan Medeiros, Adam Ni, James Reilly, David Shambaugh, and Tom Waldman. My thanks as well to my students in the 2020 Professional and Community Engagement (PACE) program at Macquarie University for their research contributions.

In addition, many colleagues in China have been generous with their time and insights over the years, helping me better understand the country and its people. Unfortunately, politics and the pandemic have combined to put greater distance between us, but I continue to learn from you.

A grateful vote of thanks also goes to the anonymous experts who, tasked by Oxford University Press, helpfully provided thorough and constructive feedback to improve the final product in numerous ways. These folks collectively contributed much to strengthening the book; the remaining flaws are my own.

I was also fortunate to affiliate with a number of institutions over the past several years that provided me with both the time and collegial intellectual atmosphere to think, test ideas, write, and publish. My former department chair Ben Schreer, with support from Deputy Vice Chancellor for Research Sakkie Praetorius and Dean Martina Möllering, brought me on board to Macquarie

University in 2017 and encouraged this book project from the start. A productive stint as the inaugural Scholar in Residence with the Asia Society Australia between 2020 and 2022 offered numerous occasions to sharpen my thinking; engage with leading experts, officials, and business executives; and promote my ideas. Many thanks to the organization's leadership—Chief Executive Officer Philipp Ivanov and Executive Director Thomas Soem—and their entire team for the opportunity to work with them. It has also been an honor and pleasure to serve since 2020 as a Senior Associate Fellow with the Royal United Services Institute (RUSI) in London, and I extend my grateful thanks to colleagues there, especially RUSI's director-general Karin von Hippel as well as Neil Melvin and Veerle Nouwens.

David McBride, my editor at Oxford University Press in New York, has supported this book from the day we first discussed its outlines in early 2020. He has marshaled a remarkable catalog on China-related topics in recent years, and I am delighted to publish with OUP once again and be a part of that tradition.

Beyond these professional circles, many others catalyzed my work and encouraged the book's progress in ways large and small. To my mates on the North Sydney Bears baseball club, thanks for the many years of friendship and making this Yank feel welcome, the chance to play the game I love, and a once-weekly respite from work-a-day worries. Our much-loved Airedale, Mojo—whether snoozing softly at my feet or encouraging me to get out for some fresh air—was a constant companion and ready reminder of the good things in life.

Three people in particular deserve special thanks. In dedicating this book to Chris Simpson and J. P. Fisher, I was drawn to the words of Kurt Vonnegut, who wrote, "Virtually every writer I know would rather be a musician." These two dear and talented friends encouraged that volition in me, for which I am forever grateful. Finally, my greatest thanks and appreciation go to Dr. Sarah Palmer, my loving wife (and resident virologist), who remains as always a never-ending source of inspiration and great joy, just as she has been since we first started life together in China more than 35 years ago.

Bates Gill
Balmain East, New South Wales, Australia
February 2022

Introduction

Understanding China's Global Ambitions
under Xi Jinping

*All the struggle, sacrifice, and creation through which the Party has
united and led the Chinese people over the past hundred years has been
tied together by one ultimate theme—bringing about the great rejuvenation of the Chinese nation.*

—Xi Jinping, July 2021[1]

Why This Book?

"What does China want from the world?" I asked. An old and dear colleague
from China, now well established in Shanghai and among the most privileged
persons in the country, responded with an unexpected passion: "To be respected
in the world and receive our due. You will have to get used to it." Despite and because of our great friendship, I was more concerned than consoled.

His forceful answer was clear. But China's future pathway is not. Increasingly
powerful, prosperous, and authoritarian, China has become a more intense
and successful competitor with the world's established powers—economically,
technologically, diplomatically, militarily, and in influencing people's hearts
and minds. But its rise and growing influence on the global stage present major
challenges to governments and societies around the world, which react with
growing concern. As large-scale polling by the Pew Research Center shows,
"While majorities in most countries agree China's influence on the world stage
has grown markedly, this has not necessarily translated into favorable views
of the country."[2] The most negative views toward China emanate largely from
Western and wealthy countries as well as from countries in China's immediate
neighborhood, including the United States, Canada, Australia, Japan, European
nations, India, and South Korea. Countries such as the United States, Canada,
the United Kingdom, Sweden, and Australia have seen particularly precipitous
drops in favorability ratings toward China in recent years.

These increased concerns about China have become more acute since
Xi Jinping's ascent to paramount leadership in 2012 and his subsequent

Daring to Struggle. Bates Gill, Oxford University Press. © Oxford University Press 2022.
DOI: 10.1093/oso/9780197545645.003.0001

consolidation of power. Under his leadership, the People's Republic of China (PRC or China) has pursued a far more ambitious foreign policy agenda with profound effects on regional security, economic and technological competition, and world order. Having celebrated the 100th anniversary of the Chinese Communist Party (CCP or Party) in 2021, Chinese leaders now turn their sights toward achieving the long-held ambition of "the great rejuvenation of the Chinese nation"—to become a fully modernized, prosperous, respected, and leading world power in the coming decades. As China's top leader, Xi personifies the country's apparent determination to do all that is necessary in order to realize such achievements. In a commonly repeated refrain, Xi calls on the Party and the Chinese people to "dare to struggle" (敢于斗争) against the many challenges he sees confronting China's aspirations at home and abroad.[3] However, in doing so, China now faces a far more contested strategic environment, and with it the rising risk of greater tensions and even conflict in the Indo-Pacific region and beyond.

Given these stakes, a deeper understanding of "what China wants"—the underlying strategic objectives that motivate Xi Jinping and his country's global ambitions—will remain a matter of intense interest to foreign policy practitioners, business leaders, China specialists, and students of global affairs, as well as interested publics around the world. That is where this book comes in, by offering a timely, comprehensive, and accessible treatment of the fundamental aims motivating China's international pursuits in the Xi Jinping era.

Yet, in spite of China's spectacular ascent on the world stage and growing impact on the daily lives of people around the globe, there are relatively few books on what drives the country's global ambitions under Xi's leadership. Moreover, fewer still would appeal to a relatively wide, well-informed audience—neither densely theoretical and academic nor resorting to polemics and populist pandering. Instead, this book aspires to complement and build on the excellent work of specialists on PRC politics and foreign policy in recent years who bridge the gap between nuanced, accessible scholarship on the one hand and real-world, practical policy relevance on the other.[4]

That said, while this book presents a coherent framework for understanding China's motivations and actions on the world stage, it does not purport to uncover a Chinese "grand strategy." Nor is the book narrowly intended to inform official policy in any one country. Rather, its analysis, findings, and recommendations aim to educate a broad audience around the globe—policymakers and diplomats, corporate executives and business owners, scholarly experts and students, and other globally engaged practitioners and observers—and do so in three broad areas.

First, this book seeks to introduce and clarify the fundamental objectives underlying Beijing's international behavior and make them plainly understood.

Contrary to the views of some observers of PRC foreign policy, this book demonstrates that Beijing's objectives are not "secret" or all that deceptive.[5] For decades, important statements from the Party, government, and other PRC institutions and individuals—including from leadership speeches, official summations of important high-level conferences, white papers, well-connected experts, and other authoritative sources—have explained the country's foreign policy objectives. Sometimes they are expressed in the arcane language of Party discourse and hence can be perceived as vague gibberish or purposeful obfuscation when read out of context, but they are readily available for analysis and interpretation and not hidden. The six fundamental drivers that form the crux of this book are not in any way an official Chinese framework, but they are distilled from openly observable expressions of strategic intent from authoritative sources on the one hand and their implementation on the ground on the other. My express hope in writing this book is that its framework for understanding PRC foreign policy brings greater clarity to China's international actions, which in turn informs and strengthens the responses of countries, societies, institutions, and individuals affected by them.

Second, the book aims to present a comprehensive picture of the many diverse measures Beijing employs on the international scene in pursuit of the six fundamental foreign policy drivers at the heart of this volume, providing an up-to-date catalog of the PRC toolkit abroad, including in the economic, diplomatic, political, military, cultural, and ideational realms. Detailing every official PRC undertaking overseas is impossible, but the book intends to give a wide-ranging sense of the growing scale and scope—and intended impact—of China's increasingly dynamic international presence in the Xi Jinping era.

Third, this book is about both the opportunities and challenges facing China's global ambitions. The PRC has never been in a stronger position to make good on its goal to emerge as a global great power—powerful, prosperous, and respected. It is also clear that the Chinese leadership is determined to seize the opportunity before them and achieve this aspiration. But as this book explains—and as the PRC leadership understands—there are many obstacles ahead in this quest and they loom larger and larger. In many respects, Beijing's very pursuit of legitimacy, sovereignty, wealth, power, leadership, and ideas has generated its own challenges as countries and societies in China's neighborhood and farther afield rethink their relationship with the rising power. And China has its own domestic problems that can thwart its leaders' expectations as well. In taking these challenges to Chinese ambitions into full account, this book aims to present a nuanced but realistic assessment of China's future role on the world stage.

What's Different about This Book?

While building on prior work, this book takes a different approach. First, rather than following a traditional structure with chapters on foreign policy issues (for example, trade relations, climate change, human rights) or certain global regions (PRC relations with Africa, the Middle East, or the United States), this book goes deeper to explore the most important strategic objectives that motivate China's foreign policy today and for the future. Doing so illuminates the fundamental nexus between strategy and action, clarifying not just the what and how, but the *why* of Chinese international behavior. Each of the core chapters, introduced here in more detail, focuses on one of the six fundamental drivers that increasingly shape Chinese foreign policy in the Xi Jinping era: legitimacy, sovereignty, wealth, power, leadership, and ideas. As shown in Figure I.1, structuring the book in this way establishes a coherent framework on which the complexities of China's expanding global presence today can be readily understood.[6]

Second, this book is purposely timed to inform our thinking about China at a critically important turning point in its contemporary history. As Xi Jinping and his supporters frequently proclaim, his ascent to power in 2012 marked the beginning of a "new era" for China, at home and abroad. By nearly all outward appearances, Xi has steadily built up the foundations of that new era—some would say for better, some would say for worse.[7] Now a decade into Xi's leadership, and as he looks ahead to sustain his power and influence for at least another decade or more, China is better positioned than ever to realize its grand ambitions. But whether it succeeds or not, and with or without Xi Jinping at the helm, China has the potential to transform global affairs more in the next

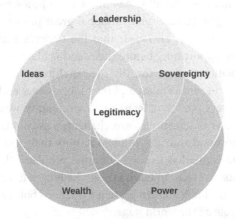

Figure I.1 Six fundamental objectives motivating PRC foreign policy

10 years than it has over the past 30. A clear understanding of the Chinese object-ives driving that transformation is needed now more than ever.

A few clarifications are in order about the book's overall approach. First, the six fundamental objectives at the center of this book—legitimacy, sovereignty, wealth, power, leadership, and ideas—are not entirely new. Many of these have been long-held goals of Chinese leaders dating back a century-and-a-half. What differentiates them in the Xi Jinping era is the relative importance each has gained as a critical element of PRC foreign policy strategy and the political and economic resources that have been devoted toward their realization.

Next, while the framework identifies six key objectives driving PRC for-eign policy, Figure I.1 illustrates they do not stand alone from one another, but in fact often overlap. This figure depicts in graphic form the reality that these goals are pursued concurrently and, if possible, synergistically. At the center of the diagram, where all six objectives most overlap, sits the highest-priority objective of all—legitimacy of the CCP—toward which all the other objectives must ultimately contribute. Readers should also take note that when describing specific PRC policy initiatives and activities abroad, the book ascribes them to one of the six fundamental foreign policy objectives. So, for example, the Belt and Road Initiative is discussed in relation to the wealth objective, and cross-Strait relations are covered largely in the chapter on sovereignty. While this approach aims for clarity and concision, it is un-derstood that some readers might categorize PRC international activities differently. With that in mind, the book regularly identifies and explains how different PRC activities abroad often serve multiple foreign policy objectives.

Organization of the Book

The core chapters of the book are preceded by a scene-setter, chapter 1. This chapter provides some background on the "period of strategic opportunity" that Chinese leaders saw before them—roughly the 20 to 25 years between the late 1990s and 2020—that would, in their view, favor China's rise and establish the foundation on which to realize the long-standing aspiration of restoring China's greatness—the so-called China Dream. The chapter places Xi Jinping's ascent to power within the larger context of that national dream and explains how Xi's background and life experiences have shaped his leadership in pursuit of it. The chapter then brings us up to date by outlining the many steps Xi has taken in his first 10 years as paramount leader, at home and abroad, to consolidate Party power, assert PRC interests more confidently, and lay the foundation for China to realize national rejuvenation.

Chapters 2 through 7 form the heart of the book and take each of the six funda-mental PRC foreign policy objectives in turn. Each of these core chapters is simi-larly organized. They begin by first defining and explaining the importance of the fundamental objective covered in that particular chapter and then going on to describe the most significant current and likely future policies, initiatives, and ac-tivities the Chinese leadership will carry out to achieve that objective. Chapter 2 addresses the most important objective driving PRC foreign policy: maintaining and bolstering the legitimacy and survival of the Chinese Communist Party. This effort means seeking the acceptance, appreciation, and even approbation of for-eign governments and societies for the PRC's system of governance, domestic policies, and pursuit of overseas interests. The chapter explains how the CCP legitimates and strengthens its rule through certain foundational foreign policy narratives: the Party alone best understands and represents the ideological tides of history that favor the continued advancement of "socialism with Chinese characteristics"; the Party alone is responsible for ending the "century of shame" at the hands of foreigners and maintaining vigilance against continuing foreign threats; the Party alone has succeeded in delivering economic development and international respect for China; and the Party alone has the rightful claim to be the steward of China's cultural heritage. Chapter 2 goes on to show how, under Xi Jinping, the pursuit of legitimacy has assumed a much more prominent place in PRC external relations, including through a more active role for the Party in developing and executing of the country's foreign policy. The centrality of CCP legitimacy as a driver of PRC foreign policy behavior is a recurring theme throughout the book.

Chapter 3 defines and explains the second fundamental driver shaping PRC foreign policy: assertion and defense of the broadest possible claims of Chinese sovereignty. This chapter adopts an expansive definition of sovereignty that includes the achievement of national unity and territorial integrity behind se-cure frontiers, immunity from foreign intimidation, and freedom from sub-version or intervention by other states and actors. But for the purposes of this book, the discussion of sovereignty also includes broader aims of securing strategic advantage and its denial to potential enemies at a regional and even global level, protecting economic assets and PRC citizens abroad, accessing resources essential for national power and economic development, and oper-ating more freely within the international system—less bound by constraints Beijing sees in a U.S.-led, Western-oriented world order. The chapter provides a background history explaining how matters of sovereignty have come to oc-cupy such a central place in the minds of Chinese leaders, and how Xi Jinping's sharper, more expansive, and riskier approach to sovereignty differs from that of his predecessors. Chapter 3 also specifically examines how the pursuit of sover-eignty in certain contested spaces—the Himalayas, South China Sea, East China

Sea, Taiwan, Xinjiang, Tibet, and Hong Kong—greatly exacerbates China's foreign relationships, deeply affects perceptions of China abroad, and could be the source of conflict in the years ahead.

Chapter 4, "Wealth," addresses the generation of national wealth and economic prosperity, the third key driver of PRC foreign policy. The chapter describes how the pursuit of economic development has been a constant element in PRC foreign policy as it bolsters CCP legitimacy and contributes to amassing national power and achieving national rejuvenation. Chapter 4 also explains why and how the pursuit of national wealth and economic prosperity depended—and continues to depend—so heavily on relations with the outside world. Subsequent sections in the chapter identify and describe critically important and persistent challenges facing the PRC economy and a number of initiatives launched by Xi Jinping to address them—including the Belt and Road Initiative and a renewed drive for indigenous innovation and technological advancement—all of which have significant implications for Beijing's foreign relations.

Turning to a fourth key driver, Chapter 5 focuses on China's pursuit of hard power and its exercise through economic leverage and military coercion. Following a discussion of what is meant by "hard power," the chapter describes how China has developed its economic leverage and military capabilities and how in turn they are linked with other fundamental foreign policy objectives such as legitimacy and sovereignty. Chapter 5 goes on to detail numerous specific examples to show how China employs its growing economic and military strength to shape the choices of others in directions that are more aligned with PRC interests and ambitions. These examples include embargoes and other punitive economic measures, economic inducements and assistance, muscle-flexing and shows of force by the People's Liberation Army (PLA), and an expanding PLA presence around China's periphery and farther afield. The chapter also argues that under Xi Jinping, Chinese leaders have increasingly embraced economic and military coercion as valuable instruments in pursuit of foreign policy interests and will likely use these tools even more actively in the years ahead.

Chapter 6 looks at China's pursuit of greater leadership roles across a range of international activities. This chapter begins with a background section explaining the PRC's approach to international leadership in the past and how, under Xi Jinping, taking on leadership roles and "moving closer to center stage" have become increasingly prominent objectives animating the country's foreign policy. Subsequent sections detail how and why the PRC has pursued greater leadership responsibilities internationally, especially under Xi, including: expanded contributions and leadership positions within the UN system; establishing new multilateral institutions such as the Asian Infrastructure Investment Bank, the New Development Bank, and the "17 + 1" process, linking China with 17 Central and Eastern European countries; and aspirations to leadership in emerging fields of governance and technology, including in mitigating climate change, managing cyberspace, addressing global health challenges, and setting standards in advanced technological fields such as artificial intelligence, quantum computing and information science, and renewable energy.

Chapter 7 focuses on ideas and opens with a discussion of how their propagation has played an important part in the PRC's engagement with the world. The chapter then examines how, under Xi Jinping, the use of ideas, influence, and images to persuade others to favor China's interests has become an essential and increasingly well-resourced element of PRC foreign relations. Subsequent sections of chapter 7 detail how Beijing goes about "telling China's story well" and seeks to build up its "international narrative (or discourse) power" (国际话语权), with a particular focus on three Party organizations—the Central United Front Work Department, the Central Propaganda Department, and the Central International Liaison Department—which have as a crucial part of their mission the dissemination of officially approved ideas and information to overseas audiences. The chapter concludes with a discussion of the "big ideas" that China is seeking to promote on the world stage and why. While many of these ideas are not necessarily new, they *are* novel in two important respects. The first is the power and presence that Beijing can bring to bear within the international system to have these ideas heard and heeded. Second, because of China's greater power and presence, its ideas have greater potential to transform the norms and practices of the international system in ways that are more conducive to PRC interests.

Chapter 8 takes each of the six key foreign policy drivers in turn and assesses the challenges China faces in pursuing them. The chapter makes the point that in spite of China's outward confidence in world affairs, the country increasingly confronts a range of problems for its foreign relations. Indeed, the very pursuit of its foreign policy ambitions—while often bolstering national confidence—creates problems at home and abroad that will hold China back and could derail Xi's vision for national rejuvenation. These challenges include increasing intolerance toward unwelcome and illegal PRC influence activities abroad, growing unhappiness with China's unfair economic practices, increasing concerns over Beijing's use of economic and military coercion, intensifying criticism of China's increasingly authoritarian political system, and mounting discomfort with China's effort to shape international institutions and norms in ways that favor PRC interests.

Taking stock of the book's findings, the concluding chapter looks ahead. It argues that in spite of the many challenges facing Xi Jinping's approach to world affairs, his overriding concern with regime security means China will double down and "dare to struggle" to overcome them. This approach will mean even stronger expectations of respect for Party legitimacy, more forceful assertions of

PRC sovereignty, more urgency in generating wealth and securing hard power, and even greater ambitions to realize Chinese leadership and ideas on the world stage. As a result, an even more contested future lies ahead for China's relations with the world. With that expectation in mind, the final chapter also considers the implications of that future for other key powers in the Indo-Pacific—especially the United States and its allies and partners in the region—and puts forward some succinct proposals in response to the PRC's foreign policy in the 2020s and beyond. The United States, its allies, and its other partners should aim to deepen their understanding of China's strengths and weaknesses, establish stronger countervailing coalitions where needed, build greater resilience against unwelcome aspects of China's international behavior, prepare for an intensifying competition of ideas with China, and where possible, continue to seek common ground with China where interests overlap. Looking ahead, we should expect—and prepare for—a continuing struggle over what China wants in the world.

1

Opportunities 机遇

Seeking National Rejuvenation

The tide of history is mighty. Those who follow it will prosper, while
those who resist it will perish. . . . A prosperous and stable world
provides China with opportunities. . . . Whether we succeed in our
pursuit of peaceful development to a large extent hinges on whether
we can turn opportunities in the rest of the world into China's
opportunities.

—Xi Jinping, January 2013[1]

A China Dream

Since the late 1970s, when Chinese leader Deng Xiaoping embraced a policy of
"reform and opening," the People's Republic of China (PRC or China) embarked
on a pathway to realize a rare and historic opportunity: regaining the country's
status as one of the world's most prosperous and powerful nations. This dream
of national rejuvenation did not originate with Deng. It had been the aspiration of countless Chinese leaders in the modern era—from Zeng Guofan and
Feng Guifen and other "self-strengtheners" of the mid-19th century, to Sun
Yat-sen and the Republican movement of the early 20th century, to the radical
ambitions of Mao Zedong and his followers, and many more—to overcome
the humiliations of China's past and restore the country to greatness. But Deng
Xiaoping and his successors saw in the fundamental circumstances of their times
an unprecedented "period of strategic opportunity" (战略机遇期) for China at
long last to realize that dream.

Deng passed away in 1997, but his ambition for China was carried forward. That year, China's top leader, Jiang Zemin, declared at the 15th Chinese
Communist Party (CCP) Congress, "As the new century is approaching, we are
faced with grim challenges and, more significantly, we are confronted with unprecedented favorable conditions and excellent opportunities"; five years later
he was more specific in saying "the first two decades of the 21st century are a period of important strategic opportunities, which we must seize tightly and which
offers bright prospects."[2] In this period, Chinese leaders and strategists rightly

Daring to Struggle. Bates Gill, Oxford University Press. © Oxford University Press 2022.
DOI: 10.1093/oso/9780197545645.003.0002

foresaw a largely favorable strategic environment for PRC security, prosperity, and development: peace and development would remain the fundamental global trend; great power war was unlikely; globalization and multipolarity would proceed apace and to China's benefit; and China would become an increasingly weighty and respected player in world affairs.[3] The aim, then, was to take fullest advantage of China's steadily advancing position in world affairs to develop its economy and improve the well-being of its people while becoming more open to—and respected by—the outside world. The two "centenary goals" were to be milestones by which China's leaders would affirm the country's progress. By 2021, the CCP centenary, China would become a "moderately well-off society." From there, for the country's 100th anniversary in 2049, China would become a fully modernized, strong, and prosperous nation.

By many indications, that rejuvenation is well underway. Between 2000 and 2020, China's gross domestic product (GDP) grew nearly ninefold.[4] As a proportion of global GDP, China grew from around 3 percent in 2000 to about 16 percent by 2020. China's nominal GDP was about equal to Italy's in 2000, and went to surpass that of France (2005), the United Kingdom (2006), Germany (2007), and Japan (2010) to become the world's second-largest economy behind the United States. In purchasing power parity terms, the size of China's economy overtook the United States' around 2014.[5] The personal incomes of Chinese citizens skyrocketed, and hundreds of millions escaped poverty. On the back of this wealth generation, the People's Liberation Army enjoyed steadily growing budgets: Chinese military spending raced past that of France, Japan, and the United Kingdom in the early 2000s and by 2019 had reached about $261 billion, second only to the United States and more than three times that of the next closest, India.[6] By the end of those two decades, China had become the world's largest trading nation, the number-one exporter, number-two importer, and the second-largest source of outbound foreign direct investment, and had amassed the largest reserves of foreign exchange and gold. It was the largest producer and consumer of electricity, and the world's greatest emitter of greenhouse gases. It was the largest internet market on the planet, with more than 95 percent of users gaining access via some 1.6 billion mobile phones in the country (another world-topping figure).[7]

Meanwhile, China's ability to influence world affairs likewise grew. Much of Beijing's influence drew from its burgeoning economic presence. For a growing list of countries around the world, China became either the leading source of imports, leading destination for exports, or both. Beijing's diplomatic presence expanded over these years as well. In 2018, China overtook the United States to have the most diplomatic posts in the world—a total of 276 embassies, consulates, and other missions.[8] At the same time, Beijing poured enormous investment into expanding the country's state-owned media footprint worldwide via print, broadcast, and digital platforms in dozens of languages.

But it was not only the physical attributes of China's growing power that had become more substantial. So too had the political will to transform that power into the full realization of the country's long-held ambition to be powerful, prosperous, and respected again. The current head of China, Xi Jinping, more than any other Chinese leader since Mao, has come to personify that will. More than any other Chinese leader since Deng, Xi has the mandate of the CCP behind him to pursue that ambition—including through a hard-hitting anticorruption campaign, social crackdowns, and accelerated centralization of authority to the Party and to Xi himself. And more than his immediate predecessors, Jiang Zemin and Hu Jintao, Xi has shown the determination and daring to achieve what he calls the "China Dream" (中国梦) and the "great rejuvenation of the Chinese nation" (中华民族伟大复兴). As noted earlier, reviving the Chinese nation has been a fervently hoped-for dream since the middle of the 19th century. But Xi Jinping has placed attainment of national rejuvenation at the very center of his leadership and legacy, and the opportunity to realize it seems closer and more pressing than ever.

Xi certainly seems to understand the opportunity before him. He and his supporters have positioned him as the most powerful PRC leader since Mao and Deng. He appears set to rule indefinitely and would likely have considerable influence even if he chooses to retire from official duties. Having marked the "first centenary goal" on the Party's 100th birthday in 2021, he seems urgent to press on toward the next major milestones: to overcome the big economic, technological, environmental, and demographic problems that still loom ahead by 2035, laying the groundwork for the PRC to become a fully modernized, powerful, respected, and world-leading nation in time for the country's centennial in 2049.[9] Whether the country achieves this grand vision or not, Xi's ambitious pursuit of it will have enormous implications for China's place in the world and the interests of nations and societies around the globe. Knowing this, it is worth taking a step back for a brief look at Xi Jinping's life—the influences, experiences, and beliefs he carries with him—and how in turn these have shaped his approach to leadership and pursuit of the China Dream.

A Princeling's Life

Xi stands out from previous PRC leaders in many ways. One of the most interesting is the fact that he is the first person to lead the People's Republic whose life has almost exactly paralleled the life of the country itself, from its founding to the present day. Xi Jinping was born in Beijing in June 1953, only a few years after the establishment of the People's Republic of China in October 1949. At the time, China was struggling to find its footing, having gone through decades of warlordism, foreign invasion and occupation by Japan, and internecine civil war over much of the first half of the 20th century. When Xi was born, China was at war on the Korean Peninsula against UN forces, led by the United States, in what the Chinese call the War to Resist America and Support Korea (抗美援朝战争).[10] More tumult and deprivation were to come with the disastrous social, political, and economic excesses of the Great Leap Forward (1958–1962) and the Great Proletarian Cultural Revolution (1966–1976) under China's powerful leader Mao Zedong.

Yet, as the son of revolutionary heroes, Xi was born to relative privilege. His mother, Qi Xin, had joined with the CCP as a teenager to combat Japan in the early 1940s. She married Xi Zhongxun in 1944, and Xi the younger was their third of four children together. The elder Xi was a first-generation Chinese Communist veteran and one of the founders of the PRC. At the time of Xi Jinping's birth, Xi Zhongxun was minister of propaganda and later served as vice premier on China's State Council from 1959 to 1962.[11] As a young boy Xi Jinping attended elite schools designated for senior cadres' children—such as the Beihai Kindergarten, the August 1st School, and the Beijing No. 101 Middle School—where he was inculcated with Party-centric ideals of conviction and sacrifice.[12] He would have also spent time inside Zhongnanhai, the CCP leadership compound adjacent to the Forbidden City in central Beijing, vacationed along with other prominent families at the Beidaihe beach retreat, and had interactions with the senior-most leaders of the time such as Mao, Zhou Enlai, and Deng Xiaoping. Throughout his early years, Xi grew up as a "red princeling" and part of the "red nobility."

This privileged childhood came crashing down in 1962. Accused by Mao of being an anti-Party rightist, Xi Zhongxun was purged from his leadership posts and put in detention where he would remain until 1975. With his father disgraced, Xi Jinping's life took a difficult turn, including a short period of incarceration at the onset of the Cultural Revolution in 1966 and then being "sent down" to the countryside to work alongside and learn from the local peasant farmers, as were millions of other educated urban youth at the time. Xi chose to go to Yan'an, in Shaanxi province, which is where his father served as a military commander of Chinese Communist forces in the 1940s and where Xi had extended family ties. He worked there for most of the next seven years, a formative period between the ages of 15 and 22. While initially unhappy there, he later claimed it was a period when he faced adversity; built up resiliency, resourcefulness, and leadership experience; and came to know the struggles of China's vast rural population. Many years later, as a rising political star at the uppermost reaches of power, Xi's time in Yan'an was touted as a life-transforming phase in his life, one that affirmed his dedication to work for the benefit of the Party and the people.[13]

In 1975, at the age of 22 and with the Cultural Revolution on the wane, Xi was able to leverage his family connections and good work reputation in Shaanxi to gain entrance to Tsinghua University to study chemical engineering. This was several years before the full reopening of China's universities in 1978; they had been largely shuttered to traditional higher education pursuits since the beginning of the Cultural Revolution in 1966. Admitted as part of the first class of "Worker-Peasant-Soldier" students, Xi spent much of his time studying Marxist-Leninist–Mao Zedong thought and tilling the fields near the university.

Upon graduation in 1979, and with his father fully rehabilitated and serving as the head of Guangdong Province under the newly installed reformist leadership of Deng Xiaoping, Xi began his ascent through government and Party ranks. His political career started—again, owing to his status as the child of a high-ranking leader—as personal secretary to Geng Biao, who at the time was secretary-general of the CCP's Central Military Commission. After three years in that role, Xi left Beijing to take up government and Party positions in provincial areas, steadily assuming larger leadership responsibilities in rapidly developing eastern provinces such as Hebei, Fujian (where he rose to governor), and Zhejiang (where he became the Party secretary) from 1981 to 2007. During this period he took his now-famous trip to Iowa in the United States in 1985—believed to be his first foreign excursion—as head of a small agricultural delegation.[14]

By 2007, he was appointed the Party chief for Shanghai, a traditional signal that he would assume national office. After an unusually short stint of only seven months in that role, he was elevated to the CCP Politburo Standing Committee at the 17th CCP Congress in October 2007, making him one of the nine most powerful men in the country. He was ranked sixth of the nine leaders and given a number of Party-, government-, and military-related responsibilities. He was the first-ranking secretary of the CCP Secretariat, an executive body of the Party tasked with conducting the day-to-day operations of the Politburo, including coordinating and carrying out its decisions. In this role he gained valuable familiarity with the inner workings and interest group politics of the country's top leaders and how decisions are made and implemented. He was also made state vice president, a largely ceremonial role, but one affording him ample opportunity to meet with foreign leaders (including when he accompanied U.S. vice president Joseph Biden for a five-day visit to China in August 2011 and Biden reciprocated as host for Xi's visit to the United States in early 2012). He was also appointed vice chairman of the Central Military Commission and president of the Central Party School, to further develop his relationships and experience in the military and ideological spheres. From these positions, he began a five-year grooming period for the top job of CCP general secretary. Culminating his rise to power, he was appointed Party general secretary and chairman of the CCP Central Military Commission in November 2012, and several months later, in March 2013, became the PRC president. Holding these three positions as head of the Party, the military, and the state, he was thus fully confirmed as paramount leader of the country, just a few months shy of his 60th birthday.

This life experience—born to the "red nobility," surviving and then thriving in the personal and physical adversities of Maoist turmoil, and becoming a resolute devotee to and ultimately an embodiment of CCP authority—has no doubt had a profound influence on Xi Jinping's worldview, leadership style, and vision for China's future. From what we can observe, Xi stands out as a true believer in the CCP, far more committed than his immediate predecessors to empower and extend the Party apparatus of ideology, authority, propaganda, and control as the indispensable instrument to pursue the national interests as the Party sees them. This is understandable. He has clearly personally benefitted as a privileged son of the Party elite. But more importantly, his life has closely paralleled the trajectory of the PRC, becoming deeply immersed in the catechism of Party ideology in his youth, then personally witnessing both calamitous periods of intra-Party strife and corruption as well as great achievements during times of Party unity and discipline.

Xi's life experience and belief in what is possible under strong Party leadership also appear to have instilled in him a greater degree of confidence, audacity, and even impatience in comparison to many other PRC leaders before him. In many respects at odds with his comparatively low-key predecessors such as Hu Jintao, Jiang Zemin, Zhao Ziyang, Hu Yaobang, and even Deng Xiaoping, Xi has made a number of risky decisions to leverage the Party's control at home and PRC power abroad in a more assertive pursuit of Chinese interests as he and other CCP leaders would define them. Such a high risk–high reward strategy marks another differentiating feature of Xi's leadership.

Relatedly, as part of his approach to leadership, Xi appears determined to consolidate and centralize political and policy decision-making power to Party organizations in general, and to himself in particular, including in relation to foreign policy. This reflects a take-charge attitude for which he became known as his career progressed, but also an apparent sense of urgency on his part to assume responsibility for advancing the ambitious plans for China's future, especially as a regional and global player. It also contributes to the aura that Xi and the Party's propaganda authorities have built around him: that he is a historically transformational figure for China, accelerating its trajectory to greatness on the world stage. With Xi's background and character traits in mind, there is much to suggest these attributes were precisely among the most important in the minds of the Party elite when they appointed him become China's paramount leader.

New Leader for a New Era

When Xi Jinping was brought to the center of Chinese power, in the first decade of the 21st century, the country's leadership faced a pivotal moment. As China scholar David Shambaugh explains, the CCP had for many decades gone through a prolonged period of atrophy.[15] The traditional instruments of Party power, authority, and control—including ideological coherence and relevance, organizational commitment and discipline, tightly managed information and propaganda, and coercive threats and action—had been increasingly weakened over much of the reform era. The CCP had been buffeted by external pressures of globalization, the information revolution, and opening to the outside world. In addition, changes at home that accompanied the country's economic trans-formation, such as growing income inequality, rising incidence of social un-rest, pervasive official corruption, and widespread environmental degradation, all contributed to weakening the Party's authority and self-confidence to rule. A senior researcher at the CCP Central Party School would later write that prior to the 2012 transfer of paramount leadership to Xi Jinping, a "unilateral em-phasis on economic construction" among Party leaders resulted in "disregard for ideological work." "This kind of belittling, neglect, or ridiculing of ideology," he wrote, could be summarized as "the three smiles": "a cold smile when hearing about Marxism, a faint smile when hearing about socialism with Chinese char-acteristics, and laughter with a smile when hearing about communism."[16]

Writing in 2007—the year Xi Jinping was promoted to the CCP Politburo Standing Committee to be groomed for paramount leadership—former U.S. State Department official and leading China watcher Susan Shirk argued that Chinese leaders had become insecure and "haunted by the fear that their days in power [were] numbered."[17] Chinese leaders in the two decades following the Tiananmen crisis of 1989 were deeply shaken by that uprising, and did not exercise the kind of authority and charismatic appeal of their near-godlike predecessors such as Mao and Deng. Jiang Zemin—considered the head of the "third generation" of leadership—was elevated from relative obscurity as Party chief of Shanghai, inserted as CCP general secretary in the immediate aftermath of Tiananmen, and held the reins of power until 2002. His successor, "fourth-generation" leader Hu Jintao, who ruled as CCP general secretary from 2002 to 2012, had been handpicked for the top position by Deng years before. Both Jiang and Hu proved to be mostly low-profile, low-risk leaders who had to be cau-tious about sharing power and not forcefully imposing dramatic change on the Party or society. Zhao Ziyang, the reform-minded CCP general secretary who was ousted following the Tiananmen crisis, described his successor Hu Jintao (as well as Hu's premier, Wen Jiabao) as "lacking ideals, lacking historical re-sponsibility, and lacking vision."[18] Under Jiang and Hu's leadership, the Party struggled to adapt to the rapid economic and social changes within China and to retain its relevance and legitimacy. Domestic challenges—particularly official corruption; social, ethnic, and religious unrest; terrorist threats at home, a slowing economic growth rate, a graying population, and decaying military capabilities—persisted.[19]

On the international front, Jiang and Hu largely adhered to Deng's strategic guidance from the late 1980s to "observe calmly, secure our position, cope with affairs calmly, hide our capacities and bide our time, be good at maintaining a low profile, and never claim leadership." By the mid-1990s, this guidance went by a shorter and slightly different interpretation to "hide one's capacities and bide one's time [or 'keep a low profile'], but also get some things done" (韬光养晦,有所作为), or "hide and bide" (hereafter hide-and-bide) for short. These phrases do not translate easily into English and are subject to various interpretations. Prominent PRC analysts argue this was a "modest," "prudent," and even "self-effacing" approach to international affairs in which the country should keep a low profile, proceed with caution, and not overreach, while also steadily developing the country's capabilities.[20] Rush Doshi argues that hide-and-bide was driven in part by a deepening concern about the United States and the threats it posed to China—especially following the Tiananmen crisis of 1989, the swift U.S. victory in the first Gulf War against Iraq in early 1991, and the collapse of the Soviet Union later that year. According to Doshi, from the early 1990s, while pursuing a hiding-and-biding strategy, Beijing remained anxiously vigilant about American power around its periphery and worked to quietly blunt it through the steady accretion of military, economic, and diplomatic strength.[21]

This strategic guidance of hide-and-bide was consistent with the overall assessment of the international situation that dominated Chinese thinking in this period: that the world was generally trending toward peace and development, the likelihood of a world war was remote, and China should take the opportunity presented by the relatively stable regional and global environment to focus on its own pressing economic development needs. Under Hu Jintao, this strategic assessment cohered into several guiding concepts intended to reassure the international community about the PRC's approach to world affairs: that China would pursue a "peaceful rise" and "peaceful development" and seek a "harmonious world."[22]

By the mid- to late 2000s, China became progressively more integrated within the international community, a member in good standing across a range of multilateral organizations, an increasingly willing adherent to global norms and established rules of the road, and an ever-more important driver of the global economy. By 2010, China's economy, as measured by gross domestic product (GDP), surpassed Japan's to become the world's second-largest, behind the United States. PRC leaders at the time sought greater access to foreign markets, capital, and technology and the contributions they could make to China's economic modernization on the one hand, and the security underpinnings of peaceable and predictable relations with neighbors and other key powers on the other. Encouraged by these developments, foreign policy leaders in the United States urged China to become a "responsible stakeholder" in the international system in partnership with Washington.[23]

However, over the period from the late 2000s to 2012—roughly overlapping the period of Xi Jinping's five-year grooming period as a newly appointed member of the CCP Politburo Standing Committee—PRC relations with the outside world began to take a sour turn even as Beijing's assertiveness and confidence appeared to grow. Beginning in March 2008, deadly demonstrations, protests, and riots erupting in Tibet and in Xinjiang helped fuel global protests against the Beijing Olympic Games that took place in August of that year. Large-scale demonstrations arose in many cities around the world along the path of the Olympic torch as it made its way to Beijing for the Summer Olympic Games, generating both anger and embarrassment for PRC leaders and citizens alike. That said, the highly successful Olympics—which Xi Jinping was given the responsibility to oversee—served as a major coming-out party for China and greatly boosted the CCP's self-image and confidence on the world stage. That confidence was further bolstered with the onset of the global financial crisis that began in the United States and went on to devastate much of the global economy over 2008–2009. Left relatively unscathed by the crisis, China emerged from it in a stronger economic position. Chinese analyses at the time pinned blame on the American neo-liberal model or market capitalism, while heaping praise on the PRC system of political and economic governance. The CCP's leading journal, *Qiushi (Seeking truth)*, explained it this way:

> Looking at the inherent cause, the crisis has revealed the intrinsic shortcomings of an absolutely free market economy, deep-rooted structural problems in economic globalization and serious defects of the irrational international economic order and the international financial system in particular. The crisis has grown into a profound global economic recession, further revealing the damage caused by the theory and practice of the neo-liberalism characterized by privatization, marketization and liberalization.[24]

In dealing with the crisis, this analysis continued, China had "displayed the superiority of its system" and "strengthened its image as a large responsible country."[25]

Meanwhile, over the period from 2009 to 2012, territorial disputes between China and neighboring claimants in the South China Sea and the East China Sea steadily grew more tense. China stepped up its naval, paramilitary, surveillance, and fishing activities in an effort to assert its claims within both waterways.

A number of incidents heightened tensions further. In September 2010, a Chinese fishing fleet captain rammed Japanese coast guard vessels in disputed waters near the Senkaku Islands (known in Chinese as the Diaoyu Islands), resulting in their arrest by Japanese authorities and subsequent widespread protests in China. The Japanese government decision in September 2012 to purchase the Senkaku Islands from private owners in September 2012 sparked more outrage in China and led to increased deterioration in Beijing-Tokyo relations. In 2011 and 2012, the PRC also stepped up harassment of Philippine and Vietnamese fishing and energy exploration vessels, including seizing Scarborough Shoal in April 2012 from the Philippines.

At the same time, relations between the United States and China were likewise entering a period of increasing tension. In the early months of President Barack Obama's first term, in March 2009, Chinese vessels conducted repeated harassment activities—some of them risking dangerous collisions—against U.S. Navy ocean surveillance ships, the USNS *Victorious* and USNS *Impeccable,* operating in the Yellow Sea and South China Sea, respectively.[26] Beijing became increasingly concerned with America's stepped-up diplomatic, economic, and military presence in the Asia-Pacific region, especially with the announcement of the U.S. "rebalance to Asia" under President Barack Obama.[27] This initiative involved a range of actions, including an expanded U.S. military footprint in the region, strengthened security ties with regional allies and other partners, and a more proactive diplomatic positioning to balance China's growing regional influence. Issues of cybersecurity and illicit cyberespionage also began to take center stage between the two powers. More broadly, the U.S.-China relationship was increasingly defined by a deepening "strategic mistrust." According to one of the most prominent Chinese experts on U.S.-China relations, in 2012, from Beijing's perspective, this strategic mistrust could be attributed to four emergent perceptions in China that reflected ongoing changes in the international system:

- Many Chinese officials believe that their nation has ascended to be a first-class power in the world and should be treated as such. Chinese leaders do not credit these successes to the United States or to the U.S.-led world order.
- The United States is seen in China generally as a declining power over the long run. America's financial disorder, alarming deficit and unemployment rate, slow economic recovery, and domestic political polarization are viewed as but a few indications that the United States is headed for decline. Beijing still sees the lack of confidence and competence of the United States on the global stage and a quite chaotic picture in U.S. national politics.
- From the perspective of China's leaders, the shifting power balance between China and the United States is part of an emerging new structure in today's world.

- It is a popular notion among Chinese political elites, including some national leaders, that China's development model provides an alternative to Western democracy and experiences for other developing countries to learn from, while many developing countries that have introduced Western values and political systems are experiencing disorder and chaos.[28]

Other developments on the world stage also posed challenges for PRC interests and international image. In December 2010, the Norwegian Nobel Committee, a nongovernmental group, awarded the Nobel Peace Prize to Chinese dissident Liu Xiaobo "for his long and non-violent struggle for fundamental human rights in China."[29] This shone a stark light on the human rights situation in the PRC, especially with regard to civil and political rights, and reinforced already negative views toward the CCP, particularly among liberal democracies. During this period, Beijing also came under increasing criticism for its poor environmental record—having become the world's largest emitter of greenhouse gases by 2007—and was widely seen in the developed world as obstructing progress at the 2009 United Nations Conference on Climate Change held in Copenhagen.[30]

Xi Takes Charge

It was into this strategic environment that the heir apparent, Xi Jinping, was formally appointed as the new Party chief in November 2012, ushering in the country's "fifth generation" of leadership. At home, Xi and the Party leadership faced moral decay and factionalism within the CCP and a range of mounting sociopolitical and socioeconomic pressures within the broader populace.

Underscoring the Party's domestic woes, the Bo Xilai scandal erupted in early 2012—in which one of China's most important and high-profile leaders was implicated in murder, corruption, and plotting against Xi Jinping—unsettling what was to be Xi's smoothly orchestrated succession process to paramount leadership. Bo, who at the time was a member of the Politburo, Party chief of the huge urban agglomeration of Chongqing in central China, and purportedly a political rival to Xi, was arrested, tried, and sentenced to life in prison.[31] In an unusual public admission, Xi later told the Party leadership that Bo—along with several other disgraced senior Party and military leaders—were "not only greedy financially and corrupt in their lifestyles, but were also politically ambitious, often agreeing in public but opposing in secret, and forming cliques for personal interests and engaging in conspiracy activities."[32]

In addition, when Xi assumed office, while Chinese leaders had become increasingly confident about China's rise and place in the world, they also encountered increasing concerns and pushback from key neighbors worried about the pace and direction of China's growing power. These concerns were related to the authoritarian nature of the CCP regime as well as how the PRC would use its power to extend its influence and assert its national interests abroad. Even within China, an active debate unfolded within political and academic circles as to how—and even whether—the country should leverage its burgeoning strength in the international system in order to gain respect for the CCP and PRC development model; assert its national sovereignty; generate greater wealth, power, and influence; and take on global leadership roles.[33]

In the face of such challenges and internal debates, once installed as the top leader in late 2012, Xi wasted little time to begin rectifying the political situation at home and launching a more proactive agenda abroad. Almost from day one, he demonstrated that he would be a different kind of leader than his immediate predecessors: far more determined, daring, and devoted to pursuing the "China Dream" and the "great rejuvenation of the Chinese nation." Within hours of his appointment in November 2012, he stood before the domestic and international press to declare.

> Ours is a great nation. . . . In modern times, however, China endured untold hardships and sufferings, and its very survival hung in the balance. Countless Chinese patriots rose up one after another and fought for the renewal of the Chinese nation, but all ended in failure. Since its founding, the Communist Party of China has made great sacrifices and forged ahead against all odds. It has rallied and led the Chinese people in transforming the poor and backward old China into an increasingly prosperous and powerful new China, thus opening a completely new horizon for the great renewal of the Chinese nation. Our responsibility now is to rally and lead the entire Party and the people . . . and in making continued efforts to achieve the great renewal of the Chinese nation, make the Chinese nation stand rock-firm in the family of nations, and make [an] even greater contribution to mankind.[34]

Rectification at Home

Within two weeks of taking office, Xi—accompanied by the other six recently installed members of the CCP Politburo Standing Committee—headed to the National Museum of China, located on Tiananmen Square. But this was not merely an educational outing. They went on a high-profile tour with *Road to Renewal*, a major exhibit telling a history of the country's past hardships during the "century of shame" (roughly from the mid-19th to the mid-20th centuries) and the subsequent achievements of the present under CCP leadership. It was there to great fanfare Xi set forth his vision of the "China Dream" and seeking the "great rejuvenation of the Chinese nation."[35] These grand concepts more than any others distinguish Xi's leadership. More broadly and more importantly, the themes of reversing China's past humiliations and reestablishing the country's greatness under the CCP came to define and validate Xi's approach to domestic and foreign policy.

On the home front, Xi used his first years in office to consolidate power to the Party and to himself as Party chief.[36] Empowering and reinvigorating its organization, disciplinary, and propaganda machinery, the Party under Xi Jinping worked to sideline his potential rivals, stoke popular support for his leadership, and take firmer decision-making control across the domestic policy spectrum. To enforce CCP discipline and loyalty, clean up the Party ranks, and remove or cow potential opposition, he unleashed the most intensive and wide-reaching anticorruption drive the country had seen in decades. His leadership also redoubled the emphasis on ideological adherence among Party members, including expressions of fealty to him as CCP leader. As shown in Table 1.1, Xi took personal charge of a number of decision-making bodies across the policy spectrum, earning him the nickname "Chairman of Everything."

In October 2016, the CCP leadership designated him as "core leader"—a title previously only given to Mao, Deng, and Jiang—and over the following two years formally included his "thought" ("Xi Jinping Thought on Socialism with Chinese Characteristics in a New Era") into both the Party and State constitutions, a distinction only Mao previously enjoyed. By 2018, term limits on his presidency were officially abolished, effectively allowing him to indefinitely retain all three of his top leadership posts—the presidency, head of the military, and Party chief. Meanwhile, Xi's popular image as leader and man of the people was elevated to near-cult status, supercharged by the pervasive CCP-run media. One quirky—if saccharine—example: a music video translated as "Xi Dada Loves Peng Mama"—which touts the love story between the Chinese leader and his wife, Peng Liyuan—became a online phenomenon, viewed tens of millions of times within days of its release.[37]

Within the broader society, however, a darker side emerged as controls over public expression and day-to-day social activity tightened under Xi. In the toughest crackdown on dissent since the Tiananmen crisis of 1989, the Party has overseen the stepped-up use of propaganda campaigns, censorship, and the growing use of harassment, detentions, and disappearances to root out and suppress contrary thinking or the introduction of sensitive ideas by independent journalists, publishers, lawyers, and others, including foreigners. A part of this ideological straitjacket included Party-sanctioned warnings to steer clear of "Western ideas" that threaten CCP authority. The "Communiqué on the Current State of the Ideological Sphere" (also known as Document No. 9), issued by the CCP General Office Party in April 2013, listed seven such "false ideological

Table 1.1. Xi Jinping's Leadership Positions, 2012–2020

Position	Year appointed
General Secretary, CCP Central Committee	2012
Chairman, CCP Central Military Commission	2012
Leader, Central Leading Group for Foreign Affairs	2012–2017*
Chairman, Central Leading Group for Taiwan Affairs	2012
President, People's Republic of China	2013
Leader, Central Leading Group for Comprehensively Deepening Reforms	2013–2017*
Leader, Central Leading Group for Financial and Economic Affairs	2013–2017*
Chairman, Central National Security Commission	2014
Leader, Central Leading Group for Internet Security and Informatization	2014–2017*
Leader, Central Leading Group for National Defence and Military Reform of the CCP Central Military Commission	2014
Commander-in-Chief, Joint Battle Command, People's Liberation Army	2016
Chairman, Central Commission for Integrated Military and Civilian Development	2017
Chairman, Central Commission for Financial and Economic Affairs	2018
Chairman, Central Commission on Foreign Affairs	2018
Chairman, Central Commission on Cyberspace Affairs	2018
Chairman, Central Commission on Comprehensively Deepening Reforms	2018

* These Leading Groups were elevated to become Central Commissions in 2018, with Xi Jinping retaining leadership over them.

trends, positions and activities": promoting Western constitutional democracy, promoting universal values, promoting civil society, promoting neoliberal economics, promoting freedom of the press, promoting historical nihilism (i.e., reassessing Party history), and questioning the PRC's reform, opening, and socialism with Chinese characteristics.[38] The messaging from this document overlapped with another propaganda campaign of Party boosterism urging the Chinese citizenry to assume "three confidences" (三个自信): confidence in the political system under the Party's rule, confidence in the Party's development path of socialism with Chinese characteristics, and confidence in the scientific basis or theory of socialism with Chinese characteristics. A fourth "confidence" was later added—confidence in the value of the Party's culture—and together this "confidence doctrine" was inserted into the CCP Constitution in 2017. Along with pursuit of the China Dream, the doctrine became one of Xi's signature strategic dictates guiding the Party.[39]

The Party's concerns about ideological adherence and confidence in CCP leadership extended to other institutions such as universities and schools, where, according to a statement by Xi in December 2015, more "ideological guidance" and a greater emphasis on Marxism were required. In early 2016, the PRC minister of education put Xi's words into action, declaring that China should "[n]ever let textbooks promoting Western values enter into our classes" and "[a]ny views that attack or defame the leadership of the party or smear socialism must never be allowed to appear in our universities." According to PRC official media, some universities were later investigated for their use of foreign textbooks, with the humanities, political science, economics, sociology, history, and journalism coming in for special scrutiny.[40] Fearful over the loyalty of the military and media, Xi demanded their leaders to publicly declare fealty to him and the Party (表态, or make one's position known) in oath ceremonies in the early part of his first term in office.[41] In touring the headquarters of *Xinhua*, the *People's Daily*, and China Central Television (CCTV) in 2016, he said that "the media run by the party and the government are the propaganda fronts and must have the party as their family name. . . . All the work by the party's media must reflect the party's will, safeguard the party's authority, and safeguard the party's unity."[42] Under Xi's leadership, press freedoms in China have further declined from an already low base. Reporters without Borders ranked China 177th out of 180 countries in its 2020 World Press Freedom Index, ahead of only Eritrea, Turkmenistan, and North Korea.[43]

All of these ideological and social controls were reinforced under Xi through the passage of a slew of stricter security and surveillance laws, far less tolerance for the activities of foreign organizations (especially media organizations), and far more extensive policing of the internet and social media. The introduction of a "social credit score"—which keeps track of individuals' behavior and reputation—was intended to identify "untrustworthy" persons and reportedly would result in various rewards and punishments depending on one's score. The authoritarian crackdown on what the Party found to be undesirable behaviors extended beyond mainland China to Hong Kong where a new set of security laws were introduced in 2020 by Beijing to criminalize activities deemed threatening to PRC security. Under Xi, China also imposed far harsher surveillance for citizens in Tibet and Xinjiang, including the establishment of "reeducation camps" to detain hundreds of thousands of Muslims from Uyghur and other ethnic groups. Even individuals far beyond China's borders became the victims of harassment and intimidation owing to their critical views of the PRC and CCP.[44]

Apparently believing the Party and PRC were dangerously adrift, the Party under Xi's leadership took a range of steps to rectify this situation by consolidating decision-making authority and political control within the Party center and to Xi himself. These measures included building up Xi's image as a strong "core leader" of the Party as well as boosting confidence within the Party and within society as to the CCP's positive role. The mobile app "Study to Strengthen the Nation" (学习强国) became required reading for Party members to review Party documents and other information, receive "study points" based on their interaction with the app, and demonstrate their adherence to the latest Party line. (It is no coincidence that the second character for the word "study" in this app's name is also the surname of Xi Jinping. Thus, the app's name is also understood to mean "study Xi to strengthen the nation.") Xi also oversaw the Party's formal approval of a landmark "resolution on history"—only the third time in the CCP's 100 years that such a resolution was issued—that hails the past successes of the Party and expresses unwavering confidence in Xi's leadership and vision for the future.[45] Having worked to build up greater confidence about their leadership at home, Xi and his team could act more confidently abroad.

Greater Confidence Abroad

Xi's China Dream and the great rejuvenation of the Chinese nation also extend to encompass foreign affairs. Once appointed as top leader, Xi took bold steps and made clear that China would act more proactively to cultivate its neighbors, while also more forcefully asserting its perceived sovereign rights and national interests. Shortly after Xi Jinping assumed leadership, the hide-and-bide guideline of his predecessors Deng, Jiang, and Hu was set aside, with the directive no longer used in internal communications and documents.[46] According to one of China's leading scholars of international relations, Yan Xuetong, while momentum had been building since the early 2000s to move away from the hide-and-bide strategy, Xi signaled the formal transformation of PRC international strategy when he spoke before a major national conference on foreign affairs in October 2013.[47] It was there that Xi said China should be "striving for achievement" (奋发有为) in its relationships abroad, foretelling of a more proactive foreign policy to come.[48] Xi aspired to "great power diplomacy" and establishing a "new model of great power relations" more aligned with China's growing power, influence, and interests in world affairs.[49]

This new confidence shines through in numerous ways. More than his predecessors, Xi has been active on the international travel circuit. According to one well-documented source, since he was appointed top leader in late 2012 and prior to the worldwide coronavirus outbreak of 2020, he had taken 42 trips abroad, making 98 country visits to 69 individual countries. Most of these travels were concentrated in the seven years from 2013 to 2019: four trips in 2013, seven in 2014, eight in 2015, six in 2016, five in 2017, four in 2018, and seven in 2019. His most repeat visits were to Russia (eight times), the United States (four), and three visits each to France, India, Indonesia, Kazakhstan, and South Africa.[50] His official travels took him to 12 of the 14 countries with which China shares land borders, as well as all nearby countries with which it shares (often disputed) maritime borders.[51] He has visited all of China's fellow members of the Shanghai Cooperation Organization (SCO) (many more than once), and nine of the 10 members of the Association of Southeast Asian Nations (ASEAN). (The coronavirus pandemic slowed Xi's travels: he spent nearly all of 2020 and 2021 without leaving China, more time staying at home than any other major world leader.[52])

One of his most memorable appearances was at the World Economic Forum, in Davos, Switzerland—the first time the leader of the CCP and paramount leader of China had done so. Speaking in early 2017, shortly before Donald Trump was inaugurated as U.S. president, and with threats of "America First" trade protectionism on the rise, Xi artfully positioned China as a force for globalization, economic openness, multilateral cooperation, and "win-win" solutions.[53] In other high-profile appearances at home and abroad, he went further to promote China's position internationally by touting the "China solution" or "China plan" (中国方案). From Xi's first known use of the phrase in March 2014, to frequent subsequent usage by him and the PRC media, the "China solution" advocates the PRC model of domestic governance, economic development, and approach to global relations to tackle domestic and international challenges of the 21st century.[54]

In another signal of the shift away from hide-and-bide, Xi took steps to assert PRC sovereignty more vigorously and leverage Chinese military and economic power more openly. In November 2013, for example, Beijing announced the establishment of its first air defense identification zone (ADIZ) in the East China Sea, which encompassed airspace over islands that Japan administers but that China claims as its own.[55] In addition to this step, Chinese naval and coast guard vessels dramatically increased their operations in waters around the disputed territories, with Japanese authorities reporting more than 1,000 such incursions in 2019 alone—a record number at the time.[56] Even more provocatively, China engaged in a massive project of island building and construction of military facilities in the South China Sea from 2013 to 2016 in order to reinforce its claims in that waterway. In July 2016, Beijing rejected a ruling of the Arbitral Tribunal, in a case brought by the Philippines, which stated that much of China's island-building and other activities in the South China Sea were in breach of the United Nations Convention on the Law of the Sea. Since Xi came to power, PRC naval and coast guard vessels continued their harassment of U.S. Navy counterparts, including in international waters, with the ships at times nearly colliding with one another.[57] In June 2017 (at Doklam) and again in June 2020 (Galwan Valley), Chinese troops attempting to construct facilities on disputed territory clashed with Indian counterparts; the latter incident resulted in significant loss of life on both sides, the deadliest confrontation between the two countries in more than 50 years.[58] With these and other steps under Xi, it became increasingly apparent that China would more actively assert its sovereign interests, even at the risk of heightening tensions and instability with its Indo-Pacific neighbors.

In visits to Kazakhstan and Indonesia in late 2013, and made official in the October 2013 foreign policy conference noted above, Xi introduced the "Silk Road economic belt" and a "maritime Silk Road" for the 21st century. This idea, which has since cohered as the "Belt and Road Initiative" (一带一路; BRI), became one of Xi's signature foreign policy creations. A strategic development undertaking of enormous scale, it aims to invest some $1 trillion in the development of ports, railroads, highways, telecommunications systems, and other infrastructure networks across the Eurasian continent, along the south Asian littoral, and including Africa and Oceania.[59] Other major international initiatives soon followed such as the Asian Infrastructure Investment Bank (AIIB) and the New Development Bank (NDB). First officially announced by Xi in 2013, and formally established in January 2016, the AIIB is headquartered in Beijing and has grown to include more than 100 members and nearly $100 billion in subscribed capital from around the world.[60] The NDB (sometimes referred as the BRICS Bank) was established in 2014, formally began operations in 2016, and brings together Brazil, Russia, India, China, and South Africa (the "BRICS" countries) as shareholders. The BRI, AIIB, and NDB represent a new and more proactive Beijing leadership to generate economic benefit for others, especially in the developing world. But they also aim to bring economic and political gains for China by placing it at the center of newly created, PRC-led economic, development, and political networks.

The more proactive foreign policy of Xi Jinping was also given increased heft by his effort to overhaul the People's Liberation Army (PLA). Launched in late 2015, the sweeping reform and restructuring of the PLA under Xi's watch had two important goals. First, from a political perspective, the restructuring was intended to reassert Party control over the Chinese military. Under Xi's predecessor, Hu Jintao, the PLA overall and its army leadership in particular had become deeply corrupt and resistant to much-needed reforms. Once in office, Xi Jinping moved to clean up the army, remove it as an obstacle to military reforms, and reinforce CCP authority over the Chinese military. In addition to the formal reform and reorganization effort launched in late 2015 and the subsequent restructuring of the PLA hierarchy, Xi saw to the arrest and disgrace on corruption charges of PLA Army generals Xu Caihou and Guo Boxiong—previously China's two most powerful military officers as vice chairmen of the Central Military Commission (CMC)—along with the removal of hundreds of other PLA officers.

Second, the reform and restructuring were intended to transform the PLA from a bloated, untested, and degraded force into a military increasingly capable of conducting joint operations; fighting and winning short, intensive, and technologically sophisticated conflicts; and doing so farther from Chinese shores. With firmer Party control and with a force restructured for joint operations, the PLA was to focus on maritime domains (both "offshore defense" and "far seas protection"); stronger capabilities in nuclear, space, and information domains; the need to project power farther away from China's borders to safeguard the country's expanding international interests, and improvements in informationized warfighting.[61] According to the PLA's timeline, it aims to have mechanization "basically achieved" by 2020, "comprehensively enhance the modernisation of military theory, organisation, personnel, and weapons and equipment" by 2035, and by 2049 build the PLA into a "world-class military" (把 人民军队全面建成世界一流军队).[62]

China's military presence abroad was stepped up under Xi as well. PRC soldiers had already been active in contributing to United Nations (UN) peacekeeping forces, with China as the largest contributor of UN peacekeepers among the Permanent Five members of the UN Security Council.[63] Under Xi, those contributions expanded from about 1,870 troops and police in late 2012 to peak at nearly 3,100 in mid-2015; the levels since remained steady at about 2,500 through 2020, consistently placing China among the top-10 contributors of UN member states.[64] The PLA has also expanded its international military presence in the form of joint training exercises and humanitarian assistance and disaster relief (HADR) operations. According to official sources, between 2012 and 2018, the PLA conducted some 66 separate joint training activities with 17 countries and organizations, while also carrying out HADR operations in 25 countries in Africa, Asia, Oceania, and South America.[65] In a groundbreaking move, in August 2016, China established its first overseas military base in Djibouti, on Africa's east coast, which serves primarily to support the PLA Navy's counterpiracy task forces operating in the Gulf of Aden.

Xi's more active efforts to pursue PRC interests abroad were not limited to leveraging the country's economic and military power. Xi gave increased priority to a third dimension—in the realm of politics and diplomacy—to exert greater influence and leadership within the international community. CCP instruments of influence projection and image projection received a more powerful mandate to operate internationally so as to—in the words of Xi Jinping—"tell China's story well, spread China's voice, and strengthen [China's] narrative power internationally."[66] This included increased resources for what is termed "external propaganda work" (对外宣传工作) for Party-authorized print, broadcast, and digital media; augmented use of social media platforms such as YouTube, Twitter, and Facebook; and increased monitoring and censorship of content on other platforms such as Sina Weibo and WeChat. But in addition to these media and information channels, numerous other CCP and state-run organizations involved in international propaganda and influence activities escalated their work under Xi, including the CCP United Front Work Department, CCP International Liaison Department, China Association for Friendship with Foreign Countries, the PRC diplomatic corps, and many others.[67]

In addition, the PRC increasingly stepped forward to play leadership roles within the international community, a far cry from Deng's admonition to "keep a low profile." This ambition was reflected in Xi's proffering of "China solutions" for the challenges the global community was facing. But in more practical terms it also meant establishing China-led institutions such as the AIIB and NDB, and lobbying for and gaining leadership roles for PRC nationals in established global organizations such as the World Bank, Interpol, and within the UN system. For China, this was a significant departure from past practice but entirely consistent with Xi's stated goal, expressed in 2018 to the Party's top leadership concerned with foreign affairs, saying that "socialism with Chinese characteristics in the new era" would require, among other key points, a diplomacy that would "lead the reform of the global governance system."[68]

Opportunity or Challenge?

Having taken the reins of power in 2012 and likely to remain as China's paramount leader for many more years to come, Xi's approach to foreign affairs has been officially elevated to the title of "Xi Jinping Thought on Diplomacy" (习近平外交思想), a vision and set of guidelines to be dutifully lauded, studied, and implemented by the Party, government, and society.[69] In 2018, at the CCP Foreign Affairs Work Conference where Xi Jinping Thought on Diplomacy was formally adopted, he gave the most important summation of his views on PRC foreign policy since he took office. In the speech, Xi appeared to exude great confidence about China's future, declaring that "China has been in the best period of development since modern times," that China "enjoys many favorable external conditions . . . at present and in the years to come," and that the country is entering a "period . . . of great significance in the historical progress of the great rejuvenation of the Chinese nation."[70] Importantly, he also spoke about how

the world is in the midst of "great changes not seen in a century" (百年未有之
大变局).

These phrases foresee positive and negative developments. On the one hand,
Xi envisions encouraging change for China: Asian dynamism, an unsteady
America amid Western decline, and the ascent of the country he leads. From this
perspective, he is telling his Party, his people, and the world the tables of international history are turning in China's favor, and China must seize the opportunity to pursue its interests more actively and, if need be, more forcefully. But the
phrase also foresees profound uncertainties in these great changes. As one highly
placed and authoritative Chinese commentator interprets Xi's view, the "great
changes" ahead include a world in which the current international system "is
collapsing and a new world order has not yet been established, bringing uncertainty, anxiety, and fear." "China," this commentator continues, "is at the center
of the international political stage and at the leading edge of the international
economic stage, but our national governance system and capabilities are far from
able to adapt to these historic changes."[71] As Xi subsequently put it, "Today, we
are closer, more confident, and more capable than ever before of making the goal
of national rejuvenation a reality. But we must be prepared to work harder than
ever to get there."[72] Recognizing the many challenges still facing the country, Xi
incessantly enjoins the Party and the Chinese people to "dare to struggle, dare to
win" (敢于斗争, 敢于胜利).[73]

As he no doubt knows, Xi is right to hedge his bets. The country's future trajectory will not unfold predictably, and many challenges and uncertainties await
China and the world. But in spite of these risks and uncertainties—or perhaps
because of them—Xi nevertheless appears bent on pursuing "major power diplomacy with Chinese characteristics," "striving for achievement," taking on a
greater leadership role in world affairs, and "moving closer to the world's center
stage." These pursuits aim to achieve the China Dream and rejuvenate the
country to become a far more respected, powerful, and influential actor on the
world stage between now and mid-century. Even if China falls short of this ambition, global affairs will be profoundly shaped nevertheless by its determination
to achieve it.

But what exactly will China's pursuit of restored greatness mean for the world?
And how will this ambition unfold over the coming decades? Again, it is difficult
to predict with precision, and even Chinese scholars and former officials heat-
edly debate not only what Xi's stated ambitions for PRC foreign affairs will mean
in practice but even how far and how fast the quest for those ambitions should
proceed.[74] Moreover, China's engagement in the world has become increasingly
multifaceted, complex, and at times contradictory as the country comes to terms
with its burgeoning power and diversity of interests.

Nevertheless, we know enough of Xi's leadership and stated objectives to cut through the uncertainty and complexity and predict the priorities for Chinese foreign relations for the coming decades. As explained in greater detail in the following chapters, we can understand China's global ambitions by examining six fundamental objectives that drive the country's approach to the world: legitimacy, sovereignty, wealth, power, leadership, and ideas. These objectives for PRC foreign policy are not necessarily new, but China today is better positioned than ever to pursue them. Together they motivate PRC action abroad and tell us what we can expect of China's global pursuits in the Xi Jinping era.

2

Legitimacy 正当性

Prioritizing the Party and Its Rule

Why did the Soviet Union disintegrate? Why did the Soviet Communist Party collapse? One important reason is that ideals and beliefs were shaken . . . . Proportionately, the Soviet Communist Party was bigger than we are. But no one was man enough, no one came out to fight.
—Xi Jinping, December 2012[1]

Legitimacy at Home and Abroad

A distinctive characteristic that dominates China's approach to foreign relations—and one that appears to have become all the more important under Xi Jinping—is the precedence given to particular matters of domestic politics. This is somewhat at odds with traditional international relations thinking, which tells us that concerns over power balances and security dilemmas between states are the most important determinants that drive the foreign policy choices of national leaders. For the People's Republic of China (PRC or China), it is not that these factors of power aggrandizement and interstate rivalry are not important; as we see throughout this book, they certainly are. Rather, certain matters of a fundamentally domestic nature are of overriding concern and indeed define the very basics of state security for the Chinese political leadership and hence how the country must engage in the international realm.

That domestic concern is preserving and strengthening the Chinese Communist Party (CCP or Party) and ensuring its long-term survival. This has to do with the nature of the CCP itself. As an unelected, authoritarian, one-party, Leninist power structure, the CCP cannot base its survival on the will of the governed as expressed through the ballot box. Rather, it must seek to gain the support of the PRC citizenry for its rule through other means, including by seeking legitimacy: convincing the populace not only to accept one-party rule but also to buy into the underlying narrative that explains and grants such a mandate. Maintaining that narrative helps ensure Party survival, but has profound effects on PRC foreign policy as well.[2] University of London scholar Steve Tsang argues that putting the Party's interest in survival at the very heart of the

Daring to Struggle. Bates Gill, Oxford University Press. © Oxford University Press 2022.
DOI: 10.1093/oso/9780197545645.003.0003

country's national interest "is a constant, not a variable, factor that underpins Beijing's foreign policy. This does not mean the changing international context is irrelevant, just that it takes secondary importance."[3] This is by no means an abstract concept. No less an authority than Xi Jinping has stated clearly that the number-one priority for PRC diplomats in conducting "external work" is to "uphold the authority of the [CCP] Central Committee as the overarching principle and strengthen the centralized, unified leadership of the Party."[4] By this interpretation, the Party interest in maintaining its authority can supersede—and is the ultimate determinant in defining—the national interest. As such, to understand what drives PRC foreign policy, we should begin with the fundamental interests of the Party and the all-important quest for legitimacy that helps sustain it.

For the purposes of this book, the foreign policy objective of "legitimacy" means gaining acceptance, respect, and approbation for continued CCP leadership of China. The other five foreign policy objectives discussed in this book flow from—but also loop back to support—this core aim. As illustrated in Figure I.1 in the Introduction, legitimacy sits at the heart of this book's framework for PRC foreign policy objectives and is where all six core objectives overlap. Because the Party lays claim to representing the Chinese nation, gaining the acceptance, respect, and approbation that legitimacy confers would be a crowning achievement in the nation's long-held dream of "rejuvenation."

Some readers may find it strange to discuss political legitimacy as an objective of foreign policy. After all, gaining legitimacy to rule is primarily about domestic politics: convincing the population at home that a given leader, party, or political movement deserves to govern. That is true, but how the Party positions itself relative to the international system and relative to foreign powers has long been a central aspect of its claims to legitimacy, especially for its domestic audiences. In addition, gaining legitimacy abroad—garnering the acceptance and approbation of foreign audiences—not only strengthens the Party's standing internationally but also plays well at home.

As a result, when the Party seeks legitimacy through its foreign policy, it has two important audiences in mind. First, and most importantly, is China's domestic population. A related—and arguably even more important—audience at home is a critical subset of China's population: the more than 90 million members of the CCP.[5] Foreigners—including government leaders, elites and opinion-shapers, and societies at large in other countries—make up the second important audience. Of the two, achieving legitimacy with the domestic citizenry, and among Party members in particular, is more important than doing so with foreign audiences. For the domestic audience, the aim of gaining legitimacy is to make the case, through its foreign interactions, that the Party should remain in power because it alone is able to defend PRC interests and restore China to a powerful, prosperous, and respected position in world affairs. For foreign audiences, the aim of gaining legitimacy has two dimensions. One is to generate acceptance and even appreciation for the CCP, its leadership of China, and its policies at home and abroad. But in addition, the CCP values such praise and approval as validation of its legitimacy in the eyes of its domestic citizenry.[6]

Further complicating the pursuit of legitimacy is the fact that domestic and foreign audiences may have entirely different interpretations of PRC actions in the international arena. For example, while China's development and deployment of two aircraft carriers is no doubt seen at home as a sign of the country's growing power and prestige—and hence benefitting the CCP's legitimacy domestically—the warships send an entirely different signal to the outside world. Rather than granting the Party greater legitimacy, many countries in China's neighborhood and beyond see them as threatening and could take steps to push back, possibly in ways that would weaken the CCP's international standing.

This leads us to several important questions about the core objective of legitimacy in PRC foreign policy: How does the CCP generate legitimacy at home and abroad as an objective of foreign policy? How have the Party's efforts changed over time with evolving domestic and international circumstances? Finally, how has the pursuit of legitimacy affected PRC foreign policy for better and for worse? It might be helpful to start with what has not changed. Throughout most of its history, even prior to establishing the PRC in 1949, the CCP has claimed to be the legitimate leader of China because it alone is able to rid China of debilitating foreign influences, defend the country against future depredations from external enemies, and return the nation to its rightful place among the world's greatest powers. This case for CCP legitimacy remains powerful today under Xi Jinping, is at the heart of the "China Dream" and the "great rejuvenation of the Chinese nation," and continues to have profound effects on PRC foreign policy. In this sense, the Party's current pursuit of the China Dream and the legitimacy it expects to derive from it differs little from how Xi's CCP predecessors sought to validate their rule in relation to the outside world.

What has changed with time is the emphasis on various narratives that have been instrumentalized and adapted for foreign policy purposes in support of CCP legitimacy. In the Weberian model, legitimacy for political systems and social orders spring from three "pure types": "rational grounds" (whereby "patterns of normative rules"—such as an accepted legal framework, natural law, or scientific reasoning—serve to justify leadership), "traditional grounds" (because leaders fit with certain "immemorial traditions" that have existed for long periods of time), and "charismatic grounds" (legitimacy arises from the "exceptional sanctity, heroism, or exemplary character" of a given leader or leadership group).[7] For the CCP, elements of all three have at different times been used as part of the PRC's foreign policy in order to generate legitimacy for the Party's continued rule. The following discussion builds out from Weber's framework to sketch four key narratives the CCP has interwoven with its foreign policy since 1949 to bolster its legitimacy both at home and abroad.

Ideological Narrative

In the early years of the PRC under Mao, the CCP gave considerable emphasis to Marxist-Leninist reasoning in order to justify and legitimate its rule. By this reasoning, the CCP deserved its position of authority in part because it best understood the scientifically determined and immutable tides of history as put forward by Marx and Lenin, and was best positioned to navigate China through them as a revolutionary party at home and abroad.[8] In this reading, the Chinese people should follow the CCP as it would put the predatory and unequal history of capitalism to rest and carry them to higher forms of human organization, namely socialism and ultimately to communism. As long as Mao led the PRC (from 1949 to his death in 1976), this ideological narrative for Party legitimacy remained a core aspect of political and economic life in the PRC, in spite of the domestic disasters and upheavals it helped foster (such as the famines of the Great Leap Forward and the chaos and destruction of the Cultural Revolution) and its ultimate failure in achieving a socialist paradise, let alone a communist utopia. Nevertheless, this line of ideological and philosophical reasoning remains central to the Party's raison d'être, as evidenced by its constitution. It states that Marxism-Leninism has "tremendous vitality [and] reveals the laws governing the development of the history of human society" to guide Party action as the vanguard of the Chinese nation. The constitution also reminds that each paramount leader of the CCP— Mao, Deng, Jiang, Hu, and now Xi—does his part in "adapting Marxism to the Chinese context."[9]

Placed in the context of mid-20th-century history—the onset of the Cold War, the collapse of colonial empires, the surge of nationalist and Communist movements worldwide—this ideological narrative became unavoidably integrated with PRC foreign relations, where, it was hoped, it could serve to help legitimate CCP rule. Often it had an opposite effect, not least for the two superpowers of the day, the United States and the Soviet Union. On the positive side for the CCP, with China's new leadership fully embracing Marxism-Leninism as a ruling philosophy and mode of governance, the Sino-Soviet alliance—formalized less than five months after the founding of the PRC—brought enormous early economic benefit and diplomatic standing to the fledgling nation (though the alliance ultimately failed by the end of the 1950s).[10] In the 1950s and 1960s, Mao also attempted to position the PRC as the rightful leader of the international Communist movement (as opposed to the Soviet Union) including through political and material support for anticolonial independence revolutions in

Asia and Africa, and especially in Southeast Asia. The CCP sought to leverage its ideological campaigns abroad as a way to improve its standing at home and internationally.[11]

Less positively for the CCP's standing in world affairs, its partnership with the Soviet Union in the 1950s meant the PRC was from its earliest days thrust into—and became a critical player within—the cauldron of U.S.-Soviet Cold War rivalry.[12] U.S.-PRC hostility was framed in part by each side in ideological terms and led to direct warfare with one another on the Korean Peninsula (1950–1953), military confrontations during the first and second Taiwan Straits crises (1954–1955 and 1958), and PRC support for North Vietnam in its war against the United States (late 1960s and early 1970s). The Sino-Soviet split, which had been brewing since the mid-1950s over ideological differences—with each accusing the other of deviating from Marxism—broke into the open by 1960, and by 1969 the two sides were on the brink of war as they engaged in armed clashes over disputed sections of their joint border. The United States and China managed to set their ideological differences aside for a period of time following Deng's opening and reforms launched in the late 1970s. However, in recent years, ideological differences have again come to the fore in U.S.-PRC relations.[13]

Narrative of Victimized Nationalism

A second important narrative in support of CCP legitimacy involves the portrayal of China as a "victim" at the hands of foreigners. In this telling, the Party aims to gain the support of the Chinese people and sympathies in some capitals abroad by reminding them that the CCP alone was able to end the "Century of National Humiliation" (百年国耻)—roughly from the mid-19th to the mid-20th centuries—when China suffered semicolonialization, invasion, occupation, and war inflicted by Western powers and Japan. Moreover, this narrative continues, once the Party rid China of these malign foreign influences and established the PRC in 1949, it would ensure such depredations would never again threaten the country—and, moreover, under CCP leadership, China would regain its rightful status as an independent and respected nation.[14] Relying on this legitimacy narrative means the Party must be seen as the defender of national dignity against the slights and depredations of outside powers. Appearing weak in the face of foreign threats to PRC interests opens the leadership to criticism and undermines one of its core claims to legitimacy. This is why, speaking from the Tiananmen rostrum on the Party's 100th anniversary in 2021, Xi Jinping declared, "Through tenacious struggle, the Party and the Chinese people showed the world that the Chinese people had stood up, and that the time in which the Chinese nation could be bullied and abused by others was gone forever."[15]

Victimized nationalism has been far more central to the CCP's justifications to rule than a reliance on Marxism.[16] Eminent historian of PRC foreign policy John Garver notes that this nationalist narrative—while always a part of the CCP playbook—has become a more prominent aspect of the Party's approach to foreign affairs since 1990. This has been especially true since the formal ideological legitimization of Marxism-Leninism began to lose its appeal following Mao's death and as the country embraced "reform and opening" and capitalist principles of economic liberalization. Indeed, stepping up patriotic education and stoking nationalist pride were seen not only as ways to strengthen CCP legitimacy but also countered an overinfatuation with Western ways, the creeping encroachment of "spiritual pollution" (Western ideas), and the possibility of "peaceful evolution" toward regime change.[17]

That said, while victimized nationalism has proven a powerful instrument for the Party, it is a double-edged sword and must be employed with great care. At times, PRC leaders have tried to manage growing nationalist sentiments—including violent public protests—for diplomatic gain.[18] However, they have also learned that aggrieved nationalism cannot be easily turned on and off, can become a force of its own, and could be turned against the CCP leadership.[19] When American warplanes mistakenly attacked the PRC embassy in Belgrade in May 1999 during NATO's Operation Allied Force against Yugoslavia, killing three Chinese citizens and injuring more than two dozen others, Chinese cities erupted in violent nationalist protest directed against the United States. In August and September 2012—just prior to Xi Jinping's appointment as the PRC's top leader—mass protests erupted in numerous cities across China to protest Japanese control over the Senkaku Islands (called the Diaoyu Islands in China) in the East China Sea. The protests turned violent with Japanese shops, factories, and automobiles vandalized and burned.[20]

On the one hand, PRC leaders could leverage this outpouring of anger to their advantage to demand amends from Washington or Tokyo. However, the Party also risked humiliation in the eyes of the protestors if they appeared too weak or did not respond forcefully enough. Worse still, discontent with how the leadership responds to a given affront to national dignity could expand to encompass other grievances the people have with the central government. The more the Party turns to nationalism as a legitimation strategy at home, the greater the risks that it can be turned against them by their own population.

Moreover, using the nationalist narrative also has significant implications for PRC relations with its neighbors, sometimes positively but more often in negative ways. On the positive side, China's leaders may believe that the nationalist narrative resonates with persons of Chinese descent living outside China, appealing to their identity as ethnic Chinese and their emotional connection—however distant—to the Chinese homeland. In condemning past Japanese militarism, demanding greater signs of remorse and contrition from Tokyo for its aggression in the first half of the 20th century, and reprising China's role in defeating Japan in World War II, Beijing hopes to burnish its legitimacy in the eyes of Asians and others who also suffered at the hands of imperial Japan. As Oxford historian Rana Mitter argues, the CCP's telling of its role in World War II aims to build an international image of China as a moral and virtuous actor in global affairs.[21] But in other respects, this narrative does not play well with foreign audiences. Of greatest concern is that the PRC leadership may take more aggressive action abroad in order to satisfy the increasingly nationalist passions at home the Party itself has fanned.

The Party's Narrative of Success

The Party has also sought to legitimize its rule by holding up the success of its approach to governance. In this rendering, the CCP's decision to pursue reform, opening, and economic growth through its interactions with the outside world brings prosperity and improved livelihoods at home and peaceful development and economic benefits to partners abroad. This has been a fundamental aspect of the Party's appeal since the Deng Xiaoping era and continues today.

Following the global financial crisis in 2008 and again following the global covid-19 pandemic in 2020, this narrative has gained in salience and popularity as the Chinese authorities compared their success in managing these crises relative to others, and especially the United States. Chinese leaders and media outlets remind both domestic and international audiences that China has achieved success without domestic chaos or refugee crises and without resorting to warfare, colonialization, or the institution of slavery, instead relying on the country's own pathway: "socialism with Chinese characteristics," the core pillar of which is the unchallenged leadership of the CCP.

As part of this messaging, the Party calls upon its members and the PRC population at large to embrace the "four confidences" (四个自信) to further strengthen its legitimacy: confidence in the rule of the CCP, confidence in the pathway of "socialism with Chinese characteristics," confidence in the scientific basis of that pathway, and confidence in China's socialist culture. According to this thinking, the advantages of the PRC governance system, under the leadership of the CCP, create the basis for having such confidence. This greater confidence is seen in PRC activity abroad, perhaps most overtly in the form of "wolf warrior diplomacy" (战狼外交), with Chinese diplomats beginning in 2019 to speak out far more forcefully to juxtapose PRC successes against political, economic, and social shortcomings in the West, especially via Twitter and other social media platforms.[22]

Cultural Narrative

In recent years, the Party has sought to justify its claims to be the rightful successor to and steward of China's cultural heritage. This claim has required considerable propagandistic acrobatics, given the Party's previous record of violently rejecting much of China's historical legacy as backward, feudalistic, shameful, and the source of past weakness. Maoist excesses, especially during the Great Proletarian Cultural Revolution (1966–1976), targeted the so-called four olds—old customs, old culture, old habits, and old ideas (旧思想, 旧文化, 旧风俗, 旧习惯)—resulting in the desecration of ancient artworks, texts, temples, and gravesites (including that of Confucius).

Today, recognizing that many Chinese cultural attributes—its millennia-long history, inventive innovations, art, language, cuisine, and more—are both a source of pride for persons of Chinese descent and of fascination to foreigners, the CCP has sought to leverage them to boost its domestic and international standing.[23] This "cultural narrative" for Party legitimacy is an increasingly important part of the country's domestic politics and external relations, especially so under Xi Jinping. Aleksandra Kubat argues that the Party's association with traditional Chinese culture is not simply to "bandwagon on the growing popularity of tradition" in China, but is rather a "new legitimacy-building strategy." "Previously relegated to the role of an ideological foe," she writes, "traditional culture is now being appreciated as a political asset."[24]

This effort is most obvious in how the Party seeks to place itself within the tradition of Confucianism. This not only connects the Party to a common tradition that resonates with China's citizenry and with other Asians, but also holds up a hierarchical, top-down system of governance very different from the Western liberal tradition that aligns well with CCP preferences for authoritarian rule.[25] Turning abroad, the CCP utilizes Confucianism to argue for Chinese particularism and the need to build its own social and political system, consistent with its history and cultural traditions. As Xi Jinping stated in 2013, the Party's propaganda work at home and abroad must make clear that every nation has different historical traditions and conditions and that "socialism with Chinese characteristics is rooted in the fertile soil of Chinese culture and reflects the wishes of the Chinese people."[26] More broadly, associating itself with ostensibly Chinese traditions—such as advocating harmony, social stability, and benevolence; revering moral virtue and self-improvement; and practicing filial piety—the CCP aims to put forward a more benign and appealing image for international audiences. Favorably equating current PRC foreign policy precepts such as "building a community of shared future for mankind" with such ancient, time-honored maxims as "世界大同" (world of great harmony or world of great togetherness) and "天下为公" (under heaven all are equal or the world is one community) is an increasingly common practice for senior government and Party officials.[27] The full name for Xi Jinping's signature infrastructure development project—the Silk Road Economic Belt and the 21st Century Maritime Silk Road (better known as the Belt and Road Initiative)—likewise links China's past glories to the modern age.

Pursuing Legitimacy in the Xi Jinping Era

The dictate that the "Party leads all" has long been a central tenet of the PRC governance system. Under Xi Jinping, this principle was officially inscribed into the CCP constitution in 2017: "Party, government, military, masses, intellectuals, east, west, south, north, center, the Party leads all" (党政军民学, 东西南北中, 党是领导一切的"). The official English translation of that passage delivers the same message: "The Party exercises overall leadership over all areas of endeavor in every part of the country."[28] Under this Leninist system, the Party and its organs preside as the most important deliberative and decision-making bodies, including in relation to foreign affairs.

As a result, three distinctive features characterize and flow from the Party's involvement in China's external relations. First, as noted above, the Party's oversight and involvement in guiding PRC foreign affairs inject a predominantly domestic set of political interests—the CCP's legitimacy and longevity—as overriding priorities in the conduct of the country's external relations. Under this system, the Party interest in maintaining its rule may supersede the national interest, including in foreign affairs. To put it another way, the Party's interest *is* the national interest as far as the CCP leadership is concerned. Second, the government agencies ostensibly responsible for aspects of China's external relations—such as the Ministry of Foreign Affairs, the China International Development Cooperation Agency, the Ministry of Defense—serve principally as day-to-day *implementers* of policy and are not involved as institutions in strategic decision-making. Third, the PRC's Leninist system of authoritarian, one-party rule weighs heavily on the conduct of China's external relations. As John Garver argues in *China's Quest*, the CCP's adoption of this "deeply dysfunctional political-economic model . . . in which a centralized and disciplined party maintains perpetual control over the state while dictatorially repressing autonomous political activity" has "deeply influenced the foreign relations of the People's Republic of China" and "has had profound implications for the legitimacy of the CCP party state and for PRC relations with liberal democratic powers."[29]

In practice, the extent of Party involvement in foreign affairs has waxed and waned since the country's founding in 1949. Since the 1990s the Party has increasingly adapted to new circumstances and steadily reinserted itself into the

PRC's governance, including in the country's external relations.[30] Indeed, all three features outlined in the previous paragraph have become more prominent under Xi Jinping. This can be ascribed to the mandate given to Xi by the Party when he assumed leadership: to ensure the CCP's legitimacy and survival by strengthening its role in the nation's governance, enforcing greater ideological adherence, and generating respect for the CCP at home and abroad as it pursues the China Dream and the rejuvenation of the Chinese nation.

In terms of foreign affairs, this mandate has been translated into action in two important ways. The first is a more prominent role for Party organizations in the deliberation and implementation of foreign policies. The second is a more intensified effort to promote the Party and its legitimacy as a central aspect of China's relations with the outside world. The following discussion takes a closer look at these important developments.

Greater Party Role Overseeing Foreign Affairs at Home

Once installed as paramount leader, Xi oversaw a number of important conceptual, constitutional, and organizational measures to expand the Party's role in PRC external affairs while centralizing control over the foreign policy process with himself as Party chief. Compared to all of his predecessors, from Mao Zedong to Hu Jintao, Xi has given foreign policy a far higher priority, has devoted more of his time and energy on external relations, has traveled more abroad, given more major speeches on foreign affairs, and conducted more "home court diplomacy" (主场外交) by hosting numerous high-profile international events in China.[31]

Further underscoring Xi's role in foreign affairs, the June 2018 Central Work Conference on Foreign Affairs endorsed "the guiding position" of "Xi Jinping thought on the diplomacy of socialism with Chinese characteristic for a new era" (习近平新时代中国特色社会主义外交思想), or simply "Xi Jinping Thought on Diplomacy." In June 2020, a new research center was established by the foreign ministry think tank, the China Institute for International Studies (CIIS), "to coordinate resources nationwide and carry out comprehensive, systematic, and in-depth studies, explanations, and introductions of the Xi Jinping Thought on Diplomacy."[32]

But to link these developments to Xi alone would overlook the explicitly expressed centrality of the Party for PRC foreign affairs. Speaking at the conference that introduced his eponymous diplomatic thinking in 2018, Xi declared that its uppermost goal is to "uphold the authority of the CPC Central Committee as the overarching principle and strengthen the centralized, unified leadership of the Party on external work."[33] In launching the new research center at CIIS in

2020, PRC foreign minister Wang Yi emphasized that the "essence" and "greatest political advantage" of Xi's thought on diplomacy is the strong, centralized leadership of the CCP.[34] Indeed, as Qian Gang and Daniel Bandurski have argued, Xi Jinping Thought on Diplomacy, rather than a fully articulated strategy, is principally a term intended for CCP consumption to signal the consolidation of Xi's power and legitimate the dominant role of the Party in shaping PRC external relations.[35]

In addition to these conceptual exertions of Party influence in foreign affairs, more tangible changes have also been made in both the CCP and PRC state constitutions. Some of the most important changes are found in revisions to the PRC state constitution that were approved by the National People's Congress in March 2018. For example, the CCP was not mentioned in any of the substantive articles of the PRC state constitution prior to 2018. However, in order to reinforce the legal basis of CCP leadership over the country, Article 1 of the PRC state constitution now declares (new language in italics): "The socialist system is the basic system of the People's Republic of China. *The leadership of the Communist Party of China is the defining feature of socialism with Chinese characteristics.*"[36] In addition, the constitution was also amended to remove the two-term limit for the president and vice president of the PRC. While these posts are largely ceremonial, lifting the term limit allows Xi Jinping to retain all three of his most important posts—Party leader, military commander in chief, and president—when he gains a third five-year term as paramount leader in 2022. Doing so underscores the unity of the Party-state and Xi's intention to ensure Party authority over the apparatus of government. Even Xi Jinping's signature foreign policy undertaking, the Belt and Road Initiative (BRI), was formally written into the CCP's constitution, integrating the BRI with the Party's "work to strengthen unity and cooperation between China and other developing countries" and "achieving shared growth through discussion and cooperation."[37]

Following the PRC constitutional changes in 2018, the Party issued a number of new directives to reorganize aspects of the country's political and administrative structure as part of a larger effort to deepen reform of Party and state institutions.[38] These moves resulted in a greater role for Party organizations in managing the affairs of state, apparently further narrowing responsibilities of PRC government bodies such as the State Council.[39] Among these changes, the Chinese Academy of Governance (a training school for mid- to senior-level public servants formerly under the authority of the State Council) was subsumed by the Central Party School—the leading educational institution for training and indoctrinating CCP cadres—to further unify and coordinate the training of Party-state leaders.[40]

Many changes announced by the Party in March 2018 have a direct bearing on the country's external relations. Four Central Committee "leading small groups," which were informal policy coordination mechanisms, were elevated to become fully fledged Central Committee commissions with greater authority to deliberate and influence policy in their respective portfolios. These are now known as the Central Commission for Financial and Economic Affairs, the Central Commission on Foreign Affairs, the Central Commission on Cyberspace Affairs, and the Central Commission on Comprehensively Deepening Reforms. The work of the Central Leading Group for Safeguarding Maritime Rights and Interests, which helped coordinate policy in relation to the PRC's maritime claims such as in the South China Sea, was merged into the elevated Central Commission on Foreign Affairs. The Central Commission on Foreign Affairs is run by the Central Office of Foreign Affairs (中央外办), which throughout Xi's first two terms as paramount leader was headed by China's senior-most diplomat, Yang Jiechi. As head of this office, as a member of the CCP's Politburo, and directly reporting to Xi, Yang is in charge of the country's foreign policy and is much more powerful in that Party role than the foreign minister.[41]

Xi is chairman of all four of these newly established commissions. These Party bodies are in addition to the CCP's Central National Security Commission (中央国家安全委员会), which began its work in 2014, which Xi also chairs, and which appears concerned with matters of internal and external security and the intersection of the two.[42] As commissions, these Party bodies are empowered to serve as "decision-making, elaboration, and coordination organization[s]" (决策和议事协调机构) and enjoy greater political authority and bureaucratic clout than the functional line ministries such as the Ministry of Foreign Affairs.[43] In the meantime, the role of the Ministry of Foreign Affairs in the development and management of PRC external relations has steadily eroded even as the country has become more active internationally, with Party organs often taking greater charge.[44]

In addition to these changes at the level of strategic policy deliberation and decision-making, the Party also strengthened its role in the day-to-day management and oversight of certain government functions. In some cases, these changes affect bodies involved in "external work." It was announced, for example, that the CCP Organization Department—the Party body concerned with personnel, professional assignments, and promotion of CCP members—would exercise greater authority over the work of civil servants across the entire public sector. The Organization Department already wields considerable power, even over the country's international companies: as James Reilly explains, "The CEOs of China's 53 largest [state-owned enterprises], which enjoy equivalent ranks with State Council ministers and province governors, are appointed directly by the Party Central Committee's Organization Department."[45] The CCP Propaganda Department enlarged its administrative control over the expansive media, publication, and film sectors, including their work abroad. The CCP

United Front Work Department assumed greater responsibility for administering ethnic, religious, and overseas Chinese affairs, which had previously been handled by organs under the PRC State Council. The CCP International Liaison Department—primarily concerned in the past with ties to communist comrades in other countries—has increasingly engaged with political parties of all stripes around the world. Each of these organizations—and especially the latter three—have important roles to play in contributing to policy development, conveying the Party line at home and abroad, and making the case for Party legitimacy to Party members, the wider Chinese society, and audiences overseas.[46] The specific foreign affairs work of these Party organizations is discussed further in later chapters (especially chapter 7).

Beyond these bureaucratic and organizational measures, the growing centrality of the CCP in the conduct of foreign affairs was also signaled through several high-profile Party-organized "work conferences" involving the country's senior leadership and the top-tier of Party and government cadres engaged in diplomacy and other forms of external work. Convening such meetings more frequently than his predecessors—three times in his first six years in office—Xi has used them to unify Party thinking on the international situation and how China should respond. The Central Work Conference on Peripheral Diplomacy, convened in October 2013, was the first such high-level meeting held in the PRC to address relations with China's immediate neighbors. In November 2014 and again in June 2018, Xi convened a Central Work Conference on Foreign Affairs. These major meetings—which brought together the entire Politburo (the two dozen or so senior-most Party officials); the country's highest-ranking military brass; most of China's ambassadors; provincial leaders; the heads of key Party propaganda, united front, and international liaison organizations; and other key figures concerned with PRC external relations—not only assessed the international situation but also underscored the centrality of the Party in the formulation of national strategy and foreign policy.[47] It was at the June 2018 conference that Xi Jinping Thought on Diplomacy was formally announced.

The Party has also inserted itself into ostensibly domestic matters in ways that have ripple effects for PRC external relations. Much of these activities have to do with intensifying efforts by Party authorities to exercise greater control over public expression and suppressing the introduction of sensitive ideas by independent-minded thinkers, including foreigners. As discussed in chapter 1, part of this effort includes Party-authorized admonitions to avoid "Western ideas" that might call CCP rule into question. Individuals outside of China who have critical views of the PRC and CCP have also been targeted with official intimidation and harassment.[48] These steps are in keeping with other measures that affect PRC external relations, such as greater oversight of foreign organizations in China, the ouster of Western journalists, banning access to Western information sources, and pressures to allow for the establishment of Party committees within foreign companies based in China.

Greater Promotion of the Party Abroad

In addition, the four legitimacy narratives noted above have also been adjusted under Xi to further burnish the Party's image and acceptability. For example, while use of the ideological narrative waned following Mao's death in 1976, it has since resurged under Xi. As Joseph Torigian explains, Xi's sense of ideological conviction sets him apart from his predecessors Hu Jintao and Jiang Zemin and forms a fundamental feature of his character.[49] Xi and the Party leadership prominently highlight their "scientific" and "correct understanding" of Marxist-Leninist interpretations of history and how this understanding not only justifies CCP rule, but firmly puts the PRC on its path toward national rejuvenation. These Marxist tides of history, as the Party vanguard interprets and acts on them, will lead to an international system more favorable to CCP interests: more equitable and marked by "peaceful development," reformed global governance, and respect for different political and social systems.[50]

Xi's ideologically informed expectations of great changes on the international scene can be heard in one of the most important summations of his views on PRC foreign policy, delivered to the Central Foreign Affairs Work Conference in June 2018. In that speech, he expressed confidence that "China has been in the best period of development since modern times," that China "enjoys many favorable external conditions . . . at present and in the years to come," and that the country is entering a "period . . . of great significance in the historical progress of the great rejuvenation of the Chinese nation."[51] All of these developments, he said, are part of a "grand transformation not seen in a century": an era of potential risk and uncertainty, but one in which China has enormous opportunity given the dynamism of Asia versus Western drift and decay.[52]

The "victimized nationalism" case for CCP legitimacy also remains powerful today under Xi Jinping. This narrative animates Beijing's imposition of tighter controls over Hong Kong and its reunification demands toward Taiwan. It also emboldens PRC efforts to control disputed territories with its neighbors in the South China Sea, with Japan in the East China Sea, and along its border with India. And it justifies the Party's insistence that "foreign influences"—especially from the West and from the United States in particular—are at work to undermine the CCP, weaken the PRC, and stymie China's rise.

Under Xi, the legitimacy narrative of CCP success has taken on a more instructive tone, with propaganda organs and Party leaders, including Xi himself, touting the PRC model of political, economic, and social governance as worthy of respect, approbation, and even emulation—a "China solution" or "China plan" (中国方案) in the words of Xi Jinping—that can address contemporary global and national challenges.[53] This narrative also supports efforts to shape the global governance system in ways more conducive to Party interests, including through leadership roles within the United Nations (UN) system and other multilateral bodies, establishing PRC-led institutions, and aiming to set global normative and technical standards—from nonintervention, to civil and human rights, to press censorship, to internet access, and more.

More so than his predecessors, Xi has also embraced the cultural narrative to bolster CCP legitimacy both at home and abroad. The rapid expansion of Confucius Institutes and Confucius Classrooms around the world is among the most high-profile and often controversial aspects of this legitimacy-seeking effort. Confucius Institutes (typically established at foreign universities) and Confucius Classrooms (established at primary and secondary schools abroad) are overseen by PRC Party and government authorities and aim to promote Chinese language and culture and support educational exchanges between China and the partner institutions. Since 2004 when the first Confucius Institute was set up in South Korea, the program has established some 540 Confucius Institutes (CIs) and 1,170 Confucius Classrooms (CCs) in 162 countries and regions around the world; those figures are up from 440 CIs and 646 CCs in 2013.[54] The PRC government budget for these programs reached $278 million a year in 2013, six times larger than in 2006.[55]

In addition to more active promotion of these legitimacy narratives under Xi Jinping, Party bodies have also enjoyed a significant boost in resources and organizational mandate to conduct their activities abroad.[56] These propaganda and influence activities are more than simply "soft power with Chinese characteristics" and are often not soft power at all.[57] They are principally intended to burnish the image of the CCP, at home and abroad, and generate respect for and alignment with the Party's interests. Even the Party's pursuit of ostensibly domestic interests often have unavoidable implications for the PRC's external relations. Taotao Zhao and James Liebold have shown that the increased role of the Central United Front Work Department in dealing with restive ethnic regions such as Tibet and Xinjiang has resulted in "the intensification of integrationist solutions" rather than more moderate policies of accommodation. This in turn affects PRC relations with countries such as India and some within the Islamic world, not to mention Western liberal democracies concerned with the crackdown on China's ethnic and religious minorities. More broadly, the Party's intensive concern with its own security and threats of foreign interference—resulting in extensive surveillance, censorship, clampdown on foreign media and other influences, intrusive and sweeping national security laws, and a host of other suppressive measures—have had a largely negative effect on international perceptions of the PRC and its leadership.

According to Kingsley Edney, all of this "external work" of the Party helps bolster CCP legitimacy, national cohesion, and ultimately regime security, and hence is a critically important aspect of the country's foreign relations.[58] This work is especially evident in the increased international activities of core CCP bodies such as the Central Propaganda Department, the Central International Liaison Department, and the Central United Front Work Department, and their subordinate organizations. The surge in these activities abroad by the Party under Xi Jinping has frequently proven problematic for PRC external relations, particularly within open societies, which find them intrusive, unwelcome, and even illegal.

Legitimacy and Xi's Foreign Policy Pursuits

This chapter focuses on the fundamentally important pursuit of Party legitimacy. Gaining legitimacy for the Party and the national interests it claims to represent is the most important objective of PRC foreign policy. Achieving legitimacy, and the respect and approbation that come with it, helps secure the Party's leadership and longevity at home and abroad and is central to Xi Jinping's China Dream and the great rejuvenation of the Chinese nation.

Over the years since the founding of the PRC, four important legitimacy narratives have formed the core channels through which the Party aims to build its legitimacy with both domestic and international audiences. Those four narratives—having to do with ideology, aggrieved nationalism, Party performance, and Chinese culture—have varied in emphasis, though today elements of all four are part and parcel of PRC international discourse under Xi Jinping. Moreover, during Xi's tenure, the Party has worked to further boost its standing by strengthening its authority and oversight over the country's international affairs, including an expansion in the resources and mandate of Party organizations to conduct activities abroad.

However, building and sustaining CCP legitimacy presents profound and even self-defeating challenges for PRC foreign policy today. For example, nationalist appeals may play well at home but they raise concerns among the neighbors about Beijing's ultimate intentions. But on the other hand, if Beijing does not follow through on increasingly nationalist positions, the leadership risks appearing spineless and ineffectual to its own people. An appeal to ideological legitimacy may motivate the Party faithful, but for open societies around the world it is a disturbing reminder of the CCP's authoritarian, Leninist, one-party rule. Likewise, trumpeting the Party's successful performance often does more to annoy or even alarm Western societies. Trying to calibrate its legitimacy messages across multiple audiences at home and abroad ends up being a tricky and often contradictory business. These and other challenges facing China's foreign policy pursuits are discussed in more detail in chapter 8.

While inherently contradictory and risky, pursuit of the core objective of legitimacy, respect, and approbation will continue to animate PRC foreign policy under Xi Jinping. Importantly, the other five key features of PRC foreign policy discussed in this book—sovereignty, wealth, power, leadership, and ideas—flow from and loop back to support the core pursuit of legitimacy in China's foreign policy. For example, by pursuing a foreign policy that builds up and flexes national wealth and power, the Party expects to solidify its support at home, ward off potential threats to its standing, and defend its expanding interests abroad. Likewise, by increasing PRC leadership globally and promoting its own ideas for how the world should work, the CCP hopes to shape the international environment to be more accepting of, respectful of, and accommodating to its one-party rule. Also very importantly, pursuing and realizing its sovereignty goals—vis-à-vis Taiwan, for example, or in the South China Sea—helps burnish and sustain the Party's legitimacy, especially in the eyes of its increasingly nationalistic public.

Legitimacy, sovereignty, wealth, power, leadership, and ideas. Each of these fundamental aspects of PRC foreign policy is interlinked with one another and together form a framework for understanding and assessing China's approach to the world under Xi Jinping. We take each of them in turn, with the next chapter focusing on sovereignty and its central importance to China's overall approach to relations with the outside world. But as we shall see, while pursuit of these goals will probably help the Party solidify its domestic power in the near term, China's international standing will face more and more challenges in the years ahead.

3

Sovereignty 主权

Achieving Territorial Integrity and Expanded "Strategic Frontiers"

Why are we so confident? Because we have developed and become stronger. China has won worldwide respect with its century-long efforts. Its prestige keeps rising, and its influence keeps expanding. Today's China forms a sharp contrast to China in the 19th century when the country was humiliated, its sovereignty was infringed upon, and its people were bullied by foreigners.

—Xi Jinping, May 2014[1]

China as Nation-State: A Work-in-Progress

Considered in the long sweep of Chinese history, the current meaning of the word "主权," or "sovereignty," is relatively new to China. That is because it emerged in its present Chinese definition from the collision of expanding Western empires—especially the British—and the faltering last Chinese dynasty, the Qing, in the mid-19th century. Until then, Chinese imperial rulers maintained their traditional Sino-centric worldview, often termed *tianxia* (天下) or "all-under-heaven." In this conception of sovereign power and authority, the Chinese emperor, having received the mandate of heaven (天命), exercised absolute and rightful political authority over the world, even including those lands and peoples beyond the direct control of the Chinese empire. Other kingdoms, fiefdoms, and clans beyond China's core homeland did not, under this worldview, possess independent sovereign agency of their own, as their authority could only derive from the emperor. The Westphalian idea that individual nation-states possess their own sovereign powers and could exist as coequals under international law was entirely alien to the *tianxia* concept.

Over the course of the second half of the 19th century, following a series of military defeats, Western gunboat diplomacy, and the imposition of one-sided treaties by foreign powers, the Qing dynasty was forced to rethink its worldview and accept Western concepts of sovereignty and the prerogatives of nation-states. Indeed, as Chinese leaders and intellectuals struggled to defend China

Daring to Struggle. Bates Gill, Oxford University Press. © Oxford University Press 2022.
DOI: 10.1093/oso/9780197545645.003.0004

from disintegration and the depredations of outside powers, they embraced Western concepts of state sovereignty, notional equality among nation-states, national self-determination, and nationhood, eventually appropriating them to assert sovereign control over former tributaries such as Tibet, Xinjiang, and Inner Mongolia.[2]

Since the beginning of its difficult transition more than a century ago from "China as empire" to "China as nation-state"—starting in 1912 as the Republic of China and after 1949 as the People's Republic of China (PRC or China)—the establishment, preservation, and expansion of nationhood, national identity, and national sovereignty has been a central aspect of the country's dealings with the outside world. Importantly for our understanding of China's contemporary foreign policy, that nation-building project continues and remains a work-in-progress.[3] Today, PRC leaders fiercely defend their conceptions of sovereignty, and its pursuit remains a fundamental driver animating and shaping PRC foreign policy.

What differentiates Beijing's approach under Xi Jinping, however, is how China's growing power and aspirations for national rejuvenation have galvanized and emboldened a far more assertive and expansive approach to matters of territorial integrity and national sovereignty. Now more than ever, the pursuit and full realization of PRC sovereignty lie at the very heart of the country's foreign relations. In examining China's approach to sovereignty, this chapter unpacks this important driver for PRC foreign policy by reviewing its historical antecedents, discussing the contemporary meaning of sovereignty in Xi Jinping's worldview and how it increasingly encompasses expanding "strategic frontiers" well beyond PRC borders, and examining a range of real-world cases—from Tibet to Taiwan to contested maritime claims—where Beijing's aspirations of sovereignty shape and drive China's foreign policy with enormous implications for the country's relations with its neighbors and beyond.

Before proceeding, a definition: while "sovereignty" is often narrowly understood as the securing of authority over a defined territorial expanse, the discussion here takes a broader view. For the purposes of this book, "sovereignty" for China certainly includes traditional aspects such as the achievement of national unity, internal control, and territorial integrity behind secure frontiers; immunity from foreign intimidation; and freedom from subversion or intervention by other states and actors. But as China's sovereign interests have grown more global in scope, so too its understanding of sovereignty has broadened. This broader understanding encompasses greater strategic autonomy and room for maneuver on the international scene and includes the securing of strategic advantage and its denial to potential enemies at a regional and even global level, protecting economic assets and PRC citizens abroad, and accessing resources essential for national power and economic development.[4] In theory, many nations seek broad autonomy and unimpeded ability to achieve national interests, even though no country can achieve absolute sovereignty in today's world. However, in contrast to much of the past two centuries, China today has both the ability and intention to achieve a far more expansive degree of sovereign autonomy as Beijing defines it—strategically, politically, economically, and territorially.

Geography, History, and the "Tyranny of Sovereignty"

For PRC leaders today, lessons learned from China's geodemographic reality and centuries-long historical experience continue to weigh heavily on their minds, shape their approach to matters of sovereignty, and have enormous consequences for China's relations with its neighbors and around the world. Historically, Chinese leaders faced the challenge of overseeing extensive and heavily populated territories, generally centered around the traditional Han heartland in what is today eastern and central China, but which at times across the dynasties expanded to encompass lands and peoples farther to the south, west, and north. China's vast territory and population over the centuries has helped generate the powerful cultural, political, economic, and military influence that Chinese rulers have historically enjoyed over much of the eastern Asian continent. However, China's territorial expanse—especially as it bumped up against other, non-Han ethnicities around its periphery—also meant the empire was regularly under threat of incursion and invasion. The Yuan (1279–1368) and Qing (1644–1912) dynasties are examples of periods in which China's emperors were descended from non-Han peoples. The vulnerability of the Chinese empire became painfully clear between the mid-19th and mid-20th centuries. As noted in chapter 2, this period—known in China as the "Century of National Humiliation" (百年国耻)—began with the steady encroachment of the country's sovereignty by foreign powers, leading to dynastic collapse, warlordism, civil war, and imperial Japan's invasion and brutal occupation of much of the country in the 1930s and early 1940s.

The establishment of the PRC in 1949 did not alleviate concerns about threats from abroad. Within less than a year, China was at war on the Korean Peninsula with forces mandated by the United Nations (UN) and led by the United States, which Beijing feared might exploit the opportunity to bring down its fledgling government. The People's Liberation Army occupied Tibet in 1951 and quelled an uprising there in 1959 against PRC rule, a rebellion Beijing blamed on India. Throughout the 1950s and 1960s, the forces of the Kuomintang under the leadership of Chiang Kai-shek—which had fled to the safety of Taiwan following their defeat in the Chinese Civil War—threatened to mount an invasion to retake the mainland. Meanwhile, the United States built up an array of alliances and treaty organizations around China's periphery—including with South Korea, Japan, the Republic of China (Taiwan), the Philippines, Thailand, Australia, and others in Southeast and South Asia—in an effort to contain and weaken Chinese communism.

PRC leaders also understand from history that the country's sovereignty has frequently been threatened from within. Indeed, dynastic transitions more often arose from internal upheaval and rebellion than from foreign invasions. Over the centuries, the Chinese have proven entirely capable of turning on themselves in bloody, convulsive chaos, overturning regimes in the process. In the past 200 years, the Taiping Rebellion (1850–1864)—which established its own sovereign kingdom in central China—as well as the warlordism of the Republican era (1912–1949) and the Chinese Civil War (1927–1949) were massive internal struggles for power and sovereign control, pitting Chinese versus Chinese, and resulting in widespread destruction and scores of millions killed. Even after the country's founding, internal struggles continued over power and policy, leading to the disasters of the Great Leap Forward (1958–1960), catastrophic famine in the early 1960s, and the Cultural Revolution (1966–1976), resulting in tens of millions of lives lost.

This calamitous history of China's entry into the Western-dominated international system shares a pattern with many other developing countries over the past century and more: a tale of overcoming imperial subjugation, experiencing internal strife and ideological struggle, and ultimately achieving national self-determination. As in many other countries with similar histories, this experience makes Chinese leaders and citizens especially sensitive to perceived slights and fiercely protective of their sovereign rights.

These lessons of geography and history have not faded with time. Rather, Chinese leaders today reckon they must continue to grapple with modern manifestations of these same challenges to PRC sovereignty. For example, China's enormous population—at about 1.45 billion—is still the largest on Earth, as it has been for more than two millennia. True, China's population will peak around that level in the mid-2020s and begin to decline over the remainder of the century as India emerges as the world's most populous country. Nevertheless, with about 18 percent of the world's population on a territory roughly the size of the United States, China's demographics will remain a burden for the country's rulers and a constant source of concern over potential domestic disgruntlement, disruption, and upheaval. Moreover, as in the past, China's rulers today need to maintain and protect extensive and far-flung borders. At nearly 14,000 miles (about 22,000 kilometers), China has the longest land border in the world. Along that lengthy expanse, China shares borders with 14 nations, the most of any country (along with Russia, which also borders 14 nations). In addition, China shares maritime borders with nine others.[5] Also interestingly, and similar to China's most expansive dynastic eras, about half of what is acknowledged as PRC territory today is made up of areas thousands of miles away from the Han heartland—Tibet, Xinjiang, Qinghai, and Inner Mongolia—traditional lands of non-Han peoples that only since the mid-20th century have come under effective Chinese control.

China's past painful experience with Western powers and Japan also weighs heavily on Beijing's views about sovereignty today. As discussed in chapter 2, the Chinese Communist Party (CCP) rests its legitimacy in part on a nationalist narrative that it alone was able to halt the depredations of foreign powers to preserve China's sovereignty and likewise is the only force that can prevent such humiliations from happening again. Accusing foreign powers such as the United States or Japan of "militarism," "hegemony," "Cold War thinking," and "interference" against Chinese interests draws a connection to that painful past, seeks to position China on the moral high ground, and shows resolve to counter encroachments on the PRC's sovereign interests. Even more pointedly, recent and ongoing sovereignty disputes have been for Beijing constant reminders of China's past weakness at the hands of foreign powers. For example, until its reversion to PRC sovereignty in 1997, Hong Kong for more than a century epitomized British colonial power and extraterritoriality on China's doorstep.

Taiwan is another example. Following China's defeat in the Sino-Japanese War of 1895, Japan occupied the island as a Japanese colony for the next 50 years. In 1949, following Japan's defeat in World War II, the CCP's bitter enemies in the Chinese Civil War, the Nationalists, fled to Taiwan as a safe haven and established the Republic of China (ROC). The ROC was a formal treaty ally of the United States between 1954 and 1979, and they continue a close security relationship today, a key factor thwarting a PRC takeover of the island. As a result of that history, while the PRC claims to be the rightful authority over Taiwan, no government on mainland China has exercised effective control over Taiwan for more than 125 years—again, a constant reminder in Beijing's thinking of how foreigners continue to infringe on Chinese sovereignty.

These lessons of geography and history also explain why the PRC has consistently maintained a "fundamentalist" and narrowly state-centric position in defense of its sovereignty and that of others. It is true that in the 1990s and early 2000s, as Cold War divisions dissipated, globalization and interdependence proceeded apace, PRC overseas interests expanded, and China sought greater engagement, acceptance, and respect in the international community, Beijing's approach to sovereignty and nonintervention began to change.[6] Domestic policy debate in the early to mid-2000s explored how China, as an emerging world power, could support a broadened definition of "legitimate intervention" and pursue a more flexible and pragmatic policy of intervention in practice, while maintaining adherence to the principle of inviolable sovereignty overall.[7]

Nonetheless, Beijing remained highly suspicious of the implications of a more "borderless" world, fearful about the insidious encroachment of unwelcome foreign ideas and the possibilities of "peaceful evolution" that could bring about political change in China. Progressive ideas that gained international currency in the early 21st century, such as the "responsibility to protect"—that the global community is morally bound to intervene when a nation-state fails to protect its own citizens from atrocities such as genocide, war crimes, ethnic cleansing, and crimes against humanity—were reluctantly and only partially accepted in Beijing.[8]

For the most part, however, Beijing has maintained a traditional, state-centric conception of sovereignty. In doing so, Beijing repeatedly references the protections of state sovereignty afforded by widely accepted international frameworks and declarations such as the United Nations Charter and the Five Principles of Peaceful Coexistence. The Five Principles first appeared in an agreement between China and India in 1954 but are most famously associated with the Bandung Conference of 1955, a high-level gathering of leaders from developing, postcolonial Asian and African states.[9] These principles—mutual respect for others' territorial integrity and sovereignty, mutual nonaggression, mutual noninterference in others' internal affairs, equality and mutual benefit, and peaceful coexistence—are thoroughly embedded in the PRC's formal worldview and have been incorporated into successive calls by Beijing for a more "just" and "equitable" international system, such as Jiang Zemin's "new security concept" of the 1990s and Xi Jinping's "community of shared future for mankind."

This fundamentalist position justifies and helps legitimate the Party's absolute rule at home, brooks no outside criticism of its political system or domestic policies, and demands that such contentious matters as Hong Kong, Tibet, Xinjiang, and Taiwan be treated as "internal affairs" free from foreign interference. Beijing claims that these sovereign rights of noninterference should be extended to all nations. In the early 1990s, a prominent scholar of China's international relations observed, "The tyranny of sovereignty looms so large in Chinese thinking and behavi[or,] inhibiting a more positive and co-operative engagement in the creation of a more just and peaceful world order."[10] Today, the tyranny of sovereignty remains strong in the minds of PRC leaders. But contrary to observation above, they would argue that a more just and peaceful world is best achieved when state sovereignty is more strongly protected, not eroded.

One final point about the lessons of history for PRC sovereignty today: according to the thinking of PRC leaders and citizens, China today remains divided and incomplete, with territories yet to be "reunited" with the motherland and brought under uncontested Chinese sovereignty. Taiwan is by far the most important of these claims for Beijing. But other contested areas loom large as well: in the South China Sea, in the East China Sea, and along disputed

Himalayan borders with India and Bhutan. In recent years, even territories widely understood as within China's sovereign borders—such as Tibet, Xinjiang, and Hong Kong—have witnessed violent pushback against Beijing's rule, activities that it often attributes to foreign "black hands" (黑手): behind-the-scenes manipulators intent on undermining Chinese sovereignty and upending China's trajectory to "national rejuvenation." As this chapter shows, in the Xi Jinping era, Chinese sovereign claims in these areas have become all the more hotly contested even as China's conception of national sovereignty has expanded.

China's Approach to Sovereignty under Xi Jinping

Under Xi Jinping, China's approach to sovereignty exhibits more continuity than change. At its core, China's conception of sovereignty remains fundamentally state-centric: opposing foreign hegemony, intimidation, and subversion and insistent on the right to pursue domestic policies in accordance with its own traditions, norms, and laws. Xi understands that sovereignty in its broadest sense is absolutely crucial to realizing China's three "core national interests": maintaining national security and stability, including preservation of the PRC's one-party political system; protecting China's territorial integrity and advancing national unification; and maintaining the international conditions for the country's continued economic prosperity and development.[11]

However, while remaining true to those overarching principles, Xi's approach to exercising national sovereignty differs in many respects from his predecessors'. Three important aspects stand out in particular: the centrality, heightened profile, and changing emphasis of sovereignty in China's international discourse; an expanding conception of sovereignty to encompass national interests and "strategic frontiers" around the globe; and more proactive and risk-taking assertions of PRC sovereignty in contested areas, both inside China and with its neighbors.

To begin, under Xi Jinping, sovereignty has gained pride of place in defining China's approach to world affairs and how it believes the world should work. It is not only a matter of territorial integrity and regaining lost territories—though that obviously remains a core element of China's approach to sovereignty. Rather, sovereignty should also be defined and defended in the broadest sense: countries should be left alone to pursue their own internal policies free from outside criticism or interference. This view does not differ from past PRC positions, but during the Xi Jinping era, official PRC statements take it a step further. It is frequently argued, for example, that when countries do interfere in the internal affairs of others, disaster too often ensues. For example, this line of reasoning goes, American interventions encouraging the Arab Spring in countries such as Syria and Libya brought chaos and widespread destruction but did little to advance the cause of human rights, let alone democracy. Here is how Le Yucheng, PRC deputy foreign minister, put it:

> The United States, citing human rights above sovereignty, started intervention[s] in countries like Syria and Libya. . . . Where is that "spring"? How many people have become refugees and lost their homes? Conflicts deprived these countries of 10 years that could have been used to develop. And those who made the intervention, were they really to protect human rights in these countries? I think they only produced human rights disasters! . . . Such tragedies shall never happen again.[12]

In a similar vein, PRC officialdom and its media point out that the PRC's system, left to its own political and social choices, has been an enormous success. Rather than criticism for its human rights record, they argue, China should be appreciated for delivering fundamental human rights in the form of economic development, poverty alleviation, and greater prosperity for the Chinese people. In this broader conception of China's sovereign rights, the country should not only be left alone, but its system should be respected and even applauded for the stability and prosperity that the protections of sovereignty have helped ensure. Relatedly, PRC official efforts at the global level—within the UN system, for example—have long contended that the international community should not pressure sovereign governments on their domestic human rights, arguing that such rights cannot exist until basic rights of human development and livelihood are first achieved. This aspect of PRC foreign policy has gained even more prominence under Xi.

This more expansive understanding of sovereignty—and the protection and implicit favor it aims to generate for the PRC's system of governance—is most prominently put forward as part of Xi's call for "building a community of shared future for mankind" (构建人类命运共同体). Such a community, he claims, would uphold diversity in cultures and political systems, allow countries to choose their own social and political pathways, and abandon "zero-sum thinking" and "Cold War mentalities." In his words,

> We should respect the diversity of civilizations. . . . We respect the right of the people of all countries to choose their own development path. We endeavor to uphold international fairness and justice, and oppose acts that impose one's will on others or interfere in the internal affairs of others as well as the practice of the strong bullying the weak.[13]

Speaking to the World Economic Forum gathering in Davos, Switzerland, Xi took up the theme again and urged world leaders to "abandon ideological prejudice" because "difference in itself is no cause for alarm. What does ring the alarm is arrogance, prejudice and hatred; it is the attempt to impose hierarchy on human civilization or to force one's own history, culture, and social system upon others."[14] As discussed further in chapter 7 (on ideas), these views on sovereignty form a fundamental part of Beijing's efforts to change the international narrative about China and, at their core, aim to protect China's authoritarian system of government and the CCP's leadership of it.

A second important distinguishing feature of Xi's approach to sovereignty has to do with China's expanding overseas interests and measures that the country takes to protect them. As China's economy went global from the late 1990s, the country's dependence on—and vulnerability to—developments in the international system became more acute. This reality was further underscored as PRC companies proved more willing and able than their counterparts from other (mostly Western) countries to invest and operate in less stable environments around the world, especially in South Asia, the Middle East, North Africa, and sub-Saharan Africa. While Chinese firms and citizens abroad had been threatened and attacked in these regions prior to 2011, that year marked a critical turning point. As Andrea Ghiselli documents, the calamitous collapse of Libya in 2011—which required the unprecedented extraction of 36,000 Chinese citizens living and working in the country and resulted in massive economic losses for PRC firms—changed how Beijing thought about its expanding "interest frontiers" (利益边疆) and how to protect them.[15] This dramatic episode for China left a deep impression on its leaders and, once in power in 2012, led Xi Jinping to alter the country's approach to matters of sovereignty and intervention.

On the one hand, following the Libya debacle, Beijing has become far less trusting of interventionism by the international community. As noted above, China traditionally championed a fundamentalist approach that strictly limits the conditions under which foreign interventions can legally take place—in part to uphold the principle of national sovereignty for all, but also a means to deflect criticism of the PRC's internal policies. While always weighing its strategic options and interests on a case-by-case basis, Beijing typically required approval by the United Nations Security Council (UNSC)(where, as one of five permanent members on that body, it has veto power) and clear consent from the government where the proposed intervention would occur. However, in the case of Libya, Beijing showed greater flexibility. As the safety of civilians in Libya deteriorated in the midst of the Libyan civil war and under pressure from regional groups including the African Union and the League of Arab States, China chose to issue an abstention—rather than a veto—on the UNSC resolution authorizing a no-fly zone against the Libyan military, even without the consent for intervention from Libya's government. Almost within days, Beijing rued this decision, claiming that the UNSC authorization had become cover for Western nations—especially those within the North Atlantic Treaty Organization (NATO) that had the mandate to impose the no-fly zone—to pursue regime change and the removal of Libya's leader, Muammar Gaddafi. In the ensuing months, Libyan rebel forces advanced with support from NATO, and by October, Gaddafi was dead.[16]

Convinced the UNSC mandate had been willfully and illegally manipulated by Western governments intent on regime change, Beijing has since hardened its position on intervention. In four UNSC resolution votes between 2011 and 2014 in response to the chaos and civil war in Syria, Beijing defied pressures from Western governments and others and vetoed actions that would have censured Syrian leader Bashir al-Assad, imposed sanctions on his regime, and referred the Syria case to the International Criminal Court (ICC). While numerous factors weighed in the balance of these decisions,[17] the "Libya effect" carried considerable weight for Beijing and continues to do so. Following this experience, the PRC has more actively wielded its veto power in the UNSC: of China's total of 16 vetoes in the UNSC between 1972 and 2021, half have been since Xi Jinping took leadership in 2012 (see Table 6.3, chapter 6). All of these vetoes prevented various proposed interventions by the international community, including referring Syria to the ICC, ceasing military activities against civilians in Syria, allowing humanitarian access to Syria, and supporting stability and restoration of democratic processes in Venezuela.[18] In short, under Xi, Beijing has been far more wary about UN measures that scrutinize the internal affairs of sovereign states generally and that could lead to regime change in particular.

But that is not the only lesson drawn from the Libya experience. Somewhat paradoxically, in addition to its hardened policies on sovereignty and intervention by the international community, Beijing has at the same time expanded its own definitions and capabilities to intervene in relation to the PRC's sovereign interests. This expansion did not begin with Xi. During the period of Hu Jintao's leadership (2002–2012), Chinese leaders and strategists already understood that the growing presence of Chinese companies and citizens around the globe would require an enhanced capacity—diplomatically and militarily—to protect them.[19] Evidence for this evolution in thinking includes Hu's call for the People's Liberation Army (PLA) to take on "new historic missions" (新的历史使命), including "preserving world peace and promoting common development"[20]; the emergence of "development interests" abroad as a core national interest[21]; and the PLA's embrace of "military operations other than war" (非战斗军事行为)—such as counterterrorism, counterpiracy, peacekeeping, disaster relief, humanitarian assistance, and search-and-rescue—as one of its three main missions in addition to deterrence and warfighting.[22]

Once in office, however, Xi built upon these conceptual changes. The country's 2013 defense white paper—the first under Xi's leadership—stated in the clearest terms yet that China's armed forces, in adapting to new threats, will "strengthen overseas operational capabilities such as emergency response and rescue, merchant vessel protection at sea and evacuation of Chinese nationals, and provide reliable security support for China's interests overseas."[23] Xi has also repeatedly referred in high-level public statements to the importance of China's interests beyond its national borders and the need to protect these "strategic frontiers" (战略边疆).[24] Interestingly, these interests go well beyond traditional geographic definitions and include sovereign interests related to cybersecurity, technology security, information security, ecological security, and resource security.[25] The expansion of Xi's signature foreign policy initiative, the Belt and Road Initiative (launched in 2013; see chapter 4), became an additional critical factor in driving the greater concern with protecting PRC assets, citizens, and other interests abroad.

In 2019, in the section on "resolutely safeguarding China's sovereignty, security, and development interests," the PRC defense white paper enumerated the principal aims of China's national defense. In addition to deterring aggression, maintaining national security and social stability, and opposing separatist activities in Taiwan, Tibet, and Xinjiang, the white paper listed several other goals that define the more expansive conception of sovereignty under Xi Jinping: safeguarding China's maritime rights and interests; safeguarding China's security interests in outer space, electromagnetic space, and cyberspace; and safeguarding China's overseas interests.[26] In meeting these aims, China's armed forces have increasingly expanded their global footprint (see chapter 5), and according to Ghiselli, Chinese private security employees serving abroad now outnumber PRC soldiers serving in UN peacekeeping operations.[27] These various declarations and developments mark a departure from Xi's predecessors, both in terms of the geographic and spatial reach of China's sovereign interests and the expressed confidence and willingness to safeguard those interests.

The third—and most visible—area of difference between Xi and his predecessors is his willingness to press harder on contentious sovereignty matters and assume greater risk of international opprobrium and even conflict in the process. Official PRC government statements have long made clear that China's sovereignty over Xinjiang, Tibet, and Taiwan is a "core national interest" over which Beijing will not compromise. The same has not been said at such an authoritative level about other contested areas—such as the South China Sea, East China Sea, and territorial disputes with India.[28] Nonetheless, whether they constitute a "core interest" or not, Beijing's relations with its internally and externally contested spaces have become more antagonistic during the Xi era, in some cases resulting in considerable loss of life.

Through it all, Xi has remained adamant. Speaking to a PLA rally, he declared, "We absolutely will not permit any person, any organization, any political party—at any time, in any form—to separate any piece of Chinese territory from China." "No one," he warned, "should expect us to swallow the bitter fruit of damage to our sovereignty, security, and development interests."[29] He speaks in equally un-yielding terms to foreign leaders as well, as when he told U.S. secretary of defense James Mattis that when it comes to sovereignty and territorial integrity, China "can't lose even one inch of the territory inherited from our forefathers."[30]

With this in mind, the following section turns to these contested spaces, the actions China has taken during the Xi era to more forcefully assert its claims in these areas, and the impact these steps have had on PRC foreign relations.

External Contestation with China's Neighbors

The bordering outline of China we see on maps today is a relatively recent con-struct, historically speaking. Owing to China's past dynastic history and *tianxia* worldview, the upheavals in its transition to national self-determination and the establishment of the PRC in 1949, and the internal political and economic chaos of nation-building in the 1950s and 1960s, the country did not emerge as the territorially defined nation-state we know today until the second half of the 20th century. Moreover, not until 1971 was the PRC admitted to the United Nations as the legal, sovereign representative of China to that international body.

Even so, PRC political sovereignty remained contested across a number of areas, a situation that continues to this day. As of early 2022, for example, 13 UN member states as well as the Holy See (the Vatican) had official diplomatic relations with Taiwan and not with the PRC.[31] In addition, several of China's international borders remain in dispute. True, as China scholar Taylor Fravel details, Beijing agreed to resolve 17 of its 23 territorial disputes over the period from 1949 to 2005, often making significant territorial concessions in order to settle differences.[32] However, numerous difficult territorial disputes remain ac-tive today involving India, Bhutan, Japan, and Taiwan. These active territorial disputes also include two sets of island archipelagos in the South China Sea—the Paracel Islands (disputed among China, Taiwan, and Vietnam) and the Spratly Islands (disputed among China, Brunei, Malaysia, the Philippines, Taiwan, and Vietnam).

As a result, China's claims of territorial sovereignty remain a matter of intense dispute and a source of tension, armed clashes, and potential conflict. These sov-ereignty disputes involve some of China's largest and most powerful neighbors—such as India, Japan, and Vietnam—and have the potential of drawing in other major powers such as the United States by dint of Washington's security commitments to allies and partners involved in such quarrels with Beijing. These tensions have escalated during Xi Jinping's time as paramount leader. Beijing jus-tifies its stepped-up territorial assertiveness as the rightful exercise of its national sovereignty in the face of unlawful foreign meddling. Outside of China, Beijing is accused of bullying and bad faith in pursuit of its sovereign claims. In many cases, peaceful settlement of these disputes has become an increasingly distant prospect as sovereignty looms ever larger as a driver of China's foreign relations.

The following discussion does not delve into the complex historical and legal details of these key sovereignty disputes, as they have been covered in depth elsewhere. Instead, we consider these contested spaces in the Xi Jinping era, the measures Beijing has taken to assert its sovereignty over them in recent years, and what those measures have meant for China's foreign relations. Following this review of "external contestation," we turn to cases of "internal contestation," including Xinjiang, Tibet, and Hong Kong.

Himalayan Hotspots: Border Disputes with India and Bhutan

In June 2020, for the first time in more than 40 years, the disputed border between China and India erupted in deadly hand-to-hand violence along the Galwan River, resulting in at least two dozen military fatalities. This clash arose out of a long-standing set of border disputes dating back to the 1950s—disputes that led to war between the two Asian giants in 1962—that remain largely unresolved today despite repeated efforts by the two sides to conduct negotiations and introduce confidence-building measures through joint working groups and other mechanisms. However, the violence in June 2020, as well as other tense border confrontations between China and India since 2013, underscore how these sovereignty disputes will continue to shape the Sino-Indian relationship for many more years to come.

Stretching 2,700 kilometers (1,650 miles), the Sino-Indian border is disputed in several areas.[33] The two largest areas under dispute border on India's far north Ladakh region and on India's far northwest region of Arunachal Pradesh. In dispute in the former is an area known as Aksai Chin, which China occupies and has controlled since 1962 but which India claims as its own. This high-altitude and sparsely populated area of some 15,000 square miles is nevertheless strategically important to China as it provides road connections between the PRC's autonomous regions of Xinjiang and Tibet. In addition, India does not accept the Chinese occupation of land adjacent to Aksai Chin—known as the Karakorum Tract—which Pakistan ceded to China in 1963. India makes the claim that sovereignty over that territory should have been settled bilaterally between Pakistan and India in the context of their dispute over Kashmir.

The other major disputed area, in India's northeast, runs along its border with Tibet. There, India claims the rightful border should be defined along the "McMahon Line," an agreed-upon demarcation reached between British India and Tibet in 1913. The PRC does not recognize this agreement and occupies and administers lands well south of that line, creating a region it calls "South Tibet." This region encompasses some 35,000 square miles. In addition, China and India have confronted one another over a disputed border between China and Bhutan, in the area of Doklam, one of two points where the borders of Bhutan, China, and India come together. Note that the Sino-Indian border disputes are historically linked to PRC efforts to occupy and suppress unrest in Tibet in the 1950s and the flight of the Dalai Lama to safety in India in 1959, which adds an additional layer of political complexity to their territorial differences.[34] Owing to the remoteness of these regions, and the fact that the borders are in dispute, the situation on the ground is fluid, with the Chinese and Indian militaries seeking to establish and sustain a presence in areas they claim through building roads and semipermanent structures.

Since 2013, these activities have increasingly raised tensions and culminated in the deadly Galwan clash of June 2020.[35] In April 2013, India claimed that Chinese troops had illegally set up an encampment many miles on the Indian side of the agreed-upon "Line of Actual Control" in the far northern part of Ladakh. Soldiers from the two sides faced off with one another but avoided physical hostilities until they withdrew about a month later. A similar standoff and peaceful withdrawal of troops occurred in September 2014 at a different point along the Ladakh border. A year later, troops from both sides faced off yet again on the northern Ladakh border when the Indians destroyed an observation tower built on the Line of Actual Control.[36] In June 2017, PLA troops and construction teams attempted to extend a road south from Chinese territory into land claimed by Bhutan. Indian troops, acting to protect their ally, crossed into Bhutan from India's Sikkim region to confront the Chinese. It resulted in a diplomatic and military stand-off for several months before Beijing and Delhi agreed to withdraw their troops from the area, but without any resolution to the territorial dispute between China and Bhutan.[37] The Galwan River Valley clashes in the Ladakh region, which began with several altercations between Chinese and Indian patrols in May and June 2020, escalated to violent hand-to-hand brawls among hundreds of troops. Twenty Indian soldiers lost their lives. The PRC at first did not report any casualties, though Indian sources claimed more than 40 PLA soldiers were killed. Months later, Beijing acknowledged that one officer and three soldiers died in the skirmish.[38]

As the Sino-Indian rivalry heats up, the two countries enter a new phase in their decades-long sovereignty disputes. Under Prime Minister Narendra Modi, who came into office in 2014, India has taken a more nationalistic turn, including more actively asserting Indian sovereign claims, especially in the Ladakh region. Likewise, under Xi Jinping, China has also been more forceful in asserting its claims, including along the Sino-Indian border, with official Indian data reporting record-high numbers of transgressions by the PLA in 2019 and 2020.[39]

These developments help explain the cooling in relations between China and India and Delhi's interest in strengthening strategic ties with other major Indo-Pacific powers, such as Australia, Japan, and the United States. That said, as the PRC continues to build up its military presence along the Sino-Indian border, and as sovereignty and territorial integrity increasingly become sine qua nons of national rejuvenation under Xi, Beijing will continue to press its claims against India and Bhutan, in spite of the strategic and tactical risks they create.[40]

Rough Waters: The South China Sea and East China Sea

China's maritime sovereignty disputes date back many decades. For instance, territorial differences between the PRC and Japan over islands in the East China Sea can be dated to the 1894 Sino-Japanese War. Two deadly clashes between China and South Vietnam over islands in the Paracel chain (in 1974) and between China and Vietnam in the Spratly Islands (1988) resulted in the loss of more than 100 Vietnamese soldiers' lives. But China's maritime disputes have come into much sharper focus in recent years, particularly since Xi Jinping assumed power, as the PRC has taken a range of more forceful actions to assert its sovereign claims in the South China Sea and East China Sea.

A number of factors make these disputes especially volatile.[41] To begin, these disputes involve nearly all of China's closest maritime neighbors—Japan in the East China Sea, and Brunei, Malaysia, the Philippines, Taiwan, and Vietnam in the South China Sea; Indonesia has also voiced concerns about illegal Chinese fishing intrusions into its Exclusive Economic Zone at the far southern reaches of the South China Sea. Figure 3.1 depicts the overlapping claims among China and its neighbors in the East and South China Seas.

Some of these disputants are treaty allies of the United States (Japan, the Philippines) or close security partners with Washington (Taiwan). Moreover, the strategic value of these waterways—as fisheries, repositories of oil and gas resources, and critical sea lanes for international trade—further raises the stakes over who exercises sovereign control over them. According to authoritative estimates, some $3.37 trillion in trade passes through the South China Sea each year, and the seabed beneath its waters holds 11 billion barrels of oil and 190 trillion cubic feet of natural gas; the East China Sea is known to hold 200 million barrels of oil and 1 to 2 trillion cubic feet of natural gas, though estimates of as-yet undiscovered amounts are substantially higher.[42] In addition, a number of outside powers—such as the United States, Australia, and others—conduct freedom of navigation and overflight operations in the South China Sea to signal their objections to territorial rights made by claimants in excess of what is allowed by international maritime law.[43] These activities, while legal under the law of the

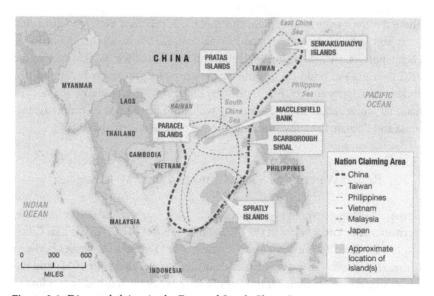

Figure 3.1 Disputed claims in the East and South China Seas

Source: Rami Ayyub, "A Primer on the Complicated Battle for the South China Sea," *National Public Radio*, April 13, 2016, https://www.npr.org/sections/parallels/2016/04/13/472711435/a-primer-on-the-complicated-battle-for-the-south-china-sea.

sea, have nevertheless resulted in highly tense and dangerous interactions, especially between the U.S. and PRC navies.

Further complicating and destabilizing matters, the PRC refuses to explicitly define the extent of its claims in the South China Sea. Instead, Beijing claims vague "historical rights" in the vast waterway, apparently roughly defined within the so-called nine-dash line. Used in official maps and other depictions, this contoured delineation, which encompasses 800,000 square miles of the South China Sea (larger than the land area of Mexico) and extends some 1,900 kilometers (1,200 miles) south of the Chinese mainland, first appeared in Chinese maps in 1948 and has been the source of territorial disagreements ever since.[44] In 2016, in a case brought against China by the Philippines under the UN Convention on the Law of the Sea (UNCLOS), the Arbitral Tribunal invalidated the nine-dash line as a basis for PRC claims in the South China Sea. The PRC did not participate in the proceeding and rejected the court's ruling (as did Taiwan). Instead, Beijing insists that territorial disputes in the South China Sea should be resolved bilaterally between the claimants, or absent such resolution, parties should shelve their disagreements and pursue "joint development" of the sea and seabed's resources. Owing to Beijing's continuing unilateral assertions of its claims, however, these efforts have gone nowhere.[45] Similarly, negotiations between Beijing and the 10 members of the Association of Southeast Asian Nations (ASEAN) on a "Code of

Conduct in the South China Sea" have dragged on since the early 2000s, even as China has steadily created "facts on the water" to bolster their claims.[46]

Indeed, since 2012, Beijing has significantly increased its efforts to assert and enforce its claims in the South China Sea. In mid-2012, just prior to Xi Jinping's appointment as top leader, China wrested control of Scarborough Shoal away from the Philippines, even though the feature is only 210 kilometers (130 miles) offshore from the Philippine main island. This action was followed by China's massive dredging and artificial island-building scheme between 2013 and 2015, which produced more than 3,000 square acres of new, above-water "territory" in the South China Sea, mostly in the Spratly Islands region, in close proximity to features claimed by Malaysia, the Philippines, and Vietnam. Moreover, Beijing has increased its military presence on and around the existing and artificial islands it claims with the construction of airstrips and aircraft hangars, naval docking and resupply facilities, and air defenses. In addition to militarizing its claimed features, Beijing has also increased the use of so-called gray zone tactics, deploying coast guard vessels, ships from the national fisheries protection authority, and ostensibly civilian—but often likened to paramilitary—fishing craft into contested regions to assert China's claims.[47] The purpose behind these coercive tactics is to compel China's neighbors to refrain from challenging PRC interests, yet doing so in a way that keeps matters beneath the threshold of conflict and does not provoke a military response, especially from other major powers in the region such as the United States.

That said, Philippine and Vietnamese fishing boats have been rammed and sunk by PRC coast guard cutters and other PRC ships belonging to its "maritime militia."[48] China deploys the world's largest coast guard, with many vessels far larger than the naval ships of some of its neighbors.[49] The Coast Guard Law of the People's Republic of China, effective in 2021, appears to authorize the maritime agency to use force, including the use of weaponry, to "stop and eliminate" threats to PRC sovereignty by foreign organizations and individuals.[50] Even more provocatively, China has also conducted major military exercises in the South China Sea, including the firing of six antiship ballistic missiles (so-called carrier killers) into the South China Sea in 2019 as a clear warning to the United States and other major naval powers of the risks they face operating in these waters.[51]

Similarly, China has in recent years increased its pressure campaign to assert its sovereign claims over islands in the East China Sea. These uninhabited features—known as the Senkaku Islands in Japan and the Diaoyu Islands in China—are an increasing source of tension between Tokyo and Beijing, both of which claim sovereignty over them. The PRC (and Taiwan) claim that these islands were a part of Chinese territory for centuries until they were wrested away as a result of Japan's victory over the Qing dynasty in the Sino-Japanese War in

1894–1895. Beijing further claims that with Japan's defeat in World War II, and its agreement to cede Taiwan back to Chinese sovereignty, so too it should have ceded sovereignty to the Senkakus, which Beijing claims were a part of Taiwan and hence a part of China. Japan rejects these claims outright and does not acknowledge a sovereignty dispute, claiming there is no evidence that China ever exercised control over these islands. Japan further claims that China's interest in exercising sovereignty over the Senkakus did not arise until the discovery of potential gas reserves nearby in the late 1960s and early 1970s. The fact that Beijing's claims are ensnarled in the painful history of Sino-Japanese relations only further enflames nationalist demands that the islands return to Chinese sovereignty.

   As chapter 5 of this volume details, since around 2009 China has increased the presence of its navy, coast guard, and commercial fishing vessels around the Senkaku Islands to asserts its sovereignty there, claiming such actions necessary in response to Japanese provocations. In 2010, Japanese coast guard vessels collided with a Chinese fishing trawler and arrested and detained its captain for illegally operating in Japanese territorial waters near the islands, sparking protests in mainland China, Taiwan, and Hong Kong. When the Japanese national government bought the islands from their private owner in 2012—claiming in doing so that it sought to deny access to them by Japanese nationalist groups—China erupted in massive and at times violent anti-Japan demonstrations that took several days to bring under control. In late 2013, Beijing declared the establishment of an Air Defense Identification Zone (ADIZ) extending off its east coast and encompassing the Senkaku Islands (and overlapping with Japanese, South Korean, and Taiwanese ADIZs in the same region) in order to "identify, monitor, control, and dispose of entering aircraft" and "guard against potential air threats."[52] Since that time, PRC coast guard and military vessels, as well as military aircraft, have maintained a near-constant presence in areas contiguous to these islands to challenge Japanese claims. With increased interactions between their military and paramilitary forces, the potential for dangerous incidents likewise increases.[53]

   From Beijing's point of view, the dispute over the Senkakus is further exacerbated by the U.S.-Japan alliance. Formally speaking, the U.S. government administered the Senkakus and other islands in the Ryukyu Island chain following the end of World War II until 1972, when their administration was handed over to Japan. Beijing claims they should have been returned to China. In recent years, successive U.S. governments—including the Obama, Trump, and Biden administrations—while acknowledging a dispute over the islands' sovereignty, have explicitly stated that they nevertheless fall under the purview of Article 5 of the U.S.-Japan security treaty, committing the United States to respond against "an armed attack against . . . the territories under the administration of Japan."[54]

Thus, Beijing's long-standing grievances about American "hegemony," "Cold War thinking," and meddling in PRC affairs are interwoven within its claims in the East China Sea.

Given Xi Jinping's overall approach to matters of national sovereignty, China will continue to press its claims in the South China Sea and East China Sea, in spite of the growing risks and the increasing pushback by other claimants and interested parties such as the United States. An exchange between the Japanese and Chinese defense ministers—during a conversation intended in part to introduce military confidence-building measures into the relationship— illustrates the problem. In speaking of the Senkaku Islands, the Japanese defense minister firmly stated that the islands "are unquestionably our territory, both in terms of history and international law." For his part, the PRC defense minister was equally clear about China's claims: "China is firmly determined to safeguard its territorial sovereignty and maritime rights and interests." Such unwavering positions in the East China Sea—and similarly unyielding positions held by claimants in the South China Sea—highlight both the growing need to find a compromise and the fading likelihood of doing so.[55]

Eyes on the Prize: Taiwan

As an island not even 1 percent the size of mainland China and with a population of about 24 million (less than the city of Shanghai), Taiwan's seemingly Lilliputian character belies its enormous historical, geopolitical, and emotional importance to the PRC. PRC leaders since Mao Zedong have insisted that the unification of Taiwan is a core national interest. Gaining sovereign control over Taiwan has been so unrelentingly defined as a matter of national pride and so deeply embedded in the collective psyche of the PRC that the CCP has left itself almost no room to fail. The firing of missiles into waters around Taiwan in 1995–1996, the passage of PRC's Anti-Secession Law in 2005, the build-up of offensive military capabilities opposite Taiwan, and dramatically increased PLA operations around Taiwan in recent years signal Beijing's determination to deter pro-independence leanings on the island and a willingness to use force to take Taiwan if necessary.[56] Importantly, Beijing considers this matter an "internal affair" and hence—in accordance with Westphalian principles—not subject to foreign pressures, interference, or negotiation.

Nevertheless, Beijing's claims of sovereignty over Taiwan are highly contested. To begin with, the island of Taiwan retains most of the trappings typically associated with a sovereign state: a permanent population, well-defined borders, a stable government exercising control within those borders, armed forces, active participation in international commerce—Taiwan ranks as the world 21st-largest economy—and an ability to enter into relations with other states.[57] While Taipei's formal diplomatic relations have dwindled, it nevertheless operates similar to a state through its more than 100 representative offices and embassies in dozens of countries around the world.[58]

China's claims of sovereignty over Taiwan are further affected by a number of other factors. The people of Taiwan have over time increasingly identified themselves not as "Chinese" but as "Taiwanese." By 2021, nearly 95 percent of the population identified as either wholly or partially Taiwanese, while slightly less than 3 percent identified as Chinese, the highest and lowest levels, respectively, at the time.[59] The fact that Taiwan, since the late 1980s, has evolved to become a robust democracy further erodes the island's political affinity with the one-party state on the mainland. Beijing's proposed framework for unification, known as "one China, two systems"—which would ostensibly allow for a significant degree of autonomy for Taiwan, as long as it accepts the PRC's ultimate sovereign authority—is the same promised to Hong Kong when it reverted to China's control. But Beijing's treatment of Hong Kong in recent years destroyed what little faith existed on Taiwan in the "one China, two systems" formula. As a result, the CCP cannot hope to use it to entice Taiwan to willingly accept a future as a sovereign part of the PRC.

Looking beyond Taiwan's own claims to self-determination, another critical factor affecting China's assertions of sovereignty over the island involves the United States.[60] Since its switch of diplomatic recognition from Taipei to Beijing and the abrogation of its security alliance with Taiwan, both in 1979, the United States has nevertheless retained a close political, economic, and people-to-people relationship with Taiwan. As to Taiwan's status, the official U.S. position neither supports Taiwan independence nor accepts that Taiwan is part of "one China."[61] Rather, Washington's position is that Taiwan's ultimate political relationship to the mainland—whether independence, absorption by China, or some other arrangement—should be achieved peacefully and with the consent of the people on Taiwan. When Washington broke official ties with Taipei, the U.S. Congress passed the Taiwan Relations Act in order to "maintain peace, security, and stability in the Western Pacific" by authorizing the continuation of unofficial relations with Taiwan. The act makes clear that U.S. policy includes "the expectation that the future of Taiwan will be determined by peaceful means"; that "any effort to determine the future of Taiwan by other than peaceful means" would be considered a threat to the region's peace and security and of "grave concern" to the United States; that the United States would provide defensive weapons to Taiwan; and that the United States would maintain the capacity to "resist any resort to force or other forms of coercion that would jeopardize the security, or the social or economic system, of the people on Taiwan."[62] Under the rubric of "strategic ambiguity," successive U.S. administrations have not openly committed to whether or how they would intervene to prevent a forceful takeover of Taiwan. Nevertheless, U.S. arms sales and the possibility that the United States might intervene to protect Taiwan add further complexity to Beijing's stated aim of incorporating Taiwan as part of China at some future point.

Under Xi Jinping, Beijing has stepped up its political and military pressures on Taiwan to assert its sovereign claims even more forcefully. Following the election of Tsai Ing-wen of the independence-leaning Democratic Progressive Party (DPP) to become Taiwan's president in 2016, Beijing restarted its campaign to isolate Taipei diplomatically by enticing eight countries to switch diplomatic recognition over to the PRC.* Since Tsai's election, Beijing has also refused to allow any form of participation by Taiwan, even in a nonstate observer capacity, in UN-related bodies such as the World Health Assembly and the International Civil Aviation Organization. Outside the United Nations, Beijing maintains constant pressures on states, international bodies, corporations, and other organizations to delegitimize and prevent Taiwan's international standing.[63] Since 2019, and as chapter 5 discusses in more detail, the PLA has increasingly conducted activities designed to intimidate Taiwan, including military aircraft incursions into Taiwan's air defense identification zone and carrying out military exercises that the PRC state media often describe as preparations for an invasion of the island. China's coercive tactics include ongoing disinformation and political warfare campaigns via social media—including efforts to influence local elections in Taiwan in 2018—intended to shape public opinion and undermine the will of the Taiwan population to resist Beijing's ultimate goal of unification.[64]

Given that about 40 percent of Taiwan's exports go to China (including Hong Kong and Macao), Beijing could also apply economic leverage to force concessions on Taipei, but it has been reluctant to do so. Aside from some high-profile exceptions—such as curtailing outbound tourism across the Taiwan Strait following Tsai's election—Beijing has preferred to stick with its strategy of deepening economic integration with the island as a means to bring it into the fold. China is also loath to disrupt either Taiwan investment in the mainland or its exports of world-class high-technology goods, especially certain high-end semiconductors, which China is currently unable to produce itself.[65]

In sum, in both rhetoric and action, since 2016 Beijing has stepped up its threats toward Taiwan in hopes of convincing Taipei that China's ultimate goal of unification will be realized one way or another. China's tougher measures under Xi Jinping are in part a response to what Beijing sees as a worsening

---

* They were Panama (in 2017), São Tomé and Príncipe (2017), the Dominican Republic (2018), Burkina Faso (2018), El Salvador (2018), Kiribati (2019), Solomon Islands (2019), and Nicaragua (2021).

situation: with the passage of time, Taiwan has drifted further away from China politically, and Beijing's preferred formula of "one China, two systems" looks increasingly less viable; at the same time, since the mid-2010s, U.S.-China relations have deteriorated and Washington has taken steps to upgrade its ties with Taiwan.

But Beijing's more forceful position toward Taiwan must also be understood as part of Xi's broader nationalist vision of "rejuvenation," which includes full realization of the PRC's sovereign interests. Xi makes this point explicit: "Our country must be reunified, and will surely be reunified. This is a historical conclusion drawn from the evolution of cross-Strait relations over the past seven decades; it is also critical to the rejuvenation of the Chinese nation in the new era."[66] China's armed forces provide a full-throated endorsement: "To solve the Taiwan question and achieve complete reunification of the country is in the fundamental interests of the Chinese nation and essential to realizing national rejuvenation."[67] Given such statements, Xi must understand that his very reputation and that of the ruling CCP will depend in no small measure on whether and how Taiwan's status is resolved in the coming years. As such, the PRC's diplomatic, economic, information warfare, and military pressures against Taiwan are likely to increase in order to force the opening of a cross-Strait negotiation process to determine the ultimate political relationship between the two. But the two sides remain very far apart as to that relationship, so the stakes over Taiwan will continue to mount as will the risks for cross-Strait confrontation and conflict.[68]

Internal Contestation in China's Borderlands

At the level of official policy, most countries in the world accept that Xinjiang, Tibet, and Hong Kong are part of China. Nevertheless, Beijing's efforts to exercise its sovereignty over these territories are contested, especially by populations within them. And while most foreign governments do not question Beijing's control over these areas, Beijing's policies within them—especially crackdowns on dissent and measures designed to suppress distinctive ethnic, religious, cultural, or political traditions—have met with harsh international criticism, punitive sanctions, boycotts, and even accusations of genocide. In response, Beijing often accuses outside forces—especially governments and organizations in advanced Western democracies—of instigating uprisings and protests against PRC rule in places like Tibet, Xinjiang, and Hong Kong. Hence, while at one level, China's sovereignty over these territories is an "internal affair," their relationship with Beijing has international implications and is profoundly intertwined with PRC foreign policy.

Xinjiang

Sparsely populated yet China's largest province by far, Xinjiang—known formally as the Xinjiang Uyghur Autonomous Region—makes up nearly one-fifth of the country's landmass. Bordering on eight countries in China's far northwest, Xinjiang is geographically, topographically, ethnically, religiously, and culturally far closer to its Central Asian neighbors than to the country's Han heartland.[†] Even its name in Chinese—新疆, meaning "new frontier" or "new borderlands"—underscores the region's separateness from the rest of China. But more than its location, what sets Xinjiang apart are its people. Xinjiang is home to many non-Han ethnicities, the largest of which are the Uyghurs, a Turkic ethnic group originating from Central Asia that predominantly professes Islam.[69] According to official PRC data, out of Xinjiang's 25 million people, nearly 64 percent are non-Han ethnicities, including the Uyghur, Kazakh, Hui, Mongol, and Tajik nationalities. Uyghurs make up about 51 percent of Xinjiang's population; Han Chinese account for about 36 percent.[70]

Xinjiang was considered a tributary or colony during the Qing dynasty, and during the first half of the 20th century, China's republican governments claimed legal sovereignty over the territory, although without effective administration to fully enforce it. With the founding of the PRC in 1949, CCP rule met with resistance as some Xinjiang local leaders sought self-determination, an aspiration that was addressed—and suppressed—by granting Xinjiang status as an "autonomous region" in 1955. Beijing's concern over its ability to effectively govern Xinjiang is evidenced by the creation of the Xinjiang Production and Construction Corps (新疆生产建设兵团) in the mid-1950s. This centrally controlled paramilitary organization operated economic enterprises, enjoyed sweeping administrative authorities, and—by funneling millions of Han Chinese to live and work in the region over the years—promoted Beijing's long-term of goal of Sinification in Xinjiang.

From the mid-1990s to the mid-2010s, a series of violent attacks attributed to Xinjiang separatists, both in China and abroad, led to increasingly harsh policies by Beijing in the region. These actions included an attack in Kashgar, just days before the 2008 Beijing Olympics, which left 16 police officers dead; a 2011 attack on a police station in the Xinjiang city of Hotan that resulted in the death of 18 persons; and a high-profile incident in 2013 in which a four-wheel-drive vehicle drove into the crowds visiting iconic Tiananmen Square—and crashed and burned, killing two pedestrians and injuring dozens. In 2014, the assaults intensified, including the killing of 31 persons at the Kunming railway station

---

[†] Xinjiang borders on Mongolia, Russia, Kazakhstan, Kyrgyzstan, Tajikistan, Afghanistan, Pakistan, and India.

by knife- and machete-wielding assailants and a series of knife and explosive attacks in 2014 in and around the Xinjiang capital of Urumuqi and elsewhere in the region, which killed more than 100 people. In many cases, Beijing blamed the attacks on a Uyghur militant group known as the East Turkestan Islamic Movement (ETIM), which seeks to establish an independent state in Central Asia that would include Xinjiang. Another group, possibly affiliated with ETIM, the Turkistan Islamic Party, took responsibility for some of the attacks.[71] In addition to these incidents, Uyghur-Han tensions exploded into large-scale riots in Urumuqi in July 2009 that killed nearly 200 people and left thousands injured.

In May 2014, following a visit to the region by Xi Jinping and his internal directives to show "absolutely no mercy" in China's "struggle against terrorism, infiltration, and separatism," Beijing launched a new "Strike Hard Campaign against Violent Terrorism" (严厉打击暴力恐怖活动专项行动), with Xinjiang as the "main battleground."[72] In addition to a stepped-up security presence and intensified use of surveillance technologies, by 2017 the clampdown came to include the massive arrest and internment of an estimated one million or more Uyghurs and other Muslim minorities in hundreds of detention centers where the PRC government claimed they received training in Mandarin Chinese, deradicalization, and patriotic education. Accounts by former detainees detail the months-long privations, punishments, and personal anguish they endured. Journalists and researchers also found that thousands of Islamic religious sites were destroyed, apparently as part of the Strike Hard campaign.[73]

By one measure, this crackdown appears to have succeeded: as of 2021, there were no reported militant attacks in China since 2017.[74] On the other hand, it has come at an extremely high cost for Uyghurs and other Muslims in the region, deepening ethnic animosities between Uyghur and Han peoples, and the pervasive portrayal of Uyghurs as a security threat in China.[75] Beijing's actions have also met with widespread international condemnation, including a formal finding on the part of the U.S. administration that China's crackdown in Xinjiang constitutes genocide (discussed further in chapter 8). Nonetheless, Xi Jinping remains determined to press on with his tough-minded policies in Xinjiang: at a 2020 CCP conference on Xinjiang he declared that the Party's strategy for governing Xinjiang is "completely correct" and must be implemented for the long term.[76]

Tibet

China's effort to extend its sovereignty over Tibet has had a likewise contentious and violent history.[77] Before 1949 and the PRC's founding, sovereign claims to

Tibet by the Republic of China government were questioned by major powers of the day, especially the United Kingdom, and for much of the first half of the 20th century, Tibet operated as a de facto independent state. Separated from the Chinese heartland by mountain ranges and located on a high-altitude plateau in China's far southwest, Tibet remains nearly homogeneous ethnically speaking; out of a population of some 3.5 million people, about 90 percent are Tibetan and 8 percent are Han Chinese.[78] For the PRC, it is a strategically important region as it shares a disputed border with India and Nepal, is rich in mineral resources, and is home to the headwaters of China's two major river systems—the Yangtze and the Yellow.

Following the establishment of the PRC, the PLA entered Tibet in 1950, defeating Tibetan armed forces in a number of skirmishes, establishing administrative control over the region by 1951, and creating the provincial-level Tibet Autonomous Region in 1965. When a Tibetan uprising was crushed by PRC forces in 1959, the 14th Dalai Lama and his ministers fled to India and set up a government in exile in Dharamshala, India, where it continues to this day. That government does not accept PRC sovereignty over Tibet, which it considers an "illegal occupation" and claims the homelands to Tibetans in China—which includes not only what Beijing defines as Tibet but also parts of other provinces where Tibetans live, such as Gansu, Qinghai, Sichuan and Yunnan—should be an independent nation. The international popularity of the 14th Dalai Lama, who won the Nobel Peace Prize in 1989, and the support for Tibetan culture and aspirations for autonomy found in India and elsewhere around the world, especially among the liberal democracies of the West, makes the issue of Tibetan sovereignty a highly sensitive one for Beijing.

Through a combination of administrative measures, tighter regulation of religious practices, cooptation of elites, a strong presence of military and other security forces, and economic development, Beijing has steadily strengthened its control over Tibetan areas—but not without international controversy and sporadic episodes of violent unrest. In the late 1980s, as the Dalai Lama and the Tibetan government in exile gained greater international sympathy, deadly riots broke out in Lhasa, Tibet's capital, between 1987 and 1989, with dozens and perhaps hundreds killed, resulting in Beijing's yearlong imposition of martial law. In March 2008, widespread rioting broke out again in Lhasa and spread to other ethnically Tibetan areas of China. Coming on the eve of the 2008 Beijing Olympics, the situation galvanized international supporters of Tibetan independence and resulted in disruptions of the international Olympic torch relay in many locations around the world and calls to boycott the games, a source of enormous irritation and embarrassment for Beijing. Since 2009, the Tibetan government in exile counts 155 Tibetans who have carried out self-immolations in China to protest PRC government policies in their homeland.[79]

Today the Tibet question remains a highly unsettling and sensitive matter for China and continues to spill over into PRC foreign affairs. When the Dalai Lama travels abroad, Beijing issues harsh warnings against government leaders not to meet with him or else face punitive measures. In spite of these admonitions from Beijing, the Dalai Lama has met with scores of world leaders—including numerous meetings with U.S. presidents Bill Clinton, George W. Bush, and Barack Obama—in an effort to draw attention to the Tibetan cause.[80] Beijing has announced that it will approve the selection of the next Dalai Lama, a move that was met with criticism from governments and organizations around the world that support greater autonomy and religious freedom in Tibet. Meanwhile, in spite of international opprobrium, PRC policy under Xi Jinping has doubled down on its assimilationist strategy in Tibet.[81] Speaking before the CCP Politburo Standing Committee at a special forum on "Tibet work," Xi emphasized "safeguarding national unity and strengthening ethnic solidarity" through incorporating patriotic education, combating separatist activities, and adapting Tibetan Buddhism to socialist society. The way forward, he said, requires "continuous efforts to enhance recognition of the great motherland, the Chinese nation, the Chinese culture, the CPC [Communist Party of China], and socialism with Chinese characteristics by people of all ethnic groups."[82]

Hong Kong

Hong Kong represents a third area of "internal contestation" for China. As noted earlier in this chapter, for more than 150 years Hong Kong has been a highly sensitive matter for Chinese sovereignty.[83] British colonial control over Hong Kong began in the 1840s, forced upon the Qing following its defeat in the First Opium War, and lasted until the enclave's reversion to Chinese sovereignty in 1997. That history is frequently invoked by China's leaders as a reminder of the country's debasement by foreigners at a time of weakness and how the PRC under CCP leadership at last regained possession of territories wrongfully wrested from Chinese sovereignty.

As part of the handover agreement with the United Kingdom, the Chinese side agreed to establish Hong Kong as a "Special Administrative Region" (HKSAR) under PRC sovereignty that would "enjoy a high degree of autonomy . . . vested with executive, legislative, and independent judicial power"; that "the laws currently in force in Hong Kong will remain basically unchanged"; that "the socialist system and socialist policies shall not be practised" in Hong Kong; and that its "previous capitalist system and life-style shall remain unchanged for 50 years" (until 2047).[84] With the agreement and under the principle of "one country, two systems," Beijing demonstrated a remarkably pragmatic flexibility in its approach to Hong Kong sovereignty—especially given the historical baggage associated with Hong Kong's past. This framework was later applied to Macao when it reverted from Portuguese to PRC sovereignty in 1999 and is the formula Beijing proposes for the unification of Taiwan.

However, Hong Kong's more open traditions—including greater freedoms of assembly and the press, the rule of law, an independent judiciary, and a vibrant civil society—as well as a Hong Kong identity distinct from the mainland, never sat comfortably alongside the PRC's authoritarian instincts and interests. Expectations for some that Hong Kong would evolve in a more democratic direction—including direct election of its executive and legislature—never eventuated. Nonetheless, Beijing's efforts to impose tighter controls on Hong Kong were met with significant dissent from the local population, including the 2014 Umbrella Movement—which opposed Beijing's efforts to interfere in Hong Kong's electoral processes—and the massive street protests of 2019–2020. Initially mobilized in opposition to a proposed law allowing for the extradition of Hong Kong citizens to face mainland China courts, the protests of 2019–2020 morphed into a pro-democracy movement demanding universal suffrage and direct elections of the HKSAR's legislature and chief executive.

With millions in the streets and much of the city's political and economic life brought to a standstill, PRC leaders were no doubt taken aback but also resolved to offer no concessions and to crush the pro-democracy movement. The PRC's legislature approved a new security law for Hong Kong that came into effect in July 2020, which, among other steps, criminalizes secession, subversion, terrorism, and collusion with foreign forces against the PRC central government and establishes a special security force within Hong Kong, answerable to Beijing and not subject to HKSAR laws.[85] In 2021, the PRC National People's Congress passed additional laws to "perfect" the Hong Kong electoral system, in effect making it impossible for pro-democracy candidates to run for office and ensuring that the territory's chief executive will be staunchly loyal to Beijing. These draconian measures—which have included the arrest and intimidation of protestors, activists, and pro-democracy leaders—effectively ended the movement and destroyed the credibility of the promised "one country, two systems" framework governing Hong Kong's relationship with the PRC.

These measures resulted in international condemnation, especially from the world's major democracies (discussed further in chapter 8). However, as in the case of Xinjiang and Tibet, the PRC leadership preferred to bear the damage these decisions have on China's international reputation rather than risk the threats to internal cohesion and Party leadership they see emanating even from a semiautonomous Hong Kong. In the words of China's foreign minister, "Sovereignty and territorial integrity are a country's core interests. Like any other country, China has no room for compromise on such a major issue of principle.

The United States should not repeatedly challenge China's rights and interests on issues related to Taiwan, Xinjiang, and Hong Kong, and at the same time expect China to cooperate with it on issues of its own concern."[86]

Deepening Dilemma

This chapter has outlined how the pursuit of sovereignty animates PRC foreign policy, especially under Xi Jinping. Matters of national sovereignty have since the mid-19th century occupied a central place in the minds of Chinese leaders. Such matters continue to do so today as China's nation-building process remains unfinished. However, what differentiates the PRC's approach to sovereignty under Xi Jinping is the intensity and scope the issue has assumed as part of Beijing's foreign policy, especially as the country gains the will and power to realize its sovereign aspirations. Under Xi Jinping, China's conception of national sovereignty forms a critical aspect of its international discourse and aspirations for how the world should work—not least in garnering respect for the Party's accomplishments and deflecting criticism of China's social and political system—and seeks to reinstitute a stronger fundamentalist norm on national sovereignty and nonintervention within the international system. At the same time, Beijing has expanded its own conceptions of what constitutes PRC sovereign interests around the globe and how to safeguard them. Moreover, Xi Jinping appears far more willing than his predecessors to press ahead in asserting China's sovereignty in contested areas on both sides of mainland China's borders, risking violence and potential conflict in the process, all in the name of achieving "national rejuvenation."

In pursuing this approach to sovereignty, however, Xi Jinping's China increasingly faces a number of dilemmas. At one level, China's more expansive geographic and spatial definition of sovereign interests exposes a "great power mentality" that Beijing officially shuns but cannot shake. China is not the first rising power to discover myriad and burgeoning interests well beyond its traditional borders. But it still struggles to reconcile the need to protect its growing global interests with its preferred image as a peaceable power intent only on "win-win" solutions and "common development." At home, PRC leaders are compelled by the imperatives of "national rejuvenation" and performance legitimacy to vigorously pursue their sovereign rights and territorial claims as they see them. However, in doing so they have boxed themselves in politically, leaving little room for compromise. Failure to defend their sovereign claims or appearing weak in the face of other claimants—such as in the East China Sea and the South China Sea—would risk a nationalist backlash and undermine the Party's mandate to rule. Moreover, in pursuing its sovereignty claims, Beijing generates distrust, pushback, and even violent conflict. China's assertions of sovereignty over Taiwan are the most complex and dangerous of all, both for what they mean to CCP standing at home and for the enormous risk of international conflict they portend if Beijing opts to use force.

But in spite of these challenges, China's expanding assertions of sovereignty under Xi Jinping will not abate. The PRC's pursuit of sovereignty draws strength from painful lessons of China's past, its remaining grievances, and its aspirations for national rejuvenation in the future. For PRC leaders and citizens today—for decades imbued with the narrative of victimhood and aggrieved nationalism—fully regaining China's sovereignty is absolutely essential to making China great again. Under Xi, there is a growing comfort in Beijing with exercising great-power prerogatives based on nationalist reasoning and muscling China's way against weaker neighbors. As China continues to grow in power and influence, we should expect matters of sovereignty to loom larger and larger in how Beijing chooses to pursue its national interests abroad.

The pursuit of sovereignty is also intertwined with the other key drivers of PRC foreign policy under Xi Jinping: legitimacy, wealth, power, leadership, and ideas. Perhaps most importantly, achieving greater sovereignty—both in terms of advancing national interests and asserting control over disputed territories—bolsters the Party's legitimacy and mandate to rule. Exerting more expansive sovereign interests abroad is also a justification for strengthening China's hard power, and increased economic and military might in turn allow Beijing to pursue its sovereignty claims more forcefully. A China more confident in its ability to achieve its sovereign interests will seek greater leadership on the world stage and promote its ideas on how the world should work. And concerns over sovereignty, economic dependency, technological self-reliance, and China's ability to protect its expanding overseas interests will be critical for the country's continuing aspirations to development and prosperity—topics to which we turn next.

4

Wealth 财富

Pursuing National Development and Prosperity

The ongoing successes of Chinese socialism signify . . . that socialism has flourished in China and opened new opportunities for development, that Chinese socialism has created a new path to modernization for developing countries, and that China is contributing its wisdom and finding solutions to the problems facing mankind.

—Xi Jinping, July 2017[1]

"To Get Rich is Glorious": Building a Modern Socialist Economy

It has long been the dream of the leaders of the People's Republic of China (PRC or China) to see the country rejoin the ranks of advanced, wealthy—and hence powerful—countries. In the earliest years of the PRC, building economic strength was a matter of national survival as the country emerged from decades of institutional collapse, foreign occupation and exploitation, and war. The post-Mao era under Deng Xiaoping emphasized "opening and reform" (改革开放), the "Four Modernizations" of industry, agriculture, science and technology, and the military; and a gradual integration with outside world. Deng's successors accelerated what he started in what has been the most spectacular economic development success story in modern times: quintupling gross domestic product (GDP) per capita from around $1,650 to over $8,250 in 20 years (1999–2019); lifting hundreds of millions above the poverty line; becoming the world's second-largest economy by 2009; and, according to China's official determination, becoming a "moderately well-off society" (小康社会) by 2020.[2] Deng's famous exhortation "To get rich is glorious" has been thoroughly and enthusiastically embraced.

Throughout these periods, three important constants characterized China's economic development. First, the Chinese Communist Party (CCP or Party) was and still is acutely aware that its domestic standing and even survival depends in no small measure on its ability to deliver continuously improved economic conditions for more and more individuals. The dynastic history of China is scattered with examples of popular uprisings spurred by economic grievance

Daring to Struggle. Bates Gill, Oxford University Press. © Oxford University Press 2022.
DOI: 10.1093/oso/9780197545645.003.0005

and hardship and the subsequent downfall of once-mighty rulers. In more recent times, such as in the aftermath of the Tiananmen crisis of 1989—in which a volatile mix of students and workers demanding greater economic certainty and political reform were violently crushed in the streets of Beijing—the Party regained its standing by implicitly promising a deal: in return for steadily improved livelihoods and economic opportunity, the people would accept the authority of the CCP. This social contract remains in place today, though it appears more stable than in the past as more and more persons have economically benefitted from it and have a major personal stake in its perpetuation. Nevertheless, it still means the Party must deliver on its promises and ensure not only continued prosperity but a prosperity that brings benefits across the entire population, burnishes the Party's mandate to rule, and sustains its legitimacy. As Xi Jinping reminded the CCP leadership in 2013:

> The historic leap forward by which China's economy rose to the second place in the world has greatly increased the enthusiasm of the Chinese people, greatly boosted the development of China's productive forces, and added great vigor to the Party and the country.[3]

Second, while the primary aim of PRC economic development is to enrich the Chinese nation, it was mostly understood that China would need to engage the outside world to access the markets, capital, resources, technologies, and know-how necessary to empower the PRC economy and propel it toward modernity. This was true even during the most autarkic and disastrous phases of PRC economic policy under Mao Zedong. In the earliest years of the PRC, the economy leaned heavily on its relationship with the Soviet Union, which provided factories, equipment, and technical assistance as well as loans to China. China's First Five-Year Plan (covering 1953 to 1957) was explicit about the important role of the Soviet Union in assisting China's nascent industrialization effort, including the well-known "156 projects" in sectors such as coal mining and processing, power generation, steel production, and heavy machinery manufacturing. With the collapse of Sino-Soviet relations by 1960, China pursued economic relations with others. China had already been in a growing trade relationship with Japan, and by 1965 Japan had become China's most important trade partner. This was true even though China and Japan were at the time still officially at war, and their diplomatic relationship was not formally restored until 1972. Japan's contributions to PRC economic development overrode the bad memories of China's wartime experience at the hands of imperial Japan.[4]

Deng Xiaoping went much further to engage the outside world as part of his economic reform and opening strategy, establishing in the 1980s and 1990s dozens of "special economic zones" and "open coastal cities"—such as Shenzhen,

Zhuhai, Xiamen, Shantou, Dalian, Tianjin, Hainan Island, and Shanghai Pudong—to attract foreign investment, managerial know-how, technology, manufacturing plants, and export facilities. From the onset of Deng's reforms in 1980, China's trade as a percentage of national GDP mushroomed from about 12 percent to its peak of over 64 percent by 2005; meanwhile, China's industrialization was highly dependent on foreign capital, with net inflows of foreign direct investment growing nearly 100-fold, from about $3.5 billion in 1990 to nearly $300 billion by 2013. Leading China economist Arthur Kroeber makes the point that China's remarkable industrialization in the 1990s and 2000s was "unique in its unusually heavy reliance on foreign investment."[5]

Under Jiang Zemin and Hu Jintao, PRC firms and investors were encouraged to "go out" (走出去), deploying China's increasing accumulation of foreign reserves to expand overseas markets and seek resource and technology acquisitions abroad. "Going out" was elevated to a national strategy by its inclusion in the 2001 10th Five-Year Plan, calling for expanding international cooperation, promoting exports, accessing new resources, and establishing research and development centers overseas.[6] An important aspect of this plan was to encourage and support—through state-subsidized loans and other preferential treatment— the acquisition of foreign firms in order to access proprietary technology and other intellectual property that Chinese firms, mostly state-owned enterprises, could absorb and utilize. During the Jiang and Hu eras of "going out," the PRC gained entry to the World Trade Organization in 2001, and between 2001 and 2012 China's exports of goods and services grew from $209 billion to over $2 trillion while its outbound investment grew more than sevenfold over that period to nearly $65 billion (it would go on to top out at $216 billion by 2016).[7] China became the world's largest exporter in 2009; the world's largest trading nation, surpassing the United States (2013); the world's second-largest source of foreign direct investment (FDI), behind the United States and ahead of the Netherlands and Japan (2016); and the largest destination for FDI, surpassing the United States (2020).[8] Opening to the outside world; accessing foreign markets, capital, technology, and supply chains; and integrating with the globalizing economy all contributed enormously to the wealth and development of China and the Chinese people. At the same time, the Party remained vigilant to the risk that international economic engagement could weaken its political authority at home.

The pursuit of national rejuvenation marks a third important constant that infuses the PRC's quest for economic development. However, while making China wealthy and powerful again has been the aspiration of Chinese leaders for more than a century, for most of that period China lacked the capacity to do so. Today presents an entirely different story. The PRC has not only built the fundamentals of a modern national economy, risen to the ranks of the world's most powerful economies, and achieved a moderately well-off society. The PRC leadership has also increasingly leveraged this wealth and development to exercise economic statecraft in the service of national strategy and its pursuit of national rejuvenation. As the following pages describe, state-owned and private companies in China are both increasingly expected to align themselves more closely with the Party's strategic and political objectives. Leveraging economic resources in pursuit of foreign policy objectives is a form of "hard power" and—as chapter 5 discusses in greater detail—is an instrument that Xi Jinping frequently employs.

Economic Challenges Ahead

Since taking power in 2012, Xi Jinping has remained focused on these three fundamental aspects of China's wealth generation and development: improve people's lives and well-being to legitimate and strengthen Party rule, maximize the benefits of international economic engagement and minimize its risks, and put China's economic power to work in achieving national strategic interests, both at home and abroad. In the simplest of terms, Xi Jinping has set out his economic priorities: "carry out reform that benefits the Party and the people, and contributes to prosperity and long-term stability."[9] But looking ahead, he understands it is not so simple. China faces a number of significant economic challenges—some long-standing in nature, others arising more recently—that demand attention if the country is to continue ascending the developmental ladder, become a high-income country, and achieve "national rejuvenation" in the next three decades.

In spite of its economic success, China may face greater economic uncertainty today than at any time since Deng Xiaoping's reform and opening strategy in the 1980s. Not only is China's pace of economic growth slowing, but the slowdown is structural and not merely cyclical. Also importantly, the slowdown has similar aspects to troubled transitions that other emerging economies failed to navigate.[10] At its heart, China's economic challenge is to change the economic growth model it has so heavily relied upon since the 1990s. China's remarkable economic sprint depended mostly on capital investments and export-led growth, fueled by the influx of rural-to-urban, inexpensive surplus labor as well as imported technology to increase efficiency. Investment in capital stock helped to build the foundations of a modern, export-led, industrial economy: power plants, telecommunication networks, highways, railways, airports, harbors, and massive urban centers.

However, continuing the pace of economic growth based on this model has become more difficult with each passing year. To begin with, China's workforce population peaked in 2012 and has been in decline since, contributing to increasing labor costs.[11] China's aging population also foretells increasing long-term pressures on the PRC's savings rate and capital formation, human capital formation, and welfare and pension systems as the country grows old before it grows rich.[12] In addition, capital investments have reached a saturation point. Constructing one more train line or high-rise urban agglomeration will add marginally less value to China's growth than in the past. If anything, China faces the problem of overcapacity: too much heavy industry, too much housing, and too much underutilized capital stock. China's future economic success needs to rely less on capital investment—which in the past was less concerned with efficient use of capital—and much more on extracting efficiencies and productivity from existing capital stock. That means gaining greater outputs per worker and unit of capital through such measures as technological innovation, allocating capital toward higher-yielding results, and shifting toward a greater consumption-led growth model.

If China can succeed in navigating these changes, it may be able to avoid the "middle-income trap."[13] This situation arises when a country reaches middle-income levels but then—owing to higher wage costs and diminishing productivity gains—fails to progress to high-income status. China's gross national income (GNI) per capita now stands at about $11,000 which, according to the World Bank, makes China an "upper-middle-income" country and on the cusp of reaching the lower rungs of the high-income ladder. However, as the World Bank reports, of the 101 middle-income economies in 1960, only 13 advanced to a high-income level by 2008.[14] In addition, it appears that a successful transition to high-income status is highly correlated with "institutional quality": greater political openness, good governance, and the rule of law. Of the 13 economies just noted, the vast majority of them—including PRC neighbors Japan, Singapore, South Korea, and Taiwan—developed high-quality political and legal institutions while transiting beyond the middle-income trap.[15] For Xi Jinping, avoiding this trap is imperative for the "great rejuvenation of the Chinese nation," but it also carries economic and political risk. Nonetheless, one of China's most acclaimed economists, former minister of finance Lou Jiwei, declared in 2015 that the country had a 50-50 chance of remaining in middle-income limbo if significant reforms were not taken.[16]

One partial solution to China's economic challenges—and one that was actively pursued from the mid-1990s to the mid-2000s—is reforming the state-owned enterprise (SOE) system by privatizing or closing loss-generating firms. However, under Xi, this reform process has slowed considerably. Indeed, the PRC leadership looks to retain and even tighten its political control over the state-owned sector and maintain SOEs' overly large role in the economy, subsidized with state debt. Doing so risks continued slowing of growth, misallocation of capital and other productive inputs, and increasing debt burdens. But on the other hand, serious reform of SOEs, including closures, downsizing, and layoffs, would be socially and politically risky. With combined assets amounting to more than 200 percent of GDP, accounting for 35 percent of China's economic output, and employing around 60 million persons, China's 170,000 SOEs make up the largest state sector of any country in the world. In 2018, 83 Chinese SOEs made the Fortune Global 500 list, including three of the four largest companies on the planet: China National Petroleum Corporation (CNPC), Sinopec, and State Grid.[17] Serious reform could mean financial losses for powerful stakeholders at the top of the PRC political and economic hierarchy who have strong incentives to maintain the system as is.

Xi is also reluctant to allow the market—with all of its unpredictability and risk—too much power in determining the most efficient allocation of resources, especially in the hulking state sector. Rather, since early in Xi's time in office, the PRC has doubled down on a hybrid strategy that maintains both the state and the market systems. In the words of a key decision taken by the Party in November 2013, market forces will play a "decisive" role determining the allocation of economic and financial resources, but the state sector will play a "dominant" role within the national economy.[18] As Arthur Kroeber concludes, "In practice, this means the government will pursue reforms that increase the role of the market in setting prices but will avoid reforms that permit the market to transfer control of assets from the state to the private sector."[19] But Chinese and Western economists agree this model is not ideal, and the achievement of sustained strong growth and significantly higher per capita incomes demand increased SOE productivity and a greater role for a thriving private sector.[20] Conversely, continued preferential political and financial treatment of SOEs means these firms will remain a drag on the overall economy.

Moreover, continued political oversight, direction, and cooptation of the private sector can also stymie entrepreneurialism and innovation. In the Xi Jinping era, private businesses have come under even more pressure to conform and demonstrate support for CCP interests.[21] The case of Jack Ma, founder of the e-commerce giant Alibaba (阿里巴巴)—one of China's most successful entrepreneurs and China's richest man—is instructive here. Amid continued political and financial scrutiny of the private sector under Xi, Ma in 2020 ran afoul of authorities by making bitingly critical—and very high-profile—remarks about China's financial regulatory system and its stifling effect on innovation. Shortly thereafter, the long-awaited initial public offering (IPO) of Ma's holding company, Ant Group, was blocked by regulators and new antitrust guidelines put in place that could lead to the break-up of his empire. Investigations later revealed that Ma's IPO might have financially benefited potential rivals to Xi Jinping.[22]

Jack Ma's empire was not the first private enterprise in China brought to heel—nor will it be the last. China's huge ride-hailing firm, Didi Chuxing (滴滴出行),

and other high-tech platforms were forced by PRC regulators in 2021 to halt the registration of new users owing to possible "national security violations." The concerns involve the security both of user data and the operation of the PRC's information technology infrastructure on which the tech platforms depend. As the state-owned *Global Times* opined at the time, "The state cannot allow [internet giants] to become rule-makers regarding the collection and use of personal information. . . . We cannot allow an internet giant to have greater control than the state over the mega-database of Chinese people's personal information."[23] Didi Chuxing and other PRC firms have raised record amounts of capital in IPOs in the United States in recent years, further raising concerns that U.S. and other foreign shareholders and regulatory agencies could have prejudicial access to the firms' data, financial records, and technological infrastructure.[24] In response to these and other concerns, PRC authorities have long preferred more compliant entrepreneurs, closely aligned with the country's political and economic interests, and employ a range of political, financial, and administrative incentives to achieve such cooperation.[25] Under Xi Jinping, it appears that compliance will be enforced even if it results in enormous economic losses: by some estimates, the investigations launched by PRC regulators into high-flying Chinese firms erased about $1 trillion from their share values.[26]

In sum, Xi Jinping faces a host of economic challenges: reforming the state-owned enterprise system and reducing its debt burden, extracting greater productivity gains even as the pace of economic growth slows, shifting from capital-intensive to consumption-led growth, and managing a difficult demographic transition featuring a far older population (by 2050, one in three people in the PRC will be over age 60) and a shrinking working-age population. Moreover, China's economic growth has generated widening socioeconomic disparities in income and education as well as between rural and urban and coastal and interior parts of the country. In addition, China will also need to develop and open markets for higher-value, higher-tech exports; free up the private sector; and become more technologically innovative and self-reliant in the face of deteriorating economic relations with advanced economies such as the United States. And Chinese leaders will try to do so while maintaining Party legitimacy and the mandate to rule, maximizing the benefits of international engagement even as economic relations with the United States worsen, and more effectively leveraging the country's economic strength to achieve national strategic goals at home and abroad. It is a tall order, and the onset of the global covid-19 pandemic in early 2020 and the sustained economic downturn worldwide that followed only further complicate these challenges for the PRC leadership. Seasoned analysts of the PRC economy are highly skeptical that the country can succeed in meeting these challenges without undertaking much more serious economic reform.[27]

Characteristically, however, Xi has launched several major initiatives that have set him apart from his predecessors and attempt to address many of these economic difficulties. These measures profoundly affect China's relations with the outside world, and not always for the better. Two sets of initiatives stand out, which, at first glance, appear somewhat contradictory. The first is a massive outward deployment of capital and infrastructure development capacity under the Belt and Road Initiative. The second is a suite of inward-focused industrial policies to promote greater reliance on China's domestic markets as an engine for innovation, technological advancement, and economic growth. Both of these initiatives reflect and reinforce the determination of China's current leadership to maintain the dominant role of the Party-state in economic—and ultimately political—affairs.[28]

Belts and Roads

The Belt and Road Initiative (BRI; in Chinese 一带一路, literally "one belt, one road") refers to the New Silk Road Economic Belt (新丝绸之路经济带) and the 21st Century Maritime Silk Road (21世纪海上丝绸之路). The "belt" tracks westward from China and extends overland across Central Asia, West Asia, and Europe. The "road" takes a maritime route south from China, extending across the archipelagos of Southeast Asia and the Western Pacific and eastward along the south Asian littoral, to Africa, and onward to southern Europe. Proposed by Xi Jinping in late 2013, and largely known as a grand international infrastructure development program, it is far and away the single most ambitious overseas undertaking of Xi's leadership and his signature strategic initiative abroad.[29] As a result, for better or worse, Xi owns the BRI, meaning the initiative will likely be an integral part of PRC foreign policy as long as he holds power. So far under his leadership, this massive undertaking has steadily gathered steam. By the end of 2020, 138 countries and 31 international organizations had signed more than 200 agreements to cooperate in developing some 2,000 BRI-labeled projects, mostly related to building infrastructure such as ports, highways, railways, power plants, and resource extraction and refining facilities.[30]

Defining the BRI

An Asian Development Bank report in 2017 estimated that developing Asia will require between $22.6 and $26.2 trillion in infrastructure investment over the 15 years between 2016 and 2030 if it is to maintain growth, eradicate poverty, and respond to climate change.[31] BRI projects could meet some of these urgent needs. However, it is unclear how much BRI infrastructure is being built or even how much BRI investment has already been spent, pledged, or made available for the future—because the BRI is broadly and vaguely defined as to its scope and duration and no official public listing of BRI projects exists. In addition, BRI projects are not strictly limited to infrastructure. The PRC government has identified "five connectivities" (五通) that BRI is intended to support: policy coordination, facilities connectivity, unimpeded trade, financial integration, and people-to-people bonds.[32] Undertakings as diverse as satellite networks, Chinese think tanks and research institutes, sports tourism, and the "Digital Silk Road" have all taken on a BRI label. Attaching the BRI name to projects equates to political and financial gain but also inflates and confuses what BRI actually means.

Adding to the confusion, governments around the world have signed memorandums of understanding (MOUs) to indicate their interest in cooperating with the BRI, but the MOUs are nonbinding and signing one does not mean those countries have to accept BRI projects. Individual projects still have to be negotiated between the countries and the companies involved. Some countries that have signed a BRI MOU do not have any BRI projects. On the other hand, countries that do not sign such an MOU can still cooperate with China in infrastructure construction and financing. In addition, previously planned, ongoing, or completed projects can be rebranded and repackaged as BRI projects. For example, the construction of the Hambantota Port in Sri Lanka, a controversial and high-profile BRI project, started in 2008, and the first phase was completed in 2010, three years before the BRI was even launched. A project in one country could be branded a BRI project while a similar project in another country may not be a BRI project, depending on whether the recipient country has signed an MOU or not.

Further muddling an accurate accounting, not all BRI projects are financed by the PRC government or its banks. True, most of the funding associated with large BRI infrastructure projects comes from PRC state financing, including the Silk Road Fund, which was established for the purpose of funding and financing the BRI, as well as China's development banks and commercial banks. However, some BRI-related projects are partly financed by multilateral development banks such as the New Development Bank and the Asian Infrastructure Investment Bank.[33]

As a result, estimates vary widely as to the total amount of PRC funding available to support BRI-related projects, with most estimates settling at around $1 trillion for the 10 years from 2016, but with some estimates reaching eight times that amount.[34] A World Bank study attempts to calculate the amount of BRI spending in 70 countries lying along the principal "corridors" of the initiative. The study found that a total of $575 billion had been invested in BRI projects by 2019, primarily focusing in the energy, electric power, transport, shipping, and chemical engineering sectors. Just eight countries—Bangladesh, Cambodia, Uzbekistan, Laos, Indonesia, Malaysia, Pakistan, and Russia—account for more than two-thirds of that funding, with the latter four alone accounting for 50 percent of the total.[35] A forward-looking study by two major consultancy groups foresees a total of $910 billion in infrastructure spending by the end of the 2020s if the BRI continues on its present trajectory, with about half of those investments going to sub-Saharan Africa and Southeast Asia.[36]

BRI Benefits

In truth, beyond the dollars invested and infrastructure built, the BRI first and foremost aims to bring economic benefit to China. For example, the BRI expects to reduce the stark regional inequalities between the wealthy eastern seaboard and the remote, poorer western regions of China. The inland belt, extending across Central Asia to Europe, also includes these less-well-off regions—such as Xinjiang, Gansu, Guangxi, and Qinghai provinces—which should gain from the investments made in transportation, telecommunications, and exporting capacity. In this respect, the BRI is an extension of the Western Development Strategy (西部大开发) started in 2000, which aimed at balancing the growing income inequities between the booming coastal east and the western reaches of the country where, still today, poverty is most concentrated. Apart from addressing poverty and reducing inequality, Beijing leaders also hope economic development generated by the BRI (and the Western Development Strategy more broadly) can contribute to stabilizing restive and potentially volatile ethnic regions in China's west, where non-Han ethnic minorities are more heavily concentrated, such as in Inner Mongolia, Guangxi, Tibet, Ningxia, and Xinjiang.

Official PRC government guidelines explicitly urge political and business leaders to harness the BRI for development of China's west.[37] By linking these "frontier regions" to neighboring countries and placing them at the heart of the BRI strategy, Beijing hopes to develop them from "dead ends" to "new crossroads." For example, more transcontinental trade overland from China to Europe could foster greater development in remote parts of Xinjiang, such as the border towns of Korgas (located on the BRI's New Eurasia Land Bridge corridor) and Kashgar (on the BRI's China-Pakistan Economic Corridor).

Another important domestic economic objective for BRI is to export excess production capacity of Chinese firms, especially chronically overleveraged and underperforming state-owned industries. As the PRC economy slowly moves from capital-intensive to consumer-oriented growth, a range of industries so vital to China's past growth—such as those building railways, roads, airports, and power plants—are less important for growth today. As early as 2010, China's State

Council announced targets for eliminating "backward production capacity," including in the electricity generation, coal, and iron and steel industries.[38] But China has struggled to manage the excess capacity challenge, which in turn has created domestic and international headaches for Beijing, which has found that it takes more and more capital investment to produce less and less growth. Declining profitability within highly leveraged industries could have knock-on effects for the stability of China's financial system—a system already under increasing stress.[39] China's excess capacity places downward pressures on global prices, such as in the steel industry, affecting the profitability of steelmakers in the United States and the European Union.[40] However, in spite of these and other problems brought on by overcapacity, state-owned firms are often deemed too big to fail for political, economic, and social stability reasons.

For Chinese leaders, the BRI offers a way to address these excess capacity problems. Through the deployment of state-owned enterprises abroad, China's overcapacity can find new markets and hopefully realize higher returns on their investments. Moving factories and infrastructure construction capacity to another country does not necessarily reduce excess capacity, so in this sense the BRI only "exports" overcapacity out of China. It is possible that—with time—growth in economic development, industrialization, and infrastructure driven by BRI projects abroad could increase global demand for steel, energy, and other commodities, thereby addressing excess capacity by increasing demand rather than reducing supply. Leading international economists have cast doubt on whether the BRI (and other major PRC initiatives such as the Asian Infrastructure Investment Bank) can adequately address the country's overcapacity problem.[41] But this remains an important domestic economic rationale to promote and expand the BRI internationally.

Another potential domestic economic benefit of the BRI derives from the acceptance in other countries of PRC technical standards, including in the construction and operation of railways, energy plants, and telecommunication networks or through the import of Chinese manufacturing facilities, heavy machinery, and industrial equipment. A prominent example of this strategy is found in the construction the Jakarta-Bandung high-speed railway in Indonesia. As one of the earliest and most high-profile BRI projects, Beijing was eager to take this railway venture on with its own financing and at a possible loss because the project would adopt Chinese standards, technology, equipment, and services, representing a major international breakthrough in an industry—high-speed rail—that China aims to dominate.[42] When other countries adopt China's standards, they might be inclined to additional imports from China in the future—rather than, say, the European Union, Japan, or the United States—because once they are invested in PRC technologies, equipment, and industry protocols, swapping them out for others might prove difficult. Furthermore, when countries enter into international negotiations to set global standards in a given field, Chinese standards would likely gain the support of those countries already using them. International adoption of PRC standards would give substantial first-mover advantage to Chinese firms. It remains too early to know whether these benefits will be fully realized, but they are a major motivation driving the BRI for now.

More broadly, the BRI may also bring strategic economic benefit to China by reducing the vulnerability of its maritime trading routes. In principle, establishing secure overland trading channels to and from China could help mitigate its "Malacca dilemma," a term coined by Hu Jintao in 2003.[43] The Malacca Strait forms the shortest, and hence least costly, maritime shipping route between the Indian Ocean, the South China Sea, and the Pacific Ocean, and is among the world's most heavily trafficked sea lanes. This maritime passageway is especially important for the Chinese economy. Some 40 percent of China's trade passes through the South China Sea, and crucially, 80 percent of the country's oil imports transit the South China Sea via the Malacca Strait.[44] Other nearby maritime corridors—such as the Lombok Straits and Sunda Strait—also form critical supply lines for China, particularly for energy and iron ore exports from Australia. Because these straits are relatively narrow—the Malacca Strait at its narrowest point is less than two miles wide—they are vulnerable to potential disruptions or even a naval blockade. Moreover, China's economic center of gravity is heavily concentrated along the country's exposed eastern seaboard, making it also vulnerable to maritime blockades and other military disruptions. Given these vulnerabilities, Chinese leaders have long sought viable alternatives. The construction of overland transport routes under the BRI banner through countries such as Myanmar and Pakistan—including energy pipelines, highways, and railways—bypasses the archipelagic mazeways and chokepoints of maritime Southeast Asia and dodges some of the geoeconomic risks they pose. (That said, many of the overland routes across Central, South, and Southeast Asia have security risks of their own that must be considered.)

Other strategic economic benefits of the BRI include the possibilities of internationalizing the Chinese renminbi currency, expanding and solidifying markets for exports and imports, and improving socioeconomic conditions in unstable neighboring countries. Through its financing mechanisms such as the Silk Road Fund and a growing economic presence in recipient countries, the BRI can play a role in promoting the internationalization of the renminbi, a goal that would also bring both strategic and fiscal benefit to the PRC economy.[45] The BRI also aims to bring strategic economic benefit to China by nurturing import and export markets, especially in the developing world. By assisting countries to develop infrastructure for the extraction, processing and export of raw materials—minerals and energy from Africa and from Central Asia, for example—China diversifies and secures supplies of much-needed commodities to help fuel its economy. If and as poorer countries can become more developed through BRI investments, they can become more lucrative markets for PRC goods and services from textiles and apparel, to consumer electronics and heavy machinery, to mobile networks. Beijing's leaders may also hope that BRI projects can bring some stability not only to their own remote regions, but also to troubled areas close to China's inland borders in places like northern Myanmar, Afghanistan, and the Baluchistan and Khyber Pakhtunkhwa regions of Pakistan.

BRI Balance Sheet

Sweeping ambitions and high expectations define the BRI. But taking it as a whole, assessing the BRI's ultimate success or failure is a tricky business. Already hundreds of billions of dollars have been invested, with hundreds of billions more likely to come. Infrastructure and development needs are enormous throughout most of the world, and these huge outlays will no doubt tackle many of them. Overall, China's overseas direct investment has risen significantly in BRI countries, especially countries along the Silk Road Economic Belt, particularly in the energy and transport sectors.[46] It is possible over the medium term that, as a result of BRI-related infrastructure improvement and economic development, some countries will become greater consumers of PRC exports. A World Bank report finds that BRI could lift tens of millions out of poverty, increase trade among participating countries, and decrease the costs of trade worldwide (though not all countries would benefit equally).[47] The biggest winner of all, though—and intentionally so—may be China. For China, the BRI has become an overarching brand for its international economic engagement, holding out the promise of geostrategic benefit, strengthened diplomatic outreach, and—most importantly—multiple drivers to generate wealth and development back home.

At the same time, the BRI has generated much controversy internationally. From an economic point of view, many critics argue the BRI does not deliver on its promised benefits. Accusations of wasteful spending, poor planning, lack of accountability and transparency, "debt-trap diplomacy," and strategic overreach have dogged the BRI from its outset. Rather than a well-oiled juggernaut as it is often portrayed, the BRI like any enormous political and economic undertaking is plagued by fragmented bureaucratic, organizational, and local self-interests and the "principal-agent" frictions between the policy intentions of central authorities on the one hand, and the actual on-the-ground implementation of those policies on the other.[48] According to a PRC Ministry of

Foreign Affairs official, the covid-19 pandemic either "seriously" or "somewhat" affected about 60 percent of BRI projects worldwide owing to disrupted travel and supply chains and local social distancing restrictions.[49] Moreover, with the global economic downturn precipitated by the viral outbreak, many recipients of BRI financing will struggle with repayments, threatening major losses for PRC lenders.

While the BRI appears to be largely welcomed abroad for the economic benefits it delivers, governments and societies along the Belt and Road increasingly see strategic risks in China's burgeoning economic footprint and the dependencies it creates. More ominously, many analysts have raised concerns about how the BRI contributes to China's strategic goals and military power projection.[50] Beijing has taken some of these criticisms to heart and since 2018 has sought to address them by introducing more accountability, scaling back some projects, being more attuned to local sensitivities, emphasizing trade or debt-laden capital construction, and initiating "softer" BRI-labeled outreach in areas of tourism, education, culture, and even religion.[51] Recognizing many of the problems with hard infrastructure projects and looking to the BRI to promote high-tech exports, Chinese officialdom gave greater emphasis to promoting diverse elements of the initiative: the "Health Silk Road" (健康丝绸之路), focusing on vaccines and other measures to combat covid-19 and other global health challenges; the "Green Silk Road" (绿色丝绸之路), focusing on environmentally friendly technologies; and the "Digital Silk Road" (数字丝绸之路), focusing on telecommunications, e-commerce, artificial intelligence, surveillance, and other advanced digital and computing technologies.[52] But in spite of these efforts, many problems remain. These challenges to the BRI and to PRC foreign economic policy more broadly are considered in more detail in this book's closing chapter.

Despite its many question marks, the BRI will remain a fundamentally important element of China's international engagement under Xi Jinping. Beyond the economic pluses and minuses of the BRI, Xi Jinping has tightly woven the project within his legacy-defining ambition to achieve the "great rejuvenation of the Chinese nation." He duly ensured the incorporation of the BRI into the CCP constitution in 2017, committing all Party members to its pursuit. Looking abroad, Xi declares this signature endeavor will "complement the development strategies of countries" and will contribute to his oft-proclaimed goal of realizing a "community of shared future for humankind."[53] The latest efforts to reshape the BRI to encompass high-tech exports, people-to-people ties, and green solutions suggests the BRI will be constantly repackaged to attract foreign partners and remain China's premier brand for foreign economic interactions. For better or worse, this is Xi's signature overseas undertaking, and enormous financial, political, and promotional resources will continue to pour into it.[54]

Drive for Innovation and Technological Advancement

As discussed earlier in this chapter, China needs to undergo an economic transformation in order to sustain its growth and join the ranks of higher-income economies: key elements in Xi Jinping's dream to realize the "great rejuvenation of the Chinese nation." Given the structural impediments to growth facing the PRC economy, new sources of productivity must be generated. But how? The BRI attempts to address some of the challenges, for example, by exporting overcapacity and developing new markets for higher-value PRC exports. Additional options exist, but many have been stymied during Xi's tenure. As discussed above, maintaining the dominance of the state sector can slow productivity gains, and the private sector remains constrained in many respects.

Innovation via Foreign Technology Acquisitions

In the past, the acquisition of foreign technology was an important pathway for introducing innovation and gaining greater efficiencies within the PRC economic model. There is nothing unusual in this. Developing countries have long used national policies to promote international technology transfers to their shores.[55] In general, a country can acquire technology via three methods—transacting, taking, and making—and China has used all of them to advance productivity gains and spur greater innovation. For much of its economic rise since the 1980s, China has relied on the first two methods. Only recently has the country begun to achieve the third by developing a greater capacity for indigenous innovation and technology development. As the following discussion shows, "transacting" and "taking" can still make an important contribution to China's economic development. However, over the course of the Xi Jinping era, this route has become increasingly strewn with obstacles and risk, particularly in the most advanced technological fields. This places all the more emphasis on generating indigenous innovation and technology for China's future.

Transacting for foreign technology often involves acquiring companies overseas that own a particular technology or other valuable intellectual property (IP). As noted earlier, this was one of the primary motivations behind the "going out" strategy during the years Jiang Zemin and Hu Jintao were in power. In many cases, the PRC government encouraged SOEs to acquire foreign companies expressly in order to access proprietary technology. For example, official overseas investment guidance in 2006 outlined three kinds of transactions that should be prioritized. One is transactions that "significantly improve China's technological research and development capabilities."[56] Support for these efforts could include inexpensive loans from state-owned banks to facilitate acquisition for private companies or state-owned enterprises, as well as preferential treatment for risk evaluation and insurance. With this kind of support, such acquisitions were not always determined purely on market factors—whether, for example, the foreign firm was a viable business or not—but could owe to larger strategic considerations of technology acquisition.

However, in more recent years, the acquisition of foreign enterprises and technologies by PRC companies has increasingly raised concerns overseas, with many countries scrutinizing these investments far more closely. More broadly, Chinese SOEs are accused of benefitting from state subsidies and gaining unfair competitive advantage. As a result, in dozens of cases since the mid-2010s, SOEs and even non-SOEs deemed too closely aligned with the PRC government have seen opportunities for investment, acquisition, and raising capital rejected on national security grounds in countries such as Australia, Canada, the United Kingdom, and the United States, and across the European Union. SOE access to critical infrastructure and technologies is a particular concern. For example, rising economic tensions between Washington and Beijing in recent years have resulted in greater restrictions on PRC investment in the United States, threats to delist Chinese firms from U.S. stock exchanges, and sanctions against PRC high-tech firms. The United States has expanded the power to review investment in critical technologies under the Foreign Investment Risk Review Modernization Act of 2018. In 2020, new U.S. regulations covering transactions involving "critical technologies" were released, meaning that foreign investments in U.S. businesses with critical technologies will trigger more mandatory screening.[57] The European Union as well as many individual European countries have also strengthened foreign investment rules. In Australia, new legislation and regulations in recent years have been passed and implemented that are designed to tighten the scrutiny of foreign investments, including the creation of a Critical Infrastructure Center, to assist the government in determining the national security implications of such acquisitions.[58] With similar national security concerns, other countries around the world are doing the same, prompted by China's burgeoning role as an overseas investor in search of advanced technology.

A prominent case in point is the Chinese telecommunications company Huawei, the world's largest manufacturer of telecommunications equipment. Huawei claims that it is a private business, independent from the CCP or PRC government. Its CEO, Ren Zhengfei, a former soldier in the People's Liberation Army (PLA), has even claimed that Huawei would never provide personal customer information to the Chinese government.[59] Nevertheless, given the firm's close ties with PRC authorities, many governments are skeptical about its autonomy. As a result, Washington and other governments have repeatedly hit Huawei with punitive measures on national security grounds. In 2008, for example, Huawei's attempted acquisition of an American producer of internet routing and networking equipment, 3Com, was denied by U.S. regulators for national security reasons as was Huawei's bid in 2011 to acquire 3Leaf, a U.S. company specializing in cloud computing technologies. In 2019 and 2020, the U.S. government went further, blocking U.S. and foreign semiconductor designers and manufacturers from providing chips to Huawei if they are developed and made using U.S. technology and blacklisting Huawei from doing business with U.S. companies—in effect barring it from doing any business in the United States or with U.S. companies abroad. In its final week in office, the Trump administration also notified Huawei suppliers—including the U.S. semiconductor producer Intel—that it would rescind a number of licenses allowing sales to the PRC telecommunications firm and would reject scores of pending applications from other firms to supply Huawei. Reports indicated these bans would halt some $400 billion in technology and equipment sales to Huawei.[60]

The Trump administration also blacklisted dozens of other Chinese companies on national security grounds. These actions bar U.S. investors from owning or trading securities related to these firms; in some cases, U.S. businesses are also restricted from providing technologies and equipment to these companies. The PRC companies affected include some of the country's largest and most technologically advanced in their fields. In addition to Huawei, other blacklisted firms include Xiaomi and China Mobile (telecommunications), China National Offshore Oil Corporation (energy exploration), Skyrizon and Aero Engine Corporation (aircraft engines), Commercial Aircraft Corporation (aircraft manufacturing), Semiconductor Manufacturing International Corporation and GOWIN Semiconductor Corporation (semiconductors), CRRC Group (high-speed rail), and others involved in drone development and manufacturing and face-recognition and other surveillance technology.[61] In addition, the Trump administration took a range of actions in response to Beijing's repressive policies in Xinjiang—including formally declaring those policies as genocide and crimes against humanity—which impose economic sanctions on certain Chinese companies and individuals and ban the import of commodities such as cotton and tomatoes from that province.[62] Upon assuming office in 2021, Joe Biden and his administration maintained these policies and in some cases added new sanctions of their own.[63]

China has also transacted for foreign technology by encouraging or forcing foreign firms to transfer valuable technologies and IP to local partners as a prerequisite for doing business in China and gaining access to its domestic market (some would see this as "taking" rather than "transacting"). Beijing agreed upon joining the World Trade Organization (WTO) in 2001 that it would not impose such conditions on investors. Even so, the United States included language banning the practice in the "Phase One" trade agreement reached between the two countries in 2020.[64] But the practice persists, and to avoid violation of WTO rules or other agreements, the pressure to transfer technology is usually informal rather than formal, and oral rather than written.[65] This form of technology acquisition has become a matter of increasing concern for foreign investors in China and over time has made them more wary of doing business there.

Another way for China to acquire foreign technology and other IP has been through talent recruitment. Initiatives such as the "Thousand Talents Program" (海外高层次人才引进计划 or 千人计划), launched in 2008, aim to attract to China high-level experts—both foreign and PRC nationals living overseas—to conduct their work and share their knowledge. The program's emphasis is on advanced scientific and technical research and development and intends, in part, to reverse a brain-drain problem for China. For example, although China is the largest source of top-tier artificial intelligence (AI) researchers in the world, only 34 percent of them end up staying in China, while 56 percent have gone to the United States to work.[66] However, the program also actively seeks to recruit highly accomplished experts who are not PRC citizens or of Chinese ethnicity, providing them with ample research support and facilities in China.

This program has also come under increased scrutiny. The U.S. Senate Permanent Subcommittee on Investigations labels the Thousand Talents Program and 200 other PRC talent recruitment schemes as threats to the U.S. research enterprise and to overall U.S. national security.[67] The U.S. government has taken legal action against American and PRC citizens involved in Chinese recruitment programs charging them with illegal exports, IP theft, misuse of U.S. government funds, and fraud while dramatically stepping up its public scrutiny of these programs. It has also tightened visa restrictions on PRC citizens seeking to conduct scientific and technology research in U.S. companies and universities.[68] In light of the negative attention, China renamed the Thousand Talents Program to the High-End Foreign Experts Recruitment Plan (高端外国专家引进计划), which lists four priority areas for its work: strategic technology development, industrial technology innovation, social and ecological construction, and agriculture and rural revitalization.[69] This foreign technology acquisition program will continue but will be monitored far more closely, especially in advanced economies, which may limit its success.

The second approach to technology acquisition is "taking," usually in the form of economic or industrial espionage, which can be done through a variety of means: from physically pilfering equipment, data, and documents to accessing information and IP via cyberintrusion. While almost all governments with the capacity to do so use espionage for intelligence gathering against other governments, China has been frequently accused of targeting foreign commercial interests in order to acquire technology. For example, an extensive independent study completed in 2013 estimated that between 50 and 80 percent of the intellectual property theft against the United States was perpetrated by PRC entities, resulting in hundreds of billions of dollars in losses.[70]

In response, the U.S. government pressed Beijing to accept an agreement whereby the two sides would refrain from conducting industrial espionage against one another, an accord apparently achieved during the Obama-Xi summit in September 2015. The White House announcement of the agreement stated that the two sides agree that "neither country's government will conduct or knowingly support cyber-enabled theft of intellectual property . . . with the intent of providing competitive advantages to companies or commercial sectors."[71] Beijing reached similar understandings with other countries, including Australia, Canada, and the United Kingdom, as well as with the Group of 7 (G7) and Group of 20 (G20) nations. However, the PRC's commitments did not last long, and by 2018 China's industrial espionage activity returned stronger than ever.[72] That year the U.S. Department of Justice launched the China Initiative, aimed at countering economic espionage and other forms of trade secret theft, specifically from China.[73] Other governments around the world have taken similar measures to protect against PRC industrial espionage, especially for the most sophisticated and cutting-edge technologies.

These protections, naming and shaming, and legal action may have some effect in limiting illegal Chinese access to foreign technologies via espionage. For China's part, there is no indication that PRC government and industry will halt this form of technology acquisition. It has been a successful effort in many respects, and Beijing appears prepared to pay a diplomatic, economic, and reputational cost to access critical technologies and IP that the country cannot otherwise obtain. But it means that advanced industrial economies—important technology sources for China—will be working harder than ever to sharply limit such access in the years ahead.

Indigenous Innovation, "Made in China 2025," and "Dual Circulation"

Innovation is important for all countries to sustain continued economic growth. But innovation is even more crucial for China if it is to move out of middle-income status and become a more prosperous and powerful country. This "innovation imperative" is what drives PRC strategies for technology acquisition.[74] However, as we have seen for China, two well-worn pathways to innovation and greater productivity—through "transacting" and "taking" foreign technology— will be more and more thicketed and even impenetrable in the years ahead. In response, industrial policy under Xi Jinping has intensified the effort to leverage both the public sector and private sector in the cause of indigenous or "independent innovation" (自主创新). According to the PRC State Council, this means "starting from enhancing the national innovation capacity, strengthen original innovation, re-innovation, and absorption of imported innovation."[75] As this definition suggests, China already has significant "national innovation capacity," including within the state-owned sector. For example, CRRC Group (中车集团), the world's largest producer of railway equipment, is best known for its development of world-leading high-speed trains. Other companies in the private sector, such as Alibaba, have transformed the world of e-commerce by leapfrogging from cash to cashless payment systems. Alibaba is also active in cutting-edge artificial intelligence research.

However, much of the intellectual property China has produced and exported over the past several decades was not indigenously developed nor the result of domestic investment. According to a leading analyst of the PRC economy, beginning in the 1990s, about one-third of PRC exports on average have been manufactured by foreign-invested companies (a figure that topped out at nearly 60 percent in 2005). For exports designated as high-tech, the proportion owing to foreign firms is even higher—persisting at around two-thirds even in 2020.[76] As Xi Jinping declared to a high-profile conference on cybersecurity in 2016:

> Our dependence on core technology is the biggest hidden trouble for us. . . .
> Heavy dependence on imported core technology is like building our house on top of someone else's walls: No matter how big and how beautiful it is, it won't remain standing during a storm.[77]

While Xi has placed more emphasis on indigenous innovation, it was an important aspect of China's science and technology development strategy well before his leadership. For example, indigenous innovation was listed as the first of four overarching principles guiding the 15-year National Medium- and Long-Term Science and Technology Development Plan, issued in 2006.[78] In exposing the vulnerabilities of China's export-led growth model, the global financial crisis of 2008 further motivated the shift to greater reliance on domestic demand and indigenous innovation for economic growth. The 11th (2006–2010) and 12th (2011–2015) Five-Year Plans were each accompanied by a plan to build out China's indigenous innovation capability. The 13th Five-Year Plan, covering 2016 to 2020, also emphasized indigenous innovation, moving up the value chain, and the importance for technology self-sufficiency. The 14th Five-Year Plan, unveiled in March 2021, has an even greater emphasis on technology and innovation, including technology self-reliance in the face of extended "decoupling" from advanced economies, especially the United States, and particularly in relation to high-end, critical technologies of the future.

In contrast to transacting or taking, "making" demands investments in research and development (R&D) to develop new technologies, including technologies that do not yet exist or technologies that are inaccessible due to trade and investment restrictions. In order to spur indigenous innovation, China has increased its R&D spending—total expenditure on R&D grew by double digits annually between 2016 and 2020[79]—and it is now the world's second-largest investor in R&D, behind the United States. In part a result of this spending spree, China surpassed America to have the largest number of patent filings worldwide in 2019 and retained the number-one position in 2020.[80] According to the World Intellectual Property Organization (WIPO), since 2012 China has been the top middle-income country for quality of innovation—measured by rankings of domestic universities, internationalization of inventions, and international citations of research. Also, when measuring sheer output of science and technology activity by innovation hubs around the world, China has three in the top 10—located in Shenzhen–Guangzhou–Hong Kong, Beijing, and Shanghai—ranked second, fourth, and ninth, respectively.[81]

However, on other indicators of R&D spending and innovation, China does not fare as well. For example, as a percentage of GDP (2.19 percent in 2018), China's R&D spending ranks behind countries including Finland, Israel, Japan, South Korea, Sweden, and the United States. Also, in spite of its world-topping number of patent applications, China ranks only 16th globally as to the quality of its innovation and does not make the top 30 in terms of innovation intensity (measured by science and technology output per capita). Beijing aims to climb up these charts by increasing its R&D spending to 3 percent of GDP by 2025.[82]

One of the most important undertakings under Xi to promote indigenous innovation is known as "Made in China 2025" (中国制造 2025). Launched by the State Council in 2015, it aims to promote indigenous innovation and help transform China into a science and technology innovation superpower by 2049.[83] It builds on concepts of indigenous innovation introduced in the 2006 long-term science and technology plan and draws inspiration from Germany's "Industrie 4.0," launched in 2011, which Chancellor Angela Merkel called "the fusion of the online world and the world of industrial production."[84] For China, it is an effort to upgrade its manufacturing base through the integration of information technology—in essence pulling together the strengths of the state-owned and private sectors—to improve productivity, increase the indigenous content of higher-end technology products, reduce reliance on foreign inputs, and position China as a global leader in critical technologies of the future.[85]

The Made in China 2025 strategy gives priority to 10 high-technology sectors:

- Next-generation information technology
- High-end numerical control machinery and robotics

- Aerospace and aviation equipment
- Maritime engineering equipment and high-tech maritime vessel manufacturing
- Advanced rail equipment
- Energy-saving vehicles and new energy vehicles
- Electrical equipment
- Agricultural machinery and equipment
- New materials
- Biopharmaceutical and high-performance medical devices[86]

Similar to priorities in past Five-Year Plans, these sectors represent areas where China has proven strengths—such as in automobile and other heavy equipment manufacturing, advanced machinery, consumer electronics and internet-based services, and high-speed rail—plus crucial industries for the future. Foreign technology acquisition, though still necessary for China, is largely downplayed in the strategy, backed up by policy tools to encourage indigenous innovation such as tax incentives, financing by state-owned banks, and direct funding for projects.[87] It is a nationwide effort, with government at the national, provincial, and local levels providing research funding and other support under the Made in China 2025 banner. As of March 2018, some 1,800 "government guidance funds" worth $426 billion were associated with Made in China 2025 projects.[88] Ostensibly, the strategy is "led by the market, guided by the government" (市场主导, 政府引导), and funding is allocated to encourage innovation within small- and medium-sized industries in the private sector. But in fact, as with many industrial policies around the world, the government has already selected the priority sectors, essentially picking winners and sometimes even certain companies for preferential treatment. Some skepticism attends these choices, including within China, on the government's ability to identify winners versus placing more trust in the market.[89]

Made in China 2025 set off alarm bells for governments and businesses around the world. Of greatest concern is the plan's associated objective of increasing the proportion of PRC domestic content across the value chain—design, manufacturing processes, technology and material inputs, and finished products—in the 10 prioritized industrial areas and their subsectors. While the PRC government has not officially announced these targets, publications and analysis by Chinese think tanks and foreign counterparts conclude they generally range between 40 percent and 80 percent, depending on the sector, with the intention of achieving these goals between 2020 and 2030.[90] To do so will mean focusing the PRC's considerable legal, regulatory, and fiscal resources on squeezing out foreign competition inside China and positioning these industries for dominant roles in the international marketplace in the coming decades. In this sense, Made in China 2025 is an offensive measure to drive innovation and grab greater market share. But for China, it is defensive as well. Xi Jinping noted that one reason to enhance the international leading position of some industries is to "tighten international production chains' dependence on China, forming a powerful countermeasure and deterrent capability against foreigners who would artificially cut off supply [to China]." Xi specifically named high-speed rail, electric power equipment, new energy, and telecommunication equipment as sectors where China already has advantages.[91]

Owing to the international criticisms of Made in China 2025, the PRC government has lowered the program's profile since 2018.[92] However, the overall strategy to become more technologically self-reliant remains in place. Indeed, the strategy has been reinforced by China's experience in the wake of the covid-19 pandemic in 2020–2021 and the continuing deterioration in economic relations with the United States over that period. In the midst of the global pandemic, in mid-2020, Xi Jinping doubled down on promoting self-sufficiency by advocating a "dual circulation" (双循环) strategy—comprising "domestic circulation" (国内循环) and "international circulation" (国际循环), also going by the terms "internal" and "external" circulation. On the one hand, the strategy will encourage the Chinese economy to rely more on its enormous internal market ("domestic circulation") for growth and technological innovation rather than on the low-value exports and imported technology that spurred the country's economic success in the past. The other half of the strategy, "international circulation," will invest greater resources in Made in China 2025 with the aim of becoming a dominant supplier of advanced technologies and manufactures of the future.

The drive for self-sufficiency gained even greater momentum as the United States took a number of measures in 2020 and early 2021 to further restrict PRC access to U.S. technologies and capital markets. Given repeated high-profile mentions of the "dual circulation" concept by Xi Jinping and other top leaders, it is a key aspect of the 14th Five-Year Plan (2021–2025). As Premier Li Keqiang declared in his work report to the NPC:

> We will give priority to domestic circulation, and work to build a strong domestic market and turn China into a trader of quality. We will leverage the flows of the domestic economy to make China a major magnet for global production factors and resources, thereby promoting positive interplay between domestic circulation and international circulation.[93]

Key elements of the strategy include increasing technological independence and innovation, securing external supply chains, and not only promoting greater reliance on China's domestic demand but also facilitating it through improvements to internal efficiencies in production and logistics. In short, the dual circulation strategy not only places greater faith in China's domestic market to drive economic growth and innovation in the years ahead, it also aims to buffer China from growing risks in the international marketplace. PRC leaders clearly recognize these risks. As Xi Jinping declared in promoting the dual circulation strategy, "Only by being self-reliant and developing the domestic market and smoothing out internal circulation can we achieve vibrant growth and development, regardless of the hostility in the outside world."[94]

Facing Headwinds?

This chapter has examined the pursuit of prosperity as an important element in PRC foreign policy under Xi Jinping. Seeking economic growth by engaging the outside world is nothing new for Chinese leaders. In many respects, Xi faces the same imperatives as his predecessors: increase society-wide prosperity and well-being to bolster the Party's claim to power and preserve social stability; maintain access to foreign capital, technology, know-how, and markets to advance economic growth; and leverage growing national economic might to achieve national strategic goals. By most indicators, China has been highly successful in meeting these imperatives, including under Xi Jinping.

The chapter has also described a number of looming economic challenges facing the Party leadership and argues that China faces greater economic uncertainty today than at any time since the dramatic shift to reform and opening in the 1980s. These challenges include transforming the PRC's economic growth model, increasing productivity, navigating the transition to a much older society, managing more difficult economic relations with the United States and other advanced economies, becoming more self-reliant technologically, and breaking through the middle-income trap to join the ranks of high-income countries. As the chapter discussed, under Xi Jinping, China has launched some significant and highly ambitious economic initiatives—such as the BRI, Made in China 2025, and the dual circulation strategy—intended to help the country meet and overcome these headwinds. However, while designed to drive continued economic growth and wealth generation, these initiatives can have a profoundly negative impact on China's international relationships.

China is a large and well-resourced economy with numerous positive advantages and a record of resilience and adaptability. Of the world's major economies, it emerged strongest from the early stages of the covid-19 pandemic. It will continue to make strides in innovation, especially if the private sector is given a greater chance to reach its potential. Chinese advancements in e-commerce, high-speed rail, drone technology, and artificial intelligence suggest promising possibilities for indigenous innovation in the future. Along with

14 other Asia-Pacific partners, China concluded the Regional Comprehensive Economic Partnership (RCEP) free trade agreement at the end of 2020. In that year, the 10-country Association of Southeast Asian Nations (ASEAN) became China's largest trading partner, followed by the European Union, with the United States coming in third.[95] These and other positive developments may help offset some of the challenges noted above by enhancing China's access to key foreign markets besides the United States. China has even put in place its own regulations to punish firms—including foreign firms—which comply with "unjustified" sanctions imposed on China.[96]

But in spite of these and other economic positives for China, persistent structural obstacles remain in place and will likely frustrate progress in realizing Xi Jinping's economic ambitions. These obstacles arise from two dilemmas, one internal and one external. Internally, the Chinese leadership will face increasing pressures to diminish the role of the state and Party within the economy, permit a greater role for the market, and introduce a legal and regulatory system that is more predictable and bound by the rule of law. But there is little sign that Xi and the Party-state are prepared to take such steps, seeing instead too much social and political risk in doing so. The past PRC growth model and approach to globalization has been an economic success by and large, but has also empowered the Party and Xi Jinping.[97] Sticking with that model—or at least significant elements of it—may bode well for the continuation of authoritarian rule, but will come at an economic cost in the years to come.

Externally, Xi and the Chinese leadership face growing pushback around the world to the country's economic policies such as the BRI and its quest for technology acquisition and indigenous innovation. A resulting bifurcation of the global economy, one that detaches elements of the PRC economy from their most prized markets and supply chains, could have a crippling effect on China's growth and economic aspirations. Having set lofty political expectations for China's economic success in the coming decades, Beijing faces the challenge of achieving increased productivity, greater self-reliance, and heightened income levels even as its economic and technological competition with other advanced countries continues to escalate. In the context of its strategic competition with the PRC, the United States has taken various measures to decouple elements of its economy from China's, as have other countries. These internal and external challenges are discussed further in the book's concluding chapter. How the PRC leadership addresses these dilemmas will have significant implications not only for China's wealth and prosperity but also for China's future role on the world stage.

But no matter how Beijing ultimately chooses to confront these dilemmas, Xi Jinping and his successors will continue to pursue national wealth as a critical aspect of PRC foreign policy. The achievement of greater prosperity makes a fundamentally important contribution to bolstering the other key elements of Xi Jinping's foreign policy highlighted in this volume. Amassing and distributing national wealth to the PRC citizenry remains a foundation stone for the Party's legitimacy and continuing hold on political power. Greater economic power is leveraged to support and enforce China's sovereignty claims and strategic ambitions. China's economic prowess also provides the necessary resources to promote the ideas and influence of the Party-state abroad and helps Beijing attain greater leadership within the international system. Perhaps most importantly, greater national wealth can be harnessed to generate economic and military hard power, a subject to which we turn in the next chapter.

5

Power 势力

Leveraging China's Growing Economic and Military Might

A wealthy country may build a strong army, and a strong army is able to safeguard the country.

—Xi Jinping, April 2013[1]

China and Hard Power

Generally speaking, power in international relations is the ability to shape the behavior of others. And, like all states, China needs power to pursue its national interests—including the six core objectives at the heart of this book. But as Harvard University professor Joseph Nye and others have explained, power is not such a simple concept. Nye is well known for distinguishing between "hard" and "soft" power. The former is the ability to affect the decisions of others through threats or inducements. For states, hard power's most common currencies are military strength and economic heft, which can be leveraged as carrots and sticks to shape another's preferences toward your own. Soft power, on the other hand, is "the ability to get what you want through attraction rather than coercion or payments."[2] (China's approach to soft power is considered in more detail in Chapters 7 and 8.)

The People's Republic of China (PRC or China) has long wielded considerable hard power. Even during its early years of nation-building and internal chaos, China was able to deploy hard power to threaten and coerce others to attain its interests. The country's entry into the Korean War in October 1950—only a year after the fledgling nation was founded—was a major factor in eventually bringing that conflict to a stalemate. With its successful detonation of an atomic weapon in 1964, China could deter nuclear blackmail at the hands of the Soviet Union and the United States. Even as one of the world's poorest countries in the 1960s and 1970s, China provided weapons to insurgent groups such as the Pathet Lao, the White Flag Communists (Burmese Communist Party), the Communist Patriotic Front in Thailand, the Front de Libération (FLN) in Algeria, the Palestine Liberation Organization, and many others to help them

Daring to Struggle. Bates Gill, Oxford University Press. © Oxford University Press 2022.
DOI: 10.1093/oso/9780197545645.003.0006

pursue goals in alignment with Beijing's anti-imperialist stance.[3] For more than 70 years PRC armed forces have been the largest in the world—today, even after repeated major troop reductions since the 1970s, the People's Liberation Army (PLA) still boasts more than two million personnel, which does not include the domestic paramilitary forces such as the People's Armed Police and Coast Guard, with some 660,000 personnel, and military reservists numbering about 510,000.[4] The prospect of facing millions of armed Chinese on or near their home turf has been and still is a powerful disincentive to would-be attackers. In more recent years, as China's economy has skyrocketed, Beijing has been able to add economic threats and inducements to its hard power toolkit.

The subject of China's power has generated considerable attention among the country's scholars and policy analysts. This has been especially true since the 1990s as China began to ascend more rapidly across many indices of national power. Using various methods and indices to define "comprehensive national power" (综合国力), numerous studies have been carried out in China over the past 25 years to rank the nation vis-à-vis other major countries. Not surprisingly, Chinese scholars generally concluded that the PRC's comprehensive national power steadily grew over the course of the 1990s and 2000s. Surprisingly, however, these Chinese analyses still ranked the country far lower than one might expect, and definitely lower than in contemporaneous rankings compiled by Western analysts. For example, a Chinese Academy of Sciences study of 13 major countries found that China rose from eighth to seventh in the international rankings of comprehensive national power between 1990 and 2000—ahead of Russia, Australia, Italy, India, Brazil, and South Africa, but trailing the United States, Japan, Canada, Germany, France, and the United Kingdom. Similarly, a 10-country study by scholars at the Chinese Academy of Social Sciences found that as of 2010, China still ranked only seventh in the world (and had actually *declined* from sixth place in 2006). Meanwhile, studies by Western analysts ranked China as high as third by 2000, behind only the United States and Russia.[5]

More recent studies by PRC scholars find that China has continued to rise in the ranks of national power, but still lags far behind the United States. One study, for example, employing a measurement of "relative national power," shows that China surpassed Japan from 2006 to 2007 to become the world's number-two, but even by 2018 China's relative power remained about half that of the United States. Another study, making projections out to 2030, ranked China second in comprehensive national power by that year, but still well behind the United States and much closer in relative terms to other major powers such as Russia (third), the United Kingdom (fourth), and Germany (fifth).[6]

The gap between Chinese and Western power rankings is attributable to the different methodologies and data used across the studies. For example, giving greater weight to gross domestic product (GDP) per capita—as was common with the Chinese studies—results in a lower ranking for China owing to its enormous population. By that indicator of relative power, China today ranks about 96th out of more than 220 states and territories worldwide.[7] In assessing PRC power more modestly, the Chinese studies in the 1990s and 2000s were also consistent with the country's broader strategic outlook at the time, which emphasized "keeping a low profile" and "biding one's time" and the then widespread view that the international system would be characterized by "one superpower [the United States] and many great powers" (一超多强), including China. But no matter how one treats these assessments, none of them dispute that China's comprehensive national power has continued to grow, surpassing other great powers and gaining relative to the United States. That enhanced ability to shape the decisions of others is crucially important to support the pursuit of the other five key foreign policy goals addressed in this book: legitimacy, sovereignty, wealth, leadership, and ideas.

Yet, even as China's power has grown, it still cannot achieve all of its aims. The Chinese Communist Party (CCP or Party) still struggles to gain legitimacy and acceptance overseas, especially within more democratic societies. The PRC has yet to extend de facto sovereignty over Taiwan, and its claims in the South China Sea remain disputed. As North Korea's principal patron state, China would seem to have enormous leverage over Pyongyang, yet Beijing has not been able to achieve its preferred outcome of a North Korea without nuclear weapons. As subsequent chapters show, China's ability to expand its ideational preferences abroad has met with growing pushback, and its aspirations to global leadership likewise face many challenges. As David Shambaugh found in his 2013 study, while China had "gone global" it nonetheless still struggled to shape and realize its preferred outcomes on the world stage and remained a "partial power."[8] However, under Xi Jinping, a combination of growing capabilities on the one hand and a greater urgency to achieve "national rejuvenation" on the other has resulted in more overt displays of hard power by Beijing to shape its strategic environment in ways that are more favorable to PRC interests.[9]

This chapter delves into some of the ways that China has sought to build and exercise power in recent years under Xi Jinping. For the purposes of this chapter, when discussing power, we focus primarily on what Nye has termed as "hard power": the ability to shape others' choices through threats, coercion, and inducements. In particular, the chapter zeroes in on the two most important aspects of PRC hard power. The first has to do with leveraging China's economic might to threaten, coerce, or buy others' alignment with PRC interests. The second concerns military power and the steps taken under Xi Jinping to strengthen and use the Chinese armed forces as a hard power instrument in PRC external relations. The chapter concludes by considering the continuing pursuit of power as a central aspect of PRC foreign policy and how it contributes to achieving the other five goals of legitimacy, sovereignty, wealth, leadership, and ideas.

Economic Leverage

In 2016, following the Arbitral Tribunal's decision to reject most PRC territorial claims in the South China Sea (see chapter 3), the Australian government joined others in the world in calling on Beijing to abide by the judges' ruling. Beijing's reaction was swift and threatening. The state-owned *Global Times* newspaper reminded Canberra that it "has inked a free trade agreement with China, its biggest trading partner, which makes its move of disturbing the South China Sea waters surprising to many." The op-ed went further, saying of the Australian government:

> It lauds Sino-Australian relations when China's economic support is needed, but when it needs to please Washington it demonstrates a willingness of doing anything in a show of allegiance. . . . China must take revenge and let it know it's wrong. Australia's power means nothing compared to the security of China. If Australia steps into the South China Sea waters, it will be an ideal target for China to warn and strike.

The rebuke concluded, "Australia is not even a 'paper tiger,' it's only a 'paper cat' at best. . . . But this paper cat won't last."[10]

A few years later, the PRC ambassador to Australia was more pointed. In response to Australia's proposal for an independent international review of the origins of the covid-19 pandemic, he said such an initiative would cause PRC tourists to have "second thoughts" about visiting "such a country while it is not so friendly to China. . . . Maybe the parents of the students would also think whether this place, which they find is not so friendly, even hostile, is the best place to send their kids to. . . . Maybe the ordinary people will think why they should drink Australian wine or eat Australian beef."[11] Setting diplomatic niceties aside, the ambassador wielded economic hard power in an attempt to shape Australian policy choices in China's favor.

Australia is not alone in facing such pressures. China's growing economic might translates into growing hard power capabilities and an increased willingness on Beijing's part to brandish and use it. In addition to military hard power, that kind of leverage can arise from a range of other sources—market access, trade relations, investment opportunities, the provision of development assistance, and threats and use of punitive measures such as sanctions, tariffs, and boycotts—all of which provide Beijing with hard power tools to help incentivize or coerce alignment with PRC policy preferences. Consider the remarkable growth in China's economy alone: over the 40 years of the post-Mao reform period, from 1979 to 2019, the country's gross domestic product grew from about $178 billion to well over $14 trillion—an astounding 80-fold increase.[12] And even though the Chinese economy contracted in early 2020 owing to the covid-19 outbreak, it went on to post strong growth between 8 and 9 percent in 2021, according to the World Bank.[13] Today, China is the world's largest trading nation and largest manufacturing economy and holds the largest foreign exchange reserves. About two-thirds of the world's economies (128 out of 190) have a larger trading relationship with China than with the United States, and in 2019 China overtook the United States as the world's biggest retail market.[14] China is the second-largest destination for foreign direct investment and the world's second-largest economy in nominal GDP terms. However, when China's economy is measured in terms of purchasing power parity, China overtook the United States as the world's largest economy around 2016.[15] China's voracious domestic market for capital, technology, commodities, and goods as well as its burgeoning number of wealthy and middle-class consumers can give the country substantial economic leverage over other economies around the world.

The PRC has become a critical exporter as well, which can also grant Beijing considerable hard power leverage. From 1999, China grew from the 23rd-largest source of outbound direct investment (ODI) to the world's second-largest (behind Japan), with over $196 billion in ODI in 2016. Beijing has since imposed tighter controls on capital outflows, but China remains a major global investor, with some $117 billion in ODI in 2019.[16] China has also become one of the world's largest providers of economic and development assistance worldwide, by some measurements outpacing the United States.[17] The PRC produces and exports the largest amount of rare earths (and has the world's largest rare earths reserves), and is also the world's greatest source of outbound students (almost 1 million in 2019) and travelers (nearly 150 million international departures from China in 2018).[18]

As Beijing amasses greater economic leverage, the nation will use this leverage as an instrument of hard power—sometimes coercively, other times with inducements—in pursuit of its interests. According to Sinologist James Reilly, Chinese leaders, strategists, and economists increasingly believe that China's economic resources should be wielded for such strategic purposes. As Reilly writes, "Confident in their government's capacity to deploy these economic resources for strategic benefit, Chinese strategists insist that the Party-state can and should mobilize an array of commercial actors to advance key policy goals abroad."[19] Countries as well as corporations around the world have been the target of such economic carrots and sticks, whether through China's threat or use of punitive measures or offerings of monetary benefit. Either way, generating and brandishing economic hard power is one of Beijing's most potent means for shaping the behavior of others and hence a tool that Xi Jinping has aimed to strengthen.

Punitive Measures

China's foreign policy under Xi Jinping is replete with the punitive use of economic power to alter the actions of others. Many other nations do the same—or try to. But a country with the economic heft and centralized state power of China can be especially well positioned to apply such pressures forcefully, if not always successfully.

One of the most of blatant examples concerns Norway. In October 2010, the Nobel Prize committee—an independent, nongovernmental body based in Norway—awarded the Nobel Peace Prize to Chinese dissident Liu Xiaobo. Beijing's reaction was swift and furious, calling on the Norwegian government to rescind the prize—even though the Norwegian government was not able to do so—or face the consequences. Oslo refused and Beijing lowered the boom, not only freezing official political relations but also placing restrictions on the import of salmon and other products from Norway, encouraging boycotts on other Norwegian goods, excluding Norway from a visa-free transit agreement extended to other European countries, and halting negotiations on a bilateral free trade agreement. It would take six years for Norway to fully overcome these punitive measures. The price to pay was an official joint declaration stating that Norway "fully respects China's development path and social system . . . attaches high importance to China's core interests and major concerns, will not support actions that undermine them, and will do its best to avoid any future damage to the bilateral relations." Tellingly, in the joint declaration, the PRC did not make the same pledges to Norway. Nonetheless, when the statement was released, the Norwegian foreign minister announced that diplomatic and economic relations would be normalized and negotiations on a free trade agreement resumed.[20]

South Korea offers another case in point. When Seoul announced plans in July 2016 allowing for the deployment of U.S. theater high-altitude air defense (THAAD) systems in South Korea to defend against North Korean missiles, Beijing's reaction was—again—swift and furious, in a dispute that would ultimately last nearly 18 months. Claiming that the system's radar could be operated to help track and destroy Chinese missiles and undermine its nuclear deterrent, the PRC government escalated the issue to be part of bilateral talks between Xi Jinping and U.S. president Barack Obama.[21] But Beijing's ire was mostly taken out on Seoul, as it encouraged boycotts of South Korean goods and brands, curtailed tourist travel to South Korea, and even banned popular South Korean films, television programs, and music. Nearly all retail stores and other facilities owned by Lotte Group in the PRC were forced to close, and the Lotte Mart chain eventually withdrew entirely from mainland China; South Korea lost more than $15 billion in tourism-related revenue from China; and Hyundai and Kia vehicle sales in China plunged by half.[22] Interestingly, however, Beijing did not significantly disrupt economic relations in important sectors where Chinese companies had few viable alternatives, such as key information technology imports from South Korea.[23]

The THAAD batteries were ultimately installed by October 2017 in spite of PRC pressures. However, to get the bilateral diplomatic and economic relationship fully back on track, Seoul announced a "three nos" policy: no additional THAAD batteries, no participation in U.S. region-wide missile defense systems, and no trilateral alliance with the United States and Japan. In applying economic hard power against South Korea, Beijing could claim a partial victory.[24]

As noted earlier in this chapter, Australia has also faced the pressures of PRC economic hard power. Australia-China relations began to deteriorate at the political level starting in 2016–2017, especially as concerns mounted about the expansion of PRC influence and interference activities down under. The Australian government responded with a slew of legislation intended to staunch what Australian prime minister Malcolm Turnbull called "covert, coercive, or corrupt" activities that crossed the line separating "legitimate influence from unacceptable interference."[25] Australia also stepped up scrutiny of foreign investment, especially in critical infrastructure; during this period, Canberra took the decision to deny the Chinese firm Huawei from involvement in the construction of Australia's fifth-generation (5G) broadband communications infrastructure. Canberra was also vocally critical of the PRC's flouting of international law in the South China Sea and Beijing's crackdowns in Hong Kong and Xinjiang. None of this sat well with Beijing. Expectations grew in Australia that Chinese authorities would lean much harder on Canberra and do so through economic hard power.

Beijing launched its most forceful economic barrage to date in 2020. Recall that in April 2020 the PRC ambassador to Canberra issued some implicit but very public threats that China could economically punish Australia's for its call for an independent international investigation into the sources of the covid-19 pandemic. By the end of the year, those warnings became reality. Australian beef, barley, timber, wine, and other agricultural exports were subjected to steep tariffs or restrictive regulatory barriers; the Chinese Ministry of Culture and Tourism issued warnings against travel to Australia; the state-run *Global Times* newspaper advised PRC students against undertaking studies in Australia; and Chinese orders for Australian coal declined.[26] Similar to the South Korean case, these restricted imports could be replaced by other suppliers to China, though not always without difficulty. For example, some Australian exports on which

China is more dependent and would find more difficult to substitute—such as natural gas and iron ore—were not affected in that wave of punitive action. If they had been, it could have been far more damaging to the Australian economy. But while Beijing could not afford to take such a step at the time, it is no doubt exploring ways to diminish dependence on these Australian imports.

In any event, Canberra can expect Beijing to continue to brandish economic hard power in an effort to coerce or induce more favorable Australian policies. To underscore this point, in the midst of the punitive economic measures, the PRC embassy in Canberra took the extraordinary step of releasing a document to Australian media outlets listing 14 reasons why the Australian government was to blame for "poisoning bilateral relations." The list of grievances covered a range of touchy subjects for Beijing, including the denial of certain Chinese investments in Australia; blocking Huawei from Australia's 5G network; funding "anti-China" think tanks in Australia; raiding the homes and offices of Australia-based PRC journalists; making unwelcome statements regarding Xinjiang, Hong Kong, Taiwan, and the South China Sea; making China the target of foreign interference legislation; and calling for an independent international investigation into the source of the covid-19 pandemic.[27] Releasing these criticisms of Australian policy while also leveling increasingly painful trade measures sent an unmistakable message from Beijing: Australia would need to change its tune toward China or expect the economic punishments to continue.

Dozens more examples illustrate how, as China's economic heft has grown, PRC leaders have increasingly turned to economic hard power to pursue the country's interests.[28] A study from the Australian Strategic Policy Institute identifies at least 54 instances of "coercive diplomacy" between 2010 and 2020 in which PRC authorities issued threats or took action against 23 governments—in Africa, Asia, Europe, and North America—to restrict trade, tourism, and investment through punitive measures, boycotts, and other activities in order to alter the target country's behavior on an issue of sensitivity to Beijing.[29] But these cases probably do not tell the entire story, as it is likely many governments self-censor and avoid provoking Beijing precisely for fear of potential economic repercussions—in essence, PRC hard power is at work without being directly applied. Some scholars have noted a "Dalai Lama effect": countries whose top leadership met with the Dalai Lama in spite of Beijing's protestations saw their exports to China decline by nearly 17 percent over the subsequent two years.[30] Others have detailed how the PRC government intervenes in its outbound tourism market as a means to further its strategic interests.[31]

It is important to note that the PRC has not only leveled economic pressures against foreign governments. They have done the same—and often for the same reasons—against international corporations and other organizations. When an executive with the Houston Rockets basketball team personally tweeted his support for pro-democracy protestors in Hong Kong, Beijing responded angrily, including by temporarily banning the broadcast of National Basketball Association (NBA) games in China. Several dozen international airlines and the hospitality giant Marriott were required by PRC authorities to change their websites and other public-facing media showing Taiwan, Hong Kong, and Macau as separate entities from China or face potential punitive measures and consumer boycotts. Many other companies—including tech majors Samsung and Apple; fashion icons Calvin Klein, Dior, and Tiffany & Co.; and even giants such as Walmart and McDonald's—faced similar threats for purporting to misrepresent the status of Taiwan and Hong Kong and "hurting the feelings of the Chinese people." Venerable academic publishers, such as Cambridge University Press (CUP), came under intense pressure to remove "sensitive" articles from its China-facing website—research on such topics as Tibet, the Cultural Revolution, Taiwan, Falun Gong, Mao Zedong, and the Tiananmen crisis—or face a ban on all of its publications. CUP relented at first but later reversed course and kept the articles online; however, other publishers that faced similar demands from Beijing complied.[32] Most of these companies issued apologies, acceded to PRC demands, and said they would be more careful in the future.[33] In these and many other cases, Beijing has shown its willingness to leverage the enormity of the Chinese market to dictate political outcomes in its favor—classic examples of economic hard power at work and an important element of PRC foreign policy under Xi Jinping.

Economic Enticements

But China's economic hard power under Xi Jinping is not only about sticks. Economic hard power also involves carrots: seeking to shape another's behavior by offering benefits or incentives—in essence, buying power. In many respects this is simply the opposite side of the same coin as economic threats: the reason economic threats can work is because of the benefits that are put at risk. In this sense, "playing along" with China in return for access to its lucrative market is a manifestation of PRC economic hard power, which Beijing expects to work of its own volition, without need for resort to threats or punitive measures. Indeed, the persistent tug of this invisible hand to the China market—the opportunity to gain from economic relations with the PRC—is probably Beijing's most powerful and effective foreign policy tool.

That said, under Xi Jinping, China has become visibly more proactive in extending economic benefits abroad as part of its economic statecraft. There are many reasons for doing so. As discussed in chapter 3 on wealth, such motivations might include exporting domestic overcapacity, opening new overseas markets, gaining access to foreign technologies and resources, and strengthening the competitiveness and branding of Chinese firms. But another reason is economic hard power: trying to shape others' behavior to align with Beijing's interests through offers of monetary benefit and other inducements. The Belt and Road Initiative—discussed in detail in the previous chapter—is one of the most obvious examples of this kind of economic hard power.

Foreign aid and overseas development assistance is another example. According to official statements, China has been a source of foreign assistance since the early 1950s, especially to poorer countries. Since that time, China has provided 166 countries and international organizations with close to 400 billion renminbi (RMB) in assistance (approximately $60 billion at today's exchange rate), delivered medical aid to 69 countries in the developing world, and sent some 600,000 aid workers abroad. According to China's 2014 official white paper on foreign aid, over the 2010–2012 period, the country provided the equivalent of $14.4 billion in foreign assistance in the form of grants, interest-free loans, and concessional loans to 121 countries: 51 in Africa, 30 in Asia, 19 in Latin America, 12 in Europe, and nine in Oceania. More recent data shows that over the 2013–2018 period, Beijing increased its annual foreign aid giving, allocating more than $39 billion to 20 international and regional multilateral organizations and 122 countries, with over 80 percent of that support going to least-developed and lower-middle-income countries.[34]

In addition, China delivers development assistance to dozens of less-developed countries to support such United Nations (UN) initiatives as the UN Millennium Development Goals, the UN 2030 Agenda for Sustainable Development, and the China-UN Peace and Development Fund. Beijing also established a South-South Cooperation Assistance Fund in 2015, which China claims has provided assistance in disaster relief, health care, environmental preservation, refugee relief, and protection for women and children to more than 30 countries in Asia, Africa, and the Americas.[35] Beijing prefers to characterize its foreign aid as "South-South cooperation" (南南合作) in order to credit its own status as a developing country while giving aid to other developing countries.

China does not provide official country-by-country data for its development aid and other official financial assistance, so it is difficult to fully verify exact amounts, recipients, and projects associated with all PRC foreign aid. Moreover, PRC foreign assistance has generally come in two forms. The first is best considered as overseas development assistance (ODA), which is support primarily intended for development purposes, provided to developing countries and multilateral institutions, and is concessional—that is, the support has a large grant component of 25 percent or more. The other form of foreign assistance is more commercial in nature and is known as "other official flows." This assistance is not primarily intended for development purposes and would not be as concessional as ODA. Examining these two types of Chinese foreign assistance, the AidData project found that between 2000 and 2014, China offered some $354 billion in aid and nonconcessional official financing to at least 140 countries and territories.[36]

As is the case for Western countries, China's concessional development assistance—as opposed to commercially oriented official financial flows—is typically linked to its foreign policy interests. Several studies have shown that Beijing targets this kind of assistance with specific political outcomes in mind, such as encouraging political alignment and support in international organizations such as the United Nations, advancing developing world solidarity, enticing senior foreign leaders to participate in high-profile events in China, and—in its dollar-diplomacy battle with Taiwan—wresting and keeping formal diplomatic recognition for Beijing rather than Taipei.[37] Concessional foreign aid in the service of political goals has become an increasingly important aspect of China's foreign aid under Xi Jinping as indicated by the establishment in 2018 of the China International Development Cooperation Agency (CIDCA), a subministerial body within the PRC State Council. Prior to CIDCA's existence, PRC foreign aid policy had been beleaguered by bureaucratic infighting, stovepiping, and lack of coordination as well as poor oversight and accountability standards, opening the door to corruption and underperforming projects. The new body is intended to overcome these problems, focus on development aid, and see to a more effective alignment of that assistance with the country's overall foreign policy strategy and goals. Importantly, CIDCA reports to the state councilor responsible for foreign affairs, meaning the agency's programs will be much more closely linked to the country's foreign policy strategy. Its establishment marks a significant shift in how China sees itself and its role in world affairs—steadily transforming from a developing-world country to a leader in the provision of assistance to the developing world.[38] If the CIDCA is successful in meeting these aims it would strengthen China's use of overseas development aid as an instrument of economic hard power.

A number of examples illustrate the importance of foreign assistance as an instrument of economic statecraft and hard power under Xi Jinping. Some analysts and prominent political leaders draw attention to "debt-trap diplomacy"—that is, a deliberate effort by Beijing to burden developing countries with loans they cannot repay in order to extract strategically valuable concessions in return for debt forgiveness. The term "debt-trap diplomacy" was first coined in 2017 by an Indian think tank following an episode in which Sri Lanka sold its majority share in the port of Hambantota to China Merchants Port Holdings, giving the firm a 99-year lease to operate the facility. Since then, the term has become a frequently invoked meme to describe PRC overseas financing schemes. However, it is a misleading and inaccurate way of looking at Chinese foreign assistance. Extensive research, data collection, and analysis provide little to no evidence that China has used loans to ensnare countries in unsustainable debt in order to gain strategic advantage or to "repossess" high-value assets.[39]

However, in other cases, it is clearer how Beijing proffers economic benefits to countries in order to advance specific political interests. China is the largest aid provider to Cambodia, and Phnom Penh is Beijing's closest partner in Southeast Asia. China's generosity appeared to pay off in 2012 when Cambodia, which at the time held the chair of the Association for Southeast Asian Nations (ASEAN), did not allow the issuance of a joint communiqué from the organization that was critical of Beijing's policies in the South China Sea. A Southeast Asian diplomat was quoted as saying, "China bought the chair, simple as that," and the PRC foreign minister later thanked the Cambodian prime minister for protecting China's "core interests."[40]

Beijing has also engaged in checkbook diplomacy as a way of wresting diplomatic recognition away from Taiwan and asserting the one-China principle. The Solomon Islands, for example, decided in 2019 to establish diplomatic relations with the PRC, breaking diplomatic ties with the Republic of China (Taiwan) that had been in place for 36 years. In recommending recognition of China over Taiwan, a bipartisan parliamentary committee considering the "China question" specifically pointed to the prospect of joining the Belt and Road Initiative and tapping into assistance promised by Beijing in more than two dozen areas— including helping with preparing for the 2023 Pacific Games; promoting trade; offering debt relief; providing scholarships for study in China; investing in the Solomon Islands' mineral, fisheries, agriculture, and tourism sectors; delivering medical assistance; and more—as justification for the decision.[41] Prior to the diplomatic switch, Beijing reportedly promised Honiara some $500 million in assistance; Taiwan had spent some $105 million in aid in the Solomon Islands over the 2011–2017 period.[42] Similarly motivated by pledges of economic assistance, the Pacific island nation of Kiribati—which had officially recognized Taiwan between 2003 and 2019—switched back to Beijing a week after the Solomon Islands had done the same.[43] As of the end of 2021, 13 members of the United Nations plus the Holy See (the Vatican) formally recognized Taiwan diplomatically. Many of these governments will be courted by Beijing, including through monetary inducements and other benefits, in a continuing game of economic hard power.[44]

China's "facemask diplomacy" during the covid-19 pandemic provides another example of leveraging economic benefits to shape favorable political outcomes. Once Beijing brought its own coronavirus outbreak under control, it poured considerable resources into shaping the global narrative in praise of China's response, downplaying its responsibility as the initial source of the disease, and demonstrating a worldwide leadership role. This became all the more important politically as Washington and Beijing traded barbs over their respective mishandling of the pandemic. According to Beijing's official tally, by mid-2020, China had dispatched 29 medical teams to 27 countries around the world and provided various forms of assistance—including personal protective equipment, ventilators, testing kits, and personnel training—to some 150 countries and four international organizations, while donating $50 million above and beyond its normal dues to the World Health Organization. In doing so, Beijing called on the international community to resist scapegoating and stigmatizing China, reject "decoupling" and deglobalization, respect China's contribution to combating the pandemic, and embrace Xi Jinping's vision of a "global community of shared future."[45] Whether China's generosity will reap these rewards remains an open question. But Beijing's facemask diplomacy stands out as one of its most concerted and high-profile efforts to deploy its economic capacity to shape the behavior of others in favor of Chinese interests.

Military Power

In October 2019, to mark the 70th anniversary of the founding of the PRC, Xi Jinping presided over the most massive military parade in the country's history. Stretching for miles along Chang'an Avenue, the spectacle featured 15,000 troops and nearly 800 pieces of military hardware. Among its most sophisticated weaponry, the military display included China's new J-20 stealth fighter, hypersonic weapons, and for the first time in public, the DF-41, the country's most powerful nuclear-armed missile. Accompanied by martial music, military flyovers, and rousing chants to service and Party loyalty, the event was a raw display of PRC hard power potential.

It also symbolized the progress made under Xi Jinping to assert Party leadership over the PLA, strengthen PLA power-projection capabilities, and deploy those capabilities with greater confidence in the pursuit of PRC interests abroad, all commensurate with the country's growing political and economic influence regionally and globally. While the PLA had been steadily modernizing since the 1990s—accelerated by double-digit increases in its budget nearly every year between 1995 and 2015—Xi has taken some particularly decisive steps his immediate predecessors were unable or unwilling to take. In so doing, he aims to transform the PLA from a bloated, corrupt, untested, and stovepiped military to a far more formidable force, absolutely loyal to the CCP, capable of fighting and winning intensive conflicts against technologically sophisticated foes, and doing so farther from Chinese shores.

The first important step Xi took regarding the military was to strengthen Party control over it. Mao Zedong's famous adage that "political power grows from the barrel of a gun" still defines the relationship between the CCP and its armed wing, the PLA. The PLA is first and foremost the Party's army but the degree of central Party control and internal PLA discipline has varied ever since the founding of the Red Army—the PLA's predecessor—in the late 1920s.[46] In the 1990s and 2000s, times of enormous social and economic change in China, the PLA drifted in a more independent and depoliticized direction. Corruption and malfeasance—facilitated through the operation of bars, brothels, and transport companies; misappropriation of funds and resources; and selling promotions— was widespread in the ranks and even reached the very top.[47] According to PLA experts Phillip Saunders and Joel Wuthnow, "The extent of corruption within the PLA—and the fact that neither political ideology nor existing supervisory mechanisms could control it—was evidence that Party control over the PLA had eroded, perhaps to dangerous levels."[48]

Within days of taking power in November 2012—including his appointment as the chairman of the Central Military Commission (CMC)—Xi and the Party leadership moved quickly to staunch these trends. In his first speech as CMC chair, speaking to an enlarged meeting of the body, he made matters clear:

> We must uphold the Party's leadership of the armed forces. This is central to the nature and mission of the armed forces, the future of socialism, the enduring stability of the Party, and the lasting peace of our country. . . . In our efforts to strengthen our armed forces we must treat theoretical and political educa-tion as our first priority, so that the Party's leadership of them will take firm root in the minds of our officers and soldiers, and the whole armed forces will follow without hesitation the commands of the Party Central Committee and the Central Military Commission at all times and under all conditions. . . . We will apply political convictions as a measure when reviewing and appointing officers to ensure that our weaponry is always in the hands of those who are re-liable and loyal to the Party.[49]

Shortly thereafter, Xi and the Party leadership took the major step of launching an anticorruption drive within the PLA. Hundreds of officers were charged and removed from their posts. These included the two most senior uniformed officers in the PLA—Generals Guo Boxiong and Xu Caihou—who, prior to their downfalls, were vice chairmen of the CMC. In addition, the Party reinvigorated ideological training and further emphasized the importance of fealty to the CCP, political indoctrination, and organizational discipline. By the time of the 19th Party Congress in 2017, Xi oversaw sweeping personnel changes across the PLA leadership, installing officers reliably loyal to him and to the Party.[50]

This opened the way to push ahead with a second major step: the introduc-tion of an across-the-board organizational overhaul for the PLA. These changes were foreshadowed in November 2013, a year after Xi took office, when the Third

Plenum of 18th Party Central Committee announced the decision to "optimize the size and structure of the army" and to improve the "joint operation command authority under the Central Military Commission and theater joint operation command system."[51] While steadily improving since the early 1990s to become a more professional and effective fighting force, the PLA nonetheless faced many challenges: as a RAND Corporation study concluded in 2015, China's military transformation remained "incomplete."[52] These problems ranged from the organizational to the operational and meant PLA capabilities fell short of the country's expanding interests and ambitions under Xi Jinping. In particular, the PLA had not sufficiently developed the ability to conduct modern, joint operations warfare and lacked combat experience and realistic training. A former U.S. Army attaché to China, Col. (retired) Larry Wortzel, agrees, finding that "even after a long period of high-intensity training for the PLA, there does not seem to be much improvement in the ability of their commanders and soldiers to operate on the modern battlefield."[53] These were problems that the Party and PLA leadership openly acknowledged, but until Xi came to power, entrenched interests within the PLA resisted the necessary reforms to address them.[54]

Formally launched in late 2015, Xi's ongoing reforms of the PLA are among the most extensive and potentially transformative in its history.[55] These changes have already had far-reaching effects on the PLA's organization, personnel numbers, force posture, command-and-control structures, and internal politics. As shown in Table 5.1, the reorganization has resulted in a significant downsizing of the PLA, though it remains the world's largest military and continues to be dominated by its land forces as opposed to naval, air, and missile forces. Looking ahead and over the longer term, it remains to be seen whether this reform and reorganization campaign can succeed in resolving all the challenges facing the PLA. But it is a clear signal of Xi's intention to vastly improve the PLA as a part of China's hard power toolkit.

Building a World-Class Military

With his military shake-up well underway, Xi outlined his expectations for the PLA in his work report to the 19th CCP Congress in October 2017:

A military is built to fight. Our military must regard combat capability as the criterion to meet in all its work and focus on how to win when it is called on. We will take solid steps to ensure military preparedness for all strategic directions, and make progress in combat readiness in both traditional and new security fields. We will develop new combat forces and support forces, conduct military training under combat conditions, strengthen the application of military

Table 5.1 Estimated Personnel in PRC Armed Forces, 2016 and 2020

PLA Active Duty	Estimated Personnel—2016 (% Active Force)	Estimated Personnel—2020 (% Active Force)
Total	2,333,000 (including uniformed Civil Cadre)	2,000,000 (including uniformed Civil Cadre)
Army	1,600,000 (69%)	975,000 (<50%)
Navy (includes Marines)	235,000 (10%)	250,000 (12.5%)
(Marines, counted as Navy)	(10,000–12,000)	(40,000) (2%)
Air Force (includes Airborne)	398,000 (17%)	395,000 (19.75%)
Second Artillery / Rocket Force	100,000+ (5%)	120,000 (6%)
Strategic Support Force	Not applicable	175,000 (8.75%)
Joint Logistics Support Force	Not applicable	85,000 (4.25%)
Reserves	510,000	510,000? (no recent reporting)
Contract Civilian Personnel	20,000	40,000? (undergoing expansion)
People's Armed Police (PAP)	660,000 (Coast Guard not included)	500,000? (includes Coast Guard, but total number not released after 2018 reform)
Total: PLA Active, Reserves, Civilians, and PAP	3,523,000	approx. 3,050,000
Militia (includes unknown number of uniformed People's Armed Forces Department Local Civilian Cadre)	8,000,000	8,000,000? (2008 number, no recent reporting)

Note: According to the 2019 white paper *China's National Defense in the New Era*, the total number of active-duty PLA personnel before the 2016 reforms was 2,300,000.

Source: *The Military Balance 2016* and author estimates for 2020.

strength, speed up development of intelligent military, and improve combat capabilities for joint operations based on the network information system and the ability to fight under multidimensional conditions. This will enable us to effectively shape our military posture, manage crises, and deter and win wars.[56]

In that same important speech, Xi set out key milestones for the PLA in a "three-step development strategy" (三步走的发展战略). In the first step, to be realized by 2020, mechanization would be "basically achieved," information technology applications would have "come a long way," and strategic capabilities would have seen a "big improvement." By 2035, Xi foresees achievement of the second step, an across-the-board modernization of military theory, organization, personnel, and weaponry. And by the mid-21st century, he said, the PLA would be fully transformed into a world-class military (把人民军队全面建成世界一流军队).[57]

To achieve these aims, the PLA has begun to invest more heavily in particular capabilities. They stress the growing importance of maritime domains (both "off-shore defense" and "far seas protection"); stronger capabilities in nuclear, aero-space, and information domains; the need to project power farther away from China's borders to safeguard the country's expanding international interests; and improvements in joint operations and informationized warfighting. The Pentagon acknowledges that the PLA has made significant strides in these and other areas over the past 20 years, progressing from a military whose forces were "mostly obsolete" and "lacked the joint organizations and training needed" to one today that has "marshaled the resources, technology, and political will . . . to strengthen and modernize the PLA in nearly every respect" and is even ahead of the United States in certain areas.[58]

For example, regarding naval construction, the PRC has surpassed the United States as having the largest navy in the world, with some 355 ships and submarines (compared to about 295 ships in the U.S. Navy) in 2020. During Xi Jinping's time as top leader, China's first aircraft carrier (the *Liaoning*) reportedly achieved "all-weather combat capability" in 2018, a second carrier was commissioned into the PLA Navy (PLAN) in 2019 (the *Shandong*, China's first entirely domestically produced aircraft carrier), and building began on a third carrier to be launched in 2021. The PLA Air Force is already the largest air force in the Asia-Pacific region and the third-largest in the world, estimated to have over 2,800 aircraft, including some 2,250 combat aircraft.[59]

The PLA Rocket Force also operates one of the world's largest and most diverse arrays of land-based conventional ballistic and cruise missiles, more than 1,200 of them and counting as of 2020, with ranges between 300 and 5,500 kilometers; the Rocket Force also deploys some 100 nuclear-armed intercontinental-range ballistic missiles (ICBMs) while the PLA Navy (PLAN) has six nuclear-armed ballistic missile submarines, each carrying 12 missiles.[60] The PLA is looking to further develop and refine its missile force, and in 2018, 2019, and 2020, conducted more ballistic missile testing and training launches than the rest of the world combined; it launched more than 250 such ballistic missile tests in 2020. Moreover, in 2020 and 2021, China built more than 200 new ICBM silos in the western provinces of Gansu and Xinjiang; if all of these silos are filled with nuclear-armed missiles, it would mark the largest single expansion ever in

China's nuclear arsenal.[61] Work also continues apace in the development and deployment of Chinese hypersonic weapons, with the PLA displaying the DF-17 missile—designed to carry hypersonic vehicles—at the PRC's 70th anniversary parade in October 2019 and is in the midst of testing the Xingkong-2 hypersonic flight vehicle.[62] In a critical breakthrough, China tested a nuclear-capable hypersonic vehicle in 2021 that circled the globe through low-orbit space before descending toward its target.[63]

In addition, with the establishment of the PLA Strategic Support Force (PLASSF) under the new reforms, the PRC has prioritized the importance of information warfare and joint operations. The PLASSF will be an especially critical instrument of the PRC as it provides the PLA with integrated strategic information support through space- and network-based capabilities, including communications, navigation and positioning, intelligence, surveillance and reconnaissance, and the protection of military information infrastructure while also conducting strategic information operations in the space, cyber-, electromagnetic, and psychological warfare spheres. Moreover, renewed efforts at home and abroad in pursuit of "military-civilian fusion" (军民融合)—which aims to gain synergies from the integration of relevant civilian- and military-use technologies—may also advance China's ongoing military modernization process.[64] Table 5.2 provides a comparative snapshot of some of the PRC's principal weapon systems in 2014 versus 2020.

In spite of these significant developments, the PLA still faces major shortcomings. However, the overhaul of the Chinese armed forces launched in late 2015 has put them on a clear path toward becoming increasingly effective in deterrence, coercion, and warfighting. Looking ahead over the next 10 to 15 years, the PLA will build up its hard power into a far more formidable force abroad, especially as it expands its offshore presence in the region and around the world.

Expanding Hard Power within the First and Second Island Chains

China's increasing hard power—the ability to achieve aims through threats, coercion, and inducements—is most readily seen in the expanded presence of Chinese armed forces in areas relatively close to the Chinese mainland in order to deter, combat, and defeat potential adversaries.[65] The Pentagon refers to these as "anti-access / area-denial" (A2/AD) capabilities. These would include land-based missiles and air power, antiship and antisubmarine warfare capabilities, an incipient—but growing—expeditionary capability, and increasingly sophisticated cyberwarfare forces. For now, these capabilities are most significant and

Table 5.2 Selected PLA Weapons Platforms, 2014 and 2020

Weapon Platform	2014	2020	Comments
Fighters			
• J-7 variants	526	512	incl. J-7 E & G
• J-8 variants	168	124	incl. J-8B, F & H
• J-11	95	95	
• Su-27 variants	75	52	incl. Su-27SK & UBK
Fighter Ground Attack			
• J-11 variants	approx. 122	approx. 202	incl. J-11B & BS
• J-10 variants	approx. 294	468	incl. J-10A, C & S
• JH-7 variants	240	120	
• Su-30	97	97	
• J-15		20	
• J-16		approx. 100	
• J-20		approx. 22	
• Su-35		24	
Bombers			
• H-6 variants	136	211	incl. H-6 A, G, H, & K
AEW&C			
• KJ series	8	25	incl. KJ-200, 500 &
• Y-8	10	4	2000
Tankers			
• H-6	13	15	incl. H-6DU & U
• Il-78	1	3	
Submarines			
• SSBN	4	6	
• SSN	5	6	
• SSK	60	46	
Surface Combatants			
• Aircraft carriers	1	2	
• Cruisers		1	
• Destroyers	23	31	
• Frigates	48	46	
Missiles*			
• ICBM	75–100 (50–75)	100 (100)	range: >5,500 kms
• IRBM	n.d.	200+ (200)	range: 3,000–5,500 kms
• MRBM	200–300 (100–125)	150+ (150)	range: 1,000–3,000 kms
• SRBM	1,000–1,200 (250–300)	600+ (250)	range: 300–1,000 kms
• GLCM	200–300 (40–55)	300+ (100)	range: >1,500 kms

Key: AEW&C: airborne early warning and control aircraft; GLCM: ground-launched cruise missile; ICBM: intercontinental ballistic missile; IRBM: intermediate-range ballistic missile; MRBM: medium-range ballistic missile; SRBM: short-range ballistic missile; SSBN: nuclear-powered ballistic missile submarine; SSK: attack submarine; SSN: nuclear-powered attack submarine; kms: kilometers; n.d.: no data.

* Data from 2016 and 2020 for surface-to-surface missiles; columns show number of missiles with number of launchers shown in ().

Sources: Institute for International Strategic Studies, *The Military Balance 2014* and *2020*; missile data drawn from Office of the Secretary of Defense, *Military and Security Developments Involving the People's Republic of China: Annual Report to Congress* (Washington, D.C.: Department of Defense, August 2020), Appendix I; and Office of the Secretary of Defense, *Military and Security Developments Involving the People's Republic of China: Annual Report to Congress* (Washington, D.C.: Department of Defense, April 2016), Appendix II.

dangerous within what is often called the "first island chain," but also include an increased ability to project deadly power to the "second island chain" and beyond into the Western Pacific and Indian Oceans.[66] Within the first island chain, China has numerous and highly contentious sovereignty and territorial disputes with its neighbors, including with Japan, Taiwan, the Philippines, and Vietnam (see chapter 3). Importantly, some of these neighbors are treaty allies (Japan, the Philippines) or close security partners (Taiwan) with the United States, which further raises the stakes of these disputes. Figure 5.1 depicts the first and second island chains.

China's actions in the South China Sea stand out as one of the most obvious examples of hard power in this contested maritime area. Since 2012 in particular, Beijing has stepped up its activities to assert its territorial claims in this vast waterway. These actions are carefully calibrated to fall below the threshold of outright war in order to diminish the likelihood for more fierce reactions from others in the region, including the United States. In mid-2012, following a

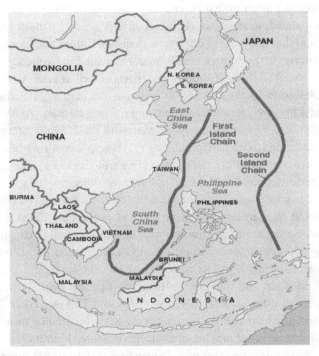

Figure 5.1 First and second island chains

Note: Boundary representations are not necessarily authoritative.

Source: Office of the Secretary of Defense, *Military Power of the People's Republic of China 2006* (Washington: Department of Defense, 2006), p. 15.

stand-off between PRC and Philippine coast guard vessels, China took effective control over Scarborough Shoal—located just 130 miles west of the Philippine mainland, but falling within Beijing's "nine-dash line"—which had been previously held by the Philippines; China has since maintained a constant coast guard presence at the shoal. Under Xi Jinping, China has further fortified its claims within the South China Sea by undertaking a massive dredging and artificial island-building project between late 2013 and mid-2015, particularly in the Spratly Island region—some 500 miles from the Chinese mainland—where Vietnam, the Philippines, and Malaysia also have claims and occupy islands. Having created some 3,200 acres of new land in the South China Sea, China has proceeded to build up its military capabilities on both existing and newly built islands, including the construction of airstrips, air defense systems, communication stations, aircraft hangars, bunkers, and port facilities suitable for naval vessels. While the construction and militarization of seven new islands in the Spratlys have received the most attention, China has also conducted landfilling operations and military upgrades on islands it occupies in the Paracel Island region of the South China Sea.[67]

By conducting major military exercises in the South China Sea, Beijing sends hard power signals to the other claimants as well to other nations such as the United States that may seek to dispute or challenge China's assertions of sovereignty. Exercises in the South China Sea have increased in frequency and complexity, involving all three of China's navy fleets as well as other services, such as the PLA Rocket Force (PLARF). In an important first, in 2019, the PLARF conducted a live-fire exercise of six antiship ballistic missiles (ASBMs) in the South China Sea, apparently in coordination with the *Liaoning* aircraft carrier task force operating nearby.[68] Conducting PLAN activities at sea while also carrying out live-fire ASBM exercises in the same area marked a significant milestone in the development of PLA hard power capabilities.

Beijing has taken pages from the same playbook in asserting its claims elsewhere around its maritime periphery, such as in the East China Sea. There China has ongoing territorial disputes with Japan (discussed in chapter 3) and has stepped up military and Chinese Coast Guard activities in this region as a way to assert its claims, signal its capabilities, conduct training and intelligence-gathering missions, and put wear-and-tear on Japanese equipment and personnel. Starting from around 2009, the PLAN and PLA Air Force (PLAAF) have significantly increased the number of its aircraft patrolling near Japanese airspace, forcing a record number of intercepts by Japanese aircraft in response. Potential Chinese intrusions prompted Japan to scramble jets 851 times in 2016. Between April 2019 and March 2020, Japan scrambled jets 675 times against Chinese patrols: a 6 percent increase over the previous year and the most since 2016. These Chinese flights are heavily concentrated in the East China Sea near the disputed Senkaku/Diaoyu Islands as well as near U.S. and Japanese military facilities at Okinawa.[69]

The Japanese Ministry of Defense also documents a steady increase in the number of Chinese government vessels—such as coast guard ships and maritime surveillance vessels, but also including ships and submarines of the PLAN—intruding in Japanese territorial waters, especially around the Senkaku Islands, as a way of routinizing PRC presence and asserting Beijing's claims. In 2019, nearly 1,100 such vessels spent a total of some 282 days in the waters contiguous to the Senkaku Islands—a record at the time; that record was surpassed the following year when Chinese Coast Guard vessels made 1,161 incursions over 333 days.[70] China and Russia also held joint naval drills in the Sea of Japan in 2017 and the East China Sea in 2019, the latter including live-fire surface-to-air missile tests—a first for China with a foreign navy. Later in 2019, Chinese and Russian long-range bombers conducted a joint flight over international waters of the Tsushima Strait between Japan and South Korea, prompting both U.S. allies to scramble jets in response.[71] These kinds of hard power displays will likely continue and probably increase in regularity, sophistication, or both in the coming years.

The ultimate prize for Beijing within the first island chain is Taiwan, and it stands out as the most important target of the PRC's hard power intimidation. It is here that Beijing has been most willing to use or threaten force in order to dissuade or prevent Taiwan from permanently thwarting China's claims to sovereignty over the self-governing island. Since the mid-1990s, as Taiwan has become a thriving democracy and the political mood there has increasingly shifted against reunification on the PRC's terms, China's response has been to ramp up its hard power capabilities vis-à-vis Taiwan. Importantly, these hard power signals and capabilities are not only intended for Taiwan. They are also designed as a signal to others, such as the United States, to deter them from political and military support for Taiwan, including military actions in defense of Taiwan in the face of PRC harassment and attack.

In 1995 and 1996, for example, in an effort to intimidate pro-independence leaders in Taiwan, China fired short-range ballistic missiles into the waters off the island's coast, followed by massive naval and amphibious landing drills—at the time some of the largest exercises of this type ever undertaken by the PLA. Since then, the Chinese military has steadily built up its military capabilities opposite Taiwan. According to the Pentagon, the PRC's Eastern and Southern Theater Commands, located across from Taiwan, deploy some 600 fighter jets, 250 bombers and ground-attack aircraft, 100 major surface combatants (including destroyers, frigates, corvettes, and one aircraft carrier), and nearly 40 submarines. These forces are augmented by well more than 1,000 Chinese medium- and short-range ballistic missiles and ground-launched cruise missiles that can reach Taiwan and beyond.[72]

With the election of Tsai Ing-wen as Taiwan president in 2016, and her reelection in 2020, Beijing has considerably increased its hard power pressure on Taiwan through a range of coercive military tactics. These measures are in addition to the hard power economic leverage noted earlier in this chapter that Beijing exercises against Taiwan. For example, since 2016, the PLAAF has increased its patrols of fighters, surveillance planes, and other aircraft near and around Taiwan, including increased H-6 heavy bomber flights circumnavigating the island. More provocatively, in March 2019, two Chinese J-11 fighters (Chinese versions of the Russian Su-27) for the first time in 20 years crossed the unofficial but customarily respected "median line" in the Taiwan Strait between China and Taiwan. A month later, the PLA's Eastern Theater Command conducted major joint training exercises east of Taiwan involving a range of aircraft and naval vessels to simulate strikes against land targets and amphibious landings.[73] Chinese military activity in and around Taiwan increased considerably in the following years, including air and naval drills and repeated crossings of the median line by Chinese warplanes.[74] In August and September 2020, the Chinese media gave high-profile coverage to PLA exercises "aimed at deterring Taiwan secessionists and the US," and over a two-day period the PLAAF sent an unprecedented number of some 40 aircraft—including fighters, bombers, and submarine hunters—across the median line and regularly kept up such pressure tactics.[75] Following the announcement of new U.S. arms sales to Taiwan in late 2020, the PRC state media kept up the pressure, saying that "future penalties" might include military flights over Taiwan, an economic blockade, strikes against the new weapons systems, and other "unprecedented pressure."[76]

Upping the ante in 2021, the PLA conducted sorties over waters southwest of Taiwan with H-6 bombers and other aircraft that simulated an antiship missile attack against the USS *Theodore Roosevelt,* a U.S. aircraft carrier that at the time was operating in the vicinity—probably the first time such a simulation was made public. The PLAN also conducted additional exercises purporting to "surround" Taiwan and thwart foreign intervention, drills Beijing said would be conducted on a regular basis. And, coinciding with the October 1 PRC National Day that year, the Chinese military conducted the largest-ever incursion into Taiwan's air defense zone with nearly 150 fighters, bombers, and other aircraft over the course of several days.[77] The PLA has also stepped up its use of other political warfare against Taiwan, employing cyber and other means in an attempt to disseminate misinformation and influence public opinion.

Through these and other military activities, Beijing seeks to shape the choices not only of Taiwan but others, including the United States—a classic use of hard power. In spite of some constraints imposed by covid-19 in 2020, the PLA stepped up its military activities along its eastern and southern periphery by 50 percent over its pace the previous year, including training exercises and maritime operations, to improve readiness and warfighting capabilities. According to prominent PRC naval analyst Li Jie, "The US Navy's intensive, provocative moves in the Taiwan Strait and South China Sea pushed the PLA Navy to increase its preparedness for a possible conflict."[78] It appears these extra efforts may be paying off: the Pentagon concludes the PLA is "developing capabilities to provide options for the PRC to dissuade, deter, or, if ordered, defeat third-party intervention during a large-scale, theater campaign such as a Taiwan contingency."[79]

In addition to these steps to increase the PLA's hard power capabilities within the first island chain—especially with regard to the South China Sea, East China Sea, and Taiwan Strait—the Chinese military has also steadily improved its ability to project power beyond those waterways. The PLAN and PLAAF increasingly conduct training and patrols in the Western Pacific, while the PLARF has developed more lethal and accurate ballistic and cruise missiles that can reach thousands of kilometers from the Chinese mainland. The PLAAF can deploy a small number of long-range bombers to conduct antiship and land attack missions between the first and second island chains. Land-attack and antiship variants of the DF-21 and DF-26 ballistic missiles—with ranges of 1,500 kilometers and 4,000 kilometers, respectively—as well as the DH-10 ground-launched cruise missile (1,500-kilometer range) reportedly allow the PLA to launch precision strikes—including against aircraft carriers—from the PRC mainland to reach targets in the Indian and Western Pacific Oceans.[80] These weapons add an increasingly formidable deterrent and warfighting capacity to China's hard power arsenal.

Developing Military Power Farther Afield

In addition to flexing such hard power muscle closer to home, the PLA conducts a range of other military-related activities offshore that also contribute to building its hard power capabilities. Globally, the PLA lacks a traditional expeditionary capability. However, by participating in UN peacekeeping operations, conducting counterpiracy task forces, evacuating noncombatants from regional hotspots, holding military exercises with other militaries, and establishing a base in Djibouti, the PLA has demonstrated a nascent ability to deploy and sustain a military presence far from the Chinese mainland. These activities contribute to PRC hard power by deploying military force against threats, gaining real-world experience, learning from foreign militaries, gathering intelligence, accessing advanced military technology, and sending deterrent signals about PLA capabilities, all of which can in turn be used to shape the behavior of others in pursuit of Chinese interests. Some of these military activities also have a soft power element to them as they aim to generate a more favorable and attractive image for the PRC and may help Beijing gain a greater say over how the United Nations uses force (discussed further in chapter 6). Beijing sees these activities not only as ways to advance PRC power, but part and parcel of broader efforts to achieve other foreign policy goals. Under Xi Jinping, the PLA has been encouraged to expand its overseas activities in order to promote and protect expanding Chinese interests around the globe.[81]

One of the most high-profile examples of the PLA's expanding presence overseas is the Djibouti Support Base (吉布提保障基地) operated by the PLAN. China announced its intention to build this base in 2015, and it formally opened in 2017. Located in the small nation of Djibouti on the east coast of Africa where the Bab al-Mandab Strait connects the Red Sea and the Gulf of Aden, this facility is China's first and (so far) only overseas military base. It was established to support the PLAN's antipiracy missions in the Gulf of Aden as well as China's growing contributions to UN peacekeeping operations in Africa. It houses approximately 2,000 military personnel, including from the PLA Navy, Marines, Army, and special forces.[82]

The Djibouti Support Base is notable for its break with the long-standing PRC practice of abjuring any permanent overseas military presence and decrying the use of foreign bases by other powers, such as the United States. It is also notable for what it could mean for China's power projection in the future. In operating the Djibouti base, the PLA gains important experience in sustaining such a presence far from Chinese shores, provides the PLA with an operational foothold in a strategically important region where Africa and the Middle East converge, and allows the PLA to more closely observe and learn from other militaries that also have a base in Djibouti, including those of the United States, France, Italy and Japan. China's Djibouti base has also fueled speculation that the PLA will establish other foreign bases in the years ahead. Much attention has focused on the port at Ream in Cambodia as a potential site, but Phnom Penh has officially denied that such a plan is in the works.[83] Looking ahead, it is possible the PLA will set up another foreign base in the future, though it is more likely in the near term that the Chinese military will continue to seek various forms of access rights—for refueling, maintenance, and logistics purposes—at airports and harbors to support the PLA's expanding presence abroad.

An important and ongoing element of the PLA's growing presence offshore is its antipiracy escort missions in and around the Gulf of Aden. Since December 2008, alongside other countries' antipiracy escort missions in this area, the PLAN has sent small task forces—usually comprising two combatants and a supply ship—for four-month rotations. As of early 2022, the PLAN had dispatched 40 such missions, involving more than 50 different naval vessels and thousands of sailors and special forces.[84] A ship from the 16th task force assisted in escorting chemical weapons out of Syria in 2014, and the 17th task force, which set sail from China in March 2014, took part in the search for the downed Malaysian Airlines flight 340. Ships from the Gulf of Aden escort missions also took part in the emergency evacuation of more than 600 Chinese citizens and nearly 300 non-Chinese citizens from war-torn Yemen in 2015.[85] These missions had escorted more than 6,600 Chinese and non-Chinese ships and assisted more than 70 ships in distress.[86] In helping combat piracy and protect vital sea lanes, these missions provide international public goods. But they also help build up the PLAN's capabilities by providing crews and headquarters staff with excellent real-world experience in extended, long-distance operations; at-sea replenishment; communications and tactical operations; and interactions with other navies. That the PLA Navy has proven capable of deploying an uninterrupted three-ship counterpiracy task force in and around the Gulf of Aden since 2008 is no small feat for a navy with comparatively little previous experience on the high seas. Given the PLAN's lack of wartime experience, these operations are the closest thing to combat on the high seas the modern PLAN has undertaken.[87]

China's involvement in UN peacekeeping operations (UNPKOs) delivers similar benefits in building PRC hard power capabilities. While avoiding contributions to UNPKOs for nearly 20 years after entering the United Nations in 1971, the PRC sent its first small team of military observers to assist the United Nations Truce Supervision Organization in the Middle East in 1990. With one major exception—China sent 400 engineering troops to carry out demining operations in support of a UN mission in Cambodia in 1992–1994—Beijing continued to keep its UNPKO contributions to between 50 and 100 military observers a year up until the early 2000s. Since 2002, however, PRC participation has grown by more than 20-fold, and since 2009 China has been the largest contributor of UN peacekeeping forces among the five permanent members of the UN Security Council and the second-largest contributor of funding to UNPKOs. The majority of Chinese blue helmet forces have provided engineering, transport, medical, and policing support, but in 2015 China deployed its first combat troops—a full infantry battalion—to a UNPKO in South Sudan.[88] At the end of 2021, China had 2,253 troops, police, experts, and staff officers in UNPKOs across nine missions, making China the ninth-largest contributor of personnel among UN members, with a little more than 1,000 of those posted to South Sudan.[89]

Since 1990, China has sent more than 40,000 personnel to 25 UNPKOs, and 16 PRC service personnel have lost their lives while operating on these missions.[90] In addition to demonstrating the PRC's international leadership (see chapter 7), the officers and troops involved in these missions have accrued valuable overseas experience, established and maintained long-distance supply chains and communications channels, honed staffing and operational skills in differing threat environments, learned from foreign military personnel, and gained other on-the-ground intelligence. These are all valued inputs as the country continues to build up its hard power capabilities.

Another means the PLA has taken to build up and demonstrate its hard power is through conducting a range of bilateral and multilateral training exercises with foreign militaries. Since the early 2000s, these activities have significantly increased in number and complexity, and become more multilateral in nature. Over time, PLA exercises with foreign militaries have also become more focused on developing combat, combat support, and counterterrorism skills. The total annual number of PLA exercises with counterparts abroad more than quintupled from eight in 2013 (Xi Jinping's first full year as paramount leader) to 45 in 2016. All told, China has carried out military exercises with nearly 60 countries since 2003, including with the United States, the United Kingdom, France, Australia, India, and Japan.[91]

China's most preferred partner for military exercises is Russia.[92] The two countries held naval drills in the Mediterranean Sea in 2015 and the Baltic in 2017, and Russia has joined with the PLAN to conduct joint exercises in the East China Sea, Yellow Sea, and South China Sea. Since 2007, China, Russia, and the other members of the Shanghai Cooperation Organization have held "Peace Mission" counterterrorism exercises involving thousands of troops—since 2010, every two years.[93] China also contributed 3,500 troops to the massive Vostok-2018 exercise, which involved an additional 300,000 Russian troops in what the Kremlin claimed at the time was its largest military drills ever. The following year, China contributed 1,600 ground and air personnel and some 30 aircraft—including H-6 bombers—to participate alongside forces from the other SCO members in the Russian "Tsentr-2019" exercise. While 2020 saw a decline in international military exercises for the PLA owing to the covid-19 pandemic, some nevertheless took place. One of the most significant was "Caucuses-2020," which brought together some 12,000 soldiers and sailors from China, Russia, Armenia, Belarus, Iran, Myanmar, and Pakistan to conduct land and sea drills in southern Russia. In its first joint military exercises inside the PRC since the covid-19 outbreak, some 10,000 personnel from China and Russia conducted a five-day set of drills involving land and air forces in the country's northwest autonomous region of Ningxia.[94] These exercises underscore a deepening military relationship between the two countries.

Conducting these exercises with foreign powers is an important element in the development and exercise of Chinese hard power. While some exercises are scripted and do not simulate conditions of real combat, they nevertheless can help commanders and soldiers improve operational experience and confidence while providing lessons learned, new skills, and intelligence, all of which bolster's China's military capabilities. More broadly, PLA involvement in exercises abroad can contribute to such strategic objectives as deepening diplomatic and security ties with key partners and signaling potential adversaries as to China's deterrent and warfighting capabilities.

In addition to their joint military exercises, China-Russia ties have made other valuable contributions to the development of PRC hard power. Russia has been by far the most important exporter of advanced weapons and military technology to China for the past 30 years. These exports have included weapons platforms as well as assistance in the development of China's indigenous arms production capacity. A small sampling of these systems would include hundreds of Su-27, Su-30, and Su-35 fighter jets; scores of advanced turbofan engines to power Chinese-built fighters, bombers, and transport aircraft; highly capable S-300 and S-400 surface-to-air missile batteries; hundreds of antiship missiles; four Sovremmeny-class destroyers; and 12 Kilo-class submarines.[95] And the PRC's first aircraft carrier, the *Liaoning*, was originally a Russian hull delivered to China in 2002 and refurbished in Chinese shipyards, becoming fully operational for combat duty in 2019. Time and time again, China has proven adept at reverse engineering and adapting these and other Russian systems to suit their own requirements and advance the development of the PRC arms industry. As Lyle Goldstein and Vitaly Kozyrev convincingly demonstrate, the military-technical relationship with Russia over three decades has been a decisive factor in the modernization of PRC maritime and air doctrine and power, and shows that the two countries are poised to develop even deeper cooperation across a range of strategic and political-diplomatic initiatives.[96] These areas of cooperation all contribute to bolstering China's hard power.

Finally, arms exports are another important means for the PRC to build up its hard power. China has consistently ranked among the top 10 arms exporters in the world since the 1980s. However, in 2012 and again in 2013, China rose to become the third-largest weapons exporting nation (behind the United States and Russia) for the first time and has since remained among the top five. Over the 20 years from 2000 to 2019, the PRC supplied a wide range of weaponry to 75 recipients worldwide, mostly to developing-world countries in Asia, Africa, and the Middle East. Over that period, the top 10 importers of Chinese weapons were, in order, Pakistan, Bangladesh, Myanmar, Algeria, Iran, Venezuela, Sudan, Thailand, Egypt, and Tanzania. These 10 accounted for nearly 80 percent of Chinese arms exports by value during that period. Since 2013, about 78 percent of Chinese exports by value went to a similar set of seven countries (in rank order): Pakistan, Bangladesh, Algeria, Myanmar, Thailand, Venezuela, and Indonesia. Chinese arms exports have become increasingly sophisticated and today include such aircraft as fighters, transports, combat helicopters, and jet trainers; frigates, submarines, patrol craft, and other naval vessels; antiship and surface-to-air missiles; armed drones; and a range of land systems such as tanks, rocket launchers, infantry fighting vehicles, and armored personnel carriers. In a sign of deepening military-technical cooperation with certain partners, some PRC export deals include the assembly or production of Chinese systems in the recipient country, such as submarines and the JF-17 Thunder fighter jet built in Pakistan, JF-17 Thunder fighters assembled in Myanmar, and T-59 tanks assembled in Sudan.[97]

Arms exports assist in the development of PRC hard power in a variety of ways. A portion of the profits generated from such sales can be plowed back into research and development of new and more advanced weapons systems. Chinese weapons producers as well as the PLA can learn how to improve their own weaponry and tactics by watching how others operate PRC platforms, including in combat, essentially looking to these importers as proving grounds. Arms exports can also help strengthen military-technical relationships between the PRC and recipient countries. China's arms export relationship with Pakistan, for example, has allowed for significant militarily relevant scientific collaboration and technology transfer between the two. Depending on the specifics of a given deal, arms exports themselves can be a form of hard power when they act as leverage to gain preferred diplomatic outcomes from recipient countries.

Hard Power and Xi's Foreign Policy Pursuits

This chapter has focused on how China builds up and uses hard power—either coercively or through inducements—as an important feature of its foreign policy strategy. As China's economic heft and military capabilities have grown, they offer new, more powerful, and more sophisticated instruments through which Beijing can affect the choices of others in directions that are more aligned with PRC interests and ambitions. In the Xi Jinping era it is clear Beijing is far more inclined than in the past to brandish and deploy hard power tools in furtherance of national interests—not only because China has amassed the resources to do so, but also because Xi and the Chinese leadership believe they are compelled to do so to achieve the aspiration of national rejuvenation.

Officially, of course, China disavows coercive tactics in the conduct of its foreign relations. In speaking of China's approach to the world, the chief spokesperson for the Ministry for Foreign Affairs, Hua Chunying, declared, "We never strong-arm others, never seek supremacy [and] never bully others." "The word 'coercion,'" she says, "has nothing to do with China."[98] However, as this chapter has shown, the PRC under Xi Jinping has bolstered its hard power capability and its willingness to use it for strategic advantage. While not always coercive, China's hard power certainly has coercive elements. Governments and corporations around the world—from Australia to Apple, from Norway to the NBA, from Taiwan to Tiffany's, and many others—can attest to that.

China's military has likewise strengthened and become an increasingly potent instrument for PRC hard power, whether that is to intimidate rival claimants in the South China Sea, discourage Taiwan independence, complicate U.S. and allied force projection close to Chinese shores, or protect China's expanding interests around the world. In the words of a major Pentagon report, "China's leaders increasingly cast the armed forces as a practical instrument to defend Beijing's expanding global interests and to advance its foreign policy goals."[99] Indeed, during the Xi era, as the PLA works to shape a more favorable security environment, it has "increasingly *displayed* military capabilities rather than downplaying them."[100]

China's acquisition and exercise of greater hard power leverage has had mixed success. The prospect of engaging with and benefiting from China's economic success story is arguably the country's single most powerful and effective foreign policy tool. But at the same time, governments and societies around the world are rethinking their economic dependencies with China for fear of the leverage they grant to Beijing. Militarily, China is in a far stronger position than in the past to dissuade, deter, and defeat opponents across a range of scenarios to assert and defend its national interests. On the other hand, as China's military hard power has grown, it has sparked a counterbalancing military response, especially by the United States, its allies, and its partners. Perhaps the best example of China's hard power challenges is Taiwan. In spite of Taiwan's economic dependence on the China market and China's military build-up in and around the Taiwan Strait, Taiwan remains resolutely opposed to unification with the PRC; if anything, politically speaking, Taiwan drifts further and further away from China with each passing year. In fact, China's hard power prospects face many challenges ahead and are discussed in further detail in the concluding chapter.

But in spite of these challenges, hard power is likely to become an increasingly prominent aspect of PRC foreign policy in the years ahead. Importantly, the pursuit and use of hard power—economically and militarily—contributes to strengthening the other key features of Xi Jinping's foreign policy discussed throughout this book: legitimacy, sovereignty, wealth, leadership, and ideas. For example, building and exercising hard power abroad helps bolster CCP legitimacy when it garners greater respect for PRC interests, aligns foreigners with Beijing's preferred outcomes, and deters outsiders' interference in China's "internal affairs." In doing so, it also helps the CCP to retain and strengthen its legitimacy in the eyes of PRC citizens—all the more so as the population assumes an increasingly nationalistic stance. Military and economic hard power are instrumental in advancing Beijing's sovereignty interests, whether that is deterring formal Taiwan independence, asserting and defending claims in the South China Sea, or gaining greater freedom of maneuver to pursue its expanding strategic interests around the globe. Leveraging economic hard power is critically important in helping to open foreign markets to generate greater wealth for China. Hard power is also at play in facilitating greater PRC influence within foreign societies and promoting greater acceptance for Chinese leadership within the international system. Given the importance of hard power in contributing to these other critical aspects of the PRC's international strategy, we should expect Beijing to leverage economic and military carrots and sticks even more actively in the years ahead.

Each of these key strands for Chinese foreign policy—legitimacy, sovereignty, wealth, power, leadership, and ideas—interweave with and promote one another. Taken together, these six aspects of PRC foreign policy provide a construct for grasping the complexities of PRC foreign policy in the Xi Jinping era and beyond. In the remaining chapters we examine leadership and ideas and their central role in PRC foreign policy today and then turn to consider the challenges that will confront Beijing's approach to the world in the future.

6

Leadership 领导权

Gaining a Greater Say in How the World Works

*Therefore, we should not be a bystander or follower, but a participant
and leader. We should enhance our international competitiveness . . .
giving China a greater voice and injecting more Chinese elements in
the formulation of international rules, so as to protect and expand the
interests of China's development.*

—Xi Jinping, December 2014[1]

Destined for Leadership?

By dint of the country's geographic and demographic heft, historical continuity,
cultural influence, and eras of great power and wealth, China's leaders over the
centuries have laid claim to the country's rightful leadership status in regional
and global affairs. The very name of "China" in Chinese—中国, which directly
translates as "middle kingdom" or "central country"—connotes consequence
and even supremacy. Through highly ritualized forms of diplomatic obeisance,
the imperial tributary system reinforced a Sino-centric worldview. But it was not
just pomp and circumstance. From the founding of the Qin dynasty in 221 B.C.,
through the rise and fall of successive dynasties, until the last emperor abdicated
in 1912, China can claim world-leading achievements in the arts and technology
and in cultural, economic, and military power. According to data compiled by
the British economist Angus Maddison, for most of the past 500 years, China
was the either the world's largest or second-largest economy, even as late as 1930;
only for a relatively short period of time, roughly the period between 1950 and
2000, did China fall out of the ranks of the world's top-five economies.[2]

China's economic difficulties in the mid-20th century did not restrain its
leaders' aspirations to leadership. Following the founding of the People's Republic
of China (PRC or China) in 1949, and under the leadership of Mao Zedong,
Beijing sought the world stage. The newly established country's coming-out
party was the first Afro-Asian Summit, also known as the Bandung Conference,
which convened in Indonesia in 1955. There, Mao's foreign minister, Zhou Enlai,
left a strong impression and began to build the PRC's bona fides as a leader of the

Daring to Struggle. Bates Gill, Oxford University Press. © Oxford University Press 2022.
DOI: 10.1093/oso/9780197545645.003.0007

developing world. As the Beijing-Moscow schism intensified in the early 1960s, Maoist China claimed to take the ideologically "correct" mantle of leadership away from the Soviet Union to head the international communist movement. Over the course of the 1960s, in its ideological struggle with the Soviet Union, China poured tens of millions of dollars in aid into countries across Asia and Africa—including arms and other military support for "people's war" insurgencies in Southeast Asia and beyond—part of Mao's bid to position himself as the "fifth deity" in the shrine of hallowed Marxist-Leninist heroes (after Marx, Engels, Lenin, and Stalin).[3]

Even as Mao's revolutionary tendencies tempered somewhat toward the end of his life, he still strongly felt that China could assert itself as a leader of the developing world in opposition to the "hegemony" of the two superpowers, the United States and the Soviet Union. In 1974, Mao selected Deng Xiaoping to lead the PRC delegation to the Sixth Special Session of the United Nations General Assembly. Deng would be the first top Chinese leader to speak before the United Nations since the PRC had replaced the Republic of China (Taiwan) as the representative of China to the international body. In his speech, Deng expounded on Mao's "Three Worlds Theory," expressing solidarity with the "Third World" of developing nations and their quest for a more just and equitable economic order free from imperialist "bullying" and "neocolonialism." It was also on this occasion that Deng memorably stated:

> China belongs to the Third World. Consistently following Chairman Mao's teachings, the Chinese Government and people firmly support all oppressed peoples and oppressed nations in their struggle to win or defend national independence, develop the national economy and oppose colonialism, imperialism and hegemonism. China is not a superpower, nor will she ever seek to be one. . . . If one day China should change her color and turn into a superpower, if she too should play the tyrant in the world, and everywhere subject others to her bullying, aggression, and exploitation, the people of the world should identify her as social-imperialism, expose it, oppose it, and work together with the Chinese people to overthrow it.[4]

Deng's words were warmly received by the developing-world delegates and helped cement China's reputation as an advocate for their interests.[5]

With Mao's death in 1976 and the ascent of Deng and other pragmatists to leadership in the PRC, the country turned its energies mostly inward in the relentless pursuit of national economic development. Recognizing the need to focus on China's own modernization and seek the benefits of constructive economic relations with the world, Deng and others around him toned down the revolutionary rhetoric and assumed a lower profile internationally. It was in the early 1980s that Deng first put forward his well-known guidance that China should "observe calmly, secure our position, cope with affairs calmly, hide our capacities and bide our time, be good at maintaining a low profile, and never claim leadership." In the 1990s, as China grew stronger and more confident in its development path, this slogan was modestly revised to "hide one's capacities and bide one's time [or 'keep a low profile'], but also get some things done" (韬光养晦,有所作为), or "hide and bide" for short. But even Deng must have known that if his modernizing vision succeeded, a time would come when China's expansive power and interests would demand it assume ever greater leadership roles.

From Hide-and-Bide to Center Stage

Even as China grew more powerful at the dawn of the 21st century and continued to ascend through the ranks of great powers, Beijing preferred to eschew overt leadership roles on the world stage. PRC leaders were well aware that China's ascendance created anxieties among other powers and sought to reassure them that China's rise would be peaceful and focused overwhelmingly on its own national development. High-level American calls in 2005 for China to become a "responsible stakeholder" in global affairs were vigorously debated in China, but treated with caution by officialdom in Beijing, with many fearing it was a trap to slow China's rise.[6]

However, since that period, three important events have shaken the international community in ways—in combination with China's growing strength and the ascent of Xi Jinping to the pinnacle of power—that have led Beijing to seek a greater leadership role across a range of activities on the international stage, from matters of governance to technological standard-setting. First, the global financial crisis of 2008–2009 marked one such important turning point. As Western economies floundered and China's economy became the engine for global growth, Chinese leaders gained greater confidence about the PRC's success and the contributions the country could make on the world stage. Recognizing an opportunity for China, but still cautious about overtly taking the lead, it was in July 2009 that Hu Jintao subtly modified the well-known Dengist axiom on foreign policy by saying that China should "uphold keeping a low profile and bide its time" but it should do so "while actively getting something accomplished." Also at this time, Hu called on PRC diplomacy to seek "more influential power in politics, more competitiveness in the economic field, more affinity in its image" and "more appealing force in morality."[7] In the speech marking his handover of power to Xi Jinping in 2012, Hu pledged that China will "get more actively involved in international affairs, play its due role of a major responsible country, and work jointly with other countries to meet global challenges." In doing so, he added, "We have promoted reform in global governance, enhanced world peace and development, secured more representation and a greater say for China in international affairs, and created favorable international conditions for China's reform and development."[8]

Once in power, Xi reinforced these themes and made them ever more prominent elements in China's approach to world affairs, increasingly calling for China to take on greater leadership roles, contributing "Chinese wisdom to the improvement of global governance," and having a greater say in how the world works. In doing so, Xi accelerated China's orientation from "keeping a low profile" to "striving for achievement." In one of his earliest speeches as top leader—one largely devoted to bolstering the Chinese Communist Party's faith in "socialism with Chinese characteristics" and defending it against foreign criticism—he urged his comrades in 2013 to "concentrate our efforts on bettering our own affairs, continually broadening our comprehensive national power, improving the lives of our people, building a socialism that is superior to capitalism, and laying the foundation for a future where we will win the initiative and have the dominant position."[9]

Later that year, Xi convened one of the most high-level foreign affairs gatherings in PRC history—attended by all members of the Politburo Standing Committee and the senior-most officials at national and provincial levels concerned with foreign affairs—and proposed that "striving for achievement" (奋发有为) should define PRC foreign policy for the future.[10] According to Chinese analysts, Xi's speech marked a milestone in Beijing's relations with the outside world by legitimating a more proactive pursuit of PRC interests, including through the exercise of political leadership.[11] In subsequent high-profile policy speeches to PRC diplomats and senior Chinese Communist Party (CCP or Party) officials between 2014 and 2016, Xi continued to stress the importance of promoting a more multilateral system (that is, one where China can play a greater role) while reforming and strengthening institutions of global governance in ways that would give greater representation and "voice" (or "narrative power," 话语权) to China.[12]

According to his summation of expert attitudes in China at the time, PRC international relations scholar Mao Weizhun concluded that taking up greater international leadership responsibilities was not a "trap," but instead should be used as an instrument of foreign policy to reassure neighbors, promote China's image, and chart new pathways for the country's development and influence.[13] However, in spite of this shift in thinking, Xi did not openly call for PRC leadership in global affairs. That would soon change.

A second important development encouraging greater PRC leadership aspirations was the advent of the Trump administration in early 2017 and its withdrawal from a range of global governance institutions. Momentum was already building for Xi's China to take a greater international leadership role; for example, playing host to the 2016 G-20 summit of the world's leading economies in Hangzhou gave Xi a major leadership platform. But America's relinquishment of many global responsibilities—especially at a time of increasing political uncertainties around the world—provided an important opening for Beijing to fill. In the months prior to Trump's inauguration, Xi had already begun to not only speak of actively constructing a global governance system that was more "just and equitable" (公正合理), but also to contribute more in the way of "Chinese wisdom" (中国智慧) to achieving that goal.[14] Also during this period, Xi hinted that as the international balance of power shifts in China's favor, so too should the patterns of global governance. As such, he said, China must improve its ability to take part in global governance, make rules, and set agendas.[15] By 2017, as he further solidified his political standing at home, Xi proclaimed the advent of a "new era," with China "blazing a new trail for other developing countries to achieve modernization" and offering "Chinese wisdom and a Chinese approach to solving the problems facing mankind." In taking on these roles, he said, China would be "moving closer to center stage" in the world and would "take an active part in leading the reform of the global governance system" (积极参与引领全球治理理体系改革).[16] In a speech given on the day Donald Trump was inaugurated, a senior strategist at China's National Defense University foresaw the significance of the event: Trump, he said, has given China a "huge gift." "As the U.S. retreats globally," he continued, "China shows up."[17]

The onset of the covid-19 pandemic in early 2020 marked a third important turning point in bolstering Beijing's ambitions for global leadership. While China was criticized for its initial handling of the outbreak and not acting quickly enough to prevent its spread overseas, it was able to rapidly bring the virus under control at home through the imposition of strict lockdown measures affecting tens of millions of people across the country. From there Beijing mobilized a broad international campaign to position China as a world leader in responding to the pandemic—both in its success on the home front and in delivering hundreds of millions of dollars in financial support, protective equipment, ventilators, vaccines, and other help to scores of countries and organizations struggling to combat the virus around the world. This record stood in stark contrast to how many other major countries failed disastrously to cope with the pandemic, including, most visibly, many of the world's leading liberal democracies such as the United States, India, the United Kingdom, and members of the European Union. A lively debate continues outside China over the praiseworthiness of its response to covid-19, its efforts to deflect criticism for its role in the global pandemic disaster and whether Beijing's international standing has improved or worsened as a result.[18] But from the PRC's perspective, it is clear that the covid-19 calamity—while deeply challenging to its image—gave Beijing an opportunity to demonstrate its leadership capacity and credentials.[19]

In the pages to follow, we delve more deeply into how China under Xi Jinping puts its leadership aspirations into practice: in established institutions such as the United Nations; by initiating new institutions such as the Asian Infrastructure Investment Bank, the New Development Bank, and the 17 + 1 process with Central and Eastern European partners; and through leadership roles in emerging areas of global governance and new technologies.

Leadership within the United Nations System

China has a checkered relationship with the United Nations (UN), to say the least. Barred from entry to the organization until 1971, when it assumed the China seat previously held by Taiwan, Beijing was in the 1950s and 1960s withering in its criticism of the world body. The PRC claimed it was simply the tool of the imperialist superpowers of the day—the Soviet Union and the United States—to run roughshod over the weaker members of the international community. Even upon entering the United Nations and taking up its position as one of the permanent five members of the UN Security Council, Beijing maintained a relatively low profile and sought to demonstrate its independence from Moscow and Washington.[20] Beijing's skepticism about the United Nations continued into the 1980s and 1990s, especially following the collapse of communism in Russia and Eastern Europe, fearing the organization would become an instrument of "hegemonism and power politics"—a reference to a triumphalist post–Cold War America—or made irrelevant and circumvented all together as was the case with the U.S.-led North Atlantic Treaty Organization (NATO) intervention against Yugoslavia in 1999.

From Skeptic to Champion

Jolted in part by the Yugoslavia intervention—in which the PRC embassy in Belgrade was accidentally bombed by NATO warplanes, with the loss of three Chinese lives—and as China's power, confidence, and diplomatic acumen grew, Beijing's attitude toward the United Nations began to change. China steadily became more supportive of the United Nations, rhetorically, financially, and in the provision of personnel and other resources. In language it has frequently repeated since 2005, China has lauded the United Nations as "the most universal, representative, and authoritative inter-governmental organization" and a "symbol of multilateralism."[21] Of course, China's special status as a permanent member of the UN Security Council and the veto power it grants over the body's strategic decision-making—a rare position of power for Beijing within the international community—reinforces its support for the United Nations.

As Oxford University scholar Rosemary Foot details, China has increased its assessed contributions to the United Nations, from covering about 2 percent of the organization's general expenses in 2004 to 12 percent by 2020. In 2015, Xi Jinping announced the formation of the 10-year, $1 billion China–United Nations Peace and Development Fund. The PRC-financed fund, which is in addition to the country's regular assessed contributions, had by 2020 invested approximately $100 million in nearly 100 projects that support the UN's work in such areas as peacekeeping, preventive diplomacy, poverty reduction, and development.[22] By 2019, China became the second-largest contributor, after the United States, to both the UN general budget and the UN peacekeeping budget.[23] Speaking before the UN General Assembly to mark the organization's 75th anniversary in 2020, Xi declared that China would step up to provide an additional $50 million for the UN covid-19 relief plan, give $50 million to the ongoing South-South Cooperation Trust Fund project between China and the UN Food and Agricultural Organization, extend the UN-China Peace and Development Fund noted above for another five years from 2025 to 2030, and will establish two new UN centers—the Global Geospatial Knowledge and Innovation Center and the International Research Center of Big Data for Sustainable Development Goals—to assist the world body in implementing the 2030 Agenda on Sustainable Development.[24]

Today, Xi Jinping frequently points out that China was not only a founding member of the United Nations but was the first country to sign its charter in 1945. Of course, in saying so, he conveniently sidesteps the fact that it was the CCP's avowed enemy, Chiang Kai-shek, leader of the Nationalist Party (Kuomintang or KMT) who, as an ally in the war against imperial Japan, sat side by side at the Cairo conference with Britain's Winston Churchill and America's Franklin Roosevelt in 1943 to map out the world's post–World War II future. Nor does Xi's claim note that the Chinese government that signed the UN Charter and helped established the postwar system and its institutions was that of the Republic of China, not the PRC. Nonetheless, the assertion, while factually inexact, illustrates how far Beijing has come to embrace the United Nations and finds in that embrace both legitimation and support for PRC interests on the world stage. Little wonder then that the CCP's media outlets give tribute to Xi Jinping as "a champion of the UN ethos."[25]

Leadership Positions

As China has come to embrace the United Nations, it has sought greater leadership roles within the organization, commensurate with its increased contributions and aspirations to put a stronger PRC stamp on global governance norms and activities. As of mid-2021, PRC nationals held the top leadership posts of four of the 15 specialized agencies of the United Nations: the International Civil Aviation Organization (ICAO),* the International Telecommunication Union (ITU), the Food and Agriculture Organization (FAO), and the UN Industrial Development Organization (UNIDO). In addition, as shown in Table 6.1, PRC citizens hold six deputy positions within the 15 principal UN agencies. In addition, since 2007, PRC citizens have held the position of undersecretary general for the UN Department of Economics and Social Affairs (DESA). Two PRC nationals serve as senior representatives of the UN secretary-general to conflict-prone regions—one to the Great Lakes Region of eastern Africa and the other in South Sudan. However, as documented by China scholars Courtney Fung and Shing-hon Lam, among the major powers of the United Nations and with the exception of Russia, the PRC holds the fewest executive positions and has never led an agency concerned with international security affairs. That said, they found that China has been steadily increasing the number of its international civil servants working within the UN system.[26]

In addition to these executive leadership roles, China has held a seat on the UN Human Rights Council (UNHRC) for most of the organization's existence since 2006.[27] China has also sought greater leadership roles in other UN agencies, such as the World Health Organization (WHO). The first PRC citizen to head a major UN agency was Margaret Chan, a native of Hong Kong, who led the WHO from 2006 to 2017.

Peacekeeping is another area where China has sought increasing leadership within the UN system.[28] China has steadily built up its contributions of troops, police, and other personnel to UN peacekeeping operations (UNPKOs) and has since the early 2000s been the largest contributor of peacekeepers to the world body among the permanent five members of the UN Security Council. Since first providing personnel to a UNPKO in 1990, China has participated in some two dozen UN peacekeeping missions and contributed more than 40,000 personnel. Importantly, it has shifted from providing primarily engineering and other support personnel to providing combat troops, demonstrating a willingness to put its soldiers in riskier situations. Since 1990, 20 PRC peacekeepers have lost their lives on duty.[29]

Following Xi Jinping's ascendance to China's top leadership posts, China began to ramp up its contributions of peacekeepers to the United Nations, from an average of fewer than 2,000 personnel in 2012 to over 3,000 per year by 2015. In 2015, China also deployed its first combat troops to a UNPKO mission—an

---

* Liu Fang, a PRC national, stepped down from her post as secretary general of the ICAO as of July 31, 2021.

Table 6.1 PRC Nationals in Key UN Leadership Posts

Name	Position	Year appointed
WANG Binying	Deputy Director General, WIPO	2009
LI Yong	Director General, UNIDO	2013
ZHU Shanzhong	Executive Director, UNWTO	2013
ZHOU Houlin	Secretary General, ITU	2014
LIU Fang*	Secretary General, ICAO	2015
ZHANG Tao	Deputy Managing Director, IMF	2016
ZHANG Wenjian	Assistant Secretary General, WMO	2016
YANG Shaolin	Managing Director/Chief Administrative Officer, WBG	2016
LIU Zhenmin	Under-Secretary General, DESA	2017
QU Xing	Deputy Director General, UNESCO	2018
QU Dongyu	Director General, FAO	2019
XIA Huang	Special Envoy of the Secretary General for the Great Lakes Region	2019
CONG Guang	Deputy Special Representative of the Secretary General and Deputy Head of the UN Mission in South Sudan	2020

Key: DESA: Department of Economics and Social Affairs; FAO: Food and Agricultural Organization; ICAO: International Civil Aviation Organization; IMF: International Monetary Fund; ITU: International Telecommunications Union; UNESCO: UN Educational, Scientific, and Cultural Organization; UNIDO: UN Industrial Development Organization; UNWTO: UN World Tourism Organization; WBG: World Bank Group; WIPO: World Intellectual Property Organization; WMO: World Meteorological Organization.

Note: Entries valid as of July 2021; Liu Fang stepped down as head of the ICAO on July 31, 2021.

infantry battalion to South Sudan. That year Beijing also responded to a call for contributions to the UN Peacekeeping Capability Readiness System—to enable more rapid deployment of trained peacekeeping personnel as needed—and established a certified standby force of 8,000 troops. Since 2015, Chinese contributions to UNPKOs have dropped somewhat, averaging between 2,000 and 2,500 personnel per year, but China continued to rank in the top 10 countries providing peacekeepers to UN missions. At the end of 2021, there were 2,253 PRC troops, police, experts, and staff in nine of the 12 UN peacekeeping

Table 6.2 Top Ten Contributors to the UN
Peacekeeping Budget

Country	Percentage
1. United States	27.89
2. China	15.21
3. Japan	8.56
4. Germany	6.09
5. United Kingdom	5.79
6. France	5.61
7. Italy	3.30
8. Russian Federation	3.04
9. Canada	2.73
10. Republic of Korea	2.26

Note: For fiscal year 2020–2021; by percentage of total UN peacekeeping budget.

Source: "How We Are Funded," United Nations Peacekeeping, https://peacekeeping.un.org/en/how-we-are-funded.

missions, primarily concentrated in Africa.[30] As detailed in Table 6.2, China is the second-largest supporter of the UN peacekeeping budget, providing around 15 percent to the UNPKO budget of $6.58 billion in the fiscal year 2020–2021.

Agenda-Setting

In these and other leadership roles across the UN system, it is possible to help shape institutional agendas, steer internal debates, and make organizational decisions, including promoting certain UN development goals and programs; adopting official statements, resolutions, and declarations; and approving budgets, procedures, procurement, hiring, and other matters related to the organizations. However, officially speaking, UN executives commit to perform their duties as neutral civil servants and not with their country's national interests foremost in mind. In addition, leaders in the United Nations face the same kind of decision-making obstacles—bureaucratic logjams, opposing coalitions, vested interests, political wrangles, funding constraints—found in any complex organization, and these will frustrate leaders' abilities to achieve their goals. Nevertheless, outside observers find that China's growing clout within the United Nations, including its growing leadership roles, have helped advance PRC national interests. As a former UN undersecretary general for political affairs writes, "Especially since Xi became China's president in 2013, Beijing has raised its profile within the very heart of the UN, specifically the peace and security pillar that motivated the signing of the UN Charter."[31]

Broadly speaking, China's growing confidence and leadership clout within the United Nations has delivered payoffs in achieving specific foreign policy aims. For example, as shown in Table 6.3, out of a total of 16 PRC vetoes cast in the UN Security Council, half have been issued since Xi Jinping took power in November 2012, including two in 2020 alone. Nearly all of China's vetoes—13 of them— have come since 2007, and in all those cases Beijing teamed up with Moscow in casting the negative vote. Nearly all these cases had to do with preventing resolutions critical of governance and human rights practices in Syria, Myanmar, Zimbabwe, and Venezuela.[32] In another example, since the election of Tsai Ing-wen as Taiwan's president in 2016 (see chapter 3), Beijing took steps within the United Nations that ultimately prevented Taiwan from participating as an observer to the governing body of the WHO, the World Health Assembly (it held that status from 2009 to 2017), and blocked Taiwan from information exchanges with the ICAO in the midst of the coronavirus outbreak in 2020.[33] The heads of both the WHO and ICAO at the time were PRC nationals.

The PRC government also succeeds in promoting Xi Jinping's signature foreign policy program, the Belt and Road Initiative (BRI), by gaining high-level official endorsements from UN leaders—including high-profile praise from the UN secretary-general[34]—as well as from a range of UN organizations. A number of UN agencies have signed memoranda of understanding with Beijing which endorse and pledge collaboration with the BRI, including the UN Environment Program, the WHO, the FAO, the UN Educational, Scientific, and Cultural Organization (UNESCO), the UN High Commissioner for Refugees (UNHCR), WIPO, ICAO, and the UN International Children's Emergency Fund (UNICEF).[35] In another example, the head of the ITU, a PRC citizen, allegedly used his position to prioritize acceptance of China's technical standards and steer business toward Chinese telecommunications firms.[36]

China also uses its position of influence within UN bodies such as the General Assembly and the UNHRC to build voting coalitions to block criticism of its policies in places such as Xinjiang and Hong Kong. Indeed, the PRC has become more active within the UNHRC, especially since 2017 when it was for the first time the main sponsor of a resolution before the body. That successfully passed resolution was one of the first formal efforts by Beijing to write into the UN record its view that human rights should be defined first and foremost by indicators of basic human development needs—access to food, shelter, livelihood—as determined by individual states and not primarily by access to universal liberties

Table 6.3 Veto Votes by the PRC in the UN Security Council

Date	Draft resolution	Issue
July 10, 2020	S/2020/667	Security in Middle East / Syria
July 7, 2020	S/2020/654	Security in Middle East / Syria
December 20, 2019	S/2019/961	Security in Middle East / Syria
September 19, 2019	S/2019/756	Security in Middle East / Syria
February 28, 2019	S/2019/186	Security in Venezuela
February 28, 2017	S/2017/172	Security in Middle East / Syria
December 5, 2016	S/2016/1026	Security in Middle East / Syria
May 22, 2014	S/2014/348	Security in Middle East / Syria
July 19, 2012	S/2012/538	Security in Middle East / Syria
February 4, 2012	S/2012/77	Security in Middle East / Syria
October 4, 2011	S/2011/612	Security in Middle East / Syria
July 11, 2008	S/2008/447	Security in Africa/Zimbabwe
January 12, 2007	S/2007/14	Security in Myanmar
February 25, 1999	S/1999/201	Security in Yugoslavia/Macedonia
January 10, 1997	S/1997/18	Security in Central America / Guatemala
August 25, 1972	S/10771	UN admission of Bangladesh

Note: As of September 2021; in reverse chronological order.

Source: "Security Council–Quick Links–Veto List," Dag Hammskjöld Library, https://research. un.org/en/docs/sc/quick.

and civil rights such as democratic expression and freedom of speech, assembly, and religion. Since then, China continues to promote a "people-centered development" within the UN system, a euphemism to uphold the sovereign rights of states over the human rights of individual citizens.[37] In what seems to be an annual ritual, China regularly mobilizes a lengthy list of supporters within the United Nations to express their official support for Beijing's harsh policies in places such as Xinjiang, Tibet, and Hong Kong. These moves usually follow formal criticisms about PRC human rights violations voiced within UN bodies by democratic states.[38] In 2020, China was also able to place one of its diplomats on the UNHRC Consultative Group, a panel of five individuals who have a key role in appointing outside experts to report to the UNHRC on a wide range of human rights issues and conditions in specific countries.[39] In expanding its voice within the UNHRC and staunchly defending state sovereignty and noninter-ference, Beijing can lay claim to representing the interests of many developing world countries who chafe at the human rights criticisms leveled at them by lib-eral democracies.[40]

Given China's critical contributions to UNPKOs—both in terms of financing and manpower— and its veto power on the UN Security Council, Beijing is more and more motivated to see that UN intervention decisions align with PRC interests. This means first and foremost a continued healthy skepticism to-ward the use of UN force and an insistence that certain preconditions are met prior to approving UNPKOs: ensuring that regime change is not the intent of such missions, having the consent of the state into which those forces would de-ploy, and generating a broad international and regional consensus in support of a given mission. Rather than readily support the intervention of UN forces, Beijing will more likely promote other pathways to stabilize troubled regions, such as through conflict resolution and economic development. That said, in ap-proving and participating in UNPKOs, Beijing stands to benefit in other ways by burnishing its international and regional image, gaining valuable on-the-ground experience and intelligence, and working with other military forces. Depending on this mix of long-standing principles, national interests, and status concerns, Beijing will exercise its leadership within the world body to either support or block the use of UN-sanctioned force.[41]

Creating New Institutions

In addition to expanding its leadership roles in existing international institutions, China has also worked to build new ones. This is motivated in part by Beijing's long-standing frustration with established multilateral bodies that the PRC had little to no hand in creating and that are often dominated by liberal Western dem-ocracies in terms of their leadership structure, principal concerns, and norms. By creating new international institutions, Beijing can have a direct say in setting their membership, guiding principles, ground rules, and priorities and see that they are aligned more closely to PRC interests. One of China's early efforts in this direction was the establishment of the Shanghai Cooperation Organization (SCO) in 2001. Starting as a regularized dialogue mechanism between China, Russia, Kazakhstan, Kyrgyzstan, Turkmenistan, and Uzbekistan, the grouping has grown to welcome India and Pakistan (in 2017) and Iran (in 2021) as full members as well as three observer states (Afghanistan, Belarus, and Mongolia). With a full-time secretariat based in Beijing and a Regional Anti-Terrorist Structure in the Uzbek capital of Tashkent, the organization has held joint coun-terterrorism exercises among its members since 2007 and now holds them every two years.[42] The SCO helps solidify PRC interests by promoting constructive re-lations with its near-neighbors, developing beneficial economic and trade ties, especially regarding energy and transport links across Central Asia, and—in the organization's words—supporting "the establishment of a democratic, fair and rational new international political and economic order."[43]

China-Led Development Banks

More recently, under Xi Jinping's leadership, China has become much more ac-tive in establishing new multilateral institutions and groupings on an even larger scale. Perhaps best known of these is the Asian Infrastructure Investment Bank (亚洲基础设施投资银行, AIIB), first proposed by Xi Jinping during a trip to Southeast Asia in 2013. Formally launched in 2015 with 57 founding members (37 from Asia; 20 from beyond the region), by 2020 it had 103 members and had approved $22 billion in financing for 108 infrastructure projects, predom-inantly in Asia and the Indo-Pacific.[44] Notably absent from AIIB member-ship are the world's largest and third-largest economies, the United States and Japan. Washington declined to join the body, mostly for geopolitical reasons, and pressured allies—mostly unsuccessfully, with the exception of Japan—to do the same.

Beijing was driven to establish the AIIB in part to help meet the enormous in-frastructure needs in Asia, including through financing of BRI-related projects. But another motivation was Beijing's exasperation with the slow pace of reform in international financial institutions such as the World Bank and International Monetary Fund (IMF).[45] Established at a time when the PRC was neither a major economy nor welcomed throughout much of the postwar international com-munity, these institutions' voting quotas, governance structures, and decision-making processes do not fairly reflect, in Beijing's view, the global economy of today and China's powerful role within it. Similarly, the Asian Development Bank is dominated by Japan and the United States. Even though China has steadily gained a greater voting share within the World Bank Group, as of 2021, in the World Bank's International Bank of Reconstruction and Development, China had the third-largest voting weight (at 5.11 percent), compared to the United States (16.03) and Japan (7.53).[46]

At the AIIB, China has subscribed nearly one-third of the bank's capital portfolio of about $97 billion (as of 2021) and retains about 30 percent of the bank's voting shares—as shown in Table 6.4, far more voting power than other members—giving it decisive sway in the strategic decision-making of the or-ganization. A PRC national, Jin Liqun, is the first president of the AIIB. He is responsible to an international board of governors and board of directors, and leads an international staff from the headquarters in Beijing.

The AIIB serves Beijing's interests in numerous ways. Contrary to many dire warnings about the bank when it was first announced, the AIIB has proven to be a welcome and well-run organization in support of much-needed infrastructure investment across Asia. The work of the multilateral development bank dovetails closely with larger PRC strategic initiatives such as the BRI, which—as discussed in chapter 4—supports a range of China's economic, political, and security goals in Asia. The AIIB also demonstrates in concrete form China's ability to lead—to set out ambitious goals, attract supporters, create multilateral institutions and agendas, and deliver public goods. But perhaps most importantly from Beijing's perspective, the AIIB reflects well on China for conceiving and launching the AIIB in the first place, and helps generate the appreciation, respect, and status China's leadership seeks on the world stage.[47]

Less well-known but with similar aims, the New Development Bank (新开发银行 or NDB) was originally proposed in 2012 and began operations in 2016. The NDB is sometimes known as the "BRICS bank" as its founding members are Brazil, Russia, India, China, and South Africa. These five nations, which have been meeting regularly at senior levels since 2006—including annual summits since 2010—decided to form the NDB in order to steer financing toward their

Table 6.4 Top Ten AIIB members, by Voting Power

Country	Percentage of Total Votes
1. China	26.56
2. India	7.60
3. Russia	5.98
4. Germany	4.16
5. Republic of Korea	3.50
6. Australia	3.46
7. France	3.18
8. Indonesia	3.17
9. United Kingdom	2.90
10. Turkey	2.50

Note: As of August 24, 2021; percentages are rounded.

Source: "Members and Prospective Members of the Bank," AIIB, https://www.aiib.org/en/about-aiib/governance/members-of-bank/index.html.

own infrastructure needs and leave open the possibility of funding development projects in other countries as well. The bank's initially subscribed capital is $50 billion divided equally across the five founding members, which also have equal voting shares. The bank is open to admitting other members and by the end of 2021, four new members had joined: Bangladesh, Egypt, United Arab Emirates, and Uruguay. However, the NDB charter ensures that the founding five members would always retain at least 55 percent of the total voting power within the organization. Interestingly, the NDB has provisions to lend in local currencies—unlike other major development banks, including the AIIB, which lend in U.S. dollars—which can protect borrowers from fluctuations in the U.S. dollar. The NDB is headquartered in Shanghai, currently headed by a Brazilian national, and led by a team of officials drawn from the five member states.[48]

By early 2022, the bank had approved some $30 billion in lending—slightly more than AIIB lending—for nearly 75 projects across a range of sectors, including clean energy, transportation, urban renewal, water, sanitation and flood prevention, public health, and communications infrastructure. The projects are distributed relatively evenly among the five NDB member states, with India receiving capital to support 18 projects, followed by China (16), Brazil (14), Russia (14), and South Africa (11).[49] China does not play the same dominant role within the NDB that it does in the AIIB. Even so, China benefits as the NDB funnels capital toward BRI projects and helps build Beijing's bona fides among the other four partner countries as a responsible supporter of their economic development. Beijing also finds value in the bank's creation, touted as the first multilateral development bank ever formed by emerging or developing world economies and an alternative to international lending bodies formed by Western powers such as the IMF. While the NDB has a lower profile internationally than the AIIB, it nevertheless stands out as a successful example of developing world initiative where China is playing a leading role.[50]

17 + 1 Process

Another multilateral mechanism Beijing helped engineer—though not without controversy—was the so-called 16 + 1 group that China established in cooperation with 16 Central and East European (CEE) countries (with Greece joining the grouping in 2019, it became known as "17 + 1").[†] Going by the formal name

---

[†] Prior to Greece's participation, the original 16 CEE countries were Albania, Bosnia and Herzegovina, Bulgaria, Croatia, Czech Republic, Estonia, Hungary, Macedonia, Montenegro, Latvia, Lithuania, Poland, Romania, Serbia, Slovakia, and Slovenia. Twelve of these countries are members of the European Union. The other five—Albania, Bosnia and Herzegovina, Macedonia, Montenegro, and Serbia, are either candidates or prospective candidates for EU membership. All of the original 16 participants are former communist states.

of "Cooperation between China and Central and Eastern European Countries" (中国-中东欧国家合作 or China-CEEC), the mechanism was proposed by Premier Wen Jiabao during his visit to Poland in 2012 and included "12 measures" devised by China to define the scope of the newly established format. These measures included forming a dedicated secretariat within the PRC Ministry of Foreign Affairs (chaired by a vice foreign minister); setting up a $10 billion fund to support joint infrastructure, technology, and environmental projects; promoting trade, investment, and tourism between China and the 16 CEE countries; providing thousands of scholarships for CEE students to study in China and paying for other academic research cooperation; and hosting a variety of cultural and other people-to-people exchanges.[51]

The 17 + 1 took a page from other China-led multilateral groupings such as the Forum on China-Africa Cooperation and the China-Arab States Cooperation Forum. In establishing these hub-and-spokes mechanisms, Beijing aims to coordinate relations with key regions, channel financial and diplomatic resources to them, and cultivate their political and business leaders, key government decisionmakers, and other elites. As China analyst Justyna Szczudlik writes in her study of the 17 + 1, the process ostensibly began as an economic endeavor to promote trade, investment, and infrastructure development, especially in relation to the BRI. However, once Xi Jinping took office in 2012, the China-CEEC also became a vehicle to promote China's political interests.[52] Beijing looked to leverage the benefits of the 17 + 1 process to deflect criticism of PRC human rights policies in places such as Xinjiang and Hong Kong, demand official adherence to the "one-China principle" to isolate Taiwan, and encourage greater respect and appreciation for the CCP. That should come as no surprise, as the Beijing-based China-CEEC secretariat, in addition to receiving input from China's economic line ministries and major banks, also takes guidance from the CCP International Liaison Department (ILD), the Chinese People's Association for Friendship with Foreign Countries of the CCP United Front Work Department (UFWD), and the CCP Youth League, all organizations whose core tasks include promotion of Party interests abroad (the ILD and UFWD are discussed further in chapter 7).[53] Some analysts argue that by engaging the less wealthy and often marginalized CEE countries of the EU, Beijing aimed to gain their support to help shape EU policies toward China in a more favorable direction.[54]

Looking ahead, while the China-CEEC process began as an ambitious and innovative leadership play on Beijing's part, the group faces cloudy prospects as some of the European members lose interest; one—Lithuania—formally withdrew in 2021.[55] Nevertheless, having mobilized his Party apparatus, bureaucracy, and state-owned enterprises to be more active in Central and Eastern Europe, and with the initiative's close association with the BRI, Xi Jinping is unlikely to abandon it just yet. Instead, not unlike adjustments to the BRI, Beijing will continue to tout its positive contributions to the China-CEEC process while quietly adjusting its strategy to lower its profile; move away from capital construction projects; focus on green, digital, and health cooperation; and improve people-to-people exchanges.

Leading in Emerging Fields of Governance and Technology

In addition to seeking leadership within a range of established and newly created institutions, China under Xi Jinping has also sought a greater leadership role to address emerging transnational governance challenges and to set the pace for the advancement of new technologies. In doing so, Beijing's greatest strength is often its sheer ability to effect change on a given issue, which in turn places Beijing in a leadership position. For example, as discussed in chapter 4, China has mobilized massive amounts of capital and excess industrial capacity in support of the BRI, which—for better and for worse—has transformed the international landscape for infrastructure financing and construction. Similarly, Beijing has shown it can rapidly deploy resources and take a leading role to provide funding, technical assistance, medicines, and equipment to combat global health challenges, and not only against covid-19. As the world's largest emitter of greenhouse gases, China must play a leading role to reduce the threat of global climate change and has begun to do so. And increasingly, by dint of its enormous domestic market and high-tech ambitions, China seeks to lead in the race to set standards and dominate the value chain in critical technologies of the future.

Global Health

Since the early 2000s, China has increasingly sought a greater leadership role on matters of global health. Important initial drivers behind this aim were the widespread emergence within China of the human immunodeficiency virus (HIV) and severe acute respiratory syndrome (SARS) in the early 2000s. In both cases, PRC authorities at first sought to downplay the severity of these diseases until domestic and international audiences increasingly became aware of their extent in China. China managed to bring both pandemics under control, but not before more than 7,000 persons were sickened and 648 persons died of SARS in China, Hong Kong, and Macau; today, about 1 million persons in China are living with HIV.[56] Coming at a time when Beijing was intent on engaging more fully with the international community, the PRC worked to build a more responsible image in the fight against these global health challenges.

Since then, China has sought greater leadership in this area. Beijing fought hard to have Margaret Chan, a PRC citizen and Hong Kong native, appointed as head of the WHO, a position she held from 2006 to 2017. In 2015, Xi Jinping announced the South-South Cooperation Assistance Fund to support developing countries in meeting the UN 2030 Sustainable Development Goals; according to official PRC data, out of the fund's $3 billion, approximately 9 percent has been allocated to improving women's and children's health and responding to health emergencies.[57] Also in 2015, Tu Youyou was a recipient of the Nobel Prize in medicine—the first time a PRC-based scientist received the award—for her work in discovering the antimalarial compound artemisinin, giving further impetus to China's world-leading efforts to eradicate malaria at home and in Africa.[58]

Most of China's health-related development assistance comes in the form of bilateral assistance and traditionally focuses on Africa—for example, dispatching thousands of medical workers, building more than 100 hospitals through foreign assistance programs, and playing an unprecedented on-the-ground role in halting the West Africa Ebola outbreak in 2014—rather than through the major international health organizations and alliances such as the WHO.[59] For example, with the covid-19 outbreak in early 2020, China made pledges of $20 million and $30 million to the WHO in March and April that year—in addition to its assessed contribution of approximately $115 million—to help the organization combat the pandemic. Yet China's assessed and voluntary contributions form a relatively small proportion, about 2.3 percent, of all WHO funding sources. Other government and nongovernment funding (both assessed and voluntary) for the WHO in 2020 included Germany ($774 million), the Bill and Melinda Gates Foundation ($756 million), the United Kingdom ($742 million), the United States ($610 million), the European Commission ($439 million), the GAVI Alliance ($353 million), and Japan ($281 million).[60]

Beijing worked hard to deploy its covid-19 response—both in containing the pandemic at home and its highly publicized efforts to assist others abroad—to position China as a leader in the face of a global health crisis. For example, in 2020, speaking before the World Health Assembly, Xi Jinping announced a new $2 billion funding commitment to help developing countries recover from the covid-19 pandemic.[61] In addition, as the world's leading producer of a range of medical supplies and equipment, Beijing heavily promoted its massive exports of these materials in the midst of the pandemic. China shipped 220 billion masks, 2.3 billion pieces of protective gear, one billion test kits, and thousands of ventilators to more than 100 countries around the globe.[62] The PRC also raced to develop a vaccine to combat the pandemic and by early 2021 announced that it had donated approved vaccines to 69 countries and two international organizations—including 300,000 jabs for UN peacekeepers—and commercially exported vaccines to 28 other countries.[63]

As a result of these and other actions, numerous commentators noted that China was stepping in to play a global health leadership role as governments in the United States and Europe struggled to contain the virus.[64] At the same time, however, China was also heavily criticized in many quarters of the globe for shipping low-quality, faulty equipment and supplies while also seeking to extract highly public expressions of appreciation from the recipients.[65] Moreover, China struggled to distance itself from the stigma of being the origin of the first major human-to-human outbreak of the disease, which quickly spread to become a global pandemic. Nonetheless, in reflecting on global developments following the covid-19 outbreak, China's senior-most diplomat, Yang Jiechi, noted that "our country has led globally in controlling the epidemic [and] expectations of and reliance on China by all parties has risen." In the same article, Yang also argued that both in spite and because of the pandemic, the international situation remains advantageous for China, "laying a more solid foundation for national rejuvenation and providing us with important assurances to lead the world's great changes and shape the external environment."[66]

Climate and the Environment

The PRC's approach to global environment and climate change issues has taken a sharp and more constructive turn since Xi Jinping took office, with Beijing trying to demonstrate global leadership. As the largest emitter of greenhouse gases and for many years having a poor international image for its environmentally unfriendly policies at home, China's cooperation and commitment to reduce its emission have been crucial in the global effort to mitigate climate change. But Beijing resisted steps to reduce its greenhouse gases, concerned that they might slow its economic development. In one of its most high-profile and controversial efforts to slow global climate change mitigation measures, PRC negotiators actively blocked a robust agreement at the Copenhagen climate summit in 2009 demanding instead that the world's developed countries—not China—shoulder most of the burden for reducing emissions. China was also heavily criticized for exporting its power production overcapacity by financing and building its capital- and energy-intensive economic model in other countries through the BRI and other infrastructure development projects. Between 2013 and 2020, for example, Chinese banks committed some $50 billion to finance the construction of nearly 27 gigawatts of coal power facilities in 152 countries as part of the BRI; as of 2021, nearly all of the 60 new coal-fired plants planned for Africa, Eurasia, and South Africa were to be financed by PRC lending.[67]

In the face of mounting international opprobrium and recognizing the debilitating health and economic effects of a looming environmental disaster at home, Chinese leaders appeared to shift gears in the early 2010s to begin improving the country's domestic and global environmental policies and seek a greater leadership role on climate issues. By 2013, China was the largest investor in new renewable energy sources and had the world's largest renewable energy generation capacity.[68] Today, while China continues to account for a quarter of greenhouse gas emissions worldwide, and consumed more coal between 2011 and 2020 than the rest of the world combined, it is also the largest producer of wind energy and has approximately a third of all solar energy generation capacity in the world.[69]

At the 2015 Paris climate summit, China played a far more constructive role, including committing, for the first time, to a verifiable cap on its emissions.[70] China ratified the Paris agreement in 2016, and it came into force the same year. It commits the parties to take measures that will help keep the increase in the global average temperature to below 2° centigrade (about 3.6° Fahrenheit) as compared to during the time of the onset of the industrial age. As part of its commitment to the agreement, China pledged to achieve peak emissions before 2030 and to increase the proportion of nonfossil energy in its primary energy supply to 20 percent by 2030 as well. In another major policy announcement, Xi Jinping declared in 2020 that China would aim to be carbon neutral by 2060. (It should be noted, however, that 124 other governments—including highly industrialized countries such as the United States, all European Union member states, Japan, South Korea, the United Kingdom, and others—pledged to meet that goal by 2050 or before.)[71] In 2021, culminating a major shift in policy that had been in the works for over a year, Xi announced that China would not build any more new coal-fired power plants abroad—an important measure that may drastically reduce international financing available for coal plants.[72]

In addition to taking a more positive position in reducing carbon emissions, Beijing is also keen to increase its development, use, and export of green and low-carbon energy technologies for the future, such as in electric vehicles, energy storage and batteries, and photovoltaics. According to a study by BloombergNEF, China had overtaken Japan and South Korea by 2020 in the lithium-ion battery supply chain and will continue to dominate this sector until at least 2025 and possibly beyond. This results from China's huge domestic demand for this energy source, and its control of 80 percent of the relevant raw material refining and 77 percent of cell and 60 percent of component manufacturing capacity.[73] China also already produces about 70 percent of solar photovoltaics worldwide, dominating this sector.[74] As discussed in chapter 4, through a number of national strategies and industrial policies—such as the Green Silk Road and Made in China 2025, Beijing has specifically targeted green energy and low-carbon technologies for priority investments in the coming years. In this way, China aims to leverage advances in green technologies to not only gain leadership positions globally but also contribute to domestic economic goals.

Technology Innovation

Across a range of other emerging and advanced technologies, China is also seeking to establish market-leading positions both in terms of supply and value chains and as a standard-setter. As discussed in chapter 4, this effort is driven by strategic, economic, and profit motives. Technologies and applications in the cyber and information fields—such as artificial intelligence (AI), quantum computing, fifth generation (5G) and next-generation wireless capability, and ultrahigh-capacity data collection, storage, and analysis—are of particular interest as they are foundational for the development of next-generation infrastructure and advanced manufacturing. These capabilities can improve productivity, speed innovative technological breakthroughs, and drive the development of smart cities, smart industrial grids, smart power transmission systems, advanced surveillance systems, and autonomous vehicles, not only in China but for export as well. These technologies are also recognized in China as critical in the development of advanced warfighting capabilities.[75] In the 14th Five-Year Plan, covering the 2021–2025 period, several of these "frontier technologies" receive top priority: AI, quantum information, semiconductors, and brain science and brain-inspired computing. These technologies will have far-reaching consequences for national power, economic development, and future governance and institutional norms.

In AI, for example, official government strategy documents call for the country to reach "world-leading" levels in AI theory, technology, and applications and become the "world's leading AI innovation center" by 2030.[76] In pursuit of that goal, China overtook the United States in the number of AI-related patent applications in 2019 and, over the 2016–2019 period, the PRC published more AI-related research articles than any other country, more than doubling its output in this field.[77] Sheer output does not equate to quality, but indicates the time and resources Chinese researchers are devoting to understanding this emerging technology. In addition, China appears to have world-leading access to a commodity critical for the advancement of AI (and other emerging technologies): data. The widening use of PRC apps, smartphones, telecommunications networks, and surveillance systems—in China itself, across Asia, and elsewhere, such as in Africa and the Middle East—mean that Chinese firms have unparalleled access to enormous amounts of data; nearly one-quarter of all cross-border data flows pass through China, nearly twice as much as for the United States.[78]

The findings of a U.S. Congress–mandated commission on artificial intelligence and national security underscore China's advances in this field:

> Many countries have national AI strategies, but only the United States and China have the resources, commercial might, talent pool, and innovation ecosystem to lead the world in AI. In some areas of research and applications, China is already an AI peer, and it is more technically advanced in some applications. Within the next decade, China could surpass the United States as the world's AI superpower.[79]

Some analysts warn against overexaggeration in assessing China's AI plans and progress. Lancaster University scholar Jinghan Zeng, for example, argues that China's AI advances result from profit-driven, bottom-up struggles among diverse and contending competitors rather than from top-down, geopolitically motivated imperatives.[80] Economic incentives are no doubt important in driving AI research: worldwide revenues for the AI market will surpass $500 billion by 2024.[81] Nevertheless, Beijing clearly recognizes the importance of AI for the country's future, including in key strategic applications such as defense, and will continue to encourage PRC leadership in this field.

Another critical area where China aims to carve out a world-leading role is in quantum computing and information science. Quantum computing remains mostly in developmental stages and is yet to enter mainstream usage. But its potential is enormous, owing to its expected speed in solving increasingly complex scientific and technological problems, with implications for a range of fields from navigation to seismology, finance, and defense. Quantum computing is also valued for its presumed superiority in decryption and encryption. Its future use could render traditional methods for secure data transmission obsolete—systems that currently secure virtually all online communications and transactions—while also possibly making future forms of data transmission impermeable to disruption, intrusion, and attack. Chinese labs are known to be developing a range of different applications for quantum computing and have had practical success in deploying them. For example, China's quantum information science made headlines with the launch of the Micius satellite in 2016 and its subsequent role in conducting the world's first-ever quantum-encrypted teleconference between parties some 7,500 kilometers apart. In 2020, the satellite was used to facilitate another first: an ultrasecure communications link between two ground stations in China, putting the country one step closer to establishing "truly unhackable" global communications.[82] China also lays claim to building the world's longest quantum fiber communications link (between Shanghai and Beijing), which will connect to additional cities in eastern China, and has begun construction on the world's largest facility for the study of quantum information science, to be based in Hefei, in Anhui province.[83]

Given strategic policy settings such as Made in China 2025 and the dual-circulation strategy, PRC investments in technological innovation have also led to a surge in patent applications. By the most basic measure—number of patent applications worldwide—China overtook the United States in 2019 and topped the rankings again in 2020. Huawei, the PRC telecommunications giant, filed the most patent proposals of any company worldwide in 2020, a position it has held since 2017.[84] By other indicators, WIPO, a UN agency focusing on intellectual property matters, has since 2012 ranked China as the top middle-income country for quality of innovation—measured by quality of domestic universities, internationalization of patents, and international citations of research. Also, when measuring sheer innovation output, of the top 10 hubs or clusters worldwide, China has three—located in Shenzhen-Guangzhou-Hong Kong, Beijing, and Shanghai—ranked second, fourth, and ninth, respectively.

However, by other indicators, China does not fare as well. For example, triadic patents—those filed for a single invention at three major patent offices (the European Patent Office, the Japan Patent Office, and the US Patent and Trademark Office)—are a better indicator of innovation because they demonstrate the global value of a patented invention. By this measurement, China lags far behind the United States and Japan. In 2019 (latest data available), Japanese innovators filed more than 17.7 million triadic patents, U.S. innovators approximately 12.9 million, and Chinese nearly 5.6 million.[85] Also, as noted in chapter 4, in spite of a large number of patent applications, China ranks only 16th globally as to the quality of its innovation and does not make the top 30 in terms of innovation intensity (measured by science and technology output per capita).[86]

Standard-Setting

As China advances across a range of critical technology sectors, Beijing also seeks a greater leadership role setting standards for these technologies of the future. In our globalized world, nearly all technologies, appliances, and other comforts in homes today—from light switches to refrigerators, wireless routers, and more—are built in conformance with certain international standards to ensure quality, functionality, and interoperability. Standards help support similar convenience and efficiencies in industrial applications as well. As wholly new technologies, gadgets, and industrial processes emerge on the scene—driven in part by the revolution in wireless and other information-based technologies—there is a lot of money to be made either through licensing fees for patents or by cornering the market in a global-standard product. For example, having come to dominate certain technology markets—such as in lithium batteries—Chinese manufacturers are in a far better position to set technological standards in this sector. The BRI and the Digital Silk Road, discussed in more detail in chapter 4, are also important conduits through which PRC standards could be established and sustained. As Chinese firms construct large infrastructure projects across Eurasia and in Africa—such as high-speed rail, telecommunications, energy plants, and power transmission systems—they can require recipients to accept PRC standards, potentially raising the costs to switch in the future to other providers with different standards.

International bodies such as the ITU, the International Standards Organization (ISO), and the International Electrotechnical Commission (IEC), which have been long-dominated by Western experts and influenced by Western governments and corporate interests, have traditionally established such standards.[87] As such, Beijing is keen to ensure that PRC nationals increasingly populate the leadership of these and related regulatory bodies at the international level in order to facilitate the acceptance and widespread use of Chinese standards in the future. With this in mind, PRC authorities have developed a number of long-term plans to strengthen the country's development and dissemination of globally recognized and approved technical standards.[88] A formal government "China Standards 2035" (中国标准 2035) blueprint, first reported in 2020, aims to establish the PRC as a standards leader in key sectors and technologies—such as blockchain, advanced cloud computing, big data, 5G, AI, Internet of Things, and smart cities—in order to overcome China's traditional weaknesses and lack of a "voice" (or "narrative power") within the highest councils of global standards decision-making.[89]

Importantly, this effort is not only about technical specifications. Beijing is also active in promoting its preferred ethical and normative standards related to the use of key technologies such as AI and 5G and their applications in such areas as internet access and communications, surveillance, and facial recognition. As Adam Segal of the Council on Foreign Relations writes, Beijing is keen to establish norms within these sectors that favor state power over the interests of individuals, the private sector, and other nonstate actors and give priority to social stability over freedom of expression and assembly.[90] As discussed in chapters 2 and 7, such state-centric positions reflect deep-seated concerns in Beijing about the security and sovereignty of the Party and the nation as a whole.

Leadership in Xi Jinping's Foreign Policy

This chapter has examined how China's foreign policy under Xi Jinping has been increasingly animated by a drive for international leadership. But what is the ultimate purpose of Beijing's desire to play a greater leadership role on the world stage? Is it largely intended for China's domestic audience—to demonstrate the Party's resolve to right past wrongs, satisfy nationalist sentiments, and tout the success of "socialism with Chinese characteristics"—in short, to bolster CCP legitimacy at home? Are Chinese leaders aiming to shoulder greater global responsibilities in order to reassure the international community and in turn gain greater respect and acceptance? Or is it to alter aspects of the international system that Beijing does not like? Perhaps the ambitions are even greater: to overturn much of the international order long dominated by the United States and other Western powers and achieve a Sino-centric system in which PRC interests and norms predominate.

To varying degrees, elements of each of these motivations can help us understand China's leadership aspirations on the international scene. Xi Jinping and other Party leaders are clear that receiving China's due on the global stage—the respect, appreciation, and deference that comes with leadership power—is part and parcel of national rejuvenation under the banner of "socialism with Chinese characteristics in the new era" (i.e., under Xi Jinping). In the past, Party legitimacy rested primarily on the delivery of economic advancement for the PRC and its population. However, while that is still a critical element of the Party's claim to rule, Chinese leaders since 2012 have raised the bar further, linking the CCP's mission of national rejuvenation to the pursuit of global governance reform, a greater "voice" in world affairs, and expanded influence and power internationally. In high-profile speeches, Xi Jinping reminds the nation that under the CCP China has "stood up," "grown rich," and now, under his leadership, is "becoming strong"—and Xi credits the Party for "propelling China into a leading position in terms of economic and technological strength, defense capabilities and composite national strength." In doing so, he argues, "China's international standing has risen as never before [and] now stands tall and firm in the East."[91] In proclaiming these points, Xi binds the Party's standing at home to China's international status in ways his immediate predecessors did not.

But Xi also knows that achieving even greater leadership on the international stage faces numerous challenges, both internal and external. In addition to having to operate in a fluid international environment of contending orders, Xi Jinping's aspirations for leadership will face other difficult realities. Analysts inside and outside of China, as well as Chinese leaders themselves, acknowledge that Beijing is not yet ready—conceptually, operationally, practically—to become a world leader, even if that is a long-term hope and expectation for some.[92] In addition, considerable pushback has mobilized within the international community to deflect, constrain, or stay ahead of China's leadership pursuits. These and other headwinds are discussed in more detail in chapter 8.

But in spite of these challenges, this chapter has made clear that Beijing will continue to push for a greater say in how the world works and do so by seeking greater global responsibilities, including leadership roles, and insisting on greater respect for and concurrence with its interests as a result. Importantly, the pursuit of leadership on the global stage contributes to the other five drivers that animate and shape PRC foreign policy under Xi. In addition to bolstering Party legitimacy at home and abroad, greater global leadership can also benefit China's assertions of sovereignty, the development of its national economy, and its exercise of hard power. Leadership can also form the foundation for pursuing another major foreign policy objective—winning hearts and minds through the competition of ideas—to which we turn in the next chapter.

7

Ideas 思想

Competing for Hearts and Minds around the Globe

Modern Chinese values are also those of socialism with Chinese char-
acteristics, representing advanced Chinese culture. China has blazed a
successful socialist path featuring Chinese characteristics. Facts prove
that our path and system, theoretical and social, are successful. More
work should be done to refine and explain our ideas.

—Xi Jinping, December 2013[1]

Seeking Traction for China's Ideas

Ideas matter. They are the conceptual seeds that, properly nurtured and propagated, can grow into intellectual movements, overturn long-accepted mindsets, and change history. They can be aspirational, attracting a society toward an ideal future—think of communist utopias or "a more perfect union." They can also be inspirational, drawing adherents to join the ranks and fight for their realization. At their most effective, ideas can exercise soft power: shaping the choices of others not by force or inducements, but rather by an idea's attractiveness and appeal. Many big ideas do not end well. Hitler's National Socialist (Nazi) ideology and lifelong dreams of Lebensraum, while claiming millions of followers, brought tragic devastation to Europe and the world. But leaders of all stripes understand the power of persuasive ideas for bringing people together, rallying them to a common purpose, and building a larger and larger circle of shared interests.

Leaders of the People's Republic of China (PRC or China) also have big ideas. Indeed, Chinese Communist Party (CCP or Party) ideology—meticulously crafted and ceaselessly promoted—is one of the core pillars upholding the edifice of Party rule. As discussed in chapter 2, Party ideology has gained a far more exalted and imperative role during the Xi Jinping era when compared to his immediate predecessors. But while CCP ideological efforts have largely targeted domestic audiences, PRC leaders have also promoted big ideas abroad in hopes of shaping foreign perceptions of China and creating more favorable conditions for its interests on the international scene.

Daring to Struggle. Bates Gill, Oxford University Press. © Oxford University Press 2022.
DOI: 10.1093/oso/9780197545645.003.0008

The best-known and most invoked of these ideas are the "Five Principles of Peaceful Coexistence." These principles were first articulated in an agreement between China and India in 1954, but gained global prominence as part of the final communiqué of the Asian-African Conference of developing-world states, held in Bandung, Indonesia, in 1955 (also known as the Bandung Conference).[2] The conference was not only a diplomatic coming-out party for the PRC. It was also an opportunity to position itself as a leading member of the postcolonial, developing world and promote ideas within the international system in support of its own interests.

Over the ensuing decades, the Five Principles have persisted as China's most consistent set of ideas for how the world should work. The principles are: mutual respect for others' territorial integrity and sovereignty, mutual nonaggression, mutual noninterference in others' internal affairs, equality and mutual benefit, and peaceful coexistence. In essence, they are a call to be left alone and allowed to pursue one's own national interests free from outside pressures and extending the same treatment to others in return. Of course, China itself has fallen short of these ideals on many occasions since their declaration at Bandung in 1955. But that has not stopped Beijing from holding them up as the defining concepts of PRC foreign relations and promoting them as ideals that others should follow as well. As discussed later in this chapter, similar incarnations of the Five Principles have formed important elements of PRC foreign policy pronouncements in recent years, including Xi Jinping's declared aim to seek "a community of shared future for mankind."

Other prominent principles associated with the PRC include Mao Zedong Thought and later Maoism. These emerged out of the experience of the Chinese revolution and civil war of the 1930s and 1940s and the establishment of the PRC in 1949. Mao attempted to "Sinify" Marxism, not only as a way to claim his Party's unique and independent revolutionary success but also to demonstrate a universal appeal for Marxism beyond its European origins and historical circumstances. This was an especially appealing idea in the postwar era as movements across the developing world rose up to demand decolonialization and independence. Many found the CCP experience and Maoist ideals powerfully attractive: a revolution arising from peasants in the countryside; destruction of feudal, landed elites and redistribution of their assets to benefit the broader population; a call for violent and radical change to destroy the old and begin anew; and promises of a future socialist paradise. In the 1960s and 1970s Maoism gained acolytes around the world, inspiring revolutionaries in Asia and Africa, in the streets of Paris and on U.S. campuses, and had a central role to play in the geopolitics of the Cold War.[3] In the 1980s, the violent insurgent movement in Peru known as Sendero Luminoso (Shining Path) drew inspiration from Maoism, pursuing guerrilla warfare in order to overthrow the government, establish a proletarian dictatorship, and become the vanguard for a new world revolution. They failed in their quest but nonetheless inspired others, such as the Communist Party of Nepal-Maoist, which waged an armed insurgency against government authorities for nearly a decade from the mid-1990s to mid-2000s. Elements of the Shining Path and Nepalese Maoist party are still active to this day. Meanwhile, in today's China, Maoist ideals of state socialism, egalitarianism, and empowerment of the working class are staging a comeback and affect Xi Jinping's thinking about political and economic reform.[4]

In the immediate post-Mao era, under the paramount leadership of Deng Xiaoping, China sought to leave Maoist excesses behind and implement the array of bold ideas that ultimately helped transform the country into the powerhouse it is today: pursuing "reform and opening" (改革开放); prioritizing the "Four Modernizations" (四个现代化) of agriculture, industry, science and technology, and defense; and further developing "socialism with Chinese characteristics" (中国特色社会主义), whereby China could economically modernize while retaining the one-party authority of the CCP. While these concepts would have a great impact on China's role in the world, they primarily targeted domestic audiences—including die-hard Maoists within the Party—to embrace the Dengist vision to shake up and transform the PRC society and economy.

As discussed in chapter 1, Deng's most famous guidance for China's international conduct in the 1980s and 1990s was to steer of clear big, splashy ideas and actions abroad. Rather, he counseled, "observe calmly, secure our position, cope with affairs calmly, hide our capacities and bide our time, be good at maintaining a low profile, and never claim leadership." But with China's unrelenting rise, PRC leaders came to recognize they could not keep a low profile for long and needed to assert a vision for regional and world affairs that would favor PRC interests. In the late 1990s, under the leadership of Jiang Zemin, Chinese officialdom put forward the idea of a "new security concept" (新安全观): a new paradigm for regional relations in Asia, which, according to its proponents, would differ from the U.S.-led system in the region and achieve stability through collective cooperation rather than through Cold War alliances. By the early 2000s, Beijing understood the need to reassure their neighbors and others, such as the United States, that its growing power would not overturn the established international system. Leaders such as Hu Jintao and Wen Jiabao promoted new concepts about China's arrival on the world stage, arguing it would be marked by a "peaceful rise" (和平崛起) and "peaceful development" (和平发展), and would contribute to a "harmonious world" (和谐世界).[5] Advancing these ideas was especially important as it indicated a greater willingness to acknowledge the concerns of China's neighbors about Beijing's strategic intentions and recognize that the PRC's emergent strength contributed to the region's intensifying security dilemma.[6]

By and large, however, for most of the period since the PRC's founding in 1949, Beijing has struggled to gain traction for its own ideas on the international stage. A part of the reason for this was the nature of the times. Relatively isolated diplomatically and economically for most of the first three decades of the Cold War, China was also consumed internally by paroxysms of Maoist fervor such as the Great Leap Forward and the Cultural Revolution. True, Beijing's message of developing world unity and the Maoist struggle to oppose American "neo-colonialism" and Soviet "revisionism" resonated with many around the world. But it was overwhelmed by the dominant ideological narrative of the time, which imposed a division of the world into two camps, pitting the "free world" against the "socialist bloc." Moreover, with Deng's reforms in the 1980s, China did not put forward a new paradigm but instead bought into much of the Western capitalist economic growth model, including Beijing's ultimate embrace of globalization. However, by the late 1990s and early 2000s, as the country's international power and interests increasingly grew, PRC leaders became more convinced of the need to be proactive in shaping how the world views China and its fundamental interests.[7] In the ensuing years, Beijing has steadily built up its capacity to do so. Today, this pursuit—using ideas, influence, and images to persuade others to favor China's interests—has become an essential and increasingly well-resourced element of PRC foreign relations under Xi Jinping.

Spreading China's Voice

Within months of assuming China's top leadership posts, at a high-profile gathering of the Party's propaganda and ideology organs, Xi made clear the need to improve how China explains itself and is seen abroad. In an extended speech, Xi bemoaned how Western countries get away with criticizing China when they themselves are far from perfect; he cited the suffering brought on by the global financial crisis, rising income inequality, and military actions in Iraq, Afghanistan, and Pakistan as examples of Western misdeeds and hypocrisy. The West gets away with this, he argued, because its governments and media are able to dominate the international narrative. In response, Xi declared, China must push back with its own narrative to "balance" against Western criticism and attacks: "waiting for them to reach such a balance is impossible, so we must do it ourselves[;] if we don't do it, others will not help us."[8] He continued:

We must meticulously do foreign propaganda work well. Following our country's economic and social development, and the rise of our international position, international society's rational knowledge of China's development path and development model is progressively deepening, but at the same time, there are still quite a few misunderstandings about us, the "China Threat Theory," the "China Collapse Theory" and other such theories linger in one's ears. . . . In the international public opinion structure, the West is strong and we are weak, Western major media control global public opinion, we often have rationales that we cannot speak out about, or once we've spoken about the[m], we can't communicate them. This problem must be resolved with great efforts.[9]

Xi concluded by saying that China must "advance the construction of international communications capabilities; innovate external propaganda methods; strengthen construction of the narrative system; focus on integrating new concepts, categories, and expressions between China and abroad; tell China's story well; spread China's voice; and strengthen our narrative power internationally."[10] Later that year, standing before the CCP Politburo, Xi advanced the same message about strengthening China's narrative power around the globe. He and other Chinese leaders have since returned repeatedly to these themes.[11] As China expert Nadège Rolland writes, Xi's emphasis on China's lack of narrative power marked a "turning point" in the country's resolve to have its voice heard and ideas respected on the global stage.[12]

Since they assumed power, it has been clear that Xi and other fifth-generation leaders value big ideas in ways that distinguish them from their third- and fourth-generation predecessors. A RAND study suggests this may be because the national leadership under Xi, while continuing to appreciate the concrete and practical dimensions of military and economic power, are also more aware of the need to compete in the abstract realm of ideas, including through the pursuit of soft power. Educational background might explain this. While previous leadership cohorts under Jiang Zemin and Hu Jintao were dominated by scientists and engineers, the majority of leaders at the very top of the Party today were educated in the social sciences and humanities, such as politics, international relations, law, history, and philosophy.[13] Another explanation may simply be (paraphrasing from Xi Jinping) that China first "stood up" under Mao Zedong; "grew rich and became strong" under Deng, Jiang, and Hu; and now must achieve "national rejuvenation," a concept not only grounded in material benefits of sovereignty, wealth, and power, but also in the success of one's culture, principles, and ideas.[14]

One of the most distinctive aspects of Xi's approach to disseminating Chinese ideas is its emphasis on building "international narrative power" (国际话语权).[15] According to a professor at the CCP Central Party School who has focused some of his work on the concept, narrative power is the ability to "use language to gain the respect and approval of others for one's own ideals and viewpoints, and to change others' thoughts and actions in non-violent and non-coercive ways."[16] This concept is relatively recent in PRC discourse, gaining currency in academic and political circles since around 2008. It was initially interpreted defensively as a power that others, such as in the West, use to criticize and weaken China. However, since Xi Jinping took charge in 2013, he and other leaders have called on high officials, intellectuals, and Party theoreticians and propagandists to build a more effective narrative system and international narrative power of China's own. Such a narrative capacity would push back against the dominant Western narrative, led by the United States, which for decades has held up such ideals as liberal democracy, the rule of law, free market capitalism, and universal human rights as the proper and ultimate aspirations for humankind. By this line of thinking, for China to be a truly great power, it must compete more actively and effectively on the world stage in a struggle over big ideas and norms, shifting the global narrative to make it more respectful and accepting of the PRC's accomplishments, its system of governance, its interests, and its preferences for how the international system should operate. Chinese leaders from Xi Jinping down recognize this will not be easy nor will it happen overnight. But they also recognize that gaining international narrative power will be a critical part of fully realizing national rejuvenation.

Telling China's Story

Recognizing the importance of ideas and the need to "tell one's story well" is one thing. It is quite another to build the capacity to voice those ideas internationally, let alone advance effective ideas that will transform global narratives and norms. The CCP has long recognized the importance of having robust organizational machinery in place to control and disseminate authorized and acceptable information while censoring, deflecting, and criticizing information that is not. At the organizational heart of the Party, three principal departments under the CCP Central Committee—the Central United Front Work Department, the Central Propaganda Department, and the Central International Liaison Department—have the dissemination of officially approved information to external audiences, including audiences abroad, as a crucial part of their mission.[17]

These three organizations have in various permutations been part of the CCP since well before the founding of the PRC in 1949, and have been critically important to the Party's narrative power, especially at home. Their relative importance within the Party hierarchy has waxed and waned along with the country's tumultuous internal politics. However, as Party organizations, they have retained considerable authority as compared to state agencies within the PRC government. Moreover, in recent years, and consistent with Xi Jinping's efforts to reinvigorate the Party's role in domestic and foreign affairs, these organizations have received a significant boost in resources and organizational mandate to build up

China's "narrative power system," expand their activities abroad, and improve the country's "international narrative power."[18] The following pages take a closer look at these important but often overlooked actors in PRC foreign relations and their role in telling China's story and promoting its ideas.[19]

International Liaison Department

The CCP Central International Liaison Department (中共中央对外联络部) (ILD) emerged from various precursor organizations within the Party and was formally established in January 1951.[20] Its core mandate is to conduct foreign relations on behalf of the Party. The ILD was traditionally known for its "quiet diplomacy" outside of government-to-government channels and was principally concerned with engaging other communist and socialist parties.[21] However, it has also played a key role, for example, in overseeing delicate diplomatic relations with North Korea and Iran over the years and in assessing the collapse of communist regimes in the Soviet Union and Eastern Europe in the 1980s and 1990s. The organization has engaged with nongoverning parties in some states, such as in Myanmar, allowing the Party to cultivate potential future leaders and gain greater insights on political developments within a given country. In addition, the ILD has also engaged in collecting intelligence, staffing PRC embassies abroad, and supporting foreign travel for other Party organizations and for central- and local-level Party members.

Like other Party organs and even the Party itself, the ILD's fortunes and influence have oscillated widely over the decades since its creation. With the onset of opening and reforms in the early 1980s, and especially following the bloody Tiananmen crisis of 1989, the ILD's star has been on the rise. From the 1990s, it has reached beyond engagement with "fraternal" parties and opened exchanges with a variety of foreign political parties and Party-affiliated organizations, politically influential figures, think tanks, and other interlocutors. According to one extensive study in the mid-2000s, the ILD had a staff at the time of about 300 persons and each year received some 200 delegations from abroad while sending about 100 groups overseas in return.[22]

However, in recent years, like other Party organizations, it has further increased its external work under Xi Jinping's watch with an eye to expanding China's voice internationally. The ILD claims to have established contact with over 400 political parties in more than 140 countries; more precise data show that the ILD was in contact with 462 political parties in 161 countries between 2002 and 2017.[23] Moreover, Christine Hackenesch and Julia Bader carefully document a steep increase in ILD exchange activities since Xi took power in 2012.[24] This includes an increasing effort by the ILD to send delegations abroad to spread the word about important CCP conferences and their outcomes: official accounts detail such missions to at least 10 countries in 2014, more than 40 countries in 2015 and 2016, and nearly 80 countries after the October 2017 CCP 19th Party Congress.[25] Xi pledged to further increase the ILD's external engagement, declaring in 2017 that between 2018 and 2022, the CCP would invite some 15,000 persons from political parties around the world to China to interact with Party representatives under the auspices of the ILD.[26] These activities present opportunities to showcase China's accomplishments, burnish the Party's credentials, and—it is hoped—expand Beijing's circle of international supporters.

An important vehicle for these increased exchanges has been the convocation of large, high-profile international dialogue meetings by the ILD to engage a range of foreign counterparts. Starting in 2014 and continuing through 2016, the ILD hosted the annual Chinese Communist Party and the World Dialogue conference. The 2016 iteration, convened in Chongqing, attracted some 300 delegates from more than 70 organizations and 50 countries.[27] This conference was upgraded to a "world political dialogue high-level meeting" in 2017, featuring a keynote address by Xi Jinping, and attended by 600 participants from 120 countries and 300 political parties and organizations, according to the concluding conference statement.[28]

This dialogue process has since been recast into "thematic meetings," held in China and abroad, to focus specifically on different regions and constituencies. For example, the May 2018 thematic meeting, held in Shenzhen, included sessions on Marxism in the 21st century, Xi Jinping Thought, and networking meetings for young African politicians and political leaders from Latin America. In July 2018, another thematic meeting invited individuals from 40 African political parties to Dar es Salaam, Tanzania, under the theme "Theories and Practices of Chinese and African Political Parties in Exploring Development Paths Suitable to National Situations."[29] The ILD has since convened numerous other large fora, such as the first Dialogue on Exchanges and Mutual Learning among Civilizations, with 100 delegates from around the world.[30]

A glance at the ILD website shows that the covid-19 outbreak did little to slow the organization's external work, though much of it was conducted virtually during the global pandemic.[31] Since early 2020, for example, the ILD donated personal protective equipment (PPE) to numerous foreign political parties; conducted training and capacity-building workshops with political parties in Africa, Latin America, and Asia; convened a virtual "cloud forum" of the Silk Road Think Tank Association; and convened major conferences via videolink— one with 200 politicians from 16 Latin American countries to tell "stories of the CCP" under the banner "Guizhou's Achievements in Practicing Xi Jinping Thought on Socialism with Chinese Characteristics for a New Era." The ILD even held a face-to-face event in Beijing in late 2020 to explain to foreign business representatives the relevant policy guidelines to emerge from a high-level CCP meeting that will shape PRC foreign economic policy over the 2021–2025 period. Meanwhile, ILD leaders liaised online and by cellphone with political party leaders around the globe.

This work by the ILD serves a number of Party objectives. First and foremost, it seeks to accomplish the organization's long-standing mandate of burnishing the image of China and its ruling party and gaining understanding, respect, and acceptance for CCP and PRC interests and positions abroad. In the words of two close observers of the ILD's activities, they aim to "reinforce[e] external and internal legitimacy by showing Chinese citizens and foreign partners that the [CCP] has longstanding friends."[32] This proselytism has long been a part of the ILD's mission, including work to "promote the international communist movement, Marxism-Leninism, socialism, and other related theories" and "increase the reputation and impact in the world of the Communist Party of China."[33]

But under Xi Jinping, the ILD has considerably expanded this work to promote CCP ideas on reforming the international system in ways that are more favorable to the Party's interests, generating international praise for the PRC social and economic model, and according to some observers, advancing "authoritarian learning and diffusion."[34] Official readouts of major ILD initiatives indicate the purpose and expected outcomes of these activities. For example, one of the principal ILD conferences for 2020 convened over 60 Arab political leaders, including the president of Syria, Bashar al-Assad, and the head of Palestine, Mahmoud Abbas. According to the ILD account, following an address by Xi Jinping, the gathered Arab leaders "highly commended" the CCP and the PRC government "for their great achievements in development, especially in fighting the COVID-19 successfully"; will "continue to firmly support China's stances on issues related to Xinjiang and Hong Kong"; "firmly oppose external interference in China's internal affairs"; and plan to work with the CCP to "step up mutual learning in exchanges of experience in party governance and state administration."[35]

The "Beijing Initiative," the declaration endorsed by the 600-plus international delegates attending the ILD-sponsored "world political dialogue high-level meeting" in December 2017, is another exemplary case of the ILD's role and expectations. While mostly a document calling for a better world, it also endorses a range of fundamental CCP concepts, slogans, ideas, and interests: promoting "a community of shared future for mankind," supporting the Belt and Road Initiative, reforming the global governance system, discarding "power politics" and the "Cold War mentality," and finding that China's "development philosophy and successful practice can offer reference" to developing countries seeking to improve their economic situation. Gaining the endorsement of the gathered leaders is an example of how the ILD and other CCP bodies seek to legitimate the Party's vision and strengthen its international narrative power.

The Beijing Initiative concludes with a full-throated endorsement of Xi Jinping and the CCP:

> We are gratified to note that the building of a community with a shared future for mankind is highlighted in the Xi Jinping Thought on Socialism with Chinese Characteristics for a New Era. It demonstrates that the Communist Party of China [CPC], as a large party with a strong sense of responsibility and global perspective, strives for both the wellbeing of the Chinese people and human progress. . . . The CPC Central Committee with General Secretary Xi Jinping as the core has unwaveringly promoted full and rigorous governance over the Party and improved the Party's ability to govern and lead, which has put in place the most solid foundation for the historic achievement and transformation in China and served as the most important guarantee for China to play its role as a responsible major country and make new and bigger contributions to the world.[36]

In short, the ILD is a highly active body on the international scene, working to promote a better image of the CCP and China more broadly, while also promoting and gaining the formal endorsement of Beijing's preferred ideas and outcomes in the international system. For the ILD, this can be done by liaising and cultivating relationships with political parties, their leaders, and other politically active individuals and high-profile opinion-shapers around the globe. As an article authored by the ILD in the Party's premier theoretical journal explains, the ILD should "showcase our party's governance achievements . . . to improve the international community's understanding, respect, and appreciation of our party [and] actively tell the story of China and the Party, so the international community can understand, recognize, and strengthen a sense of identity and closeness with the Chinese Communist Party."[37]

United Front Work Department

The CCP Central United Front Work Department (中共中央统一战线工作部) (UFWD) traces its roots to the earliest days of the Party's founding in the 1920s. In the late 1930s, the organization was tasked to engage with the rival Nationalist Party (Kuomintang), ostensibly to form a "united front" against the invasion and occupation of China by imperial Japan. It played an especially important role in the late 1940s and in the early years of the People's Republic as Communist leaders sought to solidify Party legitimacy and authority by engaging, coopting, or marginalizing non-CCP parties, interest groups, social and religious organizations, and prominent individuals inside China. However, the organization went dormant for much of the remaining period of Mao's rule. It was not revived until after his death in 1976 as the Party desperately needed to emerge from the chaos of the Cultural Revolution and reestablish and secure its legitimacy in the reform era. While going through many twists and turns over the past century, the core mission of united front work has remained unchanged. In the words of James To, an expert on united front work within the overseas Chinese community, the organization and its affiliates seek "to win over non-CCP community leaders, neutralise party critics, build temporary alliances of convenience, and systematically shut down adversaries."[38] For Xi Jinping, united front work has been an "important magic weapon" (重要法宝) for China's revolution, construction, and reform in the past, and will be one for the "great rejuvenation of the Chinese nation" now and in the future.[39]

Traditionally, the UFWD has kept tabs on non-Party domestic actors to make certain their activities and interests are aligned with the CCP's.[40] Today, the list of domestic groups that the UFWD monitors and engages includes such diverse institutions as the eight subordinate "democratic parties" (民主党派) in China, religious groups and their associations, ethnic nationalities, and the All-China Federation of Industry and Commerce. The UFWD is also active in keeping an eye on individuals and organizations in Hong Kong, Macau, and (because the Party considers it a "domestic matter") Taiwan. Importantly, the UFWD plays a critical role in helping oversee and guide what the Party identifies as its own form of consultative democracy, the highest representation of which is the annual meeting of the Chinese People's Political Consultative Conference (中国人民政治协商会议) (CPPCC). Gathering some 2,000 delegates from different parts of PRC society who are "patriotic" and loyal to the Party—such as from the "democratic parties," ethnic nationalities, religious leaders, business titans, and intellectuals—the CPPCC purports to be a meeting of the minds between the Party and non-Party elites.

Beginning in the 1980s, as the PRC opened to the outside world, the UFWD increased its international engagement, including with persons of Chinese descent living overseas, PRC workers and students abroad, and non-Chinese elites and organizations around the globe.[41] In principle, the ILD and UFWD focus on different groups overseas—political parties and organizations for the ILD and other non-CCP groups for the UFWD—but in practice their target audiences often overlap. This makes sense when we understand that it is the duty of all Party organizations and members to carry out united front work—that is, engaging non-Party members in ways that promote the Party's interests—and not only the job of the UFWD. In line with Xi's efforts to strengthen the role of the Party in domestic and foreign affairs, the UFWD has gained in status, mandate, and resources under his leadership.[42] And while much of the UFWD's focus remains on domestic groups—for example, advising on and engaging with religious groups and ethnic minorities—it has stepped up activities that directly or indirectly affect PRC external relations.

A key reason for the UFWD's reinvigoration appears to be the Party leadership's conclusion that the organization had been failing, evidenced by outbursts of unrest in Tibet in 2008, violence in Xinjiang and deadly attacks by Uyghurs elsewhere in China between 2008 and 2014, the Hong Kong "umbrella" protest movement in 2014, and the resounding election victory of Tsai Ing-wen of the pro-independence Democratic Progressive Party to become Taiwan's president in 2016. Rot at the top was another reason: not long after Xi took power in 2012, the head of the UFWD, Ling Jihua, was purged and sentenced to life imprisonment on corruption and abuse of power charges (investigations into Ling arose following a scandalous incident in which his son crashed his Ferrari on a Beijing expressway). Gerry Groot, a leading expert on the UFWD, cites at least two additional reasons for Xi's interest in reviving the UFWD: Xi's father, Xi Zhongxun, played a significant role in the organization; and Xi's leadership experience in Fujian and Zhejiang—where engaging Taiwan as well as emerging mainland entrepreneurs was a key part of his portfolio—left him with a strong impression of the importance of united front work.[43]

A number of measures have been taken under Xi to bolster the UFWD's position, including in relation to external affairs.[44] The first set of measures had to do with leadership and the political profile of united front work. To begin, in order to underscore its importance, the Party leadership has dubbed the broad united front enterprise as the "Great (or Grand) United Front" (大统一战线). To give the organization greater political heft, in 2014 Xi replaced disgraced UFWD head Ling Jihua with Sun Chunlan, a member of the Politburo—the first time since the early 1990s that such a senior political figure took charge of the department. Xi and Sun then presided over the Central Conference on United Front Work in May 2015. The last such conference was held nine years prior and at that time was termed a "national" (全国)-level meeting. Upgrading the conference to a "central" (中央), or Party, conference again signaled the leadership's intention to prioritize the CCP's efforts in this area. Following the conference, in July, the Party established the United Front Work Leading Small Group, headed by the fourth-ranking member of the CCP Politburo Standing Committee, Wang Yang, and which reportedly has some 26 Party and government agencies in its purview.[45] This was the clearest signal yet of Xi's aim to boost the mandate of united front work and ensure more powerful and coordinated Party oversight of its activities across the Party and government.[46]

Second, the Party implemented a range of internal legal and bureaucratic changes to strengthen the mandate of the UFWD and united front work overall.

Concurrent with the 2015 Central Conference noted above, the Party also developed and issued the first-ever set of "trial regulations" to govern and reinforce the mission of united front work.[47] The UFWD itself also underwent at least two reorganizations between 2015 and 2018 to better reflect the changing needs of united front work in China and abroad. In 2016 and 2017, two new bureaus were created within the UFWD: one specifically focusing on Tibet and the other targeting "new social strata" (新的社会阶层人士), such as young urban professionals, social media personalities, and cultural trend-setters. And in 2018, in a major bureaucratic reshuffling, the UFWD absorbed three organizations formerly under the State Council: the Overseas Chinese Affairs Office (OCAO), the State Administration for Religious Affairs, and the State Ethnic Affairs Commission. As a result of this reorganization, the UFWD increased its organizational capacity from nine bureaus to 12, including two focusing on overseas Chinese affairs. According to Alexander Bowe, the UFWD has added approximately 40,000 new cadres to its staff since Xi came to power.[48]

Third, since Xi was appointed paramount leader, there has been a marked increase in the work of the UFWD abroad.[49] Groups of increasing interest to united front work have been given greater priority under the Trial Regulations of 2015. Those regulations identified 12 groups as the "scope and target" of united front work. They included the growing numbers of PRC students overseas and those who have returned to China (出国和归国留学人员), overseas Chinese (especially the increasing number of recent emigrés), returned overseas Chinese and their relatives in China (华侨,归侨及侨眷), as well as "compatriots" in Hong Kong, Macau, and Taiwan and their relatives on the mainland.[50] John Dotson has also documented an expansion in the presence and activities of the Council for the Promotion of the Peaceful Reunification of China, a front organization subordinate to the UFWD around the world, with chapters in at least 91 countries and territories as well as five regional chapters encompassing several countries.[51]

Because of its oversight over religious groups in China such as those professing Catholicism, the UFWD has also been tasked to take part in the highly sensitive negotiations with the Vatican to establish official diplomatic relations between Beijing and the Holy See.[52] In addition, according to Takashi Suzuki, aspects of the 2018 bureaucratic restructuring—namely the absorption of the OCAO—gave the UFWD greater influence over the work of the sprawling network of hundreds of Confucius Institutes worldwide.[53] A number of analysts have also documented the increased role for the UFWD and affiliated organizations to promote the expansion of the Belt and Road Initiative, Xi Jinping's signature foreign policy undertaking.[54] Moreover, the UFWD's increased cultivation, cooption, and coercion work vis-à-vis Tibet, Xinjiang, Hong Kong, and Taiwan—while ostensibly "domestic" in nature—indirectly affects the PRC's external relations with countries that have interests in the political and social outcomes of those areas.[55] More broadly, with Xi's increased emphasis on the importance of united front work, PRC embassies abroad now have more individuals assigned to carry out such work, including through Chinese diaspora associations, PRC student organizations, and local media, as well through cultivating local elites such as officials and other opinion-shapers.

In sum, the UFWD is an integral player in "spreading China's voice," "telling China's story well," building up the country's international narrative power, and promoting ideas abroad consistent with the Party's interests. It does so through a broad range of subordinate organizations—such as various "overseas friendship associations," the Council for the Promotion of the Peaceful Reunification of China and its overseas branches, the China Soong Ching Ling Foundation, the China Federation of Overseas Chinese Entrepreneurs, the Overseas-educated Scholars Association of China, Chinese student and scholar associations on campuses around the world, and scores of other groups operating in China and abroad. The UFWD also operates its own media group, China News Service (中国新闻社). With a headquarters in Beijing, and providing content online and as a wire service, it has branches and journalists across China as well as in Bangkok, Kuala Lumpur, London, Los Angeles, Moscow, New York, Paris, San Francisco, Sydney, Taiwan, Tokyo, Vancouver, and Washington.[56]

In one of his studies on united front work, Alex Joske reviews official PRC documentation to identify over 90 "national-level social organizations" that are formally registered with and overseen by the UFWD and its affiliated organs, and thousands more at provincial and local levels in China.[57] Many of these organizations have overseas branches in countries around the world that engage with non-PRC individuals, with a particular focus on persons of Chinese descent living overseas. In recent years, united front work has earned a reputation for conducting unwelcome or illegal influence activities abroad—including gathering intelligence, intimidating and silencing critics, buying political favors, and monitoring the speech and activities of PRC citizens and the Chinese diaspora—all in the name of trying to build up the country's narrative power.

Central Propaganda Department

In one of his most high-profile domestic appearances as Party chief, Xi Jinping had a clear point to make when he spent a February day in 2016 visiting the PRC's three media powerhouses: Xinhua, the *People's Daily*, and China Central Television (CCTV). Accompanied on the tour by fellow CCP Politburo Standing Committee member Liu Yunshan, who oversees the Party's ideology and propaganda portfolio, Xi's message was all about loyalty to the Party and producing a positive image for China abroad. Xi reminded the executives, producers, and journalists that "media run by the party and the government are the propaganda fronts and must have the party as their family name," and that "all the work by the party's media must reflect the party's will, safeguard the party's authority, and safeguard the party's unity." Media workers, he declared, "must love the party, protect the party, and closely align themselves with the party leadership in thought, politics, and action." As for China's voice abroad, he called on the Party and its media organizations to "strengthen the building of our international communication capacity, increasing our international discourse power and focussing the proper telling of China's story . . . working to build flagship external propaganda media that have rather strong reputations internationally."[58]

For the Party and most PRC citizens, "propaganda" (宣传) does not carry the negative connotation the term bears outside of the country. Indeed, as Xi's remarks underscore, the development and conveyance of "correct" information is central to the Party's legitimacy and existence, and the control and dissemination of Party-controlled information is part and parcel of the everyday lives of China's people. In the words of leading China specialist David Shambaugh, the CCP's propaganda system was "a—if not *the*—key mechanism in Mao's and the Party's . . . efforts to transform Chinese society after 1949."[59] While the Party's emphasis on propaganda, ideology, and societal indoctrination waned in the two decades after Mao's death, they have seen a strong comeback under Xi Jinping. The propaganda system (宣传系统) in China is pervasive, overseeing nearly every aspect of information dissemination in all its forms—print, broadcast, digital, and visual—ranging from newspapers and television programming to textbooks, plays, cultural exhibitions and museums, movies and documentaries, web content, and much more. So important is propaganda for the Party that it warrants its own "leading small group" at the very pinnacle of the CCP's leadership structure that provides overall policy guidance to Party and government organs relevant to propaganda and ideology.

The CCP Central Propaganda Department (中共中央宣传部) (PD) serves as the Party's principal organ concerned with controlling the flow of information within, both disseminating correct information on the one hand and censoring, deflecting, or countermanding information deemed sensitive or dangerous on the other.[60] But it is not alone. Other Party organs as well as government agencies, from the national to local levels—such as in education, cultural affairs, tourism, Party and military training, the information technology industry, and others—are expected to play a role in developing and disseminating information consistent with the Party's overall propaganda directives.

Since its establishment in 1922, the PD has been principally focused on what it calls "internal" or domestic propaganda work. But over its century-long existence, it has also held a paramount role in conveying the CCP's messages abroad. In recent years, and especially under Xi Jinping, the PD has considerably expanded its political and bureaucratic heft and now oversees a sprawling communications and media empire that has gone global.[61] As part of this expanded external propaganda work, the PD has gained considerable financial and organizational resources. In the 2018 bureaucratic shake-up of government agencies, virtually all of China's state-run media activities were brought under tighter Party control, including overseas activities. In the reorganization, for example, the regulatory responsibilities of the State Administration of Press, Publication, Radio, Film, and Television were "reassigned" to the CCP's Propaganda Department. In addition, the reorganization established a massive new media conglomerate known as Voice of China that houses CCTV and its international arm, the China Global Television Network (CGTN), along with China National Radio and China Radio International (CRI). The enormous Xinhua News Agency was already a formal part of the Party propaganda apparatus under the PD. These outlets combined have a huge and growing international presence in both traditional and new media and form the core channels through which the Party seeks to "tell China's story well" overseas.

A few data points illustrate the growing global reach of the PD and the media it oversees. As of late 2020, Xinhua has 102 foreign bureaus across the Asia-Pacific, Eurasia, Europe, Africa, the Middle East, and North and South America; boasts 83 million Facebook followers, 12.6 million Twitter followers, and 931,000 YouTube subscribers; and produces print and digital content in 15 languages. CGTN has six channels broadcasting over the air and digitally in five languages, reaching more than 170 countries worldwide, with production centers in London, Nairobi, and Washington, D.C. It claims more than 150 million followers across multiple languages on such social media platforms as YouTube, Facebook, Twitter, and Weibo. *China Daily,* the official English-language newspaper, claims to have 200 million readers worldwide across its print and digital editions, including 73 million Facebook followers and 3.7 million on Twitter. *China Daily*'s "China Watch" insert has appeared in major newspapers in seven languages—including the *Washington Post, Wall Street Journal, Le Figaro, Sydney Morning Herald, El Pais,* and *Mainichi Shimbun*—and claims to have reached 5 million readers. CRI has nearly 70 overseas affiliate stations, 32 overseas bureaus, and 18 online radio programs, and broadcasts more than 2,700 hours of programming daily in 61 languages.[62]

These and other PRC media organizations have invested heavily in developing a multimedia online and digital presence, including through such foreign platforms as YouTube, Facebook, Instagram, and Twitter (even though these are officially banned from use inside China).[63] Other PRC social media giants such as Sina Weibo and WeChat, which are monitored for content by Chinese authorities, are also increasingly important sources of news and information for hundreds of millions of active users in China and around the world.[64] The use of Twitter by Party members, Party organizations, PRC government agencies, and other PRC state-linked entities has become more popular since 2018. The number of new accounts opened by Party and PRC government individuals and organizations ranged between two and 10 per year between 2013 and 2018. That number jumped to 65 new accounts in 2019 and was on track to reach more than 100 new accounts registered in 2020. As of late 2020, there were more than 200 Twitter accounts in active use by Chinese Party members and officials, media organizations, and government agencies.[65] Some Western research organizations have also identified the expanded use of fake Twitter accounts by Chinese agencies to generate a false illusion of support for CCP and PRC policies.[66]

Across these platforms, PRC media work to build up China's international narrative power by disseminating propaganda aligned with CCP views and interests and suppressing or censoring content that is not so aligned. A key element in this process is to gain greater control over content and information that is disseminated in countries outside of China—for example, through acquisition and ownership of local media outlets, expanding the availability of PRC media platforms within other countries, and providing China-friendly content to local media. According to Sarah Cook, a specialist on China's expanding media footprint, "these tactics have expanded over the past decade to the point that hundreds of millions of news consumers around the world are routinely viewing, reading, or listening to information created or influenced by the CCP, often without knowing its origins."[67]

Four "Big Ideas"

With greater resources and increasing activities, the ILD, UFWD, PD, and the organizations they oversee have dramatically enlarged their presence overseas and with it the capacity to shape the global narrative about China and PRC interests. As two senior PRC researchers argue, having greater international narrative power will allow China to set agendas at the global and regional level, promote Chinese norms and standards, and gain the acceptance and approval of other countries.[68] If that is the case, what agendas, norms, and endorsements—in short, what ideas—does today's China under Xi Jinping seek to promote on the global stage?

In the broadest sense, the biggest idea that PRC foreign policy wishes to promote is the legitimacy of the CCP and its claim as the PRC's rightful and unquestioned leadership. As discussed in chapter 2, the Party invests enormous resources behind this idea, especially through four crucial "legitimacy narratives," both at home and abroad. By gaining acceptance and approbation for this idea abroad, the Party not only improves its ability to achieve its interests outside China but also bolsters its standing at home, all of which translates to its long-term survival. But of course, it is not as simple as that. To have that big idea understood and accepted, many other intervening ideas and norms also need to be more widely understood and accepted within the global community. These include a list of aspirations for how the international system should operate—in Beijing's view, changes that need to be made—that will accommodate China's rise and smooth the path for its return to greatness. Some of these ideas are not new and have been long-held tenets in Chinese worldviews. Some of these ideas are new and reflect a greater confidence within China's current leadership that their experience deserves respect and even emulation. But whether old or new, what distinguishes them today is the power and presence China can bring to bear within the international system to promote them.

Drawing from Xi Jinping's key speeches on foreign relations as well as author-itative interpretations of them, at least four "big ideas" repeatedly arise and con-stitute core elements of "Xi Jinping Diplomatic Thought."[69] To begin, Xi Jinping wants the world to understand that we have entered a "new era," coincident with his leadership, in which China will fully regain its rightful place as a world-leading power and realize the "China Dream" and the "great rejuvenation of the Chinese nation." The two "centenary goals" the Party has set for the nation—becoming a moderately well-off society by the 100th anniversary of the CCP in 2021 and a "strong, democratic, civilized, harmonious and modern socialist country" by the 100th birthday of the PRC in 2049—are critical milestones on that journey. Promotion, acceptance, and the ultimate realization of this idea have enormous international consequences because by definition it results in titanic shifts in the global balance of power, especially vis-à-vis the United States, and puts pressures on the strategic framework that has ordered the international system since the middle of the 20th century. Xi Jinping frankly recognizes the world is going through "changes not seen in a century" and seems to understand the risks and opportunities they pose. He notes, for example, "that the great rejuvenation of the Chinese nation can in no way be realized easily. In fact, the stronger we be-come, the greater resistance and pressure we will encounter."[70] Nevertheless, he aims to convey his belief that China will overcome those challenges.

To offset concerns about the disruptions and uncertainties around China's rise, Xi Jinping Diplomatic Thought highlights a second set of important themes that are meant to convince the outside world of Beijing's benign intentions. One of Xi's signature concepts is the idea of building a "community of common des-tiny" (共同命运共同体). First put forward by Xi in 2013, and later officially rendered in English as "building a community with a shared future for man-kind" (构建人类命运共同体), the concept aims to remind leaders and socie-ties abroad of the common interests China shares with them—that the "dream of the Chinese people is closely connected with the dreams of the peoples of other countries" and that "by growing stronger through development, China will bring more opportunities, rather than threats, to the rest of the world."[71] In Xi's words:

> We call on the people of all countries to work together to build a community with a shared future for mankind, to build an open, inclusive, clean, and beautiful world that enjoys lasting peace, universal security, and common prosperity. We should respect each other, discuss issues as equals, resolutely reject the Cold War mentality and power politics, and take a new approach to developing state-to-state relations with communication, not confrontation, and with partnership, not alliance. We should stick together through thick and thin, promote trade and investment liberalization and facilitation, and make economic globalization more open, inclusive, and balanced so that its benefits are shared by all.[72]

In putting forward this idea of a shared future for mankind, its pursuit of mutual benefit and multilateralism through consensus-building and win-win solutions are typically juxtaposed against "old-fashioned" (and implicitly Western) concepts of global order, such as imperialism, colonialism, and the "zero-sum mentality of Cold War thinking." These thoughts dovetail with long-standing official PRC discourse casting China as a peaceable nation by tradition and by dint of its own victimization at the hands of foreign powers in the past. These ideas are intended to resonate most of all with Beijing's immediate neighbors but also with the developing world writ large in Africa, Latin America, and Asia and position China as a champion of sovereignty, development, justice, and fair play.

This concept is also linked to a third set of important ideas associated with PRC diplomacy under Xi Jinping. In addition to advocating for peace, development, and mutual benefit, the idea of a shared future for mankind also stresses "unity with diversity." That is, while the world should be united by its common pursuits of stability and prosperity, all countries have the right to choose their own social and political path toward those goals. As Xi puts it,

> We should respect the diversity of civilizations. In handling relations among civilizations, let us replace estrangement with exchange, clashes with mutual learning, and superiority with coexistence. . . . We respect the right of the people of all countries to choose their own development path. We endeavor to uphold international fairness and justice, and oppose acts that impose one's will on others or interfere in the internal affairs of others as well as the practice of the strong bullying the weak.[73]

In putting forth these ideas, Xi is restating China's long-held view about the sanctity of national sovereignty. He is also calling on the world to accept that China's "own development path"—its particular system of socialism with Chinese characteristics under the unquestioned leadership of the CCP—be treated with respect and not subjected to interference in its internal affairs. This view rejects Western conceptions of the universality of electoral democracy, human rights, and free markets and instead puts forward a positive vision of the PRC as a "major socialist country with distinctive Chinese features . . . fully confident of offering Chinese input to human exploration of better social systems."[74] As Xi declared to the 2021 World Economic Forum gathering in Davos, Switzerland, one of the world's most important tasks is to "abandon ideological prejudice" because "difference in itself is no cause for alarm. What does ring the alarm is arrogance, prejudice, and hatred; it is the attempt to impose hierarchy on human civilization or to force one's own history, culture, and social system upon others."[75]

Relatedly, PRC foreign policy under Xi has been particularly active in promoting the idea that there can be no human rights until fundamental rights of human development are first achieved. Putting the developmental prerogatives and priorities of governments ahead of the political and civil rights of individuals aligns closely with China's own state-centric conceptions of the relationship between the rulers and the ruled. As noted in chapter 6, Beijing works within international bodies such as the United Nations Human Rights Commission to gain approval for statements in which human rights are defined not as the spread of individual freedoms such as democratic expression and religious liberties, but rather by access to the basics for well-being such as food, shelter, and a living wage.

But China not only promotes these ideas within international bodies.[76] It has also become a more prominent feature of its communications with key friends as Beijing aims to disseminate its ideas more broadly as part of the international discourse. A high-profile example of this approach is found in a joint statement on global governance signed between the foreign ministers of China and Russia in early 2021. In it, the two countries agreed that "sustainable development is the basis for improving the living standards and welfare of all peoples, thereby promoting the enjoyment of human rights," that each country should determine for itself the best pathway for development that leads to human rights, and that human development leads to democracy, not the other way around. As such, they added, there is no uniform model of democracy and so countries should neither politicize the human rights of other countries nor engage in "democracy promotion" abroad.[77]

For China, this argument extends into many other realms of international and national development. For example, in relation to the cybersphere, Beijing advocates an adamantly state-centric position, privileging state security over individual access and information flows. Similar to its ideas regarding democracy promotion and human rights, Beijing argues it should be able to makes its own choices about cyber policy and not be held hostage to outside pressures and policies inconsistent with the national interest.[78] China's 2017 cyber white paper sets forth a set of principles to govern international cooperation in cyberspace, including on matters of sovereignty:

> As a basic norm in contemporary international relations, the principle of sovereignty enshrined in the UN Charter covers all aspects of state-to-state relations, which also includes cyberspace. Countries should respect each other's right to choose their own path of cyber development, model of cyber regulation and Internet public policies, and participate in international cyberspace governance on an equal footing. No country should pursue cyber hegemony, interfere in other countries' internal affairs, or engage in, condone, or support cyber activities that undermine other countries' national security.
>
> . . .
>
> National governments are entitled to enact public policies, laws, and regulations with no foreign interference. . . . No country should use [information and communication technologies (ICT)] to interfere in other countries' internal affairs or leverage its advantage to undermine the security of other countries' ICT product and service supply chain.[79]

This brings us to a fourth set of big ideas embedded in Xi's approach to world affairs: that the PRC has important inputs and solutions to offer that others in the world could follow. In many respects, this proposal marks an important departure from past practice and reflects Xi's more activist posture on the world stage. In formal settings, PRC leaders typically wish to avoid the image of imposing their model on others—exactly what Beijing criticizes others, such as the United States, of doing. That said, as early as 2014, and repeatedly thereafter, Xi Jinping and other PRC leaders have used the term "中国方案"—officially translated as "Chinese solution," "Chinese input," or "Chinese approach"—in calling for the reform of the international system, offering Chinese ideas to address 21st-century global problems, and even proposing that aspects of China's socioeconomic development model could be adopted by other countries.[80] In his speech to the 19th Party Congress in 2017, Xi explicitly suggests that the PRC governance and development model could be adopted by others, saying, "the path, the theory, the system, and the culture of socialism with Chinese characteristics have kept developing, blazing a new trail for other developing countries to achieve modernization. It offers a new option for other countries and nations who want to speed up their development while preserving their independence; and it offers Chinese wisdom and a Chinese approach [中国方案] to solving the problems facing mankind."[81]

A Contest of Ideas

This chapter has examined the pursuit and propagation of ideas in shaping PRC foreign policy under Xi Jinping. Many of the big ideas of Xi Jinping diplomacy are not all that new. They may be better understood as repackaged versions of PRC worldviews that have persisted over time and continue—though more vigorously so—during the Xi Jinping era. In particular, many of the ideas noted above echo the Five Principles of Peaceful Coexistence from the 1950s: mutual respect for others' territorial integrity and sovereignty, mutual nonaggression, mutual noninterference in others' internal affairs, equality and mutual benefit, and peaceful coexistence. It is no coincidence that in prominent speeches Xi mentions the Five Principles and the "community of shared future for mankind" in tandem.[82]

However, these ideas *are* new in two other important respects. First is the power and presence that Beijing can bring to bear within the international system to have these ideas heard and heeded. To put it another way, these ideas can carry more weight than in the past because a more powerful and influential China increasingly has the means to engage in a global contest of ideas. As China specialist Lutgard Lams colorfully puts it, "Strategies utilised to spread 'the China story' are more diverse, the conductor's baton is held more tightly, the main melody is chanted more loudly and the echoes are carried further abroad over the mountains and seas."[83] Second, because of China's more prominent position, these ideas have greater potential for transforming the norms and practices of the international system in ways that are more favorable to PRC interests.[84]

For these reasons, a vibrant debate has emerged over what strategic aims lie behind Xi Jinping's diplomatic thought. Cornell professor Jessica Chen Weiss, for example, posits that Beijing is seeking to make the world "safe for autocracy"—that is, more conducive to and accepting of CCP survival—but does not pose an existential or ideological threat to liberal, democratic societies.[85] Rather, according to this view, Xi's diplomatic ideas primarily aim to promote the Party's legitimacy and ability to pursue its own pathway of political and social development, free from outside interference and the imposition of "universal values" favored by liberal democracies. Others disagree. While in office, then–national security advisor Robert O'Brien argued that "Xi Jinping's ambitions for ideological control are not limited to his own people. The CCP's stated goal is to create a 'Community of Common Destiny for Mankind,' and to remake the world according to the CCP. The effort to control thought beyond the borders of China is well under way."[86]

This debate continues and has real-world implications for policy. However, Xi Jinping's ideas about the world do not readily lend themselves to easy, "either-or" interpretations. For the near- to medium-term—out to 2030 or 2035—Xi's ideas about the international system appear to be mostly concerned with garnering and sustaining Party legitimacy by focusing on the comparatively parochial goal of "national rejuvenation" rather than achieving a new world order. That said, as this chapter has shown, it is also true that Xi and other PRC leaders are increasingly willing and able to give greater voice to China's aspirations and to insist those aspirations be respected. If over the longer term—to 2040 and beyond—Xi's dream of national rejuvenation succeeds and China grows to become the most powerful nation on Earth, a restructuring of the world order, far more conducive to Beijing's interests, would seem almost unavoidable. Such a world—if it is to be achieved—would be more Sino-centric in nature, befitting of the country's preeminent position in the global hierarchy.

However, it is important to bear in mind that while these near- and long-term outcomes may be the *aspirations* of Xi Jinping thought on diplomacy, their *realization* faces formidable challenges. As the PRC has sought greater international narrative power and to have its voice heard—whether to promote the legitimacy of its form of governance, offer solutions to global problems based on its experience, or seek changes in how the international system operates—it has met with significant skepticism and pushback around the globe. These concerns are especially acute within liberal societies, but not exclusively. As the debate flagged above demonstrates, there is deepening skepticism and concern about whether Beijing's ideas aim to ultimately overturn the international order. Others would point to the fact that Beijing's claims to support the Five Principles of Peaceful Coexistence have proven false, especially as it increasingly employs hard power to achieve its aims, interferes in the internal affairs of other countries, and sows disinformation abroad. Societies around the world are increasingly worried about the Party's tactics as it works to have China's voice heard overseas: spreading propaganda, intimidating critics, and currying favor among influential elites. The core precept of the Party's messaging—that one-party authoritarian rule is legitimate and deserving of respect—is itself contrary to the belief systems of many. China's lack of "soft power"—that is, "the ability to get what you want through attraction" rather than coercion or inducements[87]—is a major reason it struggles to have its big ideas more widely accepted (this soft power challenge is discussed in more detail in the following chapter).

In short, as Xi implores his Party to expand China's international narrative power, a contest of ideas will increasingly define Beijing's relationship with much of the world. It is far from clear how China will fare in this battle for hearts and minds. As with the other core aspirations of PRC foreign policy under Xi

Jinping—sustaining CCP legitimacy, expanding PRC sovereignty, generating wealth and power, and becoming a global leader—China's hopes to have its ideas heard and heeded also face a mounting set of challenges. In the chapter that follows, we turn to those challenges and their implications for the PRC's role in the world now and for the future.

8

Challenges 挑战

Confronting Headwinds for the China Dream

The world today faces great changes not seen in a century. Our Party's great struggles, great projects, great undertakings, and great dreams inexorably advance. . . . We face rare historical opportunities but also great challenges. To successfully realize the goals set by our Party, we must promote the spirit of struggle and strengthen our ability to fight.
—Xi Jinping, September 2019[1]

Confidence and Contradiction

As the previous chapters show, the People's Republic of China (PRC or China) has gained momentum across the six major ambitions that shape and animate the country's foreign policy under Xi Jinping: legitimacy, sovereignty, wealth, power, leadership, and ideas. Under the Chinese Communist Party (CCP or Party), China has garnered greater respect and appreciation for its accomplishments while maintaining stability at home, increased its sovereign footprint, expanded its global economic presence and national wealth, strengthened its economic and military hard power, taken on greater and greater global leadership roles, and more actively propagated the country's ideas and international "voice." Chinese leaders exude confidence, putting forward "Chinese solutions" and basking in the glow of national success. As Xi declared in marking the Party's 95th birthday, "The whole Party should be confident in our path, theory, system, and culture. In today's world, if any party, nation, or people deserves to be confident, it is the [CCP], the PRC and the Chinese nation. . . . We shall have such courage and confidence so that we can overcome any challenges we meet, open up new horizons, and create new miracles."[2]

This confidence arises not only from the PRC's accomplishments, but also when juxtaposed against the many divisive and debilitating problems encountered by the developed and democratic world, especially since the mid-2000s: the global financial crisis, the rise of inward-looking nationalism, Brexit, the tumultuous Trump years, the devastating social and economic impact of the covid-19 pandemic, and deepening political dysfunction, discord, and upheaval. As the

Daring to Struggle. Bates Gill, Oxford University Press. © Oxford University Press 2022.
DOI: 10.1093/oso/9780197545645.003.0009

CCP marked its 100th anniversary in 2021, there was more than a bit of triumphalism in the air. A member of one of China's national parliamentary bodies, the Chinese People's Political Consultative Conference (CPPCC), and a researcher at the Academy of Military Sciences probably reflects the view of many Chinese leaders in comparing the "chaos in social and political life" in the West to what they believe the "China model" can offer:

> Nowadays, the advantages of China's system attract the world's attention like a magnet, and the community with a shared future for mankind is day by day increasingly recognized by countries of the world. Overall, the international community senses that the path of socialism with Chinese characteristics has truly offered new options, inspirations, and pathways for the development and rejuvenation of other countries and peoples. Many countries vie to study China's path and Chinese culture. It is predictable that the Chinese model will become a new hope for world development which more and more countries will choose or assimilate.[3]

Typically more circumspect, senior PRC leaders nevertheless pointedly contrast "order in the East and chaos in the West" when touting the PRC's accomplishments.[4] Even Xi Jinping reportedly stated "the biggest source of chaos in the world today is the United States," and "the East is rising and the West is in decline" (东升西降).[5] But it was China's top diplomat, Yang Jiechi, who expressed China's confidence most vividly and publicly. Speaking prior to a closed-door meeting with U.S. counterparts in Anchorage, Alaska, in 2021, Yang said:

> We believe that it is important for the United States to change its own image and to stop advancing its own democracy in the rest of the world. Many people within the United States actually have little confidence in the democracy of the United States, and they have various views regarding the government of the United States.
>
> . . .
>
> On human rights, we hope that the United States will do better. . . . The challenges facing the United States in human rights are deep-seated. They did not just emerge over the past four years, such as Black Lives Matter. It did not come up only recently. So we do hope that for our two countries, it's important that we manage our respective affairs well instead of deflecting the blame on somebody else in this world.
>
> . . .
>
> I don't think the overwhelming majority of countries in the world would recognize that the universal values advocated by the United States . . . could

represent international public opinion, and those countries would not recognize that the rules made by a small number of people would serve as the basis for the international order.

. . .

The United States does not have the qualification to say that it wants to speak to China from a position of strength.[6]

But at the same time, China's outward confidence in world affairs confronts a range of challenges as the country seeks a more respected and powerful role on the international stage. Indeed, the very pursuit of its foreign policy ambitions—while often bolstering national confidence—has also created problems both at home and abroad. These problems will hold China back and could derail Xi's vision for national rejuvenation. In public statements, Chinese leaders allude to some of these challenges and recognize that continued reforms, adjustments, and hard work are needed in order to meet and overcome them. Speaking before fellow Party members in 2019, Xi spoke at length about the many challenges facing the country, including in relation to the economy, domestic politics, the environment, the sociocultural realm, national defense and security, Taiwan, and foreign affairs. "At present and in the future," he said, "China's development has entered into a period where risks and challenges continue to increase or are becoming concentrated. The major struggles to be faced will not become less" and "will become even more complex."[7] In celebrating the Party's 100th anniversary in July 2021, he struck similar themes:

> We must carry out a great struggle with many contemporary features. Having the courage to fight and the fortitude to win is what has made our Party invincible. Realizing our great dream will require hard work and persistence. Today, we are closer, more confident, and more capable than ever before of making the goal of national rejuvenation a reality. But we must be prepared to work harder than ever to get there.[8]

Looking ahead, it appears Xi and other Chinese leaders recognize many of the challenges they face but believe they cannot compromise or accommodate, leaving them little choice but to confront the headwinds they face in the confident expectation they will prevail. Or, as Xi Jinping repeatedly exhorts, "dare to struggle, dare to win" (敢于斗争, 敢于胜利). This chapter considers those challenges, what they mean for Beijing at home and abroad, and what we can expect from PRC foreign policy in the years ahead as a result.

One basic challenge China faces has to do with its overall image in the world today. International polling suggests that China has an image problem, and Beijing still struggles to instill greater trust, confidence, and appeal in the minds of people in other countries. Notwithstanding Beijing's hopes under Xi Jinping to "tell China's story well," survey data generated over many years and across dozens of countries around the world show that unfavorable views of China have generally increased since Xi Jinping came to power, as shown in Figure 8.1. At the same time, also seen in Figure 8.1, the percentage of persons polled who expressed "not too much confidence" or "no confidence at all" in Xi Jinping to "do the right thing regarding world affairs" has also shown seen an upward trend.[9] By other indicators, China's international image likewise fares poorly. Since first published in 2016, the annual *Soft Power 30* report in 2016 has consistently placed China near the bottom of the list for its soft power appeal; China came in at 27th out of 30 in 2019.[10]

Declines in positive perceptions toward China have been especially precipitous in advanced democratic economies such as in North America, Europe, and

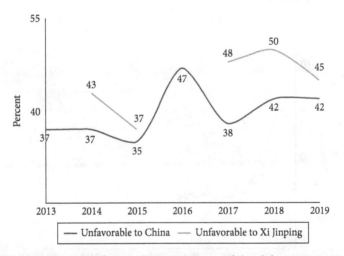

Figure 8.1 Perceptions of China and Xi Jinping around the globe, 2013–2019

Note: Median percentage shown from across the countries surveyed. For views on China, number represents those who have a "somewhat unfavorable" or "very unfavorable" opinion toward China; for views on Xi Jinping, number represents those who expressed "not too much confidence" or "no confidence at all" in Xi Jinping to "do the right thing regarding world affairs." Based on surveys in Argentina, Australia, Bangladesh, Bolivia, Brazil, Bulgaria, Burkina Faso, Canada, Chile, Colombia, Czech Republic, Egypt, El Salvador, Ethiopia, France, Germany, Ghana, Greece, Hungary, India, Indonesia, Israel, Italy, Japan, Jordan, Kenya, Lebanon, Lithuania, Malaysia, Mexico, the Netherlands, Nicaragua, Nigeria, Pakistan, Palestinian territory, Peru, Philippines, Poland, Russia, Senegal, Slovakia, South Africa, South Korea, Spain, Sweden, Tanzania, Thailand, Tunisia, Turkey, Uganda, Ukraine, the United Kingdom, the United States, Venezuela, Vietnam. Not all countries surveyed in all years. Insufficient data on views toward Xi Jinping in 2013 and 2016.

Source: "Confidence in the Chinese President," Pew Research Center Global Indicators Database, updated March 2020, https://www.pewresearch.org/global/database/indicator/69, and "Opinion of China," Pew Research Center Global Indicators Database, updated March 2020, https://www.pewr esearch.org/global/database/indicator/24.

the Indo-Pacific, but not exclusively so. Figure 8.2 tracks these trends across 14 economically advanced democracies. Negative attitudes in these countries toward China reached record levels in 2020, with a median of 73 percent saying they have an unfavorable view of the country; China's close neighbors harbored some of the strongest negative feelings: Japan (86 percent), Australia (81 percent), and South Korea (75 percent). In the same survey, an average of only 19 percent of the respondents expressed "a lot of" or "some confidence" that Xi Jinping would "do the right thing regarding world affairs."[11] Between 2018 and 2020, persons in the United States saying they feel "cold" toward China went from 46 to 67 percent; by 2021, nearly 90 percent of Americans said they see China as either a "competitor" (55 percent) or "enemy" (34 percent).[12] In a poll taken in 2021, the number of Americans expressing an unfavorable perception of China reached a record-high 79 percent.[13] This polling reflects the ongoing deterioration and intensifying competition that defines nearly all aspects of U.S.-China strategic relations.[14]

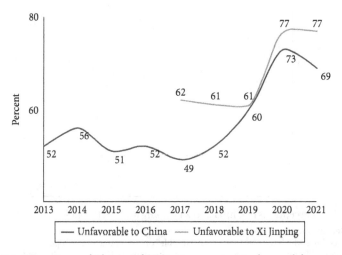

Figure 8.2 Perceptions of China and Xi Jinping among 14 advanced democratic countries, 2013–2021

Note: Median percentage shown from across the countries surveyed. For views on China, number represents those who have a "somewhat unfavorable" or "very unfavorable" opinion toward China; for views on Xi Jinping, number represents those who expressed "not too much confidence" or "no confidence at all" in Xi Jinping to "do the right thing regarding world affairs." Surveys conducted in Australia, Belgium, Canada, France, Germany, Greece, Italy, Japan, the Netherlands, South Korea, Spain, Sweden, the United Kingdom, and the United States. Belgium not surveyed 2017 to 2019; Greece not surveyed in 2020. Insufficient data on views toward Xi Jinping for 2013 to 2016.

Source: Laura Silver, "China's international image remains broadly negative as views of the U.S. rebound," Pew Research Center, June 30, 2021, https://www.pewresearch.org/fact-tank/2021/06/30/chinas-international-image-remains-broadly-negative-as-views-of-the-u-s-rebound/.

Elsewhere, surveys turn up similar findings. In the Indo-Pacific, polling shows that trust, confidence, and favorability toward China continue to slide.[15] In a survey taken across 10 Southeast Asian nations in 2021, for example, the percentage of persons surveyed who expressed distrust of China rose from 51.5 percent in 2019 to 63 percent, while more than 46 percent of respondents said, "China is a revisionist power and intends to draw Southeast Asia into its sphere of influence," up from 38 percent in 2018. In the same survey, a significant majority of those polled (61.5 percent) said they would prefer siding with the United States over China, if forced to do so as part of the Sino-American rivalry; that number was up by 8 percent from the year prior.[16]

Presumably, such negative polling and deteriorating foreign relationships should matter to PRC leaders, especially given the massive investments made to bolster the image of China and the Party leadership. In apparent recognition of China's image problem, Xi convened a Politburo study session to improve the country's international communications capabilities in June 2021. Calling for a shift in tone and approach, Xi told the Party's top leaders that they needed to be "open, confident, and humble" toward the outside world and "expand China's circle of friends," while striving to build a more "credible, lovable, and respectable image for China."[17] This will be far easier said than done: unfavorable attitudes about China and its leadership within foreign populations arise from—and in turn can undermine—the PRC's very pursuit of foreign policy goals associated with legitimacy, sovereignty, wealth, power, leadership and ideas.

Legitimacy

Chapter 2 outlines four "legitimacy narratives"—based on ideology, aggrieved nationalism, Party performance, and Chinese culture—that the Party employs and goes on to explain how the Party under Xi Jinping has expanded its involvement in the oversight, deliberation, and conduct of PRC foreign policy. These narratives and increased Party role are intended to help bolster the CCP's standing with domestic and foreign audiences. Underscoring the linkage between Party legitimacy and foreign policy, China's top diplomat and Politburo member Yang Jiechi pointedly reminded Foreign Ministry colleagues that "upholding the leadership of the CCP and socialism with Chinese characteristics is the most fundamental element of foreign affairs work."[18]

However, while the Party can probably expect to further solidify its domestic power as a result, its international standing is more open to question. Indeed, the need to secure and sustain Party legitimacy has weighty and at times risky implications for PRC foreign policy today, the outlines of which are increasingly clear. To begin, the need to please multiple audiences at home and abroad immediately raises contradictions: as Cornell professor Jessica Chen Weiss argues, a nationalistic appeal may play well at home, but will rattle the neighbors.[19] Yet a nationalist appeal can also backfire at home if the leadership is seen as feckless and weak. Nonetheless, in spite of these risks, the Party under Xi Jinping has increasingly turned to nationalist messages to legitimate its claim to power even as PRC citizens increasingly view the outside world with distrust and disdain.[20]

Furthermore, an ideological appeal to legitimacy may inspire confidence within the Party rank-and-file, but only reminds international audiences of the Leninist nature of the PRC regime. Even within the Party there continue to be difficulties in ensuring adherence to the Party line and maintaining obedience to its rule—hence the need for constantly reinforcing Party discipline, instilling ideological rigor, and fighting against "wrong thinking" within the Party ranks.[21] At the same time, legitimizing Party rule by building up domestic expectations about CCP performance is also risky. As China scholar Peter Gries points out, "The CCP has inextricably linked itself, society, and foreign policy by staking its domestic right to rule"—its legitimacy—"upon its foreign policy performance."[22] Overall, as Xiaoyu Pu convincingly shows, the CCP faces difficult challenges as it tries to calibrate its legitimacy-seeking messaging to suit multiple audiences and bolster its position at home while reassuring audiences abroad.[23]

However, the CCP's efforts to promote its legitimacy abroad often fail to reassure. Touting the superior performance of the CCP governance model—such as in the wake of the 2008 global financial crisis or in responding to the covid-19 pandemic—does more to irritate and alarm liberal societies than garner supporters within them. Moreover, governments and societies around the world—particularly but not solely liberal democracies—have found the Party's efforts to strengthen its hand at home and abroad increasingly troubling and unwelcome.[24] In the United States, the Trump administration (2017–2021) was especially active identifying an ideological challenge emanating from Xi Jinping's China. In speaking of the CCP's Marxist-Leninist nature, U.S. secretary of state Michael Pompeo stated, "General Secretary Xi Jinping is a true believer in a bankrupt totalitarian ideology. It's this ideology . . . that informs his decades-long desire for global hegemony of Chinese communism. . . . If we bend the knee now, our children's children may be at the mercy of the Chinese Communist Party, whose actions are the primary challenge today in the free world."[25] Citing concerns over Party-influenced interpretations of history and contemporary affairs, affiliations with CCP organizations, and potential censoring of free speech and academic freedoms, the Trump administration designated the Confucius Institutes as a "foreign mission" of the PRC and issued letters to university boards and U.S. state education commissions warning them about the potential "authoritarian influence" of Confucius Institutes and Confucius Classrooms in

American schools and institutions of higher learning.[26] Even prior to this official action, universities across the United States, in Europe, and in Asia had either closed their Confucius Institutes or renegotiated their agreements with them in order to exercise greater oversight over their activities. Apparently in response to the problems facing these would-be ambassadors, in June 2020 the PRC moved responsibility for managing the Confucius Institutes program to a newly formed charitable foundation named the Chinese International Education Foundation.[27] But the reputation of these institutes will struggle to recover.

These and other actions were part of the Trump administration's effort to raise awareness "about the threat posed by the Chinese Communist Party to [U.S. citizens'] livelihoods, businesses, freedoms and values." According to the U.S. National Security Advisor at the time, "The competition with which we are faced is not China versus the United States. It is the Chinese Communist Party, with its Marxist-Leninist and mercantilist vision for the world, versus freedom-loving people everywhere."[28] More than at any time since the early Cold War, ideological concerns have become an increasing source of tension in U.S.-China relations, as well as between China and other open societies around the world. A case in point: in 2020, the Inter-Parliamentary Alliance on China (IPAC) was founded, a body made up of legislators from democratic countries worldwide. According to the group's official founding statement:

> Developing a coherent response to the rise of the People's Republic of China as led by the Chinese Communist Party is a defining challenge for the world's democratic states. . . . The Chinese Communist Party repeatedly and explicitly states its intention to expand its global influence. As a direct result, democratic values and practices have come under increasing pressure. . . . The Inter-Parliamentary Alliance on China has been created to promote a coordinated response between democratic states to challenges posed by the present conduct and future ambitions of the People's Republic of China.[29]

IPAC counts about 220 legislators from 19 countries and the European Parliament as members. Through newsletters, statements, briefings, and other activities, the organization monitors developments in China and seeks to coordinate a strengthened response by democratic countries to counter illiberal and unwelcome aspects of China's domestic and foreign policies.

In assessing the Party's approach to the world, especially in the Xi Jinping era, University of London China scholar Steve Tsang argues that the regime pursues a "Party-state realism" in which the interest, authority, and survival of the CCP—and not necessarily a nonpartisan, rational assessment of national interests—come first.[30] From this fundamental characteristic flows three others that are clearly seen in how the Party pursues the core elements of PRC foreign

policy: an instrumentalist approach toward the international system to neu-
tralize criticism of the CCP, Party-centric nationalism to secure respect at
home and abroad, and a hard-nosed, realist assessment of the Party's power
versus its enemies abroad.[31] In doing so, the Party faces mounting challenges
to its legitimacy on the international scene. This in turn negatively affects the
other key pursuits of PRC foreign policy: sovereignty, wealth, power, leadership, and ideas.

Sovereignty

In discussing the second core pursuit of PRC foreign policy, sovereignty,
chapter 3 reviewed the concept's historical roots and described its more expansive meaning under Xi Jinping. The chapter also delved into a range of contemporary cases around China's periphery and farther afield to show how Beijing's
claims to sovereignty seriously affect PRC relations with its neighbors and beyond. During the Xi Jinping era, PRC sovereignty has become more hotly
contested in such areas as Tibet, Xinjiang, Hong Kong, the South China Sea, and
the East China Sea, across the Taiwan Strait, and along the Sino-Indian border.
At the same time, Xi has endorsed a broadening view of PRC sovereignty to encompass growing overseas interests and "strategic frontiers" well beyond China's
national borders.

Not surprisingly, Beijing's more assertive and expansive approach to sovereignty has helped to fuel consternation, controversy, crackdowns, and conflict
in areas around China's periphery. Overall, there is little in Xi Jinping's more
muscular approach to sovereignty that has improved Beijing's relations with its
neighbors or others farther away. Indeed, many of China's neighbors have drawn
closer in opposition to Beijing's heavy-handed tactics. Japan and the United States
have strengthened their alliance, with their leaders jointly expressing objections
to China's "unlawful maritime claims," voicing concern over the human rights
situation in Hong Kong and Xinjiang, and for the first time in more than 50 years,
underscoring the need for peace and stability across the Taiwan Strait.[32] The
Quadrilateral Security Dialogue, a partnership among Australia, India, Japan,
and the United States, held its first-ever leader-level summits in 2021 (one virtual, one in person), where they agreed to collaborate "to meet challenges to the
maritime rules-based order, including in the East and South China Seas," and to
deepen collaboration in such areas as global health, climate change, infrastructure development, and space technology. Without mentioning China directly,
the four leaders stated they would "recommit to promoting the free, open, rules-
based order, rooted in international law and undaunted by coercion, to bolster
security and prosperity in the Indo-Pacific and beyond."[33] India's greater interest

in elevating and deepening this partnership is a response to the rising tensions and deadly clashes along the Sino-Indian border during 2019–2020.

China's Southeast Asian neighbors Indonesia, Malaysia, the Philippines, and Vietnam are increasingly vocal in opposing China's attempts to take over the South China Sea. The leader of the Philippines, Rodrigo Duterte—who early in his term courted favor with Xi Jinping in spite of China's encroachment on Philippine territory—by 2021, with U.S. backing, took a tougher stance toward Beijing in the South China Sea; Washington and Manila aim to revitalize their alliance by increasing the rotational presence of U.S. military personnel and weaponry—including missile platforms—in the Philippines, a direct response to China's encroachments on the country's sovereignty.[34] Taiwan and the United States are building closer diplomatic, economic, and military relations—with the Biden administration in its early days signaling "rock solid" support for Taiwan[35]—and Washington has increased its military presence around Taiwan, including more frequent naval transits through the Taiwan Strait.[36] Oddly, Beijing squandered a strategic opportunity to burnish its international image as a provider of public goods by forcibly asserting its sovereign claims with several of its neighbors—including India, Japan, Taiwan, Vietnam, and other claimants in the South China Sea—during the 2020 covid-19 outbreak.[37] Around the globe, countries are rethinking their relationship with Beijing and seeking ways to preserve their own sovereignty and freedom to maneuver in the face of China's growing power and influence.[38]

China's crackdowns in internally contested areas of its territory have likewise sparked international criticism and punitive measures. These developments have driven a steep downturn in China's relations with key counterparts, especially in North America and Europe, and with India and Taiwan. For example, the U.S. government formally accused Beijing of genocide and crimes against humanity for its treatment of Uyghurs and other Muslim minorities in Xinjiang.[39]

Among other measures, Washington imposed export restrictions on nearly 40 PRC government agencies and companies deemed to be complicit in the Xinjiang repression campaign, halted the import of goods from PRC companies accused of using forced Uyghur labor, and banned certain PRC officials from travel to the United States. In 2021, the European Union (EU) issued human rights sanctions against China, the first EU sanctions targeting China since the Tiananmen crackdown in 1989. Beijing has pushed back hard on this criticism—including the issuance of sanctions on U.S. and European individuals and entities—justifying its actions in Xinjiang as necessary to counter a serious terrorist threat and stabilize its vast northwestern region.[40] When more than 20 countries submitted a letter to the United Nations Human Rights Council (UNHRC) urging China to scale back its repressive policies in Xinjiang, China responded by mobilizing a counterletter with 37 signatory nations, praising

Beijing's actions against terrorism and radicalization. A similar set of dueling letters was submitted to the United Nations in 2020. Interestingly, PRC supporters comprise a range of Muslim-majority countries—including Egypt, Iran, Iraq, Morocco, Pakistan, Saudi Arabia, and Syria—but not Central Asian neighbors bordering on Xinjiang such as Afghanistan, Kazakhstan, and Kyrgyzstan.[41] Beijing also met with harsh scrutiny from a group of independent experts appointed by the UNHRC who expressed concern over reports that Uyghurs had been subjected to arbitrary detentions, human trafficking, forced labor, and enslavement, which, if true, would constitute "grave human rights abuses."[42]

In Tibet, in anticipation of the Dalai Lama's passing, Beijing declared that identification of the next Dalai Lama "must comply with Chinese laws [and] regulations";[43] this contravenes Tibetan tradition, whereby the living Dalai Lama instructs his followers where to locate his reincarnation and rightful successor. As a result, there will be two Dalai Lamas—one in China and one (probably) in India—which will further intensify divisions between Beijing on the one hand and the Tibetan community and its international supporters on the other. In a sign of such controversies ahead, the Trump administration signed a law stating that U.S. policy holds that future Tibetan religious leaders can only be selected by Tibetans and calling for sanctions against PRC officials who interfere in the process.[44]

In responding to Beijing's harsh policies in Hong Kong, the United Kingdom, Australia, and the European Union all leveled criticism and in some cases sanctions against Hong Kong and against PRC individuals and entities involved in Hong Kong policy. Washington issued sanctions and travel bans on individuals charged with implementing the tougher measures in Hong Kong, withdrew Hong Kong's preferential trade status with the United States, and threatened financial sanctions against foreign financial institutions conducting certain activities with Hong Kong counterparts. The United Kingdom and Australia offered "lifeboat visas" to allow Hong Kong residents a pathway to citizenship in those countries. The EU and some European nations restricted trade in surveillance and other sensitive technologies with Hong Kong and China.

China's actions in asserting greater control over Hong Kong have spillover effects for its biggest sovereignty dispute of all—Taiwan. In effectively banning the "one country, two systems" formula in Hong Kong, Beijing cannot credibly continue to propose that same framework for resolving its differences with Taiwan. That formula was already in serious doubt, given the ongoing changes in public opinion in Taiwan on the question of future relations with the mainland. Consistent polling since the mid-1990s has tracked attitudes on Taiwan toward the questions of independence, reunification, or maintaining the status quo.[45] In this polling, "reunification as soon as possible" has never been expressed by more than 5 percent of Taiwan's population; the most recent data show this number at about 1 percent. Rather, the vast majority of respondents prefer some of form of the status quo for now—that is, neither independence nor reunification. More than half of those polled in 2020 (54.6 percent) preferred that the status quo be maintained "indefinitely" or until it can be "decided at a later date." However, those opinions have been in decline in recent years, with the fastest-growing proportion of respondents voicing support to "maintain the status quo" while "moving toward independence." The percentage of persons expressing that view has grown steadily from just 8 percent in 1994 to over a quarter (25.5 percent) of respondents as of early 2021. More ominously for Beijing, opposition to reunification is especially high among young persons on Taiwan, with an average of 89 percent of persons under 40 years of age stating they prefer either the status quo or outright independence.[46] When asked, "Would you fight for Taiwan if China uses force against Taiwan for unification?" almost 80 percent of persons surveyed in Taiwan responded affirmatively.[47]

Nonetheless, Xi Jinping appears outwardly tone-deaf to these realities. In high-profile messages to "Taiwan compatriots" he states the "principles of 'peaceful reunification' and 'one country, two systems' are the best approach for realizing national reunification," though he also does not rule out the use of force to compel reunification if necessary. This position remains official PRC policy, even though it is now a nonstarter for Taiwan.[48]

Broadly speaking, in pursuing its sovereignty claims, Beijing immediately confronts and impinges upon the sovereignty concerns of rival claimants—precisely the kind of "hegemonic" and interfering behavior that Beijing condemns in others. More to the point, China's encroachments on others' sovereignty generates distrust, pushback, and even violent conflict. The most troubling potential outcomes arise from remaining territorial disputes in the Himalayas, with Taiwan, and in the East China and South China Seas. However, unlike with China's past territorial settlements, Xi Jinping does not appear open on these remaining sovereignty disputes to finding compromise that might allow for long-term peaceful coexistence, which raises perhaps the greatest dilemma of all. Stripped to its bare essentials, China's approach to its remaining territorial claims—and especially regarding Taiwan—seem to leave only two outcomes: triumph or catastrophe. Either result can only come at a very high cost.

Wealth

Chapter 4 examined the pursuit of national wealth and prosperity as one of the key ambitions propelling PRC foreign policy under Xi Jinping, the domestic imperatives driving that ambition, and some of Xi's major economic initiatives—such as the BRI and Made in China 2025—which underpin this element of

Chinese foreign policy. During the Xi Jinping era, China has enjoyed enormous economic success, claiming the eradication of abject poverty at home while also overtaking the United States on a number of economic indicators: China's economy is already larger than the United States' based on purchasing power parity calculations and could become the world's largest economy in nominal gross domestic product (GDP) terms by the mid- to late 2020s.[49]

Nevertheless, in spite of these positive developments for China's wealth and prosperity, difficult challenges lie ahead for the country's economy. Some of these are long-standing structural challenges and will prove difficult to surmount. Others have arisen more recently. How PRC leaders choose to address these challenges will have profound effects on China's foreign relations—at times for the better but also for the worse—as the very solutions Beijing has in mind will exacerbate preexisting tensions in China's foreign economic relationships with developed and developing countries alike.

These economic challenges arise from two dilemmas, one internal and one external. Internally, moving up the prosperity ladder to avoid the middle-income trap and become a high-income country will continue to be a pressing priority but also an ongoing challenge. Following a burst of year-on-year growth in 2021 following the steep downturn induced by covid-19, China's economic growth will nevertheless remain well below its previous pace in future years as significant increases in gross domestic product (GDP) per capita will become more and more difficult to achieve. China's demographics are an immutably big reason for this as the growing number of elderly will need to be supported by a dwindling working-age population.[50] In addition, as Stanford University scholars Scott Rozelle and Natalie Hell argue, the deepening socioeconomic inequalities in China accompanying its economic growth—such as in education and income, and between urban and rural areas—may also stymie the country's goal of escaping the middle-income trap.[51]

China's slowing productivity is another domestic challenge that will affect future national wealth. According to the International Monetary Fund, China's post-covid-19 recovery relied very heavily on government financial support, which only extended the burden of poorly performing, capital-intensive SOEs. On the whole, PRC SOEs operate about 20 percent less productively than their private counterparts.[52] But because of their social, political, and economic significance within the Chinese system, SOEs still retain privileged access to resources such as capital and land while putting a disproportionate drag on the economy. State-sector reforms are much needed and should include the closure of loss-making firms, stricter budgetary controls on SOEs, and allowing the market to have a greater say in the allocation of resources. More broadly, pressures will mount for the state and Party to reduce their role in the economy, allow for greater market-driven choices to allocate factors of production—such as capital and land—and strengthen a more predictable legal and regulatory system governed by the rule of law.

But for the current PRC leadership, doing what is necessary to address these internal challenges appears to be too politically and socially risky. If anything, state and Party intervention in the economy has increased, including the governance of SOEs and the private sector. Empowered and made confident by the PRC's economic success of the past two decades, the Party under Xi Jinping seems reluctant to diminish its role in the economy. This probably augurs well for the Party's grip on power for the near to medium term, but may stall China's effort to escape the middle-income trap.[53]

Externally, China's future economic trajectory faces challenges as well. For example, access to foreign inputs to help improve productivity and economic growth—such as technology, capital, and markets—has also become increasingly problematic for Beijing in recent years. In response, Beijing seeks greater indigenous innovation, a process that has intensified under Xi Jinping as reflected in Made in China 2025; promotion of consumption-led growth and higher-value, high-tech exports; and a focus on "domestic circulation." However, despite these efforts, China is far from technological self-sufficiency and remains dependent on foreign technologies, market access, and high-end talent, especially in certain foundational technologies, such as semiconductors, which will be crucial to the development of other advanced industrial sectors. China scholar Mathieu Duchâtel points out that the value of PRC imports of semiconductors is higher than its total imports from the European Union and more than its oil imports, and that the country only produces about 15 percent of its domestic requirements. He writes, "The world's largest consumer market for semiconductor and integrated circuits depends on foreign suppliers not only for finished processors and other chips, but also for critical equipment and software at each stage of the value chain."[54] In this critical sector and others, the intensifying and more protectionist technological competition between China and other major economies—such as the United States, Japan, and Germany—will complicate Beijing's pursuit of greater productivity, innovation, and self-sufficiency.

Tellingly, the major initiatives under Xi intended to address these challenges— such as the BRI and promoting indigenous innovation—have generated their own headwinds and pushback, further complicating China's economic prospects. In spite of its high profile, high spending, and potential benefits, it is still too early to know whether, when compared to alternative policies, the BRI will address China's long-term socioeconomic challenges or actually exacerbate the country's structural economic inefficiencies.[55] Moreover, international concerns continue to shadow this massive initiative, including the lack of transparency, accountability, and sustainability of BRI projects; corruption and kickbacks associated with BRI deals; lack of quality infrastructure; environmental damage; and use of

Chinese rather than local labor to build and operate BRI projects.[56] As the strategic and security implications of the BRI become increasingly evident, alarm bells are going off in capitals around the world.[57] In one prominent example, the Australian federal government in 2021 terminated the BRI agreement reached a few years earlier between the PRC and the Australian state of Victoria, citing concerns over national security and foreign interference. In the midst of growing apprehensions about the BRI's impact on European Union (EU) internal cohesion, economic competitiveness, and regional security interests, 27 of the EU member states' 28 ambassadors to China (Hungary being the only holdout) co-signed a report in 2019 criticizing the BRI for its lack of transparency, discriminatory practices against foreign businesses, and poor record for fiscal and environmental sustainability.[58]

A number of studies have debunked accusations that Beijing intentionally burdens BRI partners with unsustainable debt—so-called debt-trap diplomacy.[59] Nonetheless, China has not succeeded in shaking off the stigma as many countries (including Djibouti, Kyrgyzstan, Laos, the Maldives, Mongolia, Montenegro, Pakistan, and Tajikistan) are facing debt distress as a result of BRI-related financing.[60] Despite much international and domestic pressure, China has not joined the Paris Club, a group of countries that coordinate debt relief.[61] These and other criticisms prompted Beijing to pull back and adjust the BRI's ambition and focus. However, even some efforts to rebrand the BRI—for example, placing an emphasis on digital technologies rather than infrastructure construction—raise concerns about the export of PRC surveillance, monitoring, and censoring technologies to bolster "technology-enabled authoritarianism" across parts of the Middle East, Africa, and Asia.[62] The BRI's inroads across Eurasia and into Africa have spurred other governments—such as the United States, the EU, Australia, India, Japan, New Zealand, South Africa, and South Korea—to expand their own economic assistance and infrastructure development programs in these regions both unilaterally and in concert with other like-minded partners.[63] In short, while the BRI will remain the core element of China economic statecraft, it will face intensified scrutiny, competition, and pushback as governments and societies around the world rethink the cost-benefit ratio of engagement with this signature foreign policy initiative under Xi Jinping.[64]

Likewise, China's pursuit of technological innovation—whether through foreign acquisitions or home-grown efforts such as Made in China 2025—faces a range of potential chokepoints both at home and abroad. U.S.-China economic competition intensifies this challenge as it moves beyond trade to encompass technology and financial markets. U.S. actions have included the restriction of exports to key PRC technology firms, banning investments in Chinese companies deemed to have links with the PLA, delisting major PRC companies from U.S. stock exchanges, trying to compel the sale of PRC companies to U.S. competitors, ordering the possibility of sanctions against financial institutions doing business in Hong Kong, stemming the flow of PRC scientists and technical experts seeking to work and study in the United States, and stepping up scrutiny of PRC talent recruitment programs.

Other advanced economies, including the EU, individual European governments, and Australia, have stepped up their scrutiny of PRC investments and other technology acquisition channels. In a major blow to China's expectations for improved economic relations with Europe, the anticipated approval of the EU-PRC Comprehensive Agreement on Investment (CAI) was indefinitely postponed by the European Parliament after Beijing sanctioned five of its members (as well as other European institutions and individuals) for their views on the human rights situation in Xinjiang.[65] As these and other advanced economies take up similar measures, China's access to foreign technology, capital and expertise will be increasingly constrained, especially in cutting-edge fields. This will be all the more so if and as PRC government and business entities increasingly turn to covert measures to acquire illicitly critical technologies they cannot access otherwise. In the words of Brookings Institution scholar Ryan Haas, "The more adversarial Beijing's relationship with other advanced powers becomes, the more longshot will its attempts be to achieve technological self-reliance."[66] How this strategic competition unfolds will profoundly affect China's future economic prospects, especially in highly sensitive areas of advanced technology.

A resulting bifurcation of the global economy, one that detaches elements of the PRC economy from their most prized markets and supply chains, could have a crippling effect on China's growth and economic aspirations. Having set lofty political expectations for economic success in the coming decades, Beijing faces the challenge of achieving increased productivity, greater self-reliance, and heightened income levels even as its economic and technological competition with other advanced countries continues to escalate. More broadly, Chinese leaders will continue to struggle to overcome the country's deficiencies in the fundamental building blocks of long-term wealth generation—produced capital, human capital, and natural capital—where China lags far behind its principal competitor, the United States.[67] These challenges for PRC's continued pursuit of expanded wealth and prosperity will remain difficult—and perhaps insurmountable—obstacles on the road to national rejuvenation.

Power

Chapter 5 outlined how China pursues and exercises hard power as a critical aspect of its engagement with the rest of the world, with a particular focus on economic leverage and military coercion. All countries seek to wield hard power in order to shape the choices of others, and China is no exception. The difference during the Xi Jinping era is the convergence of vastly increased economic and military might on the one hand and the intensified focus on realizing the "great rejuvenation of the Chinese nation" on the other. As a result, Beijing more frequently turns to its hard power toolbox to threaten, coerce, or buy others' alignment with its preferences and shape a strategic environment more favorable to PRC interests.

China's ability to wield economic leverage against others is arguably its single most powerful advantage on the international playing field. Nations large and small are keen to benefit from economic ties with China, whether that is by supplying its enormous and increasingly wealthy domestic market, enjoying the benefits of PRC investments and exports, or establishing profitable partnerships. As a result, these countries can be more sensitive to PRC interests for fear of losing out on opportunities for economic gain. As the world's largest trading nation and largest manufacturing economy, with the largest foreign exchange reserves, and as one of the largest sources of outbound investment and development assistance, Xi's China has understandably built and brandished economic hard power as a core element in the country's foreign policy strategy. Militarily too, the PRC today is far more capable and far more willing to employ coercive hard power means around its periphery—in the East China Sea, across the Taiwan Strait, in the South China Sea, in the Himalayas—and beyond to shape the decisions of others in Beijing's favor.

However, these advances in PRC hard power have not gone unchallenged nor have they all been successful.[68] To begin with, many uses of PRC hard power have backfired, not only failing to gain Beijing's preferred outcomes but in many cases hardening the positions of the intended target—in essence making an already unfavorable situation even worse for PRC interests. The plummeting perceptions of China and its leadership noted above, especially in advanced democratic countries, can be partially explained by Beijing's overreach in trying to shape others' behavior through threats, punishments, and inducements. In Europe, for example, neither the inducements of the China market nor the imposition of Chinese sanctions has resulted in certain preferred outcomes for Beijing in its relations with the EU: the European supragovernment has not recognized China as a "market economy" to facilitate trade and investment ties; it has not lifted the embargo on arms sales to the PRC; the EU and many individual European governments have criticized Beijing and issued sanctions against PRC entities for abuses in Xinjiang and Hong Kong; and (as noted above) Brussels has indefinitely suspended approval of the CAI. Taiwan appears to be another example: in spite of China's stepped-up campaign of intimidation, Taiwan's public opinion has not shifted at all in favor of reunification—in fact, quite the opposite. It is true that PRC economic inducements—such as access to the China market, technology exports, infrastructure projects, development assistance, and other "positive" goods—help maintain a favorable image for the country in many parts of the world and help ensure alignment with Beijing's interests. But at the same time, much of the world is pushing back against unwelcome forms of PRC hard power and doing so in ways that will undermine China's ambitions.

This backlash appears most prominently in the form of hard power responses *against* China. The United States has been most active in taking punitive hard power measures of its own as a way of constraining Chinese power. At the strategic level, the U.S. National Security Strategy, issued in December 2017, identifies China as a "revisionist power" that aims to "shape a world antithetical to U.S. values and interests" and that "seeks to displace the United States in the Indo-Pacific region, expand the reaches of its state-driven economic model, and reorder the region in its favor."[69] Similarly, the 2018 U.S. National Defense Strategy considers China as a long-term strategic competitor "which seeks Indo-Pacific regional hegemony in the near-term and displacement of the United States to achieve global pre-eminence in the future."[70] In response, in 2020 alone, the Trump administration took more than 200 different actions against PRC interests, including blacklisting PRC firms and government agencies for human rights violations, closing the PRC consulate in Houston, issuing restrictions on PRC journalists and media platforms in the United States, curbing entry visas for PRC scientists and other scholars, designating telecom giants Huawei and ZTE as national security threats, indicting and arresting Chinese citizens for espionage and other illegal activities, introducing tighter restrictions on companies associated with the PRC military from doing business with U.S. firms, and issuing sanctions against 90 PRC entities and individuals. These actions were part of the Trump administration's "whole-of-government" approach, launched with the aim of protecting the interests of the United States and its partners against what it termed a "revisionist" and "increasingly assertive China."[71]

The Biden administration left many of these orders in place and took actions of its own.[72] For its part, the U.S. Congress deliberated the Strategic Competition Act of 2021, which, in the words of the Senate Foreign Relations Committee chairman, presents "an unprecedented bipartisan effort to mobilize all U.S. strategic, economic, and diplomatic tools for an Indo-Pacific strategy that will allow our nation to truly confront the challenges China poses to our national and economic security." The legislation, he said, "is a recognition that this moment demands a unified, strategic response that can rebuild American leadership, invest in our ability to out-compete China, and reground diplomacy in our core values."[73]

The U.S. government encourages other countries to restrict PRC economic activities deemed threatening to the interests of the United States, its allies, and other partners. Most prominent in this regard are restrictions levied against

Huawei and other PRC telecommunications companies involved in the development of fifth-generation (5G) wireless networks around the world. Governments and communications companies in countries including Australia, the Czech Republic, Denmark, Estonia, France, Greece, India, Japan, Latvia, Poland, Romania, South Korea, Spain, Sweden, and the United Kingdom have taken steps to limit or entirely prohibit Huawei and other PRC telecommunications firms from participating in 5G networks, offering mobile telephone services and applications, or providing core equipment in telecommunications systems.[74]

Beijing also faces pushback in the form of military hard power. Announced in 2011, the Obama administration's "pivot" or "rebalance" to Asia committed to deploy 60 percent of U.S. naval power to the Asia-Pacific, established a rotating presence of several thousand U.S. Marines to train each year with counterparts near Australia's northern city of Darwin, and strengthened alliance cooperation with Japan. The Trump administration continued this trend, increasing U.S. naval and air presence in and over the South China Sea and around Taiwan. It also expanded arms sales to Taiwan, including announcements for a planned $5.1 billion in weapons exports in 2020 alone and deepening defense ties with Taipei; the Biden administration further strengthened political and defense ties with Taiwan.[75] When the Trump administration announced in 2019 its withdrawal from the Intermediate-range Nuclear Forces (INF) agreement—citing Russia's noncompliance with the accord—it also flagged China's deployment of intermediate-range missile systems and their threats to U.S. interests in the Asia-Pacific as an additional reason for leaving the INF treaty. Since then, the United States has initiated previously restricted ballistic and cruise missile development programs in order to range PRC targets, in addition to other offensive and defensive systems to counter Chinese missile threats.[76] The Biden administration likewise signaled its resolve to maintain and strengthen its military deterrent vis-à-vis China by continuing the "Pacific Deterrence Initiative." This multiyear, multibillion-dollar plan aims to build a "forward-deployed, defense-in-depth posture" by bolstering defenses around America's major bases in the Western Pacific, such as in Guam, and deploying and dispersing ground-based missiles, radar and other communications systems, logistics, maintenance and refueling facilities, and other military assets around the region, all with China very much in mind.[77]

Other governments, unilaterally and in partnership with others in the region, also announced their intention to improve and expand their military presence in the Indo-Pacific, including in and around the South China Sea. Over 2020 and 2021, the United Kingdom, France, and Germany all sent naval forces on extended tours to the region. These visits included joint exercises with Asia-Pacific partners such as the United States, Japan, and Australia.[78] In a major announcement, Australia, the United Kingdom, and the United States formed the AUKUS partnership, a pact that will have as its flagship program the provision of nuclear-powered attack submarines to Australia and include additional trilateral defense cooperation in cyber, quantum, and artificial intelligence technologies.[79] While these activities are not openly linked to China, all of these governments have repeatedly expressed their concerns about the PRC's assertive activities in the region and the need to peacefully resolve disputes in accordance with international law.

As Scott Kastner and Margaret Pearson show in their research, it is often difficult to clearly determine the intentions, mechanisms, agents, and outcomes of PRC economic influence.[80] The same could be said about aspects of military hard power. Nonetheless, numerous episodes strongly suggest that China's foreign policy under Xi Jinping is increasingly willing and able to brandish hard power as an instrument of statecraft. Moreover, those measures have often been met with harsh, negative reactions, including hard power economic and military pushback. Overall, Beijing's relations with many of its near neighbors and other key partners—especially those who have borne the brunt of PRC hard power—have grown more problematic during Xi Jinping's time in office. These developments not only make China's pursuit and use of hard power more challenging, but also complicate Beijing broader aspirations for national rejuvenation. However, as discussed further below, in spite of these risks, Beijing will continue to exercise coercive economic and military power in pursuit of its interests in the belief that not doing so is even riskier.

Leadership

As discussed in chapter 6, Chinese leaders over the centuries have traditionally asserted China's centrality and preeminence befitting its geographic and demographic weight; historical continuity, achievements, and influence; long periods of dynastic wealth and power; and even divine authority—the so-called mandate of heaven. Even during decades of decline and chaos from the mid-19th to the mid-20th centuries, including the turbulent years of Mao Zedong's rule, Chinese leaders sought the global stage and yearned to regain the country's "rightful place" among the world's leading nations. As China ascended the ranks of national power, and especially once Xi Jinping took the reins in 2012, Beijing set aside the low-profile approach of his immediate predecessors, took advantage of developments on the international scene that weakened other major powers such as the United States, and asserted China's right to a place at the center of the world stage. Today, the PRC shoulders greater leadership responsibilities within the UN system and other international bodies, plays a leadership role in new institutions it has helped found and build, takes the lead in pioneering critical new technologies, and aims to set agendas and shape decisions on pressing international governance challenges such as global health and climate change. Under Xi Jinping, China's pursuit of leadership—seeking a greater role in governing how the world operates—stands out as an indispensable element of PRC foreign policy.

However, while China's aspirations to global leadership have met with considerable success and are welcomed in many quarters, they are hampered by a number of challenges that arise from both internal and external sources. Internally, PRC leaders need only look at the experience of the United States to understand that international leadership can be burdensome and costly, not only in financial terms, but also in potential reputational cost and even the loss of Chinese lives. Such risks to CCP legitimacy will be taken on only with great caution. Moreover, scholars and officials (current and former) express concern about whether the PRC is truly prepared—strategically, conceptually, practically—to take on greater leadership roles. Renmin University professor and prominent international relations scholar Shi Yinhong strikes this cautionary note:

> As a direct result of current trends in global governance, China's chances of filling the vacuum created by the Trump administration's abandonment of America's original "global leadership role" are limited, and indeed smaller than many at home and abroad had predicted. The appeal of China's "soft power" in the world, the resources and experience available to China, are quite limited, and the domestic and international obstacles that China will encounter, including the complexities created by the coronavirus pandemic, are considerable.[81]

Shi and other experts fear China may be asserting itself too soon and too forcefully, prompting a backlash from other powers.[82]

And these experts have good reason for thinking so. In the United Nations, for example, where Beijing makes heavy political and financial investments, the PRC still meets with pushback against its aspirations for leadership within the organization. When China put forward its own candidate to run the World Intellectual Property Organization (WIPO) in 2020—which would have put the PRC in the unusually dominant position of having its citizens heading five out of 15 UN agencies—a number of countries, led by the United States, mobilized to successfully place an alternative candidate, from Singapore, in the role. The United States and others were also concerned given China's spotty record in intellectual property rights protections. The vote in the WIPO governing body was 55 to 28 against the PRC candidate, Wang Binyang, who had been a deputy director general of the organization since 2009.[83]

In another episode, China was reelected to join the UNHRC in 2020, but by its lowest vote tally ever; the 139 votes were the lowest level of support among the 15 countries up for election to the UNHRC that year and 43 fewer than Beijing received in its previous election to the body in 2016.[84] In the same year, the U.S. Department of State assigned a new envoy to the United Nations, tasked to curb China's growing influence within the UN system.[85] The incoming Biden nominee to be ambassador to the UN pledges similar vigilance. In her confirmation hearing, Linda Thomas-Greenfield said, "We know China is working across the UN system to drive an authoritarian agenda that stands in opposition to the founding values of the institution—American values. Their success depends on our continued withdrawal. That will not happen on my watch." Under subsequent questioning, Ambassador Thomas-Greenfield called China a "strategic adversary" and added, "I see what they're doing at the United Nations as undermining our values. . . . I will be working aggressively against China."[86]

Given China's critical contributions to UN peacekeeping operations (UNPKOs)—both in terms of financing and manpower—the PRC clearly wants a greater say in why and how these forces are deployed on behalf of the international community. Nonetheless, both because and in spite of these steps to expand China's contributions to UN peacekeeping, Beijing remains frustrated that it unfairly lacks the power it should have to affect decisions on UNPKOs and on broader questions of how to stabilize regions in conflict.[87] Moreover, Beijing would like to increase its leadership within the UN peacekeeping system by taking up more powerful posts with its administrative and individual mission command structure, which have traditionally been held by other countries, but has been stymied from doing so.[88]

Similarly, Beijing confronts obstacles in its efforts to build and lead its own international institutions. True, U.S. efforts failed to dissuade other governments—including some close U.S. allies—from joining the Asian Infrastructure Investment Bank (AIIB). China also hosts a number of other multilateral confabulations such as the Forum on China-Africa Cooperation and the China–Arab States Cooperation Forum. However, other such mechanisms have not fared as well in spite of significant bureaucratic, political, and financial investments. Beijing's 17 + 1 initiative in Central and Eastern Europe (CEE), for example, while making some economic inroads for China, became a political liability.[89] Many heavily promoted infrastructure projects under the initiative stalled, with a number of CEE countries complaining that China had not delivered on its investment promises. Pressures have also mounted from other EU countries, the European Commission, and the United States to convince CEE capitals to consider the political and security risks involved in a deepening relationship with China. EU leaders repeatedly express concerns that 17 + 1 is a deliberate attempt by Beijing to sow division within the EU. In many respects,

China's growing economic presence within CEE countries only exacerbated political concerns about Beijing's longer-term aims.[90]

For the 17 + 1 2021 summit, its ninth, Beijing announced the gathering would be upgraded and hosted by Xi Jinping, rather than by Premier Li Keqiang. However, in a snub to the PRC hosts, the leaders of six EU countries—Bulgaria, Estonia, Latvia, Lithuania, Romania, and Slovenia—declined to turn up, assigning lower-level representatives to attend instead, even though the virtual meeting did not require long-distance travel. Following early Chinese hype, high-profile promises, and assertions of leadership to make the 17 + 1 "a gateway" for China to Europe, the initiative instead has been likened by prominent East European observers to a "zombie"—still staggering forward but without any life.[91] Moreover, one of the European members of the group, Lithuania, formally withdrew, with the Lithuanian foreign minister openly stating that "the 17 + 1 format . . . is not useful for Europe, it is dividing Europe, because some countries have a different opinion on China than others."[92]

As noted in the previous section on wealth, governments and private sector enterprises around the world are rethinking their economic and business ties with China, concerned over the long-term implications of its aspirations to dominate the value chain for critical technologies through such efforts as Made in China 2025 and the "dual circulation" strategy. Open societies are also concerned over Beijing's attempts to establish agendas, standards, and rules in the tech sector—for example, in relation to the internet, uses of big data, and applications of surveillance technologies—which align with its authoritarian preferences. In 2020, UK prime minister Boris Johnson announced his intention to establish a "D10" group of democracies (the G7 countries of Canada, France, Germany, Italy, Japan, the United Kingdom, and the United States, plus Australia, India, and South Korea) to escape reliance on China for 5G network and other technologies and develop alternative technical and policy options.[93]

However, in spite of and because of these and other challenges to PRC leaders, Xi Jinping appears determined to continue his country's pursuit of a greater say in how the world works. China has long voiced its dissatisfaction with how the international system operates, calling it inequitable and unfair. When PRC leaders say they wish to apply Chinese wisdom to solving global challenges, they mean they wish to change the international system in ways that reflect the shifting global balance of power, and especially China's growing importance economically, diplomatically, militarily, and technologically. Xi Jinping has declared that "reforming and improving the current international system does not mean entirely replacing it, but instead developing it in a more just and reasonable direction," a message he has delivered at home and abroad on a number of occasions.[94] Nonetheless, much of the international community remains skeptical and will continue pushing back against China's expectations for global leadership.

Ideas

The PRC's pursuit and promotion of ideas formed the central focus of chapter 7. The chapter showed how big ideas have long been an important element in the PRC's approach to the world and how the strategic deployment of ideas, influence, and images to promote alignment with CCP and PRC interests is today such an important and well-resourced aspect of China's foreign relations under Xi Jinping. Unhappy with how the international competition of ideas seems to favor the interests of advanced democratic countries—especially the United States—and overlooks or disparages the PRC's accomplishments, Xi has invested enormous resources to improve China's "international narrative power" and its ability to "tell China's story well." Through the work of key CCP organs and other elements of the Party-state, Xi has promoted four big ideas in particular in an effort to shape global norms and discourse in ways more favorable to China's interests:

- A "new era" has dawned for China and the world in which China, under the CCP, will fully assume its rightful place as a respected, modernized, powerful, and world-leading nation.
- China's rise will bring about a "community of shared future for mankind" with opportunities and win-win outcomes for all.
- The world should embrace "unity with diversity" in which all countries have the right to choose their own political and social systems free from outside interference or a "one size fits all" approach privileging universal values, democracy, and free markets.
- The PRC experience has important lessons and solutions to address global problems and the national development needs of others.

However, Beijing faces a threefold challenge in having these ideas heard and heeded within the international community. First, governments and societies around the world have begun to push back, exposing and restricting many of the channels by which the Party seeks to convey its messages and ideas. In the United States and the United Kingdom, for example, a number of measures have been put in place that identify major PRC media firms as "foreign missions" and "propaganda outlets"—which allows for much government greater scrutiny of their activities—or suspend their local licenses to operate altogether.[95] With the influence activities of Party-affiliated individuals and organizations in mind, Australia has introduced a suite of legislation expressly aimed at monitoring and deterring their work.

Second, even in the absence of such restrictions, PRC propaganda faces a number of fundamental contradictions. The Party struggles to achieve much-coveted soft power and acceptance for its ideas because its attempts to gain respect and approbation are so transparently intended to serve the CCP's claim to unchallenged one-party rule and are more often than not acts of co-ercion or inducement, and hence not soft power at all.[96] In his study of China's diplomatic corps, Peter Martin explains that it is designed to be "effective at for-mulating demands, but poorly equipped to win hearts and minds," and a "system that's better at silencing critics than persuading others to share its point of view, a system that leaves the Party with tremendous international influence but few true friends."[97] The survey data at the outset of this chapter and extensive addi-tional research underscore how China's poor image in many parts of the world means Beijing's efforts to promote its ideas already face a skeptical audience, in part owing to the very messengers themselves.[98] As a result, this effort by the Party has often proven problematic for PRC external relations, particularly within open societies that find the PRC's activities intrusive, unwelcome, and even illegal.

Showcasing these tendencies in recent years, some PRC officials and media outlets have become more forthright—even combative—in criticizing Western ideals and asserting the superiority of the Chinese system. This battle of ideas has intensified during Xi Jinping's time as paramount leader. This was especially true in the early months of the covid-19 pandemic when Chinese diplomats and newspaper editorials took to the Twittersphere and other social media platforms to conduct what became known as "wolf warrior diplomacy" (战狼外交), named after a series of blockbuster action movies featuring the fictional exploits of a PRC special forces team.[99] Chinese officials touted the PRC government response to the pandemic—both in terms of quelling it at home and offering billions of dollars in assistance to international organizations, governments, and aid organizations abroad—while lambasting the response in Western countries and attacking critics who questioned the PRC's initial handling and subsequent outbreak of the disease. Chinese efforts included disinformation campaigns suggesting the deadly virus was planted in China by the U.S. military, accusing French health workers of leaving their patients to "die of hunger and disease," lobbying the Wisconsin legislature to pass a resolution commending Beijing's covid-19 response, and issuing controversial and threatening statements in other countries such as Brazil, India, Iran, Kazakhstan, Singapore, Sri Lanka, and across Europe.[100] This official Chinese ham-handedness led the European Union's chief diplomat to warn of an emergent "global battle of narratives . . . including a struggle for influence through spinning and the 'politics of generosity.' "[101] Moreover, the enormous effort to raise doubt about the virus' country of or-igin failed miserably: a survey of some 26,000 people across 25 countries found that overwhelming majorities (except in China) identify China as the source of covid-19.[102]

In seeking to defend and demand respect for the CCP and its governance of China, this more assertive official nationalism is an increasingly prominent aspect of PRC diplomacy under Xi Jinping. As Chinese nationalism flares, PRC wolf-warrior diplomats may believe they accurately represent views among their country's citizenry and the preferences of Party leaders. But they also amplify the very reasons why other countries are increasingly wary of China's rise on the world stage, thereby undermining their ability to convey positive and attractive ideas.

A third factor encumbering the promotion and acceptance of the CCP's big ideas within the international system has to do with the complexity of the system itself and the difficulty that China—and all nations—have in shaping it. This challenge sits at the heart of an intense debate over the PRC's ultimate abilities and intentions to change the world order in the decades to come. Some prominent analysts find that Xi Jinping's ideas and ambitions have a troubling vision in mind: to establish an alternative, China-centric global order, inspired by an "all under heaven" or *tianxia* (天下) tradition of ancient Chinese governance.[103] Liza Tobin, a China analyst with the U.S. government, writes, "If Beijing succeeds in realizing this ambitious vision . . . [a] global network of partnerships centered on China would replace the U.S. system of treaty alliances, the international community would regard Beijing's authoritarian governance model as a superior alternative to Western electoral democracy, and the world would credit the Communist Party of China for developing a new path to peace, prosperity, and modernity that other countries can follow."[104] Drawing in part from these views, a publication from the U.S. Department of State Policy Planning Staff in 2020 concluded that Beijing's grand vision calls for "displacing the United States as the world's foremost power and restructuring world order to conform to the CCP's distinctive way of empire."[105]

These ambitions may well reflect China's long-term aims and come to define Xi's grand idea of the "great rejuvenation of the Chinese nation." But we cannot with confidence predict that it will be so. Rather, in the near to medium term, a far more complex reality confronts China, reflecting the mix of PRC power, interests, and the opportunities and constraints of the global environment in which it must operate. Faced with these realities, Beijing must first of all pursue a multifaceted strategy to promote and implement its preferred ideas in different ways with different institutions and aspects of the international system, depending on how well they align with PRC interests and norms. For example, Beijing will try to protect and strengthen existing global governance institutions such as the United Nations Security Council, the World Trade Organization, and the Paris climate accords because they are seen as instruments through which China can effectively pursue its ideas and interests. Alternatively, the PRC might establish new institutions and operate them in an inclusive way in accordance with recognized global standards as a way to promote its strategic narratives—the AIIB stands out as a good example.[106] But Beijing will also work to change the rules and norms of some institutions if they are deemed contrary to China's national interests. China's efforts to reshape the priorities of the UNHRC, establish state-centric norms for internet governance, and gain a greater say on global technology standards illustrate its aim to establish new rules of the road.

University of Pennsylvania professor Avery Goldstein described this strategy as a mix of "reassurance, reform, and resistance."[107] Others find that Beijing's decisions to "accept," "hold up," or "invest in" the workings of global order will depend on the strategic setting of the particular global issue to be addressed by a given institution, what other options China may have, and the relative importance of China's contributions to the success of this or that regime.[108] After all, as another world-leading China scholar, Alastair Iain Johnston, argues, there is no single "world order," but instead a "world of orders." China will see benefit in supporting some of them; for others, it will seek change or just learn to live with them.[109] In sum, if indeed it is Beijing's intention to impose its ideas on the world system, it faces a highly complicated and contested road ahead, and success is far from guaranteed.

What Way Forward?

This chapter has detailed the problems Beijing's foreign policy will continue to face in its pursuit of the China Dream and national rejuvenation. These include challenges to CCP legitimacy and to its sovereignty claims, to its goals for wealth generation and the exercise of hard power, and to its aspirations for leadership and promotion of big ideas aligned with its interests. In addition, in spite of enormous investments by the Party-state to burnish China's image internationally, the country and its leadership still struggle to generate widespread positive impressions around the world. China can often wield influence to get what it wants, but has a hard time winning over friends through trust, attraction, and soft power—in short, Beijing is more feared than loved. These challenges arise from a range of sources, including long-standing structural trends within China, built-in contradictions of China's one-Party system, and increasing pushback from other countries and societies concerned with the direction of PRC strategies at home and abroad.

This is not to say that PRC foreign policy under Xi Jinping has been unsuccessful. To the contrary, Xi can rightly point to significant achievements in preserving and promoting PRC interests through the pursuit of legitimacy, sovereignty, wealth, power, leadership, and ideas. China can claim greater respect, economic heft, strength, and influence as it has moved closer to the world's center stage. The question for the future is how and whether these successes can continue in the way Xi hopes, especially given the increasing challenges he faces. Will Xi continue to pursue the six core elements of foreign policy in the same way as in the past? Or should we expect adjustments—even accommodation—in the face of the challenges ahead? And how should other countries respond to the choices Beijing makes? The concluding chapter tackles these questions.

Conclusion

A Contested Future

The great rejuvenation of the Chinese nation has reached a critical phase. The risks and challenges we face are clearly increasing. To wish for a peaceful life without struggle is unrealistic. We must fight bravely . . . and safeguard the national interests of sovereignty, security and development.

—Xi Jinping, September 2021[1]

Looking Ahead

Xi Jinping indelibly marks the foreign policy of the People's Republic of China (PRC or China). In his first decade in power, he consolidated foreign policy decision-making more closely to himself, formally enshrined "Xi Jinping Thought on Diplomacy" (习近平外交思想), and empowered organs of the Chinese Communist Party (CCP or Party) to assume even more active roles in deliberating and implementing PRC policies abroad. He drives an unabashedly more muscular approach to foreign affairs, demands greater respect for the CCP's domestic and international achievements, and asserts China's territorial claims and sovereign interests even at the risk of incurring bloody confrontations at home and with neighbors in the process. He champions bold economic ideas such as the Belt and Road Initiative and the Asian Infrastructure Investment Bank, even as China has made greater use of economic leverage as an instrument of statecraft. China's military capabilities and international footprint continue to expand. And far more than his predecessors, Xi urges the country to take on greater international leadership responsibilities while promoting "Chinese solutions" and aiming to "tell China's story well" to the world.

With Xi's continuing influence on PRC foreign policy, should we anticipate more of his muscular approach to foreign affairs? Will matters of legitimacy, sovereignty, wealth, power, leadership, and ideas remain as important for foreign policy, and will PRC leaders pursue in them in the same way as in Xi's first decade in power? Or, given the many challenges confronting PRC foreign policy, should we expect major course adjustments? How should other governments

Daring to Struggle. Bates Gill, Oxford University Press. © Oxford University Press 2022.
DOI: 10.1093/oso/9780197545645.003.0010

and societies weigh these choices by Chinese leaders, and how should these governments and societies respond? Drawing from the book's findings, this concluding chapter briefly addresses these questions and recommends how the world should prepare for an even more contested future with China in the years ahead.

Continued Struggle

In addition to the many challenges for Xi Jinping's foreign policy ambitions, his domestic agenda is likewise problematic. Two inbuilt and unresolved tensions will overshadow political, social, and economic developments on the home front for the remainder of the 2020s and will deeply affect Beijing's approach to foreign affairs. First, Xi and his leadership colleagues will confront the same dilemma as their predecessors have faced since the 1980s: any significant and sincere attempt to implement more far-reaching political and economic reforms to ensure the PRC becomes a more secure, prosperous, and contented country will by definition weaken the Party's grip. However, while past leaders could count on fast-paced economic growth to raise all boats; mitigate political, social, and economic tensions; and underpin Party legitimacy, today those prospects are less assured. Nevertheless, Xi Jinping and the Party leadership do not seem at all inclined to undertake such reform measures. Instead, he has overseen the increasing empowerment of the Party-state by bringing politics and ideology to the fore, restraining market reforms, imposing intrusive surveillance and censorship, and cracking down on dissent, intellectual freedoms, and political and religious expression. It is a risky gambit with dwindling room for maneuver, even as the CCP has irreversibly committed to achieving the "China Dream" and the "great rejuvenation of the Chinese nation."

Xi has another domestic challenge to address as well: succession politics. The transfer of power in authoritarian regimes is often messy and perilous, and the PRC is certainly no exception.[2] Ensconced in power until the late 2020s and possibly beyond, Xi nevertheless must be concerned for his future and his legacy. If, as Xi ages, he and the Party leadership continue to postpone a formal handover to a new leader, it could open the door to a destabilizing succession struggle, and all the more so if Xi experiences an unexpected demise—either physically or politically. It is possible he could orchestrate a smooth transfer of his powers and positions to a trusted successor, or he may choose to retain certain roles, such as chairman of the Central Military Commission—a post Jiang Zemin held onto for two years after he stepped down as Party chief in 2002. Or if Xi retains good health, he may wish to stay in official positions of power beyond the 2020s or even for life. (By way of comparison, Xi would not turn 80 until 2033, younger than U.S. president Biden will be at the end of his first elected term in 2025). Even if he formally steps down, he would undoubtedly want to retain considerable behind-the-scenes influence for as long as possible. In all of these scenarios, he will have his personal security and longer-term legacy foremost in mind—before, during, and after whatever succession process eventuates.

The convergence of these internal tensions with the range of foreign policy challenges detailed in chapter 8 make it increasingly clear that domestic regime security will assume an ever more central role in the PRC's geopolitical strategy going forward. PRC budgetary priorities already underscore the concern with domestic security. According to available data, since 2010 Beijing has spent more on domestic security (including on the People's Armed Police, local police and public security organs, the courts, and prosecutors) than on national defense, with that gap rising under Xi Jinping. In Xinjiang alone, spending on internal security rose 10-fold between 2007 and 2017.[3] Xi and other Party leaders are also clear about potential external threats to regime security. Xi has explicitly identified the United States as "the biggest threat to China's development and security."[4] He also openly acknowledges China-directed enmity in the international system in arguing, "Only by being self-reliant and developing the domestic market and smoothing out internal circulation can we achieve vibrant growth and development, regardless of the hostility in the outside world."[5] His recognition that the world is going through "great changes not seen in a century" (百年未有之大变局) envisions opportunities for China, but also foresees serious uncertainties and threats.[6]

Paradoxically, the very measures Xi and comrades will employ to preserve regime security—a tightening grip at home and assertiveness abroad—will likely generate further resentfulness domestically and internationally. It is possible CCP leaders will heed more temperate voices within their ranks. It is also possible that, having solidified his leadership for an indefinite period to come or having anointed a trusted successor, Xi and his closest advisors will have the confidence to adopt greater reform at home and more moderate policies abroad. But that seems unlikely. Moderate voices have been largely silenced by a Party-state under Xi that is less open to adjustment and more sensitive to criticism. Moreover, Xi Jinping has fully committed himself and the CCP to more aggressively pursuing the Party's interests at home and overseas. Xi firmly owns this strategy and has the Party's blessing to implement it. So, having promised a timeline to rejuvenation and with a triumphant nationalism increasingly in the air, a course alteration by Xi—or worse, backing away—would be a sign of weakness not only for the general population but for friends and foes alike, waiting in the wings as would-be successors. Instead, in the face of these domestic and external challenges, expect Xi and the Party faithful to double down. As Xi makes clear,

> A range of risks and challenges threaten the leadership of the Chinese Communist Party and our country's socialist system . . . threaten our country's sovereignty, security, and development interests . . . [and] threaten our country's core interest and most important principles. As long as these risks and challenges . . . come, we must resolutely fight and win the struggle.[7]

At home, this will mean increased intolerance and repression of dissent, independent-mindedness, or other signs of disloyalty, real or fabricated. This will be especially true for populations deemed insufficiently trustworthy, such as Hong Kongese, intellectuals, religious and ethnic minorities, and those suspected of sinister foreign ties, including Chinese citizens and foreign journalists, researchers, and nongovernmental organizations. Because regime legitimacy and security are closely intertwined with the six core ambitions driving PRC foreign policy, affronts to their realization will be met with even more vigorous pursuit of them. We should expect Beijing to continue pushing its sovereignty claims and ratcheting up pressure on Taiwan. We will see more urgency in generating wealth and securing hard power and leveraging that might to cajole and coerce others to align with PRC interests. Beijing will be even more forceful in promoting the legitimacy and acceptance of the Party, its form of domestic rule, and its aspirations to leadership and promotion of China-friendly ideas and norms within the international system.

This paints an ugly picture. The PRC approach objectively contributes to substantial and increasingly irredeemable deterioration in some of Beijing's most important foreign relationships. With much of the international community already concerned over the trajectory of China's domestic and foreign policy, and with many major countries taking steps to condemn and counteract those policies, these contested relationships look set to worsen. More troublingly, in an atmosphere of spiraling suspicion and combativeness, the possibilities increase for overreach and miscalculation. If the Party's performance narrative begins to falter and its appeals to ideological and cultural legitimacy ring hollow, it will increasingly stake its claim to leadership on nationalist appeals, further aggravating relationships with marginalized and "suspect" populations within China, with China's neighbors, and with countries farther afield. Nonetheless, it appears Xi has concluded that a more forceful assertion of Party-state interests at home and abroad—even as it imperils key relationships—poses less risk to regime security than alternative, more accommodating positions.

Navigating a Contested Future

With regime security foremost in mind, China's foreign policy appears determined to force a stark choice on most countries: accept and respect the Party's domestic rule and undertake policies that do not challenge—or better yet, align more closely with—PRC interests as Beijing defines them or face difficult consequences. Given this hardline position, how should other countries respond? Obviously, different countries will have different responses depending on their political, economic, security, and cultural relations with China and how they interplay with that country's domestic politics. Some countries—especially smaller and less powerful ones—have little choice but to accede to Beijing's preferences and will seek to reap rewards in doing so, such as infrastructure projects, development assistance, high-level political visits, and diplomatic support. Larger and more powerful nations will have more room for maneuver, can push back, or can strike a difficult balance that aims to maximize the benefits of relations with China while defending their interests and values when they diverge from Beijing's. Under Xi Jinping, China's foreign policy has become less and less tolerant of this latter group, which will likely face a future of increasing pressures from Beijing to accept its preferred options.

Understanding Strengths and Weaknesses

To navigate this more contested future with China, governments, businesses, and societies worldwide should keep five key points in mind. First, it is important to acknowledge and understand China's strengths and weaknesses, how the underpinnings for China's success are changing, and the contradictions increasingly confronting PRC foreign policy. This perspective recognizes that China's trajectory is not likely to be unstoppably upward and that many potential pitfalls await. These include China's slowing economic growth, diminishing productivity, aging population, and the possibility of failing to transition to high-income status. In addition, contradictions arising from Xi's policies will become more acute and apparent. For example, economic policies favoring a strong role for the Party-state raise serious medium-term concerns about China's future growth prospects, as well as the prospects for foreign businesses seeking greater access to the Chinese market. China's rapidly growing economy was a source of strength in the past but will be less so in the future, which in turn could negatively affect the Party's standing at home and Beijing's ability to wield economic clout against other major economies. Tensions also exist between China's reassurances of peaceful intent and win-win solutions on the one hand and its more forceful assertions of sovereign claims on the other. Beijing's increasing efforts to monitor, stifle, and punish critics abroad belies its ostensible commitment to noninterference in others' internal affairs. Exposing and exploiting these weaknesses and contradictions—for example, by restricting China's access to foreign sources of capital, technology, and know-how—could serve as leverage to moderate Beijing's increasingly unwelcome behaviors.

Gaining Strength in Numbers

Second, in seeking to maximize benefits in relations with China while discouraging its unwelcome behaviors, governments will find strength in numbers. This is easier said than done, as countries have differing interests vis-à-vis China—disparities Beijing will readily seek to exploit. But no one nation—not even the United States—can single-handedly succeed in resisting China's encroachments on its interests and values. In response to PRC ambitions, governments and societies globally should strengthen ongoing cooperation, as well as establish new collaborative mechanisms, as a way of countering or coopting Beijing across a range of policy areas.

Some governments will prefer to do so in existing multilateral fora, finding safety in numbers as a means to constrain or embed China with agreed-upon norms and rules of the road. In the economic realm, organizations such as the World Trade Organization (WTO), the Regional Comprehensive Economic Partnership, the Asian Infrastructure Investment Bank, the Asian Development Bank, and the Comprehensive and Progressive Trans-Pacific Partnership (CPTPP) may be able to play this role and should be strengthened for this reason. Other formal and informal multilateral and "minilateral" groupings—such as the Association of Southeast Asian Nations Regional Forum, the East Asia Summit (EAS), the Asia-Pacific Economic Cooperation (APEC) forum, and security partnerships such as the Trilateral Security Dialogue (Australia, Japan, the United States), the Quadrilateral Security Dialogue (the "Quad," involving Australia, India, Japan, and the United States), and the Australia–United Kingdom–United States (AUKUS) pact—should likewise aim to strengthen their role and capacity to shape PRC behaviors in the region to the greatest extent possible.

It will be especially important for the United States to significantly step up its engagement at the global level—such as at the United Nations and in the WTO—and in the region. This must include regular, substantive, high-level appearances in the Indo-Pacific region, including the President at the annual leadership meetings of the EAS and APEC. While politically difficult for now, the United States should nonetheless keep open the possibility of joining the CPTPP at some point in the future. Such engagement should aim to strengthen the ability of these various multilateral bodies to elicit more constructive and stabilizing actions from Beijing. There is much work to be done, as the Trump administration's skepticism and even hostility to multilateralism allowed Beijing to strengthen its role and influence across a range of global and regional bodies.

It will also mean greater engagement of American Indo-Pacific allies and partners and higher expectations that they do more—unilaterally, bilaterally with the United States, and multilaterally with other like-minded governments—to counterbalance Beijing's ambitions. It will be critically important that the United States and its allies continue to develop and deploy military capabilities that will deter PRC aggression and channel Beijing's nationalist energies toward peaceably negotiated solutions for its outstanding sovereignty disputes, especially over Taiwan. This need not be done with great fanfare, but pursued quietly and firmly. Washington needs to understand that Indo-Pacific political leaders and officials in Canberra, New Delhi, Tokyo, Seoul, Taipei, and other U.S.-friendly capitals will need to walk a fine line between Beijing and Washington. They should pursue regular high-level consultations with one another and with Washington via existing mechanisms across a host of common issues—security and military affairs, trade and investment, infrastructure and development assistance, societal resilience, and other aspects of the international rules-based order—to coordinate in response to PRC actions. Governments that are close partners with the United States—such as Australia, Japan, the Philippines, South Korea, Taiwan, and European allies—should be prepared for increased pressures from Beijing, including overt and behind-the-scenes efforts to adjust their policies to be more accommodating to PRC interests. This will include continuing hard power pressures to rethink their strategic relationship with Washington in order to put more political distance between them and the United States. Regional coordination among like-minded capitals should develop means to resist these wedge tactics.

Building Greater Resilience

Third, governments and societies around the world should continue building greater resilience to withstand pressures from Beijing to align more closely with PRC ambitions. Greater resiliency begins with a higher degree of societal understanding and awareness of the nature of the CCP and the aims of its activities abroad. A stronger light should be shone on the Party's united front, propaganda, and influence activities, including its work involving traditional and new media platforms and disinformation campaigns. Continued close scrutiny should be brought to bear on PRC efforts to access advanced technologies, know-how, and capital through investments, acquisitions, talent recruitment, stock market listings, and other means. Governments, businesses, and social organizations will need to strengthen their defenses against disruptive cyber activities and exfiltrations of sensitive information emanating from the PRC. There should also be greater efforts to reduce economic dependency on China as a way to diminish Beijing's ability to coerce or induce cooperation.

Advanced economies that have the resources to develop and deploy these measures should assist others where possible—especially in the developing countries of Africa, South Asia, and Southeast Asia, and among Pacific island nations—so they can also better withstand pressures from Beijing. For example, in the area of infrastructure construction and development assistance, such initiatives as Japan's Bay of Bengal Industrial Growth Belt and Asia-Africa Growth Corridor, the U.S.-Japan-Australia trilateral partnership for infrastructure investment in the Indo-Pacific, and the collaboration among Australia, Japan, New Zealand, and the United States to build a reliable electric power grid for Papua New Guinea represent efforts to provide developing-world countries with alternatives to China's Belt and Road Initiative (BRI). In taking these measures to build resiliency, governments and societies must avoid demonizing and alienating their fellow citizens and residents of Chinese descent who not only share concerns about unwelcome PRC activities at home and abroad, but can also be a source of insight on how to best counter them.

Preparing for the Competition of Ideas

A fourth key point concerns the nature of the competition ahead. The world has come to know China as a fierce economic competitor. Through such programs as the BRI and Made in China 2025, the dual circulation strategy, and successfully achieving high-end indigenous innovation, Xi Jinping expects China to become even more competitive economically, dominating the market across key technologies of the future. Under Xi, China has also made great strides in its military modernization to outgun nearly all of its Asian neighbors and become a near-peer competitor with the United States. This military competition will continue as China gains ground in new frontiers for military technology such as artificial intelligence and big data, autonomous systems, cyber capabilities, and hypersonic weapons.

But in addition to economic and military competition, Xi has opened a third front: a 21st-century battle for hearts and minds. This will not be a Cold War-style ideological struggle in which two major blocs—capitalists on one side led by the United States, communists on the other led by the Soviet Union—actively seek to spread their systems and expand their network of like-minded satellite states. The ideological competition with China will be more subtle and characterized by two important elements. The first will be the Party's effort to demonstrate the superiority of its political and economic system compared to others—and especially in comparison to liberal democracies—in delivering fundamental societal needs of security and prosperity. Asserting this superiority is not so much to supplant other systems as to make the point that there is not one "universal" (i.e., "Western") model for national success.

From that element of competition emerges a second: the effort to affirm that the PRC's system of Party-state authoritarianism deserves to be respected and accepted—even valued—as a legitimate form of governance to meet the challenges of the 21st century. As far as Beijing is concerned, if other nations choose to adopt aspects of the PRC model, so be it. But most importantly, from Beijing's perspective, other countries should not challenge or undermine the Party's rule. Coming from the PRC—soon to be the world's largest economy and an increasingly powerful diplomatic, military, technological, and cultural force—these ideas present a formidable challenge to democratic identity and confidence. This is all the more so as democratic countries around the world—including the United States—struggle with political dysfunction, social incohesion, and economic difficulties. Sensing an opportunity to win over converts in support of its line of thinking, Beijing will continue to drive these ideas home.

As this battle of ideas becomes a more and more prominent part of the competition with China in the years ahead, liberal societies around the world have a lot of work to do. First and foremost is the task of reinvigorating the promise of liberal societies as centers of democracy, equity, justice, dignity, cohesion, innovation, opportunity, and prosperity. In the absence of such self-reflection and -improvement, the attractiveness of liberal governance models will falter and fail. Efforts to criticize and undermine the "Party" as distinct from "the Chinese people" will also fall flat as long what the Party offers, for all of its shortcomings, nevertheless compares favorably to what PRC citizens see in parts of the democratic world.

Seek Common Ground

A fifth point involves the need to find common ground. We have entered an era of "bounded engagement," where the parameters of the possible for ties with Beijing steadily narrow and capitals around the world rethink the balance of values and interests in their relationship with a more ambitious China.[8] However, while we should prepare for a more contested future with Beijing, that should not foreclose possibilities for cooperation and mutual benefit. Economic interactions will continue. But both China and many of its economic partners are looking for ways to reduce their dependency on one another. In other areas—such as in mitigating climate change; stabilizing conflict-prone regions; coordinating development assistance; strengthening international trade and investment rules; improving disease responses; countering illegal trafficking in people, drugs, and other contraband; and limiting proliferation of weapons of mass destruction—there should be more room for cooperation and coordination. Given the chilly political climate between China and many other major powers—especially the United States—look for Beijing to devote greater resources to tackling these global challenges through its own forums with developing-world countries in Africa, the Middle East, Central Asia, and Southeast Asia where China can play a lead role and pursue outcomes conducive to PRC interests. Ideally, the world's two leading powers, the United States and China, can overcome some of their differences and put their formidable resources to work in tandem to combat the problems they share in common. But the strategic competition between the two has reached a point that makes such cooperation politically difficult and even risky in both Beijing and Washington.

Long Struggle Ahead

This book began with a question: "What does China want from the world?" My well-placed friend in Shanghai was clear in response: "To be respected in the world and receive our due. You will have to get used to it." This foresight was mostly correct.

On the one hand, under Xi Jinping, the PRC has demanded greater respect for its interests and struggled to regain its place as a world-leading power. Looking ahead, Xi will drive a foreign policy that first and foremost seeks to solidify the Party's power—unchallenged, accepted, and respected at home and abroad. He will vigorously pursue the expansion of PRC influence and hard power to become the preeminent force in critical areas around its land and maritime periphery, and especially within the first island chain and its approaches, to include the South China Sea, East China Sea, and Taiwan Strait. He will continue the quest to reconcile China's dissatisfaction with an international system it feels has wrongfully relegated it to second-class status: to fully control its sovereign claims, gain wealth and might to become an unquestioned global power, and have China's voice heard and heeded by a system of norms and rules more conducive to the Party-state's interests.[9] Along the way, he hopes to notch some wins in China's strategic competition with the United States. In the near to medium term, these pursuits will not mean achieving global supremacy or remaking the world in China's image. In spite of the outward confidence of PRC leaders, they probably understand the dangerous risks and burdensome responsibilities entailed in such ambition.

But on the other hand—and getting back to my Chinese colleague's prediction—the world has definitely not gotten "used to it." Instead, much of the world will be in an extended period of uneasy contestation with China. For China's part, having staked their future on realizing the long-wished-for goal of national rejuvenation, Xi Jinping and other PRC leaders will continue their quest for legitimacy, sovereignty, wealth, power, leadership, and ideas. The international community should welcome this if it leads to more open, productive, and mutually beneficial relations with Beijing and gives rise to a China that is increasingly prosperous, stable, just, and resolved to peacefully settling its regional and global disputes. But Chinese leaders and their counterparts around the world increasingly recognize such positive outcomes are unlikely. A long struggle lies ahead over what China wants.

Notes

Introduction

1. "Full Text: Speech by Xi Jinping at a Ceremony Marking the Centenary of the CPC," *Xinhua*, July 1, 2021, http://www.xinhuanet.com/english/special/2021-07/01/c_131 0038244.htm.
2. "People around the Globe are Divided in their Opinions of China," Pew Research Center, December 5, 2019, https://www.pewresearch.org/fact-tank/2019/12/05/peo ple-around-the-globe-are-divided-in-their-opinions-of-china/.
3. Since he became paramount leader, the imperative of "struggle" (斗争, also translated as "fight") has been a common theme throughout Xi Jinping's public statements. A search of a *People's Daily* database identifies more than 1,200 uses of the term in Xi's major speeches and in media coverage of those speeches between 2012 and 2021. See "习近平系列重要讲话数据库" ["Collection of Xi Jinping's Important Speeches Database"], at http://jhsjk.people.cn/result?searchArea=0&keywords=斗争&isFu zzy=0. I am grateful to Evan Medeiros for sharing his thoughts and research on the topic.
4. See Elizabeth C. Economy, *The World according to China* (Cambridge: Polity Press, 2022); Rush Doshi, *The Long Game: China's Grand Strategy to Displace American Order* (New York: Oxford University Press, 2021); Robert G. Sutter, *Chinese Foreign Relations: Power and Policy of an Emerging Global Force*, 5th ed. (Lanham, MD: Rowman and Littlefield, 2020); David Shambaugh, ed., *China & the World* (New York: Oxford University Press, 2020); John Garver, *China's Quest: The History of the Foreign Relations of the People's Republic of China* (New York: Oxford University Press, 2016); Thomas J. Christensen, *The China Challenge: Shaping the Choices of a Rising Power* (New York: W. W. Norton, 2016). Two other recent books are primarily aimed at an academic audience, but are among the first to explicitly interpret PRC foreign policy under Xi Jinping: Zhiqun Zhu, *A Critical Decade: China's Foreign Policy (2008–2018)* (Singapore: World Scientific Press, 2019); Hoo Tiang Boon, ed., *Chinese Foreign Policy under Xi* (Abingdon: Routledge, 2017).
5. For example, the book by Michael Pillsbury, *The Hundred-Year Marathon: China's Secret Strategy to Replace America as the Global Superpower* (New York: St. Martin's Publishing, 2016), claims to have unearthed heretofore unknown Chinese strategems and describes a long-term, secret plan to overtake the United States. Another book in a similar vein by Bill Gertz, *Deceiving the Sky: Inside Communist China's Drive for Global Supremacy* (New York: Encounter Books, 2019), describes a strategic Chinese deception campaign abetted by a purposeful American naiveté in the face of PRC ambition.

6. Writing in 2005, Feiling Wang proposed a shorter list of three drivers—political preservation of the Party, economic prosperity, and pursuit of power and prestige. See Feiling Wang, "Preservation, Prosperity and Power: What Motivates China's Foreign Policy?," *Journal of Contemporary China* 14, no. 45 (2005): 669–694. More recently, former Australian prime minister and foreign minister Kevin Rudd outlined seven "strategic priorities" in Xi Jinping's worldview: Party survival, national unity, economic growth with environmental sustainability, China's 14 bordering neighbors, China's maritime periphery, the developing world, and the global rules-based order. See Kevin Rudd, *The Avoidable War: Reflections on U.S.-China and the End of Strategic Engagement,* Asia Society Policy Institute, January 2019, pp. 20–25, https://asiasociety. org/sites/default/files/2019-01/The%20Avoidable%20War%20-%20Full%20Report. pdf. Oxford professor Rana Mitter suggests four factors driving the PRC's behavior internationally: authoritarianism, consumerism, global ambitions, and technology. See Rana Mitter, "The World China Wants: How Power Will—and Won't—Reshape Chinese Ambitions," *Foreign Affairs* 100, no. 1 (January/February 2021): 161–174.

7. On the less favorable side, see Elizabeth C. Economy, *The Third Revolution: Xi Jinping and the New Chinese State* (New York: Oxford University Press, 2018), and Carl Minzner, *End of an Era: How China's Authoritarian Revival Is Undermining Its Rise* (New York: Oxford University Press, 2018). More positive views of Xi Jinping's leadership are found in Eric X. Li, "Xi Jinping Is a 'Good Emperor,'" *Foreign Policy*, May 14, 2020, https://foreignpolicy.com/2020/05/14/xi-jinping-good-emperor-coronavirus/, and Eric X. Li, "A Tale of Two Political Systems," TED Global 2013, n.d., https://www. ted.com/talks/eric_x_li_a_tale_of_two_political_systems/discussion#t-1042237.

Chapter 1

1. From Xi Jinping, "Strengthen the Foundation for Pursuing Peaceful Development" [speech delivered at the third group study session of the Politburo of the 18th Chinese Communist Party Central Committee], January 28, 2013, in *Xi Jinping: The Governance of China* (Beijing: Foreign Languages Press, 2014), n.p.

2. Quotes from Jiang Zemin, "Hold High the Great Banner of Deng Xiaoping Theory for an All-Round Advancement of the Cause of Building Socialism with Chinese Characteristics into the 21st Century," report delivered to the 15th National Congress of the Communist Party of China, September 12, 1997, http://www.bjreview.com. cn/document/txt/2011-03/25/content_363499.htm, and "Full text of Jiang Zemin's Report at 16th Party Congress on Nov. 8, 2002," Ministry of Foreign Affairs of the People's Republic of China, November 18, 2002, https://www.fmprc.gov.cn/mfa_eng/ topics_665678/3698_665962/t18872.shtml.

3. Evan S. Medeiros, *China's International Behavior: Activism, Opportunism, and Diversification* (Santa Monica, CA: RAND, 2007), pp. 21–44.

4. Data are in current prices, using purchasing power parity terms. All dollar amounts refer to U.S. dollars. See World Economic Outlook Database, International Monetary

Fund, April 2020, https://www.imf.org/external/pubs/ft/weo/2020/01/weodata/weoselgr.aspx.

5. World Economic Outlook Database, International Monetary Fund, April 2020.

6. SIPRI Military Expenditure Database, Stockholm International Peace Research Institute, https://www.sipri.org/databases/milex.

7. These rankings drawn from "China," Central Intelligence Agency, *The World Factbook*, https://www.cia.gov/library/publications/the-world-factbook/geos/ch.html. See also "China Becomes World's Second-Largest Source of Outward FDI: Report," *Xinhua*, June 8, 2017, http://www.xinhuanet.com/english/2017-06/08/c_136350164.htm.

8. "Global Diplomacy Index 2019 Country Ranking," Lowy Institute, https://globaldiplomacyindex.lowyinstitute.org/country_rank.html.

9. On Xi's urgency, see Jude Blanchette, "Xi's Gamble: The Race to Consolidate Power and Stave Off Disaster," *Foreign Affairs* 100, no. 4 (2021): 10–19.

10. A cessation of hostilities was formally reached with the Korean Armistice Agreement of July 27, 1953. Because no peace treaty has been signed to conclude the Korean War, the parties to the conflict are still technically at war.

11. This and subsequent information on Xi Jinping's parents, upbringing, and youth is drawn from Alfred L. Chan, *Xi Jinping: Political Career, Governance, and Leadership, 1953–2018* (New York: Oxford University Press, 2022), chapter 2. See also Kerry Brown, *CEO, China: The Rise of Xi Jinping* (London: I. B. Tauris, 2016); Evan Osnos, "Born Red," *The New Yorker*, April 6, 2015, http://www.newyorker.com/magazine/2015/04/06/born-red; Chris Buckley, "From Pampered Schoolboy to Survivor: Chinese President Xi Jinping's Difficult Early Years," *Sydney Morning Herald*, October 2, 2015, https://www.smh.com.au/world/from-pampered-schoolboy-to-survivor-chinese-president-xi-jinpings-difficult-early-years-20150925-gjulpa.html.

12. Joseph Torigian, "Historical Legacies and Leaders' Worldviews: Communist Party History and Xi's Learned (and Unlearned) Lessons," *China Perspectives*, nos. 1–2 (2018): 7–15.

13. Xi discusses this period of his life in an interview filmed in 2004 by the Yan'an Educated Youth Cultural Research Association [延安知青文化研究会]. See "2004 年习近平专访:我是延安人 [2004 Xi Jinping interview: I am a Yan'an man], YouTube, posted August 25, 2014, https://www.youtube.com/watch?v=jHz7_IIVQ2M. The interview is discussed in Chris Buckley, "An Interview with Xi, Long before He Was China's Leader," *New York Times*, June 12, 2014, https://sinosphere.blogs.nytimes.com/2014/06/12/an-interview-with-xi-long-before-he-was-chinas-leader/.

14. Chan suggests that Xi may have accompanied Geng Biao to the United States for an official military-to-military visit in May 1980. See Chan, *Xi Jinping*, chapter 3.

15. David Shambaugh, *China's Communist Party: Atrophy and Adaptation* (Berkeley: University of California Press, 2008).

16. 黄相怀 [Huang Xianghuai], "重视和加强党的意识形态工作" [Emphasizing and strengthening the Party's ideological work], 中心组学习参考资料 [*Central Group Study Reference Materials*], no. 8 (2018), trans. Jude Blanchette, "Strengthening the CCP's 'Ideological Work,'" Center for Strategic and International Studies, August 13, 2020, p. 7, https://www.csis.org/analysis/strengthening-ccps-ideological-work.

17. Susan L. Shirk, *China: Fragile Superpower* (Oxford: Oxford University Press, 2007), p. 7.

18. Zhao quoted in Torigian, "Historical Legacies," p. 10, citing 宗凤鸣 [Zong Fengming], 赵紫阳软禁中的谈话 [Zhao Ziyang: Captive conversations] (Hong Kong: Kaifang Publishing, 2007), p. 348.

19. Carl Minzner, *End of an Era: How China's Authoritarian Revival Is Undermining Its Rise* (Oxford: Oxford University Press, 2018), pp. 223–28; C. Fred Bergsten, Bates Gill, Nicholas R. Lardy, and Derek Mitchell, *China: The Balance Sheet: What the World Needs to Know Now about the Emerging Superpower* (New York: PublicAffairs, 2006), chapter 3. On PRC concerns with terrorism, see Michael Clarke, ed., *Terrorism and Counterterrorism in China: Domestic and Foreign Policy Dimensions* (London: Hurst & Company, 2018).

20. See 王缉思 [Wang Jisi], "中国的国际定位问题与 '韬光养晦, 有所作为' 的战略思想" [China's international position and the strategic principle of "keeping a low profile while getting some things done"], 国际问题研究 [*International Studies*], no. 2 (2011); Huang Youyi, "Context, Not History, Matters for Deng's Famous Phrase," *Global Times*, June 15, 2011, http://www.globaltimes.cn/content/661734.shtml.

21. Rush Doshi, *The Long Game: China's Grand Strategy to Displace American Order* (New York: Oxford University Press, 2021), chapter 3.

22. Some prominent official pronouncements and explanations of these concepts include Zheng Bijian, "China's 'Peaceful Rise' to Great-Power Status," *Foreign Affairs* (September–October 2005), pp. 18–24, https://www.foreignaffairs.com/articles/asia/2005-09-01/chinas-peaceful-rise-great-power-status; *China's Peaceful Development Road* (Beijing: Information Office of the State Council, December 2005), https://www.chinadaily.com.cn/english/doc/2005-12/22/content_505678.htm; "Build Towards a Harmonious World of Lasting Peace and Common Prosperity," Statement by H.E. Hu Jintao, President of the People's Republic of China at the United Nations Summit, New York, September 15, 2005, https://www.un.org/webcast/summit2005/statements15/china050915eng.pdf. See also Bonnie S. Glaser and Evan S. Medeiros, "The Changing Ecology of Foreign Policy-Making in China: The Ascension and Demise of the Theory of 'Peaceful Rise,'" *China Quarterly* 190 (2007): 291–310, doi: 10.1017/S0305741007001208.

23. "Whither China?: From Membership to Responsibility," remarks by Deputy Secretary of State Robert Zoellick to the National Committee on U.S.-China Relations, New York, September 21, 2005, https://www.ncuscr.org/content/robert-zoellicks-responsible-stakeholder-speech.

24. Liu Yunshan, "How China Is Dealing with the Global Financial Crisis," *Qiushi* 2, no. 2 (April 2010), http://english.qstheory.cn/magazine/201002/201109/t20110920_111426.htm. At the time of writing this article, the author was head of the CCP Central Propaganda Department.

25. Liu, "How China Is Dealing with the Global Financial Crisis."

26. See a detailed discussion of these incidents in Michael Green et al., *Countering Coercion in Maritime Asia: The Theory and Practice of Gray Zone Deterrence* (Washington, D.C.: Center for Strategic and International Studies, May 2017), pp. 52–65.

27. "Remarks by President Obama to the Australian Parliament," White House Office of the Press Secretary, November 17, 2011, https://obamawhitehouse.archives.gov/the-press-office/2011/11/17/remarks-president-obama-australian-parliament;   Hillary Clinton, "America's Pacific Century," *Foreign Policy,* October 11, 2011, https://foreig npolicy.com/2011/10/11/americas-pacific-century/.

28. Kenneth G. Lieberthal and Wang Jisi, *Addressing U.S.-China Strategic Distrust,* John L. Thornton China Center Monograph Series, no. 4 (Washington, D.C.: Brookings Institution, March 2012), pp. 8–10, https://www.brookings.edu/wp-content/uplo ads/2016/06/0330_china_lieberthal.pdf.

29. "Nobel Peace Prize 2010," accessed June 16, 2020, https://www.nobelprize.org/prizes/peace/2010/summary/.

30. John Vidal and David Adam, "China Overtakes US as World's Biggest CO2 Emitter," *The Guardian,* June 19, 2007, https://www.theguardian.com/environment/2007/jun/19/china.usnews; John M. Broder, "Poor and Emerging States Stall Climate Negotiations," *New York Times,* December 16, 2009, https://www.nytimes.com/2009/12/17/science/earth/17climate.html.

31. Alice L. Miller, "The Bo Xilai Affair in Central Party Politics," *China Leadership Monitor* 38 (Summer 2012), https://www.hoover.org/research/bo-xilai-affair-cent ral-leadership-politics; Andrew Jacobs and Chris Buckley, "Chinese Official at Center of Scandal Is Found Guilty and Given a Life Term," *New York Times,* September 21, 2013, https://www.nytimes.com/2013/09/22/world/asia/bo-xilai-official-is-found-guilty-of-all-charges-and-given-life-term.html.

32. Cary Huang, "Chinese President Accuses Fallen Top Officials of 'Political Conspiracies,'" *South China Morning Post,* January 2, 2017, https://www.scmp.com/news/china/policies-politics/article/2058767/chinese-president-accuses-fallen-top-officials.

33. The research project led by Kai He and Feng Huiyun of Griffith University, in collab-oration with Yan Xuetong of Tsinghua University, titled "How China Sees the World," provides excellent and extensive research and analysis on this debate in China. See "How China Sees the World," Griffith Asia Institute, https://www.griffith.edu.au/asia-institute/our-research/how-china-sees-the-world.

34. Xi Jinping, "Remarks on the Occasion of Meeting with the Chinese and Foreign Press by Members of the Standing Committee of the Political Bureau of the Eighteenth Central Committee of the Communist Party of China," *China.org.cn,* November 16, 2012, http://www.china.org.cn/china/18th_cpc_congress/2012-11/16/content_2 7130032.htm.

35. "习近平总书记深情阐述 '中国梦'" [General Secretary Xi Jinping's heartfelt elab-oration of the "China Dream"], *Xinhua,* November 30, 2012, http://www.xinhuanet.com//politics/2012-11/30/c_124026690.htm; "Xi Pledges 'Great Renewal of Chinese Nation,'" *Xinhua,* November 30, 2012, http://en.people.cn/90785/8040389.html.

36. The following paragraphs draw in part from previous work by the author. See Bates Gill, "China's Future under Xi Jinping: Challenges Ahead," *Political Science* (2017): pp. 1–15, doi: 10.1080/00323187.2017.1313713.

37. Kiera Lu Huang, "Xi and Peng Now Have a Song of Their Own," *South China Morning Post,* November 24, 2014, https://www.scmp.com/news/china/article/1647806/xi-and-peng-now-have-song-their-own.

38. This document was translated and can be found here: "Document 9: A ChinaFile Translation," *ChinaFile,* November 8, 2013, https://www.chinafile.com/document-9-chinafile-translation.

39. *Constitution of the Communist Party of China,* revised and adopted at the 19th National Congress of the Communist Party of China, October 24, 2017, http://www.xinhuanet.com//english/download/Constitution_of_the_Communist_Party_of_China.pdf; Gloria Davies, "To Prosper or Perish," in *China Story Yearbook 2017: Prosperity,* edited by Jane Golley and Linda Jaivin (Canberra: Australian National University Press, 2018), chapter 7, especially pp. 236–239.

40. Tang Xue and Zhao Xinying, "Ministry Scrutinizes University Textbooks," *China Daily,* March 19, 2015, http://www.chinadaily.com.cn/china/2015-03/19/content_19852013.htm; Jamil Anderlini, "'Western Values' Forbidden in Chinese Universities," *Financial Times,* January 31, 2015, https://www.ft.com/content/95f3f866-a87e-11e4-bd17-00144feab7de. See also Alice Su, "Spied On. Fired. Publicly Shamed. China's Crackdown on Professors Reminds Many of Mao Era," *Los Angeles Times,* June 27, 2020, https://www.latimes.com/world-nation/story/2020-06-27/in-chinas-universities-targeted-attacks-on-intellectuals-raise-memories-of-the-cultural-revolution.

41. Edward Wong, "Xi Jinping's News Alert: Chinese Media Must Serve the Party," *New York Times,* February 22, 2020, https://www.nytimes.com/2016/02/23/world/asia/china-media-policy-xi-jinping.html.

42. "Xi Jinping Asks for 'Absolute Loyalty' from Chinese State Media," *The Guardian,* February 20, 2016, https://www.theguardian.com/world/2016/feb/19/xi-jinping-tours-chinas-top-state-media-outlets-to-boost-loyalty.

43. Reporters without Borders, *2020 World Press Freedom Index,* n.d., https://rsf.org/en/ranking/2020.

44. On these measures, see Chris Buckley, Keith Bradsher, and Elaine Yu, "Law Will Tighten Beijing's Grip on Hong Kong with Chinese Security Force," *New York Times,* June 20, 2020, https://www.nytimes.com/2020/06/20/world/asia/china-hong-kong-security-law.html; Emma Graham-Harrison and Juliette Garside, "'Allow No Escapes': Leak Exposes Reality of China's Vast Prison Camp Network," *The Guardian,* November 25, 2019, https://www.theguardian.com/world/2019/nov/24/china-cables-leak-no-escapes-reality-china-uighur-prison-camp; *The Long Arm of China: Exporting Authoritarianism with Chinese Characteristics,* Hearing before the Congressional-Executive Commission on China, 115th Congress, 2nd Session, December 13, 2017, https://www.cecc.gov/sites/chinacommission.house.gov/files/documents/GPO%20Transcript.pdf.

45. "Full Text: Communique of 6th Plenum Session of the 19th CPC Central Committee," *Xinhua,* November 11, 2021, http://www.news.cn/english/2021-11/11/c_1310305166.htm. See also, Chris Buckley et al., "Eyeing His Future, Xi Jinping Rewrites the Past," *New York Times,* November 11, 2021, https://www.nytimes.com/2021/11/11/world/asia/xi-jinping-china-third-term.html. The first such resolution, issued in 1945

under the leadership of Mao Zedong and titled "Resolution on Certain Issues in the History of the Chinese Communist Party," reviewed and rectified the Party's experience from its founding in 1921. The second, issued during the paramount leadership of Deng Xiaoping in 1981, was titled "Resolution on Certain Questions in the History of the Chinese Communist Party since the Founding of the People's Republic of China," acknowledged the mistakes of the Mao era but credited Mao for his revolutionary leadership and ideological guidance in founding the PRC.

46. Bonnie S. Glaser and Deep Pal, "Is China's Charm Offensive Dead?," *China Brief* 14, no. 15 (July 2014), https://jamestown.org/program/is-chinas-charm-offensive-dead/.

47. Yan Xuetong, "From Keeping a Low Profile to Striving for Achievement," *Chinese Journal of International Politics* 7, no. 2 (Summer 2014): 153–184, doi: 10.1093/cjip/pou027.

48. "Xi Jinping: Let the Sense of Community of Common Destiny Take Deep Root in Neighboring Countries," Ministry of Foreign Affairs of the People's Republic of China, October 25, 2013, https://www.fmprc.gov.cn/mfa_eng/wjb_663304/wjbz_663308/activities_663312/t1093870.shtml.

49. "Xi Eyes More Enabling Int'l Environment for China's Peaceful Development," *Xinhua*, November 30, 2014, http://en.people.cn/n/2014/1130/c90883-8815967-3.html.

50. "List of International Trips Made by Xi Jinping," Wikipedia, accessed June 25, 2020, https://en.wikipedia.org/wiki/List_of_international_trips_made_by_Xi_Jinping.

51. The only land- or maritime-bordering countries he did not visit were Afghanistan and Bhutan. China and Bhutan do not maintain formal diplomatic relations.

52. "Xi Jinping Hasn't Set Foot outside China for 600 Days," *Bloomberg News*, September 9, 2021, https://www.bloomberg.com/news/articles/2021-09-09/xi-jinping-hasn-t-set-foot-outside-china-for-600-days.

53. "Full Text of Xi Jinping Keynote at the World Economic Forum," *CGTN America*, January 17, 2017, https://america.cgtn.com/2017/01/17/full-text-of-xi-jinping-keynote-at-the-world-economic-forum.

54. See, for example, "Speech by H.E. Xi Jinping, President of the People's Republic of China at the Körber Foundation," Berlin, Germany, March 28, 2014, https://www.fmprc.gov.cn/mfa_eng/wjdt_665385/zyjh_665391/t1148640.shtml; "习近平：完全有信心为人类对更好社会制度的探索提供中国方案" [Xi Jinping: Fully confident to provide China solutions in humankind's search for better social systems], *Xinhua*, July 1, 2016, https://www.thepaper.cn/newsDetail_forward_1492012 (from Xi's speech to commemorate the 95th anniversary of the CCP); "人类命运共同体为全球治理提供'中国方案'" [Community of human destiny provides a "China Plan" for global governance], *Qiushi*, October 24, 2019, http://www.qstheory.cn/dukan/hqwg/2019-10/24/c_1125147150.htm.

55. "Special: China's Air Defense Identification Zone Triggers Mixed Response," *China Daily*, November 27, 2013, https://www.chinadaily.com.cn/china/2013-11/27/content_17135438.htm; for a more in-depth analysis, see Ian E. Rinehart and Bart Elias, *China's Air Defense Identification Zone (ADIZ)*, Congressional Research Service,

January 30, 2015, https://china.usc.edu/sites/default/files/article/attachments/crs-2015-china-air-defense-identification-zone.pdf.

56. "Chinese Incursions near Japan-Held Islands Top 1,000 to Hit Record, up 80% on Last Year," *Japan Times,* December 6, 2019, https://www.japantimes.co.jp/news/2019/12/06/national/politics-diplomacy/china-incursions-japan-held-islands-hit-record/.

57. Anna Mulrine, "USS Cowpens: Why China Forced a Confrontation at Sea with US Navy," *Christian Science Monitor,* December 13, 2013, https://www.csmonitor.com/World/Security-Watch/2013/1213/USS-Cowpens-Why-China-forced-a-confrontation-at-sea-with-US-Navy; Ben Blanchard and Andrea Shalal, "Angry China Shadows U.S. Warship near Man-Made Islands," *Reuters,* October 28, 2015, https://www.reuters.com/article/us-southchinasea-usa/angry-china-shadows-u-s-warship-near-man-made-islands-idUSKCN0SK2AC20151028; Ben Werner, "Destroyer USS Decatur Has Close Encounter with Chinese Warship," *USNI News,* October 1, 2018, https://news.usni.org/2018/10/01/37006.

58. M. Taylor Fravel, "China's Sovereignty Obsession: Beijing's Need to Project Strength Explains the Border Clash with India," *Foreign Affairs,* June 26, 2020, https://www.foreignaffairs.com/articles/china/2020-06-26/chinas-sovereignty-obsession.

59. Bruno Maçães, *Belt and Road: A Chinese World Order* (London: Hurst & Company, 2018). For a PRC perspective, see Wang Yiwei, *The Belt and Road Initiative: What Will China Offer the World in Its Rise* (Beijing: New World Press, 2016).

60. "Who We Are," Asian Infrastructure Investment Bank, n.d., https://www.aiib.org/en/about-aiib/index.html.

61. Phillip C. Saunders et al., eds., *Chairman Xi Remakes the PLA: Assessing Chinese Military Reforms* (Washington, D.C.: National Defense University Press, 2019); Bates Gill, Adam Ni, and Dennis Blasko, "The Ambitious Reform Plans of the People's Liberation Army: Progress, Prospects and Implications for Australia," *Australian Journal of Defence and Strategic Studies* 2, no. 1 (2020).

62. "决胜全面建成小康社会夺取新时代中国特色社会主义伟大胜利"　[Decisive victory, build a well-off society in an all-round way, win the great victory of socialism with Chinese characteristics in the new era], *PLA Daily,* October 19, 2017; see also Xi Jinping, *Secure a Decisive Victory in Building a Moderately Prosperous Society in All Respects and Strive for the Great Success of Socialism with Chinese Characteristics for a New Era,* report delivered at the 19th National Congress of the Communist Party of China, October 18, 2017, p. 48, http://www.xinhuanet.com/english/download/Xi_Jinping's_report_at_19th_CPC_National_Congress.pdf.

63. The other five permanent members of the United Nations Security Council are France, Russia, the United Kingdom, and the United States. See Bates Gill and Chin-hao Huang, *China's Expanding Role in Peacekeeping: Prospects and Implications,* SIPRI Policy Paper 25 (November 2009), https://www.sipri.org/sites/default/files/PP/SIPRIPP25.pdf.

64. "Troop and Police Contributors," United Nations Peacekeeping, https://peacekeeping.un.org/en/troop-and-police-contributors.

65. See the PRC defense white paper *China's National Defense in the New Era* (Beijing: State Council Information Office, July 2019), Tables 6 and 9.

66. "网传习近平8-19讲话全文" [Full text of Xi Jinping's 8-19 speech on the web], *China Digital Times,* November 4, 2013, https://chinadigitaltimes.net/chinese/2013/11/网传习近平8·19讲话全文：言论方面要敢抓敢管敢/ (author's translation).

67. Larry Diamond and Orville Schell, eds., *China's Influence and American Interests: Promoting Constructive Vigilance* (Stanford, CA: Hoover Institution Press, 2019); Zhou Xin, "It's the Mysterious Department behind China's Growing Influence across the Globe. And It's Getting Bigger," *South China Morning Post,* March 21, 2018, https://www.scmp.com/news/china/policies-politics/article/2138196/its-mysterious-department-behind-chinas-growing; James Kynge, Lucy Hornby, and Jamil Anderlini, "Inside China's Secret 'Magic Weapon' for Worldwide Influence," *Financial Times*, October 26, 2017, https://www.ft.com/content/fb2b3934-b004-11e7-beba-5521c713abf4?mhq5j=e7; Anne-Marie Brady, *Magic Weapons: China's Political Influence Activities under Xi Jinping* (Washington, D.C.: Woodrow Wilson Center, September 18, 2017).

68. "Xi Urges Breaking New Ground in Major Country Diplomacy with Chinese Characteristics," *Xinhua,* June 24, 2018, http://xinhuanet.com/english/2018-06/24/c_137276269.htm. For a Chinese-language summary of this speech to the 2018 Central Foreign Affairs Work Conference, see "习近平在中央外事工作会议上强调坚持以新时代中国特色社会主义外交思想为指导 努力开创中国特色大国外交新局面" [Xi Jinping stresses adherence to the guidance of diplomatic thought of socialism with Chinese characteristics in the new era, strive to create a new phase of major power relations with Chinese characteristics], *Xinhua,* June 23, 2018, http://www.ccdi.gov.cn/toutu/201806/t20180623_174367.html.

69. An early explanation of Xi Jinping Thought on Diplomacy is written by China's most senior diplomat, Yang Jiechi, "Study and Implement General Secretary Xi Jinping's Thought on Diplomacy in a Deep-Going Way and Keep Writing New Chapters of Major-Country Diplomacy with Distinctive Chinese Features," *Xinhuanet,* July 19, 2017, http://www.xinhuanet.com/english/2017-07/19/c_136456009.htm; see also the speech by PRC foreign minister Wang Yi, "Study and Implement Xi Jinping Thought on Diplomacy Conscientiously and Break New Ground in Major-Country Diplomacy with Chinese Characteristics," Ministry of Foreign Affairs of the People's Republic of China, July 20, 2020, https://www.fmprc.gov.cn/mfa_eng/zxxx_662805/t1799305.shtml.

70. "Xi Urges Breaking New Ground" and "Xi Jinping stresses adherence."

71. This quotation is from Yuan Peng, president of the China Institutes of Contemporary International Relations, one of the country's premier research centers for international affairs, affiliated with the Ministry of State Security. 袁鹏 [Yuan Peng], "世界'百年未有之大变局'之我见" [My view on the world's "great changes not seen in a century"], 现代国际关系 [*Contemporary International Relations*], no. 1 (2020). For other authoritative interpretations of the "great changes," see "百年未有之大变局:重识中国与世界的关键" [Profound changes not seen in a century: The key to understanding China and the world], 探索与争鸣 [*Exploration and Free Views*] 1, no. 1 (2019): 4–31; "从大历史视野看百年未有之大变局" [Looking at the profound changes not seen in a century from a grand historical perspective], Central

Commission for Discipline Inspection, May 14, 2020, http://www.ccdi.gov.cn/lswh/lilun/202005/t20200514_217207.html; and 袁鹏 [Yuan Peng], "新冠疫情与百年变局" [The new coronavirus epidemic and the once-in-a-century transformation], *Aisixiang,* June 17, 2020, available in English at Yuan Peng, "Corona Virus Pandemic," *Reading the China Dream,* n.d., intro. and trans. David Ownby, https://www.readingthechinadream.com/yuan-peng-coronavirus-pandemic.html.

72. "Full Text: Speech by Xi Jinping at a Ceremony Marking the Centenary of the CPC," *Xinhua,* July 1, 2021, p. 9, http://www.xinhuanet.com/english/special/2021-07/01/c_1310038244.htm.

73. See, for example, his use of this phrasing in the speech celebrating the 100th anniversary of the CCP. "习近平：在庆祝中国共产党成立100周年大会上的讲话" [Xi Jinping: Speech at the celebration commemorating the 100th anniversary of the Chinese Communist Party], 新华社 [*Xinhua*], July 1, 2021, http://www.xinhuanet.com/2021-07/01/c_1127615334.htm.

74. Some excellent examples and analysis of this debate appear in a special issue titled "China Debates Its Global Role," *Pacific Review* 33, nos. 3–4 (2020): 357–696. See also "How China Sees the World," Griffith Asia Institute, https://www.griffith.edu.au/asia-institute/our-research/how-china-sees-the-world.

Chapter 2

1. Quoted from a speech given during his "southern tour" in December 2012, and analyzed in 聞 路 [Wen Lu], "習近平南巡內部講話" [Xi Jinping southern tour internal speech], *Open,* March 8, 2013, http://www.open.com.hk/content.php?id=1197#.X1Xbzi17GYX.

2. John Garver's magisterial volume focuses on these "internal-international linkages" as a coherent analytical framework for understanding much of the seven-decade sweep of PRC foreign policy. See John W. Garver, *China's Quest: The History of the Foreign Relations of the People's Republic of China* (New York: Oxford University Press, 2016). Likewise, Pu describes the complex linkages between an all-important concern with domestic legitimacy on the one hand and pursuit of international status on the other. See Xiaoyu Pu, *Rebranding China: Contested Status Signaling in the Changing Global Order* (Redwood City, CA: Stanford University Press, 2019).

3. Steve Tsang, "Party-State Realism: A Framework for Understanding China's Approach to Foreign Policy," *Journal of Contemporary China* 29, no. 122 (2020): 305, https://doi.org/10.1080/10670564.2019.1637562.

4. "Xi Urges Breaking New Ground in Major Country Diplomacy with Chinese Characteristics," *Xinhua,* June 24, 2018, http://xinhuanet.com/english/2018-06/24/c_137276269.htm. For a Chinese language summary of this speech to the 2018 Central Foreign Affairs Work Conference, see "习近平在中央外事工作会议上强调坚持以新时代中国特色社会主义外交思想为指导 努力开创中国特色大国外交新局面" [Xi Jinping stresses adherence to the guidance of diplomatic thought

of socialism with Chinese characteristics in the new era, strive to create a new phase of major power relations with Chinese characteristics], *Xinhua*, June 23, 2018, http://www.ccdi.gov.cn/toutu/201806/t20180623_174367.html.

5. "2019 年中国共产党党内统计公报" [2019 Chinese Communist Party internal Party statistical bulletin], *Xinhua*, June 30, 2020, http://www.chinamil.com.cn/jmy wyl/2020-06/30/content_9843712.htm.

6. On China's pursuit of "status" and "prestige" within the international system, see, for example, Alastair Iain Johnston, *Social States: China in International Institutions, 1980–2000* (Princeton, NJ: Princeton University Press, 2008); Yong Deng, *China's Struggle for Status: The Realignment of International Relations* (Cambridge: Cambridge University Press, 2008); Pu, *Rebranding China*.

7. Max Weber, *The Theory of Economic and Social Organization*, ed. A. M. Henderson, trans. A. M. Henderson and Talcott Parsons (London: Collier-Macmillan, 1947), p. 328.

8. Garver, *China's Quest*, 5–10, 13–18.

9. *Constitution of the Communist Party of China*, revised and adopted at the 19th National Congress of the Communist Party of China, October 24, 2017, http://www.china.org.cn/20171105-001.pdf.

10. Odd Arne Westad, ed., *Brothers in Arms: The Rise and Fall of the Sino-Soviet Alliance, 1945–1963* (Washington, D.C., and Stanford, CA: Woodrow Wilson Center Press and Stanford University Press, 1998); Austin Jersild, *The Sino-Soviet Alliance: An International History* (Chapel Hill: University of North Carolina Press, 2014).

11. Garver, *China's Quest*, pp. 171–173.

12. Chen Jian, *Mao's China and the Cold War* (Chapel Hill: University of North Carolina Press, 2001).

13. See, for example, the speech by U.S. secretary of state Michael R. Pompeo, *Communist China and the Free World's Future*, delivered at the Richard Nixon Presidential Library and Museum, Yorba Linda, California, July 23, 2020, https://www.state.gov/commun ist-china-and-the-free-worlds-future/.

14. Peter Hays Gries, *China's New Nationalism: Pride, Politics, and Diplomacy* (Berkeley: University of California Press, 2004), especially chapter 3.

15. "Full Text: Speech by Xi Jinping at a Ceremony Marking the Centenary of the CPC," *Xinhua*, July 1, 2021, http://www.xinhuanet.com/english/special/2021-07/01/c_131 0038244.htm.

16. Peter Gries, "Nationalism, Social Influences, and Chinese Foreign Policy," in David Shambaugh, ed., *China & the World* (New York: Oxford University Press, 2020), chapter 4.

17. Garver, *China's Quest*, pp. 10–12. On the instrumentalization of nationalism for Party legitimacy, see also Thomas Christensen, "Chinese Realpolitik," *Foreign Affairs* 75, no. 5 (1996): 37–52.

18. Jessica Chen Weiss, *Powerful Patriots: Nationalist Protest in China's Foreign Relations* (Oxford: Oxford University Press, 2014); James Reilly, *Strong Society, Smart State: The Rise of Public Opinion in China's Japan Policy* (New York: Columbia University Press, 2012).

19. Gries, "Nationalism, Social Influences, and Chinese Foreign Policy."

20. "UPDATE 5: China Struggles to Curb Anger as Protests Denounce Japan," *Reuters,* September 16, 2012, https://www.reuters.com/article/2012/09/16/china-japan-idUSL3E8KG02T20120916?type=marketsNews.

21. Rana Mitter, *China's Good War: How World War II Is Shaping a New Nationalism* (Cambridge, MA: Harvard University Press, 2020).

22. The term "wolf warrior diplomacy" draws from the titles of two blockbuster action films that depict the patriotic exploits of Chinese special forces commandoes. One of the earliest uses of the term appears to be in "中美外交官推特骂战再起,中国外交愈趋'战狼化'?" [China-U.S. diplomatic Twitter feud escalates, China diplomacy increasingly "wolf warrior-esque"?], *BBC News* [Chinese-language service], July 17, 2019, https://www.bbc.com/zhongwen/simp/world-49012321. See also "West Feels Challenged by China's New 'Wolf Warrior' Diplomacy," *Global Times,* April 16, 2020, https://www.globaltimes.cn/content/1185776.shtml; Alex W. Palmer, "The Man behind China's Aggressive New Voice," *New York Times Magazine,* July 7, 2021, https://www.nytimes.com/2021/07/07/magazine/china-diplomacy-twitter-zhao-lijian.html.

23. Anne-Marie Brady, "State Confucianism, Chineseness, and CCP Propaganda," in Anne-Marie Brady, ed., *China's Thought Management* (New York: Routledge, 2012), pp. 57–75.

24. Aleksandra Kubat, "Morality as Legitimacy under Xi Jinping: The Political Functionality of Traditional Culture for the Chinese Communist Party," *Journal of Current Chinese Affairs* 47, no. 3 (2018): 47–86, quotes from 49–50.

25. Delia Lin, "The CCP's Exploitation of Confucianism and Legalism," in Willy Lo-Lap Lam, ed., *The Routledge Handbook of the Chinese Communist Party* (London: Routledge, 2017), pp. 47–58.

26. Xi Jinping speaking at the 2013 National Conference on Propaganda and Ideological Work, quoted in "习近平总书记关于'文化自信'的重要论述" [Important statements of General Secretary Xi Jinping on "cultural confidence"], Information Office of the State Council of the People's Republic of China, August 30, 2016, http://www.scio.gov.cn/tt/Document/1489005/1489005.htm.

27. 王毅 [Wang Yi], "深入学习贯彻习近平外交思想不断开创中国特色大国外交新局面" [Deeply study and implement Xi Jinping Thought on Diplomacy, continue innovations in major power diplomacy with Chinese characteristics], *Qiushi* 15 (2020), http://www.qstheory.cn/dukan/qs/2020-08/01/c_1126305967.htm.

28. 中国共产党章程 [*Constitution of the Chinese Communist Party*], October 24, 2017, http://www.12371.cn/2017/10/28/ARTI1509191507150883.shtml; *Constitution of the Communist Party of China,* revised and adopted at the 19th National Congress of the Communist Party of China, October 24, 2017, 10, http://www.xinhuanet.com//english/download/Constitution_of_the_Communist_Party_of_China.pdf.

29. Garver, *China's Quest,* 1.

30. Suisheng Zhao, "China's Foreign Policy Making Process: Players and Institutions," in Shambaugh, *China & the World,* chapter 5; Garver, *China's Quest.* On rebuilding

the Party, see David Shambaugh, *China's Communist Party: Atrophy and Adaptation* (Berkeley: University of California Press, 2008), especially chapters 7 and 8.

31. Zhimin Lin, "Xi Jinping's 'Major Country Diplomacy': The Impacts of China's Growing Capacity," *Journal of Contemporary China* 28, no. 115 (2019): 31–46, https://doi.org/10.1080/10670564.2018.1497909; Suisheng Zhao, "China's Foreign Policy Making Process: Players and Institutions," in Shambaugh, *China & the World*, 90–91.

32. "Xi Jinping Thought on Diplomacy Research Center Inaugurated," *Xinhua*, July 20, 2020, http://www.xinhuanet.com/english/2020-07/20/c_139227032.htm.

33. "Xi Urges Breaking New Ground."

34. Wang Yi, "Deeply study and implement Xi Jinping Thought on Diplomacy"; David Bandurski, "A Diplomatic Bow to Xi Jinping," China Media Project, August 3, 2020, https://chinamediaproject.org/2020/08/03/wang-yis-discourse-of-diplomacy/.

35. Qian Gang, "Diplomatic Moves toward 'Xi Thought,'" China Media Project, July 27, 2020, http://chinamediaproject.org/2020/07/27/diplomatic-moves-toward-xi-jinping-thought/; David Bandurski, "Wang Yi and the 'Ghost of McCarthyism,'" China Media Project, August 6, 2020, http://chinamediaproject.org/2020/08/06/wang-yi-and-the-ghost-of-mccarthyism/.

36. "Amendment to the Constitution of the People's Republic of China," National People's Congress of the People's Republic of China, March 11, 2018, http://www.npc.gov.cn/englishnpc/constitution2019/201911/36a2566d029c4b39966bd942f82a4305.shtml; for the full amended constitution, see *Constitution of the People's Republic of China*, as amended March 11, 2018, http://www.npc.gov.cn/englishnpc/constitution2019/201911/1f65146fb6104dd3a2793875d19b5b29.shtml.

37. *Constitution of the Communist Party of China*, revised and adopted at the 19th National Congress of the Communist Party of China, October 24, 2017, 8, http://www.xinhuanet.com//english/download/Constitution_of_the_Communist_Party_of_China.pdf.

38. "CPC Releases Plan on Deepening Reform of Party and State Institutions," *Xinhua*, March 22, 2018, http://en.people.cn/n3/2018/0322/c90000-9440252.html. See the analysis of these sweeping changes in Alice Miller, "Only Socialism Can Save China; Only Xi Jinping Can Save Socialism," *China Leadership Monitor*, no. 56 (Spring 2018), https://www.hoover.org/research/only-socialism-can-save-china-only-xi-jinping-can-save-socialism.

39. Susan V. Lawrence, *China's Communist Party Absorbs More of the State*, Congressional Research Service, March 23, 2018, https://crsreports.congress.gov/product/pdf/IF/IF10854.

40. See the website of the Central Party School (in Chinese), https://www.ccps.gov.cn. Xi is closely familiar with the work of the Party School and its importance in training the next generation of CCP leaders; during his preparation for paramount leadership, he served as president of the school from 2007 to 2012.

41. On the Central Office for Foreign Affairs and its growing authority under Xi Jinping, see Guogang Wu, "The Emergence of the Central Office of Foreign Affairs: From Leadership Politics to 'Greater Diplomacy,'" *China Leadership Monitor* 69 (Fall 2021), https://www.prcleader.org/wu-1.

42. Note that a number of analysts translate the Chinese name of the commission (中央国家安全委员会) as the "Central State Security Commission." See Zhao, "China's Foreign Policy Making Process," 93; Steve Tsang, "Party-State Realism: A Framework for Understanding China's Approach to Foreign Policy," *Journal of Contemporary China* 29, no. 122 (2020): 307, https://doi.org/10.1080/10670564.2019.1637562. On the commission, see Joel Wuthnow, "China's New 'Black Box': Problems and Prospects for the Central National Security Commission," *China Quarterly* 232, no. (2017): 886–903; Hu, "Xi Jinping's 'Big Power Diplomacy' "; David M. Lampton, "Xi Jinping and the National Security Commission: Policy Coordination and Political Power," *Journal of Contemporary China* 24, no. 95 (2015): 759–777.

43. Zhao, "China's Foreign Policy Making Process," pp. 93–94.

44. Jing Sun, "Growing Diplomacy, Retreating Diplomats: How the Chinese Foreign Ministry Has Been Marginalized in Foreign Policymaking," *Journal of Contemporary China* 26, no. 105 (2017): 419–433, https://doi.org/10.1080/10670564.2016.1245895.

45. James Reilly, *Orchestration: China's Economic Statecraft across Asia and Europe* (New York: Oxford University Press, 2021), p. 41.

46. For an overview of CCP United Front Work Department, the CCP Propaganda Department, and the CCP International Liaison Department and their growing influence on and involvement in international matters, see Anne-Marie Brady, *Magic Weapons: China's Political Influence Activities under Xi Jinping* (Washington, D.C.: Woodrow Wilson Center, September 18, 2017), https://www.wilsoncenter.org/article/magic-weapons-chinas-political-influence-activities-under-xi-jinping; Julia G. Bowie, "International Liaison Work for the New Era: Generating Global Consensus?"; David Shambaugh, "China's External Propaganda Work: Missions, Messengers, and Mediums"; and Anne-Marie Brady, "Exploit Every Rift: United Front Work Goes Global," all in Julia Bowie and David Gitter, eds., *Party Watch Annual Report 2018,* Center for Advanced China Research (October 2018), https://www.ccpwatch.org/single-post/2018/10/18/Party-Watch-Annual-Report-2018; Zhou Xin, "It's the Mysterious Department behind China's Growing Influence across the Globe. And It's Getting Bigger," *South China Morning Post*, March 21, 2018, https://www.scmp.com/news/china/policies-politics/article/2138196/its-mysterious-department-behind-chinas-growing; James Kynge, Lucy Hornby, and Jamil Anderlini, "Inside China's Secret 'Magic Weapon' for Worldwide Influence," *Financial Times*, October 26, 2017, https://www.ft.com/content/fb2b3934-b004-11e7-beba-5521c713abf4?mhq5j=e7. A broad overview of these organizations' role in PRC foreign relations is also available from Zhao, "China's Foreign Policy Making Process," 98–100.

47. These meetings do not typically generate in-depth reports for public consumption. Summaries of the deliberations with their key messages are usually disseminated by the official media, Party organizations, and government agencies. See, for example, on the October 2013 Central Work Conference on Peripheral Diplomacy, "Xi Jinping: Let the Sense of Community of Common Destiny Take Deep Root in Neighbouring Countries," Ministry of Foreign Affairs of the People's Republic of China, October 25, 2013, https://www.fmprc.gov.cn/mfa_eng/wjb_663304/wjbz_663308/activities_663

312/t1093870.shtml; on the November 2014 Central Work Conference on Foreign Affairs, "The Central Conference on Work Relating to Foreign Affairs Was Held in Beijing," Ministry of Foreign Affairs of the People's Republic of China, November 29, 2014, https://www.fmprc.gov.cn/mfa_eng/zxxx_662805/t1215680.shtml; on the June 2018 Central Work Conference on Foreign Affairs, "Xi Urges Breaking New Ground."

48. *The Long Arm of China: Exporting Authoritarianism with Chinese Characteristics,* Hearing before the U.S. Congressional-Executive Commission on China, 115th Congress, 2nd Session, December 13, 2017, https://www.cecc.gov/sites/chinacom mission.house.gov/files/documents/GPO%20Transcript.pdf.

49. Joseph Torigian, "Historical Legacies and Leaders' Worldviews: Communist Party History and Xi's Learned (and Unlearned) Lessons," *China Perspectives,* nos. 1–2 (2018): 7–15.

50. On the ideological emphasis in CCP foreign policy, see Tanner Greer, "The Theory of History That Guides Xi Jinping," *Palladium,* July 8, 2020, https://palladiummag. com/2020/07/08/the-theory-of-history-that-guides-xi-jinping/; Daniel Tobin, *How Xi Jinping's "New Era" Should Have Ended U.S. Debate on Beijing's Ambitions,* Center for Strategic and International Studies, May 2020, especially Part II, https://www. csis.org/analysis/how-xi-jinpings-new-era-should-have-ended-us-debate-beijings-ambitions; Bandurski, "A Diplomatic Bow to Xi Jinping." See also Wang Yi, "Deeply study and implement Xi Jinping Thought on Diplomacy."

51. "Xi Urges Breaking New Ground."

52. Among the numerous authoritative interpretations of the "grand transformation," see 袁鹏[Yuan Peng], "新冠疫情与百年变局" [The new coronavirus epidemic and the once-in-a-century transformation], *Aisixiang,* June 17, 2020 and available in English at Yuan Peng, "Corona Virus Pandemic," *Reading the China Dream,* n.d., intro. and trans. David Ownby, https://www.readingthechinadream.com/yuan-peng-coronavi rus-pandemic.html; "百年未有之大变局:重识中国与世界的关键" [Great trans-formation not seen in a century: the key to understanding China and the world], 探索与争鸣 [*Exploration and Free Views*] 1, no. 1 (2019): 4–31; "从大历史视野看百年未有之大变局" [Looking at the great transformation not seen in a century from a grand historical perspective], Central Commission for Discipline Inspection, May 14, 2020, http://www.ccdi.gov.cn/lswh/lilun/202005/t20200514_217207.html.

53. "Full Text of Xi Jinping Keynote at the World Economic Forum," *CGTN America,* January 17, 2017, https://america.cgtn.com/2017/01/17/full-text-of-xi-jinping-keyn ote-at-the-world-economic-forum; "Speech by H.E. Xi Jinping President of the People's Republic of China at the Körber Foundation," Berlin, Germany, March 28, 2014, https://www.fmprc.gov.cn/mfa_eng/wjdt_665385/zyjh_665391/t1148640. shtml; "习近平:完全有信心为人类对更好社会制度的探索提供中国方案" [Xi Jinping: Fully confident to provide China solutions in humankind's search for better social systems], *Xinhua,* July 1, 2016, https://www.thepaper.cn/newsDetail_forward_ 1492012 (from Xi's speech to commemorate the 95th anniversary of the CCP); "人类命运共同体为全球治理提供'中国方案'" [Community of human destiny provides a "China Plan" for global governance], *Qiushi,* October 24, 2019, http://www.qsthe ory.cn/dukan/hqwg/2019-10/24/c_1125147150.htm.

54. "关于孔子学院/课堂" [About Confucius Institutes/Classrooms], Confucius Institute Headquarters, http://www.hanban.org/confuciousinstitutes/node_10961. htm. According to this website, 39 Asian countries and regions host 135 Confucius Institutes (CIs) and 115 Confucius Classrooms (CCs); 46 African countries host 61 CIs and 48 CCs; 43 European countries and regions host 187 Confucius Institutes and 346 CCs; 27 countries in the Americas host 138 CIs and 560 CCs; and seven countries in Oceania host 20 CIs and 101 CCs. See also "Confucius Says," *The Economist*, September 13, 2014, https://www.economist.com/china/2014/09/13/confucius-says.

55. "Confucius Says."

56. Shaun Breslin, "China's Global Cultural Interactions," in Shambaugh, *China & the World*, chapter 7; Nadège Rolland, *China's Vision for a New World Order* (Washington, D.C.: National Bureau of Asian Research, January 2020); *Hearing on The Long Arm of China: Exporting Authoritarianism with Chinese Characteristics*, before the U.S. Congressional-Executive Commission on China, 115th Cong. (December 13, 2017), https://www.cecc.gov/events/hearings/thelong-arm-of-china-exporting-authorita rianism-with-chinese-characteristics; Brady, *Magic Weapons*; Bates Gill and Linda Jakobson, *China Matters: Getting It Right for Australia* (Melbourne: Black Inc. / Latrobe University Press, 2017), chapter 4.

57. Bates Gill, "China's Global Influence: Post-COVID Prospects for Soft Power," *Washington Quarterly* 43, no. 2 (2020): 97–115, https://doi.org/10.1080/ 0163660X.2020.1771041. For an extensive analysis and critique of PRC "soft power," see Kingsley Edney, Stanley Rosen, and Ying Zhu, eds., *Soft Power with Chinese Characteristics: China's Campaign for Hearts and Minds* (Abingdon: Routledge, 2019).

58. Kingsley Edney, "Building National Cohesion and Domestic Legitimacy: A Regime Security Approach to Soft Power in China," *Politics* 35, nos. 3–4 (2016): 259–272, https://doi.org/10.1111/1467-9256.12096. See also Kingsley Edney, "Soft Power and the Chinese Propaganda System," *Journal of Contemporary China* 21, no. 78 (2012): 899–914, https://doi.org/10.1080/10670564.2012.701031.

Chapter 3

1. From Xi Jinping, "Young People Should Practice Core Socialist Values," speech delivered to students at Beijing University, May 4, 2014, in *Xi Jinping: The Governance of China* (Beijing: Foreign Languages Press, 2014), n.p.

2. Maria Adele Carrai, *Sovereignty in China: A Genealogy of a Concept since 1840* (Cambridge: Cambridge University Press, 2019), especially chapters 3 and 4.

3. Bill Hayton, *The Invention of China* (New Haven: Yale University Press, 2020).

4. The author thanks Chas Freeman for his insights during a helpful exchange on this topic.

5. Traveling counterclockwise from its northeast, China shares land borders with North Korea, Mongolia, Russia, Kazakhstan, Kyrgyzstan, Tajikistan, Afghanistan,

Pakistan, Nepal, Bhutan, India, Myanmar, Laos, and Vietnam. Continuing in this direction, China has maritime borders with Vietnam, Malaysia, Indonesia, Brunei, the Philippines, Taiwan, Japan, South Korea, and North Korea.

6. An in-depth analysis on the rigidity and flexibility of China's approach to sovereignty is in Allen Carlson, *Unifying China, Integrating with the World: Securing Chinese Sovereignty in the Reform Era* (Stanford, CA: Stanford University Press, 2005). See also Bates Gill, *Rising Star: China's New Security Diplomacy* (Washington, D.C.: Brookings Institution Press, 2010), chapter 4.

7. Chen Zheng, "China Debates the Non-Interference Principle," *Chinese Journal of International Politics* 9, no. 3 (2016): 349–374, doi: 10.1093/cjip/pow010; Camilla N. T. Sørensen, "That Is *Not* Intervention; That Is Interference with Chinese Characteristics: New Concepts, Distinctions, and Approaches Developing in the Chinese Debate and Foreign and Security Policy Practice," *China Quarterly,* no. 239 (2019): 594–613.

8. Courtney J. Fung, "China and the Responsibility to Protect: From Opposition to Advocacy," United States Institute of Peace, June 8, 2016, https://www.usip.org/publi cations/2016/06/china-and-responsibility-protect-opposition-advocacy. Also see Fung's in-depth analysis of China's evolving approach to intervention by the international community and the conditions by which Beijing will or will not support such intervention in *China and Intervention at the UN Security Council: Reconciling Status* (New York: Oxford University Press, 2019).

9. The Five Principles were first articulated in "Agreement between the Republic of India and the People's Republic of China on Trade and Intercourse between the Tibet Region of China and India," Peking, China, April 29, 1954, https://digitalarch ive.wilsoncenter.org/document/121558. The Bandung Conference of 1955 issued a declaration that included the Five Principles: "Final Communiqué of the Asian-African Conference of Bandung (24 April 1955),"https://www.cvce.eu/en/obj/final_ communique_of_the_asian_african_conference_of_bandung_24_april_1955-en-676237bd-72f7-471f-949a-88b6ae513585.html.

10. Samuel S. Kim, "Sovereignty in the Chinese Image of World Order," in Ronald St. John Macdonald, *Essays in Honor of Wang Tieya* (London: Kluwer Academic, 1993), p. 442.

11. On the PRC's "core national interests," see Andrew Scobell et al., *China's Grand Strategy: Trends, Trajectories, and Long-Term Competition* (Santa Monica, CA: RAND, 2020), pp. 12–14.

12. "Transcript of Vice Minister Le Yucheng's Exclusive Interview with the Associated Press of the United States," Ministry of Foreign Affairs of the People's Republic of China, April 18, 2021, https://www.fmprc.gov.cn/mfa_eng/wjbxw/t1869649.shtml.

13. Xi Jinping, "Secure a Decisive Victory in Building a Moderately Prosperous Society in All Respects and Strive for the Great Success of Socialism with Chinese Characteristics for a New Era," speech delivered to the 19th CCP National Congress, Beijing, October 18, 2017, p. 53, http://www.xinhuanet.com/english/download/Xi_ Jinping's_report_at_19th_CPC_National_Congress.pdf.

14. Xi Jinping, "Let the Torch of Multilateralism Light Up Humanity's Way Forward," speech to the World Economic Forum, Davos, Switzerland, January 25, 2021, https://www.fmprc.gov.cn/mfa_eng/zxxx_662805/t1848323.shtml.

15. Andrea Ghiselli, *Protecting China's Interests Overseas: Securitization and Foreign Policy* (New York: Oxford University Press, 2021).

16. Fung, *China and Intervention at the UN Security Council,* chapter 5.

17. Fung, *China and Intervention at the UN Security Council,* chapter 6.

18. Texts of the draft resolutions are available at "Security Council-Quick Links-Veto List," Dag Hammskjöld Library, https://research.un.org/en/docs/sc/quick.

19. Jonas Parello-Plesner and Mathieu Duchâtel, *China's Strong Arm: Protecting Citizens and Assets Abroad* (London: Routledge, 2015); Mathieu Duchâtel, Oliver Bräuner, and Zhou Hang, *Protecting China's Overseas Interests: The Slow Shift away from Non-Interference,* Stockholm International Peace Research Institute Policy Paper 41, June 2014, https://www.sipri.org/publications/2014/sipri-policy-papers/protecting-chi nas-overseas-interests-slow-shift-away-non-interference.

20. James Mulvenon, "Chairman Hu and the PLA's 'New Historic Missions,'" *China Leadership Monitor* 27 (2009), https://www.hoover.org/research/chairman-hu-and-plas-new-historic-missions.

21. Ghiselli, *Protecting China's Interests Overseas,* pp. 30–33.

22. 军事战略研究部, 解放军军事科学院 [Military Strategy Research Department, PLA Academy of Military Science], 战略学 [*Science of Military Strategy*] (Beijing: Military Science Press, 2013), pp. 6–7.

23. *The Diversified Employment of China's Armed Forces* (Beijing: Information Office of the State Council, 2013), section I.

24. Ghiselli, *Protecting China's Interests Overseas,* p. 2.

25. "习近平谈建设更高水平的平安中国" [Xi Jinping discusses building a higher level of security in China], 党建网 [*Party Building Net*], January 9, 2021, https://www.chinanews.com/gn/2021/01-09/9382624.shtml; "习近平：坚持总体国家安全观 走中国特色国家安全道路" [Adhere to the comprehensive national security concept and follow the path of national security with Chinese characteristics], 新华网 [*Xinhuanet*], April 15, 2014; Xi Jinping, "A Holistic View of National Security," speech delivered at the first meeting of the Central National Security Commission, Beijing, April 15, 2013, in Xi Jinping, *The Governance of China* (Beijing: Foreign Languages Press, 2014), n.p.

26. *China's National Defense in the New Era* (Beijing: State Council Information Office of the People's Republic of China, 2019), section II, http://www.xinhuanet.com/english/2019-07/24/c_138253389.htm.

27. Ghiselli, *Protecting China's Interests Overseas,* pp. 1, 180–181. For a fascinating study of PRC private security companies, see Niva Yau and Dirk van der Kley, "The Growth, Adaptation, and Limitations of Chinese Private Security Companies in Central Asia," Oxus Society for Central Asian Affairs, October 13, 2020, https://oxussociety.org/the-growth-adaptation-and-limitations-of-chinese-private-security-companies-in-central-asia/.

28. Scobell et al., *China's Grand Strategy,* pp. 12–14.

29. "Highlights of Xi's Speech at Rally Marking PLA's 90th Anniversary," *China Daily*, August 2, 2017, https://www.chinadaily.com.cn/china/2017-08/02/content_30327 309.htm.

30. Yang Sheng, "Xi Delivers Clear Message on Rights to Mattis," *Global Times*, June 27, 2018, https://www.globaltimes.cn/content/1108655.shtml.

31. The 13 countries are Belize, Eswatini (Swaziland), Guatemala, Haiti, Honduras, the Marshall Islands, Nauru, Palau, Paraguay, Saint Kitts and Nevis, Saint Lucia, Saint Vincent and the Grenadines, and Tuvalu.

32. M. Taylor Fravel, "Regime Insecurity and International Cooperation: Explaining China's Compromises in Territorial Disputes," *International Security* 30, no. 2 (2005): 46–83. Those settlements were with Burma, Nepal, North Korea, Pakistan, Mongolia, Afghanistan, Russia (three separate border disputes), Laos, Vietnam (two disputes), Kazakhstan, Kyrgyzstan, Tajikistan, the United Kingdom (Hong Kong), and Portugal (Macao).

33. The Indian government officially claims that its border with China is 3,488 kilometers. However, this figure includes the border between China and parts of the territory of Kashmir, which India claims but is held by Pakistan. The U.S. Central Intelligence Agency *World Factbook* states that the Sino-Indian border is 2,659 kilometers, or approximately 1,650 miles.

34. John W. Garver, *China's Quest: The History of the Foreign Relations of the People's Republic of China* (New York: Oxford University Press, 2016), pp. 146–153, 175–182; Fravel, "Regime Insecurity and International Cooperation," pp. 66–69.

35. Will Green, "Conflict on the Sino-Indian Border: Background for Congress," U.S.-China Economic and Security Review Commission Issue Brief, July 2, 2020, https://www.uscc.gov/sites/default/files/2020-07/Conflict_on_Sino-Indian_Border.pdf.

36. On the 2013, 2014, and 2015 incidents, see "India and China 'Pull Back Troops' in Disputed Border Area," *BBC News*, May 6, 2013, https://www.bbc.com/news/world-asia-india-22423999; Hari Kumar, "India and China Step Back from Standoff in Kashmir," *New York Times*, September 26, 2014, https://www.nytimes.com/2014/09/27/world/asia/india-china-ladakh-dispute.html; and "India, China Hold Flag Meet along Line of Actual Control," *NDTV*, September 15, 2015, https://www.ndtv.com/india-news/india-china-hold-flag-meet-along-line-of-actual-control-1218022.

37. Steven Lee Myers, Ellen Barry, and Max Fisher, "How India and China Have Come to the Brink over a Remote Mountain Pass," *New York Times*, July 26, 2017, https://www.nytimes.com/2017/07/26/world/asia/dolam-plateau-china-india-bhutan.html.

38. Liu Xin and Guo Yuandan, "China Reveals Truth of Galwan Valley Clash after Half a Year, Showing the Country as 'a Lion with Wisdom and Kindness,'" *Global Times*, February 19, 2021, https://www.globaltimes.cn/page/202102/1215947.shtml.

39. Sushant Singh, "Explained: What Does the Increase in Chinese Transgressions Mean?," *Indian Express*, June 16, 2020, https://indianexpress.com/article/explained/chinese-transgressions-ladakh-line-of-actual-control-6421855/.

40. Arzan Tarapore, "The Crisis after the Crisis: How Ladakh Will Shape India's Competition with China," Lowy Institute, May 6, 2021, https://www.lowyinstit

ute.org/publications/crisis-after-crisis-how-ladakh-will-shape-india-s-competit ion-china.

41. The Asia Maritime Transparency Initiative at the Center for Strategic and International Studies hosts an excellent website, https://amti.csis.org, providing satellite imagery, maps, and analyses on political, military, territorial, and legal developments in maritime Asia.

42. "China's Maritime Disputes," Council on Foreign Relations, https://www.cfr.org/ chinas-maritime-disputes/#!/; "East China Sea," United States Energy Information Administration, September 17, 2014, https://www.eia.gov/international/analysis/ regions-of-interest/East_China_Sea.

43. See Eleanor Freund and Andrew Facini, "Freedom of Navigation in the South China Sea: A Practical Guide," Harvard Kennedy School Belfer Center for Science and International Affairs, June 2017, https://www.belfercenter.org/publication/freedom- navigation-south-china-sea-practical-guide.

44. Carrai, *Sovereignty in China,* p. 124.

45. Ralf Emmers, "China's Influence in the South China Sea and the Failure of Joint Development," in Evelyn Goh, ed., *Rising China's Influence in Developing Asia* (Oxford: Oxford University Press, 2016), chapter 7.

46. Viet Hoang, "The Code of Conduct for the South China Sea: A Long and Bumpy Road," *The Diplomat,* September 28, 2020, https://thediplomat.com/2020/09/ the-code-of-conduct-for-the-south-china-sea-a-long-and-bumpy-road/; Felix K. Chang, "Uncertain Prospects: South China Sea Code of Conduct," Foreign Policy Research Institute, October 6, 2020, https://www.fpri.org/article/2020/10/uncertain- prospects-south-china-sea-code-of-conduct-negotiations/.

47. Steven Lee Myers and Jason Gutierrez, "With Swarms of Ships, Beijing Tightens Its Grip on South China Sea," *New York Times,* April 3, 2021, https://www.nytimes.com/ 2021/04/03/world/asia/swarms-ships-south-china-sea.html.

48. Kristen Huang, "China and Vietnam 'Likely to Clash Again' as They Build Maritime Militias," *South China Morning Post,* April 12, 2020, https://www.scmp.com/news/ china/diplomacy/article/3079436/china-and-vietnam-likely-clash-again-they- build-maritime.

49. Office of the Secretary of Defense, *Military and Security Developments Involving the People's Republic of China 2020: Annual Report to Congress* (Washington, D.C.: Department of Defense, August 2020), p. 71, https://media.defense.gov/2020/ Sep/01/2002488689/-1/-1/1/2020-DOD-CHINA-MILITARY-POWER-REPORT- FINAL.PDF.

50. "Force Majeure: China's Coast Guard Law in Context," Center for Strategic and International Studies Asia Maritime Transparency Initiative, March 30, 2021, https:// amti.csis.org/force-majeure-chinas-coast-guard-law-in-context/.

51. Amanda Macias and Courtney Kube, "Chinese Military Conducts Anti-Ship Missile Tests in Hotly Contested South China Sea," *CNBC,* July 1, 2019, https://www.nbcn ews.com/news/china/chinese-military-conducts-anti-ship-missile-tests-hotly- contested-south-n1025456; "Defence Ministry's Regular Press Conference on June

27," *PLA Daily*, June 27, 2019, http://eng.chinamil.com.cn/view/2019-06/27/cont
ent_9541430.htm.

52. Michael Green et al., "Counter-Coercion Series: East China Sea Air Defense
Identification Zone," Center for Strategic and International Studies Asia Maritime
Transparency Initiative, June 13, 2017, https://amti.csis.org/counter-co-east-china-
sea-adiz/.

53. Mike Mochizuki and Jiaxiu Han, "Is China Escalating Tensions with Japan in the
East China Sea?," *The Diplomat*, September 16, 2020, https://thediplomat.com/2020/
09/is-china-escalating-tensions-with-japan-in-the-east-china-sea/; Linda Sieg and
Kiyoshi Takenaka, "Japan Protests to China after Radar Pointed at Vessel," *Reuters*,
February 6, 2013, https://www.reuters.com/article/us-china-japan-idUSBRE914
10Q20130205.

54. *Treaty of Mutual Cooperation and Security between Japan and the United States of
America*, January 19, 1960, https://www.mofa.go.jp/region/n-america/us/q&a/ref/
1.html. See also "U.S.-Japan Joint Leaders' Statement: 'U.S.-Japan Global Partnership
for a New Era,'" The White House, April 16, 2021, https://www.whitehouse.gov/brief
ing-room/statements-releases/2021/04/16/u-s-japan-joint-leaders-statement-u-s-
japan-global-partnership-for-a-new-era/.

55. Junnosuke Kobara, "Japan Defense Chief Calls for China's Restraint on the Senkakus,"
Nikkei Asia, December 15, 2020, https://asia.nikkei.com/Politics/International-relati
ons/Japan-defense-chief-calls-for-China-s-restraint-on-the-Senkakus;   "Chinese
Defense Minister Holds Video Talks with His Japanese Counterpart," *China Military
Online*, December 14, 2020, http://eng.mod.gov.cn/news/2020-12/14/content_4875
458.htm.

56. Article 8 of the Anti-Secession Law states, in part, "In the event [of] 'Taiwan independence' . . . or that possibilities for a peaceful reunification should be completely
exhausted, the state shall employ non-peaceful means and other necessary measures
to protect China's sovereignty and territorial integrity" ("Full Text of Anti-Secession
Law," *People's Daily*, March 14, 2005, http://en.people.cn/200503/14/eng20050314_
176746.html).

57. Economic ranking based on "GDP, Current Prices," International Monetary Fund,
April 2021, https://www.imf.org/external/datamapper/NGDPD@WEO/OEMDC/
ADVEC/WEOWORLD.

58. For details, see "Embassies and Missions," at the website of Taiwan's Ministry of
Foreign Affairs, https://en.mofa.gov.tw.

59. "Changes in the Taiwanese/Chinese Identity of Taiwanese as Tracked in Surveys by
the Election Study Center, NCCU (1992-2021.06)," Election Study Center, National
Chengchi University, July 20, 2021, https://esc.nccu.edu.tw/PageDoc/Detail?fid=
7800&id=6961. The survey asks, "In our society, there are some people who call themselves 'Taiwanese,' some who call themselves 'Chinese,' and some who call themselves
both. Do you consider yourself to be 'Taiwanese,' 'Chinese,' or both?" Responses were
then tallied into one of four responses: Taiwanese, Chinese, both, or no response.

60. For an in-depth review and analysis of the history and centrality of the "Taiwan
question" in U.S.-China relations, see Alan D. Romberg, *Rein In at the Brink of the*

Precipice: American Policy toward Taiwan and U.S.-PRC Relations (Washington, D.C.: Henry L. Stimson Center, 2003).

61. On this point, the most authoritative statement of the U.S. position is that it "*acknowledges* the Chinese position that there is but one China and Taiwan is part of China." See "Joint Communique on the Establishment of Diplomatic Relations between the United States of America and the People's Republic of China," December 15, 1978 (emphasis added), https://photos.state.gov/libraries/ait-taiwan/171414/ait-pages/prc_e.pdf.

62. Taiwan Relations Act, Public Law 96-8, April 10, 1979, https://uscode.house.gov/statutes/pl/96/8.pdf.

63. Taiwan's Ministry of Foreign Affairs keeps a detailed listing of such activities. See "Instances of China's Interference with Taiwan's International Presence," Ministry of Foreign Affairs, Republic of China (Taiwan), https://en.mofa.gov.tw/cl.aspx?n=1510.

64. Nathan Beauchamp-Mustafaga and Jessica Drun, "Exploring Chinese Military Thinking on Social Media Manipulation against Taiwan," *China Brief* 21, no. 7 (2021), https://jamestown.org/program/exploring-chinese-military-thinking-on-social-media-manipulation-against-taiwan/.

65. Bonnie Glaser and Jeremy Mark, "Taiwan and China Are Locked in Economic Co-Dependence," *Foreign Policy,* April 14, 2021, https://foreignpolicy.com/2021/04/14/taiwan-china-econonomic-codependence/.

66. Xi Jinping, "Working Together to Realize Rejuvenation of the Chinese Nation and Advance China's Peaceful Reunification," speech marking the 40th anniversary of the Issuance of the Message to Compatriots in Taiwan, Beijing, January 2, 2019, http://www.gwytb.gov.cn/wyly/201904/t20190412_12155687.htm.

67. From the 2019 PRC defense white paper, *China's National Defense in the New Era,* State Council Information Office of the People's Republic of China, July 2019, section II, http://english.www.gov.cn/archive/whitepaper/201907/24/content_WS5d3941ddc6d08408f502283d.html.

68. For an insightful, well-informed prognosis on the future of PRC-Taiwan relations, see John Culver, "The Unfinished Chinese Civil War," *Lowy Interpreter,* September 30, 2020, https://www.lowyinstitute.org/the-interpreter/unfinished-chinese-civil-war. See also Richard C. Bush, *Difficult Choices: Taiwan's Quest for Security and the Good Life* (Washington, D.C.: Brookings Institution Press, 2021).

69. For more in-depth assessments of Xinjiang's past, present, and future, see David Tobin, *Securing China's Northwest Frontier: Identity and Insecurity in Xinjiang* (Cambridge: Cambridge University Press, 2020), and James A. Millward, *Eurasian Crossroads: A History of Xinjiang* (New York: Columbia University Press, 2007).

70. Data calculated from "An Analysis Report on Population Change in Xinjiang," *Global Times,* January 7, 2021, https://www.globaltimes.cn/page/202101/1212073.shtml.

71. Michael Martina and Megha Rajagopalan, "Islamist Group Claims China Station Bombing: SITE," *Reuters,* May 14, 2014, https://www.reuters.com/article/us-china-xinjiang/islamist-group-claims-china-station-bombing-site-idUSBREA4D07H20140514; Jonathan Kaiman, "Islamist Group Claims Responsibility for Attack on China's Tiananmen Square," *The Guardian,* November 25, 2013, https://www.theg

uardian.com/world/2013/nov/25/islamist-china-tiananmen-beijing-attack. In 2002, the United States and China joined with other countries and the United Nations in formally designating ETIM as a terrorist organization. In 2020, the Trump administration rescinded this designation. Sha Hua, "China Irate after U.S. Removes 'Terrorist' Label from Separatist Group," *Wall Street Journal,* November 6, 2020, https://www.wsj.com/articles/china-irate-after-u-s-removes-terrorist-label-from-separatist-group-11604661868.

72. "公安部开展严厉打击暴力恐怖活动专项行动" [Ministry of Public Security launches Strike Hard Campaign against violent terrorist activities], 新华社 [*Xinhua*], May 25, 2014, http://www.gov.cn/xinwen/2014-05/25/content_2686705.htm. Xi quotations from Austin Ramzy and Chris Buckley, "'Absolutely No Mercy': Leaked Files Expose How China Organized Mass Detentions of Muslims," *New York Times,* November 16, 2019, https://www.nytimes.com/interactive/2019/11/16/world/asia/china-xinjiang-documents.html.

73. Chris Buckley and Austin Ramzy, "China Is Erasing Mosques and Precious Shrines in Xinjiang," *New York Times,* September 25, 2020, https://www.nytimes.com/interactive/2020/09/25/world/asia/xinjiang-china-religious-site.html; Nathan Ruser et al., *Cultural Erasure: Tracing the Destruction of Uyghur and Islamic Spaces in Xinjiang* (Canberra: Australian Strategic Policy Institute, 2020), https://www.aspi.org.au/report/cultural-erasure. See also, for example, the detailed personal account of Anar Sabit in Raffi Khatchadourian, "Surviving the Crackdown in Xinjiang," *The New Yorker,* April 5, 2021, https://www.newyorker.com/magazine/2021/04/12/surviving-the-crackdown-in-xinjiang.

74. For a detailed assessment of China's shifting approach to counterterrorism in Xinjiang, see Sheena Chestnut Greitens, Myunghee Lee, and Emir Yazici, "Counterterrorism and Preventive Repression: China's Changing Strategy in Xinjiang," *International Security* 44, no. 3 (2020): 9–47, doi: 10.1162/ISEC_a_00368.

75. David Tobin, "A 'Struggle of Life or Death': Han and Uyghur Insecurities on China's North-West Frontier," *China Quarterly* no. 242 (2020): 301–323, doi: 10.1017/S030574101900078X.

76. "习近平：坚持依法治疆团结稳疆文化润疆富民兴疆长期建疆　努力建设新时代中国特色社会主义新疆" [Xi Jinping: Continue governing Xinjiang according to the law, unite to stabilize Xinjiang culture, enrich Xinjiang for people's prosperity, rejuvenate and build Xinjiang for the long term, and build a Xinjiang of socialism with Chinese characteristics in the new era], 新华社 [*Xinhua*], September 26, 2020, http://www.xinhuanet.com/politics/leaders/2020-09/26/c_1126544371.htm.

77. A classic work on Tibet in the 20th century is the four-volume opus by Melvyn C. Goldstein, *A Modern History of Tibet,* Volume 1: *1913–1951: The Demise of the Lamaist State* (Berkeley: University of California Press, 1989); *A History of Modern Tibet,* Volume 2: *The Calm before the Storm: 1951–1955* (Berkeley: University of California Press, 2007); *A History of Modern Tibet,* Volume 3: *The Storm Clouds Descend, 1955–1957* (Berkeley: University of California Press, 2013); and *A History of Modern Tibet,* Volume 4: *In the Eye of the Storm, 1957–1959* (Berkeley: University of California Press, 2019). A briefer analysis on modern Tibet is Melvyn C. Goldstein,

Tibet, China, and the United States: Reflections on the Tibet Question, Atlantic Council of the United States Occasional Paper Series, April 1995, https://case.edu/affil/tibet/documents/ReflectionsontheTibetQuestion1995.pdf.

78. "Population at Year-End by Region," *China Statistical Yearbook 2020* (Beijing: China Statistics Press, 2020), http://www.stats.gov.cn/tjsj/ndsj/2020/indexeh.htm; Palden Nyima and Daqiong, "Majority Tibetan Population Continues to Grow," *China Daily,* July 17, 2020, https://www.chinadaily.com.cn/a/202007/17/WS5f115e48a31083481 725a55e.html.

79. "Self-Immolation Fact Sheet," Central Tibetan Administration, last updated February 19, 2021, https://tibet.net/important-issues/factsheet-immolation-2011-2012/.

80. With advancing age—he was born in 1935—and the onset of the covid-19 pandemic, the Dalai Lama's international travel schedule was dramatically curtailed; following a trip to Japan in late 2018, he has not travelled abroad since. "Schedule," His Holiness the 14th Dalai Lama of Tibet, https://www.dalailama.com/schedule.

81. For a remarkable, independent, and on-the-ground account of life for Tibetans in China, see Barbara Demick, *Eat the Buddha: Life and Death in a Tibetan Town* (New York: Random House, 2020).

82. "Xi Focus: Xi Stresses Building New Modern Socialist Tibet," *Xinhua,* August 29, 2020, http://www.xinhuanet.com/english/2020-08/29/c_139327765.htm.

83. On the history of Hong Kong's relationship with the PRC, see Stephen Vines, *Defying the Dragon: Hong Kong and the World's Largest Dictatorship* (London: Hurst & Company, 2021).

84. "Joint Declaration of the Government of the United Kingdom of Great Britain and Northern Ireland and the Government of the People's Republic of China on the Question of Hong Kong," December 19, 1984, in *United Nations Treaty Series,* vol. 1399, no. 23391, pp. 61–73, https://treaties.un.org/doc/Publication/UNTS/Vol ume%201399/v1399.pdf.

85. "English Translation of the Law of the People's Republic of China on Safeguarding National Security in the Hong Kong Special Administrative Region," *Xinhua,* July 1, 2020, http://www.xinhuanet.com/english/2020-07/01/c_139178753.htm; see also "Hong Kong Security Law: What Is It and Is It Worrying?," *BBC,* June 30, 2020, https://www.bbc.com/news/world-asia-china-52765838.

86. Wang Yi, "Focusing on Cooperation and Managing Differences: Bringing China-U.S. Relations back to the Track of Sound and Steady Development," remarks to the Council on Foreign Relations, Ministry of Foreign Affairs of the People's Republic of China, April 23, 2021, https://www.fmprc.gov.cn/mfa_eng/zxxx_662805/t1871285. shtml.

Chapter 4

1. Xi Jinping, "Complete a Moderately Prosperous Society and Realize the Chinese Dream," from a speech at the opening ceremony of a study session for provincial and

ministerial-level leaders on the guiding principles of Xi Jinping's speeches in the run-up to the 19th CCP National Congress, July 26, 2017, in Xi Jinping, *The Governance of China II* (Beijing: Foreign Languages Press, 2017), p. 65.

2. "GDP per Capita (Constant 2010 US$)—China," World Bank, https://data.worldbank.org/indicator/NY.GDP.PCAP.KD?end=2019&locations=CN&start=1999; "GDP (Current US$)—China, United States, Japan," World Bank, https://data.worldbank.org/indicator/NY.GDP.MKTP.CD?end=2019&locations=CN-US-JP&start=1995.

3. From Xi Jinping, "Align Our Thinking with the Guidelines of the Third Plenary Session of the 18th CPC Central Committee," from a speech at the second Plenary Meeting of the Third Plenary Session of the 18th CPC Central Committee, November 12, 2013, in Xi Jinping, *The Governance of China* (Beijing: Foreign Languages Press, 2014), n.p.

4. On postwar Sino-Japanese economic relations, see Amy King, *China–Japan Relations after World War Two: Empire, Industry and War, 1949–1971* (Cambridge: Cambridge University Press, 2016). According to King, "In framing Japan, Chinese policymakers downplayed Japan's wartime atrocities and typically referred to the war only as a way of highlighting China's contribution to the defeat of Japanese imperialism. Chinese officials also argued that the Japanese people were victims of US imperialism." King, *China-Japan Relations*, p. 51. According to Yinan He, "Most young Chinese [in the 1970s] had minimal knowledge about Japanese war atrocities, for the state-controlled textbooks rarely mentioned them and academic research on this topic was banned." Yinan He, "History, Chinese Nationalism, and the Emerging Sino-Japanese Conflict," *Journal of Contemporary China* 15, no. 50(2007): 1–24, quotation from p. 6.

5. Data on trade and inbound investment in "Trade (% of GDP)—China," World Bank, https://data.worldbank.org/indicator/NE.TRD.GNFS.ZS?locations=CN, and "Foreign Direct Investment, Net Inflows (BoP, Current US$)—China," World Bank, https://data.worldbank.org/indicator/BX.KLT.DINV.CD.WD?locations=CN. Quotation from Arthur R. Kroeber, *China's Economy: What Everyone Needs to Know* (New York: Oxford University Press, 2020), p. 69; on the role of foreign direct investment in China's industrial development, see Kroeber, *China's Economy*, pp. 80–84.

6. 中华人民共和国国民经济和社会发展第十个五年计划纲要 [Outline of the 10th Five-Year Plan for National Economic and Social Development of the People's Republic of China], March 15, 2001, http://www.gov.cn./gongbao/content/2001/content_60699.htm. For an in-depth analysis on the "going out" strategy, see Min Ye, *The Belt Road and Beyond: State-Mobilized Globalization in China: 1998–2018* (New York: Cambridge University Press, 2020), chapter 4.

7. "Foreign Direct Investment, Net Outflows (BoP, Current US$)—China," World Bank, https://data.worldbank.org/indicator/BM.KLT.DINV.CD.WD?locations=CN; "Exports of Goods and Services (BoP, Current US$)—China," World Bank, https://data.worldbank.org/indicator/BX.GSR.GNFS.CD?locations=CN.

8. Angela Monaghan, "China Surpasses US as World's Largest Trading Nation," *The Guardian*, January 10, 2014, https://www.theguardian.com/business/2014/jan/10/china-surpasses-us-world-largest-trading-nation; on foreign direct investment, see

United Nations Conference on Trade and Development, *World Investment Report 2017: Investment and the Digital Economy* (Geneva: United Nations, 2017), Annex Table 1, https://unctad.org/system/files/official-document/wir2017_en.pdf; "Global Foreign Direct Investment Fell by 42% in 2020, Outlook Remains Weak," United Nations Conference on Trade and Development, January 24, 2021, https://unctad.org/news/global-foreign-direct-investment-fell-42-2020-outlook-remains-weak.

9. Xi Jinping, "Improve Governance Capacity through the Socialist System with Chinese Characteristics," a speech at a seminar of provincial-level officials to study and implement the decisions of the Third Plenum of the 18th CCP Central Committee, February 17, 2014, in *The Governance of China*, n.p.

10. Arthur Kroeber, "Can China Avoid the Japan Trap?," presentation for the China Matters National Meeting, Sydney, Australia, April 6, 2016, http://chinamatters.org.au/wp-content/uploads/2016/04/Dinner-keynote-speech-China-Matters-National-Meeting-Sydney-6-April-2016.pdf.

11. Li Hongbin et al., "The End of Cheap Chinese Labor," *Journal of Economic Perspectives* 26, no. 4 (2012): 57–74, doi: 10.1257/jep.26.4.57.

12. Lei Xiaoyan, "Grey Matter: Its Aging Population Is an Issue of Major Concern for China Requiring Policy Changes to Address It," *China Daily*, November 13, 2020, https://global.chinadaily.com.cn/a/202011/13/WS5fadcebda31024ad0ba93c88.html.

13. This term is defined by Indermit Gill and Homi Kharas in *An East Asian Renaissance—Ideas for Economic Growth* (Washington, D.C.: World Bank Group, 2007).

14. The World Bank and the Development Research Center of the State Council of the People's Republic of China, *China 2030: Building a Modern, Harmonious, and Creative Society* (Washington, D.C.: World Bank Group, 2013), p. 12, http://documents1.worldbank.org/curated/en/781101468239669951/pdf/China-2030-building-a-modern-harmonious-and-creative-society.pdf.

15. The 13 economies are Equatorial Guinea, Greece, Hong Kong, Ireland, Israel, Japan, Mauritius, Portugal, Puerto Rico, Singapore, Spain, South Korea, and Taiwan. On the correlation between "institutional quality" and breaking out of the middle-income trap, see Michael Witt, "How China Can Avoid the Middle-Income Trap," *INSEAD Knowledge*, April 12, 2016, http:// knowledge.insead.edu/blog/insead-blog/how-china-can-avoid-the-middle-income-trap-4629.

16. Chen Qingqing, "China May Hit Middle-Income Trap—Minister," *Global Times*, April 26, 2015, http://www.globaltimes.cn/content/918760.shtml.

17. Data on SOEs are drawn from Kroeber, *China's Economy*, pp. 129–132.

18. This language is taken from "Communiqué of the Third Plenary Session of the 18th Central Committee of the Communist Party of China," adopted at the Third Plenary Session of the 18th Central Committee of the Chinese Communist Party, Beijing, November 12, 2013, http://www.china.org.cn/china/third_plenary_session/2014-01/15/content_31203056.htm.

19. Kroeber, *China's Economy*, p. 284.

20. Lixing Li, "Changing Ownership Structure of the Economy," and Yong Wang, "Role of Government and Industrial Policies," both in David Dollar, Yiping Huang, and Yang Yao, eds., *China 2049: Economic Challenges of a Rising Global Power* (Washington,

D.C.: Brookings Institution Press, 2020), chapters 8 and 11; Nicholas R. Lardy, *The State Strikes Back: The End of Economic Reform in China?* (Washington, D.C.: Peterson Institute of International Economics, 2019); Kroeber, *China's Economy*, chapters 7 and 14.

21. Anna Holzmann and Caroline Meinhardt, "The CCP Tightens Its Grip on the Private Economy," MERICS China Industries Briefing—September 2020, October 5, 2020, https://merics.org/en/briefings/merics-china-industries-briefing-september-2020.

22. On Jack Ma's fall from grace, see Lulu Yilun Chen and Coco Liu, "How China Lost Patience with Jack Ma, Its Loudest Billionaire," *Bloomberg Businessweek*, December 23, 2020, https://www.bloomberg.com/news/features/2020-12-22/jack-ma-s-emp ire-in-crisis-after-china-halts-ant-group-ipo; Lingling Wei, "China Blocked Jack Ma's Ant IPO after Investigation Revealed Likely Beneficiaries," *Wall Street Journal*, February 16, 2021, https://www.wsj.com/articles/china-blocked-jack-mas-ant-ipo-after-an-investigation-revealed-who-stood-to-gain-11613491292.

23. "国家要求滴滴出行下架整改为何深得人心" [State requirement to remove Didi Chuxing from the shelves a popular move], 环球时报 [*Global Times*], July 4, 2021, https://opinion.huanqiu.com/article/43o4K21Rxr5.

24. Christian Shepherd and Yuan Yang, "China Targets More Tech Groups after Didi Crackdown," *Financial Times*, July 6, 2021, https://www.ft.com/content/771f6d40-ecd2-4855-8193-d0550f1d2e3d.

25. On the CCP's strategy of cooptation of the PRC private sector, see Bruce Dickson, *Wealth into Power: The Communist Party's Embrace of China's Private Sector* (New York: Cambridge University Press, 2008), and Neil Thomas, "The Red Capitalist: Lessons for Jack Ma on Doing the Party's Business, from Rong Yiren," *The Wire*, January 10, 2021, https://www.thewirechina.com/2021/01/10/the-red-capital ist/. For more in-depth analysis of how the Party and state leadership employ state and private firms in the pursuit of economic statecraft, see William J. Norris, *Chinese Economic Statecraft: Commercial Actors, Grand Strategy, and State Control* (Ithaca, NY: Cornell University Press, 2016), and James Reilly, *Orchestration: China's Economic Statecraft across Asia and Europe* (New York: Oxford University Press, 2021).

26. "Factbox: China Crackdown Wipes Hundreds of Billions off Top Companies' Values," *Reuters*, September 16, 2021, https://www.reuters.com/world/china/china-crackd own-wipes-hundreds-billions-off-top-companies-values-2021-09-13/.

27. See, for example, Daniel H. Rosen, "China's Economic Reckoning: The Price of Failed Reforms," *Foreign Affairs* 100, no. 4 (2021): 20–29, https://www.foreignaffairs.com/articles/china/2021-06-22/chinas-economic-reckoning.

28. On the resurgence of the role of the state in the PRC economy since Xi Jinping took power, see Lardy, *The State Strikes Back*.

29. "President Xi Jinping Delivers Important Speech and Proposes to Build a Silk Road Economic Belt with Central Asian Countries," Ministry of Foreign Affairs of the People's Republic of China, September 7, 2013, https://www.fmprc.gov.cn/mfa_eng/topics_665678/xjpfwzysiesgjtfhshzzfh_665686/t1076334.shtml; "'Belt and Road' Incorporated into CPC Constitution," *Xinhua*, October 24, 2017, http://www.xinhua net.com/english/2017-10/24/c_136702025.htm. For an excellent overview of the

BRI, see Nadège Rolland, "A Concise Guide to the Belt and Road Initiative," National Bureau of Asian Research, April 11, 2019, https://www.nbr.org/publication/a-guide-to-the-belt-and-road-initiative/. See also her extensive book-length assessment; Nadège Rolland, *China's Eurasian Century? Political and Strategic Implications of the Belt and Road Initiative* (Seattle: National Bureau of Asian Research, 2017).

30. "已同中国签订共建'一带一路'合作文件的国家一览" [List of countries that have signed a "Belt and Road" cooperation document with China], Belt and Road Portal, April 12, 2019 (updated December 17, 2020), https://www.yidaiyilu.gov.cn/info/iList. jsp?tm_id=126&cat_id=10122&info_id=77298; "特稿:同筑共赢之路共迎美好明天--共建'一带一路'全景扫描" [Feature article: Building a win-win road together and welcoming a better tomorrow—Overview of BRI], *Xinhua*, September 13, 2020, http://www.xinhuanet.com/world/2020-09/13/c_1126486680.htm.

31. *Meeting Asia's Infrastructure Needs*, Asian Development Bank, February 2017, p. xiii, https://www.adb.org/publications/asia-infrastructure-needs.

32. "'一带一路'内涵丰厚 意义深远" [Belt and Road Initiative has rich meaning and far-reaching significance], *Xinhua*, March 29, 2015, http://www.xinhuanet.com/world/2015-03/29/c_127632204.htm. See also "Full Text: Vision and Actions on Jointly Building Belt and Road," *Xinhua*, April 10, 2017, http://www.beltandroadfo rum.org/english/n100/2017/0410/c22-45.html.

33. *China's Belt and Road Initiative in the Global Trade, Investment and Finance Landscape*, OECD Finance Outlook 2018 (Paris: OECD Publishing, 2018), https://www.oecd. org/finance/Chinas-Belt-and-Road-Initiative-in-the-global-trade-investment-and-finance-landscape.pdf.

34. Jonathan E. Hillman, "How Big Is China's Belt and Road?," Center for Strategic and International Studies, April 3, 2018, https://www.csis.org/analysis/how-big-chinas-belt-and-road. See also "China's New Silk Route," PwC's Growth Market Centre, February 2016. https://www.pwc.com/gx/en/growth-markets-center/assets/pdf/china-new-silk-route.pdf.

35. The six BRI "corridors" identified by the PRC government are the China-Mongolia-Russia Economic Corridor, the New Eurasian Land Bridge, the China–Central Asia–West Asia Economic Corridor, the China–Indochina Peninsula Economic Corridor, the China-Pakistan Economic Corridor, and the China-Myanmar Economic Corridor. See *Belt and Road Economics: Opportunities and Risks of Transport Corridors* (Washington, D.C.: World Bank Group, 2019), p. 3. Data on investment amounts, sectors, and country recipients are from *Belt and Road Economics*, pp. 37–40.

36. "BRI & Beyond Forecast," BakerMcKenzie, September 2019, https://www.bakerm ckenzie.com/-/media/files/insight/publications/2019/09/bm_bri_infographic_ m.pdf?la=en.

37. See, for example, "关于新时代推进西部大开发形成新格局的指导意见" [Guiding opinions on promoting the Western development strategy in the new era], State Council of the People's Republic of China, May 17, 2020, http://www.gov.cn/zhengce/2020-05/17/content_5512456.htm.

38. "国务院关于进一步加强淘汰落后产能工作的通知" [State Council notice on fur-ther strengthening the elimination of backward production capacity], State Council

of the People's Republic of China, April 6, 2010, http://www.gov.cn/zwgk/2010-04/06/content_1573880.htm.

39. Logan Wright, Lauren Gloudeman, and Daniel H. Rosen, *The China Economic Risk Matrix*, Center for Strategic and International Studies, September 2020, https://csis-website-prod.s3.amazonaws.com/s3fs-public/publication/200921_RiskMatrix_FullReport_0.pdf.

40. *Global Forum on Steel Excess Capacity Report*, Federal Ministry for Economic Affairs and Energy (Germany), November 30, 2017, https://www.bmwi.de/Redaktion/EN/Downloads/global-forum-on-steel-excess-capacity-report.pdf?__blob=publicationFile; "G20 Leaders' Communique Hangzhou Summit," Ministry of Foreign Affairs of the People's Republic of China, September 6, 2016, http://www.g20chn.org/English/Dynamic/201609/t20160906_3396.html.

41. David Dollar, "The AIIB and the 'One Belt, One Road,'" Brookings Institution, Summer 2015, https://www.brookings.edu/opinions/the-aiib-and-the-one-belt-one-road/.

42. Peter Cai, *Understanding China's Belt and Road Initiative*, Lowy Institute, March 2017, https://www.lowyinstitute.org/publications/understanding-belt-and-road-initiative

43. Marc Lanteigne, "China's Maritime Security and the 'Malacca Dilemma,'" *Asian Security* 4, no. 2 (2008): 143–161, doi: 10.1080/14799850802006555. For Chinese PRC analyses on the Malacca dilemma, see, for example, 薛力 [Xue Li], "'马六甲困境'内涵辨析与中国的应对" [Analysis of the "Malacca Dilemma" and China's response], 世界经济与政治 [*World Economics and Politics*] no. 10 (2010): 117–140; 张洁 [Zhang Jie], "海上通道安全与中国战略支点的构建" [Sea lane security and constructing China's strategic fulcrum], 国际安全研究 [*International Security Research*] no. 2 (2015), http://cdn.ccps.ducway.com/51412015/342029000002/51412064.pdf.

44. "How Much Trade Transits the South China Sea?," China Power Project, August 2, 2017, updated August 26, 2020, https://chinapower.csis.org/much-trade-transits-south-china-sea/.

45. Lindsay Marie Thill, "RMB Internationalization and the BRI: Reality or Fantasy?," Real Instituto Elcano, November 13, 2020, https://blog.realinstitutoelcano.org/en/rmb-internationalization-and-the-bri-reality-or-fantasy/.

46. Julan Du and Yifei Zhang, "Does One Belt One Road Initiative Promote Chinese Overseas Direct Investment?," *China Economic Review* 47 (2018): 189–205.

47. *Belt and Road Economics*, p. 21.

48. James Reilly, *Orchestration: China's Economic Statecraft across Asia and Europe* (New York: Oxford University Press, 2021), chapter 2; Ye, *Belt Road and Beyond,* especially chapters 1 and 2.

49. "China Says One-Fifth of Belt and Road Projects 'Seriously Affected' by Pandemic," *Reuters,* June 19, 2020, https://www.reuters.com/article/us-health-coronavirus-china-silkroad-idUSKBN23Q0I1.

50. Daniel R. Russel and Blake H. Berger, *Weaponizing the Belt and Road Initiative* (New York: Asia Society, 2020), https://asiasociety.org/policy-institute/weaponizing-belt-and-road-initiative.

51. Gregory V. Raymond, "Religion as a Tool of Influence: Buddhism and China's Belt and Road Initiative in Mainland Southeast Asia," *Contemporary Southeast Asia* 42, no. 3 (2020): 346–371, doi: 10.1355/cs42-3b.

52. "发改委:共建'一带一路'合作取得积极进展呈现十足韧性" [National Development and Reform Commission: Constructive "One Belt One Road" cooperation makes positive progress, shows resilience], 人民网 [*People's Daily Online*], November 17, 2020, http://finance.people.com.cn/n1/2020/1117/c1004-31934058. html; see also Alice Han and Eyck Freymann, "Coronavirus Hasn't Killed Belt and Road," *Foreign Policy,* January 6, 2021, https://foreignpolicy.com/2021/01/06/coro navirus-hasnt-killed-belt-and-road/.

53. Xi Jinping, "Full Text of President Xi's Speech at Opening of Belt and Road Forum," May 14, 2017, http://www.xinhuanet.com//english/2017-05/14/c_136282982.htm; 赵周贤, 刘光明 [Zhao Zhouxian and Liu Guangming], "'一带一路':中国梦与世界梦的交汇桥梁" ["One Belt One Road": Connecting bridge between the China Dream and the world dream"], *People's Daily,* December 24, 2014, http://theory. people.com.cn/n/2014/1224/c40531-26265185.html. See also Rolland, "A Concise Guide."

54. For an extensive assessment of the BRI from the perspective of U.S. interests, see Jacob J. Lew et al., *China's Belt and Road: Implications for the United States,* Independent Task Force Report No. 79 (New York: Council on Foreign Relations, March 2021), https://www.cfr.org/report/chinas-belt-and-road-implications-for-the-united-states/.

55. Kamal Saggi, Keith E. Maskus, and Bernard Hoekman, "Transfer of Technology to Developing Countries: Unilateral and Multilateral Policy Options," World Bank Group Policy Research Working Paper No. 3332 (2004), https://openknowledge. worldbank.org/handle/10986/14181.

56. "国家发展和改革委员会,商务部,外交部等关于印发 '境外投资产业指导政策'的通知" [Notice on National Development and Reform Commission, Ministry of Commerce, Ministry of Foreign Affairs and others printing and issuing "Guidance Policy for Overseas Industry Investment"], 中华人民共和国商务部 [Ministry of Commerce of the People's Republic of China], July 5, 2006, http://tradeinservices.mof com.gov.cn/article/zhengce/hyfg/201710/447.html.

57. "Fact Sheet: CFIUS Final Regulations Revising Declaration Requirement for Certain Critical Technology Transactions," U.S. Department of the Treasury, September 11, 2020, https://home.treasury.gov/system/files/206/Fact-Sheet-Final-Rule-Revising-Mandatory-Crit-Tech-Declarations.pdf.

58. On the European Union and Australia, see "New EU Screening Framework Also Targeting Chinese FDI Is Finally in Place," Mercator Institute for China Studies, October 22, 2020, https://merics.org/en/short-analysis/new-eu-screening-framework-also-targeting-chinese-fdi-finally-place, and Melissa Clarke, "Foreign Investment Review Board to Be Given Greater Approval Powers amid Increasing National Security Risk," Australian Broadcasting Corporation, June 5, 2020, https:// www.abc.net.au/news/2020-06-05/foreign-investment-restrictions-tighten-austral ian-businesses/12324276.

59. "Huawei's Founder Ren Zhengfei: Huawei Will Never Provide Government with Customer Information," Huawei, January 15, 2019, https://www.huawei.com/en/facts/voices-of-huawei/interview-with-ren-zhengfei.

60. Karen Freifeld and Alexandra Alper, "Exclusive: Trump Admin Slams Huawei, Halting Shipments from Intel, Others—Sources," *Reuters,* January 18, 2021, https://www.reuters.com/article/usa-huawei-tech/exclusive-trump-admin-slams-chinas-huawei-halting-shipments-from-intel-others-sources-idUSL1N2JT054.

61. U.S. Department of Commerce, "Addition of Entities to the Entity List, Revision of Entry on the Entity List, and Removal of Entities from the Entity List," *Federal Register,* 85 FR 83416, December 18, 2020, https://www.federalregister.gov/documents/2020/12/22/2020-28031/addition-of-entities-to-the-entity-list-revision-of-entry-on-the-entity-list-and-removal-of-entities. See also "DOD Releases List of Additional Companies, in Accordance with Section 1237 of FY99 NDAA," U.S. Department of Defense, January 14, 2020, https://www.defense.gov/Newsroom/Releases/Release/Article/2472464/dod-releases-list-of-additional-companies-in-accordance-with-section-1237-of-fy/.

62. Edward Wong and Chris Buckley, "U.S. Says China's Repression of Uighurs Is 'Genocide,'" *New York Times,* January 19, 2021, https://www.nytimes.com/2021/01/19/us/politics/trump-china-xinjiang.html.

63. For example, see Humeyra Pamuk and David Shepardson, "U.S. Set to Add More Chinese Companies to Blacklist over Xinjiang," *Reuters,* July 9, 2021, https://www.reuters.com/world/china/exclusive-us-set-add-more-chinese-companies-blacklist-over-xinjiang-2021-07-09/.

64. *Economic and Trade Agreement between the Government of the United States of America and the Government of the People's Republic of China,* Office of the United States Trade Representative, January 15, 2020, chapter 2, https://ustr.gov/sites/default/files/files/agreements/phase%20one%20agreement/Economic_And_Trade_Agreement_Between_The_United_States_And_China_Text.pdf.

65. *Findings of the Investigation into China's Acts, Policies, and Practices Related to Technology Transfer, Intellectual Property, and Innovation under Section 301 of the Trade Act of 1974,* Office of the United States Trade Representative, March 22, 2018, https://ustr.gov/sites/default/files/Section%20301%20FINAL.PDF.

66. Ishan Banerjee and Matt Sheehan, "America's Got AI Talent: US' Big Lead in AI Research Is Built on Importing Researchers" *Macro Polo,* June 9, 2020, https://macropolo.org/americas-got-ai-talent-us-big-lead-in-ai-research-is-built-on-importing-researchers. A more comprehensive assessment of the PRC's brain-drain challenge is in David Zweig, "Competing for Talent: China's Strategies to Reverse the Brain Drain," *International Labour Review* 145 (2006): 65–90.

67. U.S. Senate Permanent Subcommittee on Investigations, "Threats to the U.S. Research Enterprise: China's Talent Recruitment Plans," 2019, https://www.hsgac.senate.gov/imo/media/doc/2019-11-18%20PSI%20Staff%20Report%20-%20China%27s%20Talent%20Recruitment%20Plans.pdf.

68. For example, see "Harvard University Professor and Two Chinese Nationals Charged in Three Separate China Related Cases," U.S. Department of Justice, January 28,

2020, https://www.justice.gov/opa/pr/harvard-university-professor-and-two-chin ese-nationals-charged-three-separate-china-related, and "Former Cleveland Clinic Employee and Chinese 'Thousand Talents' Participant Arrested for Wire Fraud," U.S. Department of Justice, May 14, 2020, https://www.justice.gov/opa/pr/former-clevel and-clinic-employee-and-chinese-thousand-talents-participant-arrested-wire-fraud. A comprehensive take on the problem by the director of the Federal Bureau of Investigation is Christopher Wray, "The Threat Posed by the Chinese Government and the Chinese Communist Party to the Economic and National Security of the United States," speech delivered to the Hudson Institute, Washington, D.C., U.S. Federal Bureau of Investigation, July 7, 2020, https://www.fbi.gov/news/speeches/ the-threat-posed-by-the-chinese-government-and-the-chinese-communist-party-to-the-economic-and-national-security-of-the-united-states.

69. "National High-End Foreign Experts Recruitment Plan (2019 Annual Call)," China Innovation Funding, http://chinainnovationfunding.eu/project/2019-high-end-fore ign-experts-recruitment-plan/.

70. *The IP Commission Report: The Report of the Commission on the Theft of American Intellectual Property* (Washington, D.C.: National Bureau of Asian Research, 2013), https://www.nbr.org/wp-content/uploads/pdfs/publications/IP_Commission_Rep ort.pdf.

71. "Fact Sheet: President Xi Jinping's State Visit to the United States," White House Office of the Press Secretary, September 25, 2015, https://obamawhitehouse.archives. gov/the-press-office/2015/09/25/fact-sheet-president-xi-jinpings-state-visit-united-states.

72. Lorand Laskai and Adam Segal, "A New Old Threat: Countering the Return of Chinese Industrial Cyber Espionage," Council on Foreign Relations, December 6, 2018, https://www.cfr.org/report/threat-chinese-espionage.

73. "The China Initiative: Year-in-Review (2019–20)," U.S. Department of Justice, November 16, 2020, https://www.justice.gov/opa/pr/china-initiative-year-rev iew-2019-20.

74. Andrew Kennedy and Darren Lim, "The Innovation Imperative: Technology and US-China Rivalry in the Twenty-First Century," *International Affairs* 94, no. 3 (2018): 553–572.

75. 中华人民共和国国务院 [State Council of the People's Republic of China], 国家中长期科学和技术发展规划纲要 (2006–2020年) [National Medium- and Long-Term Program for Science and Technology Development (2006–2020)], 国务院公报 [*State Council Bulletin*], no. 9 (2006), section 2.1, http://www.gov.cn/gongbao/cont ent/2006/content_240244.htm.

76. Kroeber, *China's Economy*, p. 81.

77. "Core Technology Depends on One's Own Efforts: President Xi," *People's Daily Online,* April 19, 2018, http://en.people.cn/n3/2018/0419/c90000-9451186.html.

78. The other three principles were "leapfrogging in priority areas" by taking advantage of the country's existing technological strengths, "enabling development" in crucial areas of social and economic need, and "leading the future" with cutting-edge

technologies and basic research to create new industries and markets. See National Medium- and Long-Term Program, section 2.1.

79. "China's Spending on R&D Rises to Historic High," *Xinhua*, August 27, 2020, http://www.xinhuanet.com/english/2020-08/27/c_139322217.htm.

80. Rintaro Hosokawa, "China Beats US in Patent Filings for Second Straight Year," *Nikkei Asia*, March 3, 2021, https://asia.nikkei.com/Business/Technology/China-beats-US-in-patent-filings-for-second-straight-year.

81. Soumitra Dutta, Bruno Lanvin, and Sacha Wunsch-Vincent, eds., *Global Innovation Index 2020: Who Will Finance Innovation?* (Geneva: World Intellectual Property Organization, 2020), https://www.wipo.int/edocs/pubdocs/en/wipo_pub_gii_2020.pdf.

82. Data in this paragraph drawn from Dutta, Lanvin, and Wunsch-Vincent, *Global Innovation Index 2020*; United Nations Economic, Social and Cultural Organization Institute for Statistics, http://uis.unesco.org/apps/visualisations/research-and-development-spending/; and Wang Tao, "China's Next Five-Year Plan to Prioritize Technology, Innovation," *Caixin Global*, September 25, 2020, https://www.caixinglobal.com/2020-09-25/wang-tao-chinas-next-five-year-plan-to-prioritize-technology-innovation-101609731.html.

83. For an excellent analysis of Made in China 2025 and its implications, Josh Wübbeke et al., *Made in China 2025: The Making of a High-Tech Superpower and Consequences for Industrial Companies,* MERICS Papers on China no. 2 (Berlin: Mercator Institute for China Studies, December 2016); Max J. Zenglein and Anna Holzmann, *Evolving Made in China 2025: China's Industrial Policy in the Quest for Global Tech Leadership,* MERICS Papers on China no. 8 (Berlin: Mercator Institute for China Studies, July 2019). See also Scott Kennedy, "Made in China 2025," Center for Strategic and International Studies, June 1, 2015, https://www.csis.org/analysis/made-china-2025.

84. Merkel quoted in Demetrius Klitou et al., *Germany: Industrie 4.0* (Brussels: European Commission, 2017), p. 3.

85. "'Made in China 2025' Industrial Policies: Issues for Congress," Congressional Research Service, August 11, 2020, https://crsreports.congress.gov/product/pdf/IF/IF10964/6.

86. "国务院关于印发 '中国制造2025' 的通知 [State Council notice on the issuance of Made in China 2025], 中华人民共和国国务院 [State Council of the People's Republic of China], May 8, 2015, http://www.gov.cn/zhengce/content/2015-05/19/content_9784.htm.

87. Zenglein and Holzmann, *Evolving Made in China 2025*.

88. "'Made in China 2025' Industrial Policies."

89. Kinling Lo, "'Made in China 2025' All Talk, No Action and a Waste of Taxpayers' Money, Says Former Finance Minister Lou Jiwei," *South China Morning Post*, March 7, 2019, https://www.scmp.com/news/china/diplomacy/article/2189046/chinas-tech-strategy-all-talk-no-action-and-waste-taxpayers.

90. In-depth details on Made in China 2025 as well as details of its domestic content goals are provided in *Made in China 2025: Global Ambitions Built on Local Protections* (Washington, D.C.: United States Chamber of Commerce, 2017), especially Appendix

3, https://www.uschamber.com/sites/default/files/final_made_in_china_2025_repo rt_full.pdf.

91. Xi Jinping, "国家中长期经济社会发展战略若干重大问题" [Certain major issues for our national medium- and long-term economic and social development strategy], 求是 [*Seeking Truth*], October 31, 2020, https://web.archive.org/web/20201111020 608/http://www.qstheory.cn/dukan/qs/2020-10/31/c_1126680390.htm. This article is translated by Etcetera Language Group at https://cset.georgetown.edu/research/ xi-jinping-certain-major-issues-for-our-national-medium-to-long-term-economic- and-social-development-strategy/.

92. Michael Martina, Kevin Yao, and Yawen Chen, "Exclusive: Facing U.S. Blowback, Beijing Softens 'Made in China 2025' Message," *Reuters*, June 25, 2018, https://www. reuters.com/article/us-usa-trade-china-madeinchina2025-exclu-idUSKBN1JL12U.

93. Li Keqiang, *Report of the Work of the Government,* delivered at the Fourth Session of the 13th National People's Congress of the People's Republic of China, March 5, 2021, p. 10, http://en.people.cn/n3/2021/0313/c90000-9828536.html.

94. Quoted in Kristen Huang and Kinling Lo, "Xi Jinping Says 'Time and Momentum on China's Side' as He Sets Out Communist Party Vision," *South China Morning Post,* January 12, 2021, https://www.scmp.com/news/china/politics/article/3117314/xi- jinping-says-time-and-momentum-chinas-side-he-sets-out.

95. Ryan Hass, "How China is Responding to Escalating Strategic Competition with the U.S.," *China Leadership Monitor,* no. 67 (2021), https://www.prcleader.org/hass.

96. Tom Mitchell, "China Launches Measures to Protect Companies from US Sanctions," *Financial Times,* January 9, 2021, https://www.ft.com/content/33c307b7-7157-442d- 90b4-f48308429d02.

97. Ye, *Belt Road and Beyond,* chapter 8.

Chapter 5

1. From Xi Jinping, "A Holistic View of National Security," speech delivered at the first meeting of the Central National Security Commission, April 15, 2013, in Xi Jinping, *The Governance of China* (Beijing: Foreign Languages Press, 2014), n.p.

2. Joseph S. Nye Jr., *Soft Power: The Means to Success in World Politics* (New York: PublicAffairs, 2004), chapter 1; quote from p. x.

3. R. Bates Gill, *Chinese Arms Transfers: Purposes, Patterns and Prospects in the New World Order* (Westport, CT: Praeger, 1992), pp. 56, 60.

4. From "China, People's Republic of (PRC)," in *Military Balance* (London: International Institute for Strategic Studies, 2020).

5. On Chinese studies of comprehensive national power, see Qi Haixia, *From Comprehensive National Power to Soft Power: A Study of the Chinese Scholars' Perception of Power,* The Griffith-Tsinghua "How China Sees the World" Working Paper Series no. 7 (2017), https://www.griffith.edu.au/__data/assets/pdf_file/0022/ 206644/Griffith-Tsinghua-WP-7-final-web.pdf. See also Michael Pillsbury, *China*

Debates the Future Security Environment (Washington, D.C.: National Defense University Press, 2000), especially chapter 5.

6. These data draw from 杨原, 张宇燕 [Yang Yuan and Zhang Yutiang], "新冠肺炎疫情下的全球政治与安全" [Global politics and security during the coronavirus epidemic], 吉林大学国家发展与安全研究院 [Jilin University Institute for National Development and Security Studies], February 6, 2021, http://indss.jlu.edu.cn/info/1010/1291.htm; 高红卫 [Gao Hongwei], "2030 年中国综合国力模型构建与预测" [Construction and application of a model for China's comprehensive national strength for 2030], 管理观察 [*Management Observer*], no. 32 (November 2016): 49–68. The author is grateful to Alastair Iain Johnston for bringing these articles to his attention.

7. This data point drawn from "China," *The World Factbook*, U.S. Central Intelligence Agency, n.d., https://www.cia.gov/library/publications/the-world-factbook/geos/ch.html.

8. David Shambaugh, *China Goes Global: The Partial Power* (Oxford: Oxford University Press, 2013).

9. For an excellent and in-depth assessment of China's power and how it is and is not translated effectively into influence across a number of case studies in Asia, see Evelyn Goh, ed., *Rising China's Influence in Developing Asia* (Oxford: Oxford University Press, 2016).

10. "'Paper Cat' Australia Will Learn Its Lesson," *Global Times*, July 30, 2016, https://www.globaltimes.cn/content/997320.shtml.

11. "Transcript of Chinese Ambassador CHENG Jingye's Interview with Australian Financial Review Political Correspondent Andrew Tillett," Embassy of the People's Republic of China to the Commonwealth of Australia, April 27, 2020, http://au.china-embassy.org/eng/gdtp_16/t1773741.htm.

12. "GDP (Current US$)—China," World Bank, https://data.worldbank.org/indicator/NY.GDP.MKTP.CD?locations=CN.

13. "China Economic Update—June 2021," World Bank, June 29, 2021, https://www.worldbank.org/en/country/china/publication/china-economic-update-june-2021.

14. Alyssa Leng and Roland Rajah, "Chart of the Week: Global Trade through a US-China Lens," *The Interpreter*, December 18, 2019, https://www.lowyinstitute.org/the-interpreter/chart-week-global-trade-through-us-china-lens; Daniel Shane, "China Will Overtake the US as the World's Biggest Retail Market This Year," *CNN*, January 23, 2019, https://edition.cnn.com/2019/01/23/business/china-retail-sales-us/index.html.

15. "GDP, PPP (Current International $)—China, United States," World Bank, https://data.worldbank.org/indicator/NY.GDP.MKTP.PP.CD?end=2019&locations=CN-US&start=2008.

16. "What Was the State of Chinese Outbound Investment in 2019?," EY Greater China, February 1, 2020, https://www.ey.com/en_cn/china-opportunities/what-was-the-state-of-chinese-outbound-investment-in-2019.

17. "China's Global Development Footprint," AidData, https://www.aiddata.org/china-official-finance.

18. On rare earths, see "Does China Pose a Threat to Global Rare Earth Supply Chains?," China Power Project, Center for Strategic and International Studies, https://chinapo wer.csis.org/china-rare-earths/. On outbound students, see "Global Flow of Tertiary-Level Students," United Nations Educational, Scientific and Cultural Organization Institute for Statistics, http://uis.unesco.org/en/uis-student-flow#slideoutmenu. On outbound departures, see "International Tourism, Number of Departures—China," World Bank, https://data.worldbank.org/indicator/ST.INT.DPRT?locations=CN.

19. James Reilly, *Orchestration: China's Economic Statecraft across Asia and Europe* (New York: Oxford University Press, 2021), p. 1.

20. "Full Normalisation of Relations with China," Ministry of Foreign Affairs of Norway, December 19, 2016, https://www.regjeringen.no/en/aktuelt/normalization_china/ id2524797/.

21. "Xi Jinping Meets with President Barack Obama of US," Ministry of Foreign Affairs of the People's Republic of China, September 3, 2016, https://www.fmprc.gov.cn/mfa_ eng/zxxx_662805/t1395073.shtml.

22. Jung-min Hee, "Lotte Mart Decided to Withdraw from the China Market," *BusinessKorea,* September 15, 2017, http://www.businesskorea.co.kr/news/articleV iew.html?idxno = 19316; "THAAD Row with China Costs S. Korea Dear: Report," *Yonhap News Agency,* September 15, 2017, https://en.yna.co.kr/view/AEN201709 15008300320; Vince Courtenay, "Missile Dispute Shooting Down Hyundai, Kia in China," *Wards Auto,* July 11, 2017, https://www.wardsauto.com/industry/missile-dispute-shooting-down-hyundai-kia-china, accessed on the 27th September 2020.

23. Jeongseok Lee, "Back to Normal?: The End of the THAAD Dispute between China and South Korea," *China Brief* 17, no. 15 (2017), https://jamestown.org/program/ back-normal-end-thaad-dispute-china-south-korea/.

24. For more details and analysis on this case, see Darren J. Lim and Victor Ferguson, "Chinese Economic Coercion during the THAAD Dispute," *The ASAN Forum,* December 28, 2019, http://www.theasanforum.org/chinese-economic-coercion-dur ing-the-thaad-dispute/.

25. Malcolm Turnbull, "Speech Introducing the National Security Legislation Amendment (Espionage and Foreign Interference) Bill 2017," December 7, 2017, www.malcolmturnbull.com.au/media/speech-introducing-the-national-security-legislation-amendment-espionage-an.

26. Fergus Hanson, Emilia Currey, and Tracy Beattie, *The Chinese Communist Party's Coercive Diplomacy,* Australian Strategic Policy Institute, Report no. 36 (2020), pp. 21, 29–33, https://www.aspi.org.au/report/chinese-communist-partys-coercive-diplomacy; Sonali Paul and Kirsty Needham, "Sour China-Australia Ties Hit Talks over LNG Deal, Says Woodside," Reuters, November 12, 2020, https://www.reuters. com/article/australia-china-trade/update-1-sour-china-australia-ties-hit-talks-over-lng-deal-says-woodside-idUKL1N2HY087; "China Seeks Alternatives after Ban on Australian Coal," *Argus Media,* November 11, 2020, https://www.argusmedia. com/en/news/2158794-china-seeks-alternatives-after-ban-on-australian-coal.

27. Jonathan Kearsley, Eryk Bagshaw, and Anthony Galloway, "'If You Make China the Enemy, China Will Be the Enemy': Beijing's Fresh Threat to Australia," *Sydney*

Morning Herald, November 18, 2020, https://www.smh.com.au/world/asia/if-you-make-china-the-enemy-china-will-be-the-enemy-beijing-s-fresh-threat-to-austra lia-20201118-p56fqs.html.

28. Peter Harrell, Elizabeth Rosenberg, and Edoardo Saravalle, *China's Use of Coercive Economic Measures* (Washington, D.C.: Center for a New American Security, June 2018).

29. Hanson, Currey, and Beattie, *The Chinese Communist Party's Coercive Diplomacy,* Appendix Table 1.

30. Andreas Fuchs and Nils-Hendrik Klann, "Paying a Visit: The Dalai Lama Effect on International Trade," *Journal of International Economics* 91 (2013): 164–177, doi: 10.1016/j.jinteco.2013.04.007.

31. Darren J. Lim, Victor A. Ferguson, and Rosa Bishop, "Chinese Outbound Tourism as an Instrument of Economic Statecraft," *Journal of Contemporary China* 29, no. 126 (2020): 916–933, doi: 10.1080/10670564.2020.1744390.

32. Matthew Y. H. Wong and Ying-ho Kwong, "Academic Censorship in China: The Case of *The China Quarterly*," *PS: Political Science and Politics* 52, no. 2 (2018): 287–292, doi: 10.1017/S1049096518002093.

33. More details on these and other cases in Hanson, Currey, and Beattie, *The Chinese Communist Party's coercive diplomacy,* Appendix Table 2.

34. Data in this paragraph drawn from *China's Foreign Aid (2014)* (Beijing: State Council Information Office, July 2014), http://english.www.gov.cn/archive/white_paper/ 2014/08/23/content_281474982986592.htm; *China's International Development Cooperation in the New Era* (Beijing: State Council Information Office, January 2021), http://www.xinhuanet.com/english/2021-01/10/c_139655400.htm.

35. *China and the World in the New Era* (Beijing: State Council Information Office, September 2019), http://english.www.gov.cn/archive/whitepaper/201909/27/con tent_WS5d8d80f9c6d0bcf8c4c142ef.html.

36. Axel Dreher et al., *Aid, China, and Growth: Evidence from a New Global Development Finance Dataset,* AidData Working Paper no. 46 (Williamsburg, VA: AidData, 2017), http://aiddata.org/data/chinese-global-official-finance-dataset.

37. Axel Dreher and Andreas Fuchs, "Rogue Aid?: An Empirical Analysis of China's Aid Allocation," *Canadian Journal of Economics* 48, no. 3 (2015): 988–1023, doi: 10.1111/ caje.12166; Axel Dreher et al., "Apples and Dragon Fruits: The Determinants of Aid and Other Forms of State Financing from China to Africa," *International Studies Quarterly* 62, no. 1 (2018): 182–194, doi:10.2139/ssrn.2855935.

38. Marina Rudyak, *The Ins and Outs of China's International Development Agency,* Carnegie Endowment for International Peace, September 2, 2019, https://carnegieen dowment.org/2019/09/02/ins-and-outs-of-china-s-international-development-age ncy-pub-79739; Denghua Zhang and Hongbo Ji, "The New Chinese Aid Agency after Its First Two Years," *DevPolicyBlog,* April 22, 2020, https://devpolicy.org/the-new-chinese-aid-agency-after-its-first-two-years-20200422-2/.

39. Kevin Acker, Deborah Brautigam, and Yufan Huang, *Debt Relief with Chinese Characteristics,* China Africa Research Initiative Policy Brief no. 46 (2020); Agatha Kratz, Allen Feng, and Logan Wright, *New Data on the "Debt Trap" Question,* The

Rhodium Group, April 29, 2019, https://rhg.com/research/new-data-on-the-debt-trap-question/; Deborah Brautigam, "Misdiagnosing the Chinese Infrastructure Push," *The American Interest*, April 4, 2019, https://www.the-american-interest.com/2019/04/04/misdiagnosing-the-chinese-infrastructure-push/.

40. Jane Perlez, "Asian Leaders at Regional Meeting Fail to Resolve Disputes over South China Sea," *New York Times*, July 12, 2012, https://www.nytimes.com/2012/07/13/world/asia/asian-leaders-fail-to-resolve-disputes-on-south-china-sea-during-asean-summit.html.

41. *Report of the Bi-Partisan Task-Force: Review of Solomon Islands Relations with People's Republic of China and Republic of China* (Honiara: Office of Prime Minister and Cabinet, 2019), https://drive.google.com/file/d/1Av3YhQy4980b8X83nhLt9xORN-5M3qYb/view.

42. Natalie Whiting, Christina Zhou and Kai Feng, "What Does It Take for China to Take Taiwan's Pacific Allies? Apparently, $730 Million," *ABC News*, September 19, 2019, https://www.abc.net.au/news/2019-09-18/solomon-islands-cuts-ties-with-taiwan-in-favour-of-china/11524118.

43. Christopher Pala, "Kiribati Re-Embraces China," *Policy Forum*, August 17, 2020, https://www.policyforum.net/kiribati-re-embraces-china/.

44. The 14 governments that recognize Taiwan (as of the end of 2021) are Belize, Eswatini (formerly known in English as Swaziland), Guatemala, Haiti, the Holy See, Honduras, the Marshall Islands, Nauru, Palau, Paraguay, Saint Kitts and Nevis, Saint Lucia, Saint Vincent and the Grenadines, and Tuvalu. On China-Taiwan checkbook diplomacy, see Denghua Zhang, "Comparing China's and Taiwan's Aid to the Pacific," *DevPolicyBlog*, January 20, 2020, https://devpolicy.org/comparing-chinas-and-taiwans-aid-to-the-pacific-20200120/.

45. *Fighting Covid-19: China in Action* (Beijing: State Council Information Office, June 2020), http://english.scio.gov.cn/whitepapers/2020-06/07/content_76135269.htm.

46. Harlan Jencks, *From Muskets to Missiles: Politics and Professionalism in the Chinese Army, 1945–1981* (Boulder, CO: Westview Press, 1982); David Shambaugh, *Modernizing China's Military: Progress, Problems, and Prospects* (Berkeley: University of California Press, 2003), especially chapter 2; Michael Kiselycznyk and Phillip C. Saunders, *Civil-Military Relations in China: Assessing the PLA's Role in Elite Politics*, China Strategic Perspectives 2 (Washington, D.C.: National Defense University Press, 2010), http://ndupress.ndu.edu/Portals/68/Documents/stratperspective/china/ChinaPerspectives-2.pdf.

47. James Mulvenon, *Soldiers of Fortune: The Rise and Fall of the Chinese Military-Business Complex, 1978–1998* (Armonk, NY: M. E. Sharpe, 2001); John Garnaut, "Rotting from Within: Investigating the Massive Corruption of the Chinese Military," *Foreign Policy*, April 16, 2012, https://foreignpolicy.com/2012/04/16/rotting-from-within/.

48. Phillip C. Saunders and Joel Wuthnow, "Large and in Charge: Civil-Military Relations under Xi Jinping," in Phillip C. Saunders et al., eds., *Chairman Xi Remakes the PLA: Assessing Chinese Military Reforms* (Washington, D.C.: National Defense University Press, 2019), chapter 13, quote from p. 521.

49. From Xi Jinping, "Build Up Our National Defense and Armed Forces," November 16, 2012, in Xi Jinping, *The Governance of China* (Beijing: Foreign Languages Press, 2014), n.p.

50. Joel McFadden, Kim Fassler, and Justin Godby, "The New PLA Leadership: Xi Molds China's Military to His Vision," in Saunders et al., *Chairman Xi Remakes the PLA*, chapter 14; Bates Gill and Adam Ni, "Expect a Shake-Up of China's Military Elite at the 19th Party Congress," *The Conversation,* October 16, 2017, https://theconve rsation.com/expect-a-shakeup-of-chinas-military-elite-at-the-19th-party-congr ess-84060.

51. "China to Optimize Army Size, Structure: CPC Decision," *CCTV,* November 16, 2013, http://english.cntv.cn/20131116/100749.shtml.

52. Michael Chase et al., *China's Incomplete Military Transformation: Assessing the Weaknesses of the People's Liberation Army (PLA)* (Santa Monica, CA: RAND Corporation, 2015).

53. Larry M. Wortzel, "What the Chinese People's Liberation Army Can Do to Thwart the Army's Multi-Domain Task Force," Association of the United States Army Land Warfare Paper No. 126, July 2019, 10–11, https://www.ausa.org/sites/default/files/ publications/LWP-126-What-the-Chinese-People's-Liberation-Army-Can-Do-to-Thwart-the-Armys-Multi-Domain-Task-Force.pdf. Wortzel continued, "It is clear, then, that while the PLA understands multi-domain warfare conceptually and has a robust doctrine for these forms of operations, it is stymied in attempts to apply such operations in practical scenarios."

54. Authoritative, critical assessments of the PLA repeatedly appear in PRC media and official publications. Some examples include, "学习习近平总书记关于强军目标的重要论述" [Study General Secretary Xi Jinping's exposition on the goal of strengthening the military], *People's Daily,* July 22, 2013, http://theory.peo ple.com.cn/n/2013/0722/c40531-22275029.html; "破解一支军队所向披靡的脉动密码" [Crack an army's password], *PLA Daily,* July 28, 2014, http://www.81.cn/ 2014-content_18620/2014-07/28/content_6173099.htm; State Council Information Office, *China's National Defense in the New Era,* July 2019, http://eng.mod.gov.cn/ news/2019-07/24/content_4846443.htm. On official self-assessments of the PLA, see Dennis J. Blasko, "PLA Weaknesses and Xi's Concerns about PLA Capabilities," testimony before the U.S.-China Economic and Security Review Commission, February 7, 2019, https://www.uscc.gov/sites/default/files/Blasko_USCC%20Test imony_FINAL.pdf.

55. For more details on these PLA reforms, see Bates Gill, Adam Ni, and Dennis Blasko, "The Ambitious Reform Plans of the People's Liberation Army: Progress, Prospects and Implications for Australia," *Australian Journal of Defence and Strategic Studies* 2, no. 1 (2020): 5–26, http://www.defence.gov.au/ADC/publications/AJDSS/volu me2-number1/ambitious-reform-plans-of-the-PLA.asp. See also Saunders et al., *Chairman Xi Remakes the PLA;* Michael S. Chase and Jeffrey Engstrom, "China's Military Reforms: An Optimistic Take," *Joint Forces Quarterly* 83 (2016): 49–52; Roger Cliff, "Chinese Military Reforms: A Pessimistic Take," *Joint Forces Quarterly* 83 (2016): 53–56.

56. Xi Jinping, *Secure a Decisive Victory in Building a Moderately Prosperous Society in All Respects and Strive for the Great Success of Socialism with Chinese Characteristics for a New Era*, report delivered at the 19th National Congress of the Communist Party of China, October 18, 2017, http://www.xinhuanet.com/english/special/2017-11/03/c_136725942.htm.

57. Xi, *Secure a Decisive Victory*; see also "决胜全面建成小康社会夺取新时代中国特色社会主义伟大胜利" [Decisive victory, build a well-off society in an all-round way, win the great victory of socialism with Chinese characteristics in the new era], *PLA Daily*, October 19, 2017. For an insightful discussion on the concept of a "world-class military," see M. Taylor Fravel, "China's 'World-Class' Military Ambitions: Origins and Implications," *Washington Quarterly* 42, no. 4 (2020): 85–99, doi: 10.1080/0163660X.2020.1735850.

58. Office of the Secretary of Defense, *Military and Security Developments Involving the People's Republic of China 2020: Annual Report to Congress* (Washington, D.C.: Department of Defense, August 2020), p. i, https://media.defense.gov/2020/Sep/01/2002488689/-1/-1/1/2020-DOD-CHINA-MILITARY-POWER-REPORT-FINAL.PDF.

59. On naval, missile, and air force weaponry, see Office of the Secretary of Defense, *Military and Security Developments Involving the People's Republic of China 2021: Annual Report to Congress* (Washington, D.C.: Department of Defense, November 2021), https://media.defense.gov/2021/Nov/03/2002885874/-1/-1/0/2021-CMPR-FINAL.PDF; "Chinese Aircraft Carrier Forming All-Weather Combat Capability with Successful Night Takeoff and Landing," *Global Times*, May 28, 2018, https://www.globaltimes.cn/content/1104460.shtml; Liu Xuanzun, "China's Third Aircraft Carrier 'Progressing Smoothly,'" *Global Times*, September 13, 2020, https://www.globaltimes.cn/content/1200749.shtml.

60. Unless otherwise noted, information in this paragraph draws from *Military and Security Developments Involving the People's Republic of China 2021*, pp. 49, 60–62, and Appendix I.

61. Matt Korda and Hans Kristensen, "China Is Building a Second Nuclear Missile Silo Field," Federation of American Scientists, July 26, 2021, https://fas.org/blogs/security/2021/07/china-is-building-a-second-nuclear-missile-silo-field/.

62. 杨凡凡 [Yang Fanfan], "东风-17常规导弹方队 东风劲旅剑开新刃" [DF-17 conventional missile formation: Dongfeng sword's new sharp edge], 中国军网综合 [*China Military Online*], October 10, 2019, http://www.81.cn/jmywyl/2019-10/02/content_9642720.htm; *Military and Security Developments Involving the People's Republic of China 2021*, p. 60.

63. Phil Stewart, "Top U.S. General Confirms 'Very Concerning' Chinese Hypersonic Weapons Test," *Reuters*, October 28, 2021, https://www.reuters.com/business/aerospace-defense/top-us-general-confirms-very-concerning-chinese-hypersonic-weapons-test-2021-10-27/.

64. Eric Daniel Hagt, *China's Civil-Military Integration: National Strategy, Local Politics* (Ph.D. dissertation, Johns Hopkins University School of Advanced International Studies, 2020); Alex Stone and Peter Wood, *China's Military-Civil Fusion Strategy*,

China Aerospace Studies Institute, June 15, 2020, https://www.airuniversity.af.edu/CASI/Display/Article/2217101/chinas-military-civil-fusion-strategy/; see also the four articles available in Richard A. Bitzinger, Yoram Evron, and Zi Yang, "Roundtable: China's Military-Civil Fusion Strategy: Development, Procurement, and Secrecy," *Asia Policy* 16, no. 1 (2021): 1–64.

65. On China's "near seas," see Andrew S. Erickson, "China's Near-Seas Challenges," *The National Interest*, January 13, 2014, https://nationalinterest.org/article/chinas-near-seas-challenges-9645.

66. "First island chain" refers to the line of major archipelagos immediately east of the Asian mainland, extending from the Kamchatka Peninsula in the north to the Malaysian Peninsula in the south, and encompassing the Yellow Sea, East China Sea, Taiwan Strait, and South China Sea. These archipelagic features include the Kuril Islands, the main Japanese islands, the Ryukyu Islands, Taiwan, the northern and western Philippines, Borneo, and the Indonesian Riau Islands. The "second island chain" refers to a line roughly extending from the Japanese home islands to the Mariana Islands, which include, importantly, the U.S. territory of Guam, and continuing southward to Papua New Guinea.

67. The Asia Maritime Transparency Initiative at the Center for Strategic and International Studies hosts an excellent website, https://amti.csis.org, providing satellite imagery, maps, and analyses on political, military, territorial, and legal developments in maritime Asia.

68. Amanda Macias and Courtney Kube, "Chinese Military Conducts Anti-Ship Missile Tests in Hotly Contested South China Sea," *CNBC*, July 1, 2019, https://www.nbcnews.com/news/china/chinese-military-conducts-anti-ship-missile-tests-hotly-contested-south-n1025456; "Defence Ministry's Regular Press Conference on Jun. 27," *PLA Daily*, June 27, 2019, http://eng.chinamil.com.cn/view/2019-06/27/content_9541430.htm.

69. *Defense of Japan 2020* (Tokyo: Ministry of Defense, 2020), p. 27, https://www.mod.go.jp/e/publ/w_paper/wp2020/DOJ2020_EN_Full.pdf; "Japan ASDF Jets Scrambled 947 Times in FY 2019," *Jiji Press,* April 9, 2020, https://www.nippon.com/en/news/yjj2020040900904/japan-asdf-jets-scrambled-947-times-in-fy-2019.html.

70. *Defense of Japan 2021 Digest* (Tokyo: Ministry of Defense, 2021), p. 3, https://www.mod.go.jp/en/publ/w_paper/wp2021/DOJ2021_Digest_EN.pdf; *Defense of Japan 2020*, pp. 73–74.

71. On these China-Russia activities, see "China-Russia 'Joint Sea–2019' Exercises Makes Two 'First Times,'" *China Military Online,* May 5, 2019, http://eng.chinamil.com.cn/view/2019-05/05/content_9495927.htm; Mike Yeo, "Russian-Chinese Air Patrol Was an Attempt to Divide Allies, Says Top US Air Force Official in Pacific," *Defense News,* August 23, 2019, https://www.defensenews.com/global/asia-pacific/2019/08/23/russian-chinese-air-patrol-was-an-attempt-to-divide-allies-says-top-us-air-force-official-in-pacific/.

72. *Military and Security Developments Involving the People's Republic of China 2021,* Appendix I.

73. *Military and Security Developments Involving the People's Republic of China 2020*, p. 95; *Military and Security Developments Involving the People's Republic of China 2021*, p. 98.

74. John Dotson, "Military Activity and Political Signaling in the Taiwan Strait in Early 2020," *China Brief* 20, no. 6 (2020): 1–7, https://jamestown.org/wp-content/uploads/2020/04/Read-the-04-01-2020-CB-Issue-in-PDF.pdf.

75. "PLA's 'Unprecedented Drills' in Taiwan Straits for Deterrence, Actual Combat: Observers," *Global Times,* August 13, 2020, https://www.globaltimes.cn/content/1197716.shtml; Liu Xuanzun, "PLA Holds Concentrated Military Drills to Deter Taiwan Secessionists, US," *Global Times,* August 23, 2020, https://www.globaltimes.cn/content/1198593.shtml; Lawrence Chung, "Taiwan under Psychological Attack as Chinese Warplanes Cross Median Line, Analysts Say," *South China Morning Post,* October 3, 2020, https://www.scmp.com/news/china/diplomacy/article/3103985/taiwan-under-psychological-attack-chinese-warplanes-cross. The Taiwan Ministry of National Defense maintains a website tracking these regular intrusions: https://www.mnd.gov.tw/PublishTable.aspx?Types=即時軍事動態&title=國防消息.

76. "社评: 能否治住美国对台军售? 当然也必须能" [Editorial: Can American military sales to Taiwan be brought to an end? Of course they must be], 环球时报 [*Global Times*], October 27, 2020, https://opinion.huanqiu.com/article/40SOGIRxqDe.

77. For these activities in 2021, see Liu Xuanzun, "PLA Carrier Enters S. China Sea after American Flattop Exercise amid Taiwan Tensions," *Global Times,* April 11, 2021, https://www.globaltimes.cn/page/202104/1220779.shtml; Liu Xuanzun, "PLA Carrier, Warplanes Surround Taiwan in Drills, in Show of Capability to Cut Off Foreign Intervention," *Global Times,* April 6, 2021, https://www.globaltimes.cn/page/202104/1220377.shtml; Kathrin Hille and Demetri Sevastopulo, "Chinese Warplanes Simulated Attacking US Carrier near Taiwan," *Financial Times,* January 29, 2021, https://www.ft.com/content/e6f6230c-b709-4b3d-b9a2-951516e52360; "Record Number of China Planes Enter Taiwan Air Defence Zone," *BBC,* October 5, 2021, https://www.bbc.com/news/world-asia-58794094.

78. "How Covid-19 Affected U.S.-China Military Signaling," Center for Strategic and International Studies Asia Maritime Transparency Initiative, December 17, 2020, https://amti.csis.org/how-covid-19-affected-u-s-china-military-signaling/; Li Jie quoted in Minnie Chan, "China-US Tensions Keep PLA Sailors at Sea for an Extra Four Months in 2020," *South China Morning Post,* December 25, 2020, https://www.scmp.com/news/china/military/article/3115328/china-us-tensions-keep-pla-sailors-sea-extra-four-months-2020.

79. *Military and Security Developments Involving the People's Republic of China 2020*, p. 72.

80. *Military and Security Developments Involving the People's Republic of China 2020*, p. 56.

81. *Military and Security Developments Involving the People's Republic of China 2020*, p. 7; Kenneth Allen, Phillip C. Saunders, and John Chen, *China's Military Diplomacy, 2003–2016: Trends and Implications,* China Strategic Perspectives 11 (Washington, D.C.: National Defense University Press, 2017).

82. Jean-Pierre Cabestan, "China's Military Base in Djibouti: A Microcosm of China's Growing Competition with the United States and New Bipolarity,"

Journal of Contemporary China 29, no. 125 (2019): 731–747, doi: 10.1080/ 10670564.2019.1704994; Dennis J. Blasko and Roderick Lee, "The Chinese Navy's Marine Corps, Part 2: Chain-of-Command Reforms and Evolving Training," *China Brief*, February 15, 2019, https://jamestown.org/program/the-chinese-navys-mar ine-corps-part-2-chain-of-command-reforms-and-evolving-training/.

83. Jeremy Page, Gordon Lubold, and Rob Taylor, "Deal for Naval Outpost in Cambodia Furthers China's Quest for Military Network," *Wall Street Journal,* July 22, 2019, https://www.wsj.com/articles/secret-deal-for-chinese-naval-outpost-in-cambodia- raises-u-s-fears-of-beijings-ambitions-11563732482; Sopheng Cheang, "Cambodia Denies New Speculation about Chinese Base Plans," *Associated Press,* October 6, 2020, https://apnews.com/article/thailand-china-archive-cambodia-345a88965b1c0 272448c2270e966fc39; "China Refutes Report of Cambodia Naval Base," *Associated Press,* July 24, 2019, https://apnews.com/article/e69191b4bc5a4bcd93892e17c 04b83c4.

84. "40th Chinese Naval Escort Task Force Departs for Gulf of Aden," *China Military Online,* January 16, 2022, http://english.chinamil.com.cn/view/2022-01/16/content_ 10123678.htm. Further details on the PLAN Gulf of Aden missions available in Bates Gill, Dennis Blasko, Adam Ni and Ben Schreer, *Assessing the Ambitious Reform Plans of the Chinese People's Liberation Army: Progress, Problems, and Prospects*, report submitted to the Australian Department of Defence, March 30, 2020, Appendix 2 (available on request from the author).

85. *China's National Defense in the New Era*, 21.

86. *China's National Defense in the New Era*, 51.

87. On the value of the Gulf of Aden missions to the PLAN, see Andrew S. Erickson and Austin M. Strange, *No Substitute for Experience: Chinese Antipiracy Operations in the Gulf of Aden,* United States Naval War College China Maritime Studies Institute Red Books no. 10 (2013).

88. Bates Gill and Chin-hao Huang, "The People's Republic of China," in Alex J. Bellamy and Paul D. Williams, eds., *Providing Peacekeepers: The Politics, Challenges, and Future of United Nations Peacekeeping Contributions* (Oxford: Oxford University Press, 2013), chapter 6; Richard Gowan, "China's Pragmatic Approach to UN Peacekeeping," Brookings Institution, September 14, 2020, https://www.brookings. edu/articles/chinas-pragmatic-approach-to-un-peacekeeping/.

89. Data as of November 2021 and drawn from the United Nations Peacekeeping website, https://peacekeeping.un.org/en.

90. *China's Armed Forces: 30 Years of UN Peacekeeping Operations* (Beijing: State Council Information Office of the People's Republic of China, September 2020), Preface and Annex III, http://english.www.gov.cn/archive/whitepaper/202009/18/content_WS5 f6449a8c6d0f7257693c323.html.

91. *China's Military Diplomacy, 2003–2016*, 29–33, Table 6 and Appendix.

92. On China-Russia joint exercises, see Richard Weitz, "Assessing Chinese-Russian Military Exercises: Past Progress and Future Trends," Center for Strategic and International Studies, July 2021, https://www.csis.org/analysis/assessing-chinese- russian-military-exercises-past-progress-and-future-trends.

93. The Shanghai Cooperation Organization (SCO) was announced in 2001 and was made up of six members: China, Kazakhstan, Kyrgyzstan, Russia, Tajikistan, and Uzbekistan. Two additional members, India and Pakistan, joined in 2017 and took part in the Peace Mission exercises in 2018. "A Quick Guide to SCO and Its Military Cooperation," *CGTN,* June 5, 2018, http://english.scio.gov.cn/infographics/2018-06/05/content_51673238.htm. On "Peace Mission–2018," see Daniel Urchick, "What We Learned from Peace Mission 2018," *Small Wars Journal,* October 3, 2018, https://smallwarsjournal.com/jrnl/art/what-we-learned-peace-mission-2018.

94. On "Vostok-2018," see "Russia Begins Its Largest Ever Military Exercise with 300,000 Soldiers," *The Guardian,* September 12, 2018, https://www.theguardian.com/world/2018/sep/11/russia-largest-ever-military-exercise-300000-soldiers-china. On "Caucuses-2020," see Ben Wolfgang, "Russia, China, Iran to Hold Massive Joint Military Exercise," *Washington Times,* September 10, 2020, https://www.washingtontimes.com/news/2020/sep/10/russia-china-iran-hold-massive-joint-military-exer/. On the exercises in Ningxia in 2021, "China-Russia Drill Signals New Era in Joint Exercises: Spokesperson," *Global Times,* August 27, 2021, https://www.globaltimes.cn/page/202108/1232623.shtml.

95. Data for 1990 through 2019 from Stockholm International Peace Research Institute Arms Trade Database, https://armstrade.sipri.org/armstrade/page/trade_register.php.

96. Lyle J. Goldstein and Vitaly Kozyrev, "China-Russia Military Cooperation and the Emergent U.S.-China Rivalry: Implications and Recommendations for U.S. National Security," *Journal of Peace and War Studies,* 2nd ed. (2020): 24–48. On the early years of Russian arms exports to China, see Bates Gill and Taeho Kim, *China's Arms Acquisitions from Abroad: A Quest for "Superb and Secret Weapons"* (Oxford: Oxford University Press, 1995), especially chapter 3.

97. Data in this paragraph are through 2019 and drawn from Stockholm International Peace Research Institute Arms Trade Database, https://armstrade.sipri.org/armstrade/page/toplist.php, https://armstrade.sipri.org/armstrade/page/values.php, and https://armstrade.sipri.org/armstrade/page/trade_register.php. For a historical overview of PRC arms exports up to the early 1990s, see Gill, *Chinese Arms Transfers.*

98. "Foreign Ministry Spokesperson Hua Chunying's Regular Press Conference on October 23, 2019," Ministry of Foreign Affairs of the People's Republic of China, October 23, 2019, https://www.fmprc.gov.cn/mfa_eng/xwfw_665399/s2510_665401/t1710130.shtml.

99. *Military and Security Developments Involving the People's Republic of China 2020,* p. 24.

100. *China's Military Diplomacy, 2003–2016,* p. 58.

Chapter 6

1. Xi Jinping, "Implement the Free Trade Zone Strategy," speech at the 19th group study session of the Political Bureau of the 18th CCP Central Committee, December 5,

2014, in *Xi Jinping: The Governance of China II* (Beijing: Foreign Languages Press, 2017), pp. 106–107.

2. Wendell Cox, "500 Years of GDP: A Tale of Two Countries," *Newgeography,* September 21, 2015, https://www.newgeography.com/content/005050-500-years-gdp-a-tale-two-countries.

3. John W. Garver, *China's Quest: The History of the Foreign Relations of the People's Republic of China* (New York: Oxford University Press, 2016), pp. 171–175, 196–231; Julia Lovell, *Maoism: A Global History* (New York: Alfred A. Knopf, 2019), especially chapter 4.

4. "Speech by Chairman of the Delegation of the People's Republic of China, Deng Xiaoping, at the Special Session of the U.N. General Assembly," April 10, 1974, https://www.marxists.org/reference/archive/deng-xiaoping/1974/04/10.htm.

5. Ezra F. Vogel, *Deng Xiaoping and the Transformation of China* (Cambridge, MA: Belknap Press of Harvard University Press, 2011), pp. 83–84.

6. "Whither China: From Membership to Responsibility?," remarks by Deputy Secretary of State Robert B. Zoellick to the National Committee on U.S.-China Relations, September 21, 2005, https://2001-2009.state.gov/s/d/former/zoellick/rem/53682.htm. For a PRC scholar's perspective on the "responsible stakeholder" debate in China, see Weizhun Mao, "Debating China's International Responsibility," *Chinese Journal of International Politics* 10, no. 2 (2017): 173–210, doi: 10/1093/cjip/pox006.

7. For an analysis of Hu Jintao's formulations, see Bonnie S. Glaser and Benjamin Dooley, "China's 11th Ambassadorial Conference Signals Continuity and Change in Foreign Policy," *China Brief* 9, no. 22 (November 4, 2009), https://jamestown.org/program/chinas-11th-ambassadorial-conference-signals-continuity-and-change-in-foreign-policy/.

8. "Firmly March on the Path of Socialism with Chinese Characteristics and Strive to Complete the Building of a Moderately Prosperous Society in All Respects," report by General Secretary Hu Jintao to the 18th National Congress of the Communist Party of China, November 8, 2012, http://www.china.org.cn/china/18th_cpc_congress/2012-11/16/content_27137540.htm.

9. Xi Jinping, "Uphold and Develop Socialism with Chinese Characteristics," speech to members and alternative members of the CCP Central Committee, January 5, 2013, trans. at Tanner Greer, "Xi Jinping in Translation: China's Guiding Ideology," *Palladium,* May 31, 2019, https://palladiummag.com/2019/05/31/xi-jinping-in-translation-chinas-guiding-ideology/#xv.

10. "习近平在周边外交工作座谈会上发表重要讲话" [Xi Jinping delivers important speech at the Conference on Diplomatic Work toward Neighboring Countries], 新华网 [*Xinhuanet*], October 25, 2013, http://www.xinhuanet.com//politics/2013-10/25/c_117878897.htm.

11. For analysis by PRC scholars of this shift in orientation, see, for example, Yan Xuetong, "From Keeping a Low Profile to Striving for Achievements," *Chinese Journal of International Politics* 7, no. 2 (2014): 153–184, doi: 10.1093/cjip/pou027; Qin Yaqing, "Continuity through Change: Background Knowledge and China's

International Strategy," *Chinese Journal of International Politics* 7, no. 3 (2014): 285–314, doi: 10.1093/cjip/pou034.

12. "习近平出席中央外事工作会议并发表重要讲话" [Xi Jinping attends Central Foreign Affairs Work Conference and delivers important speech], 新华网 [*Xinhuanet*], November 29, 2014, http://www.xinhuanet.com/politics/2014-11/29/c_1113457723.htm; "Xi Stresses Urgency of Reforming Global Governance," *Xinhua*, October 14, 2015, http://www.chinadaily.com.cn/china/2015-10/14/content_22182 736.htm; "Xi Calls for Reforms on Global Governance," *Xinhua*, September 29, 2016, http://www.chinadaily.com.cn/china/2016-09/29/content_26931697.htm.

13. Mao, "Debating China's International Responsibility."

14. "习近平在庆祝中国共产党成立95周年大会上的讲话" [Xi Jinping's speech to the conference commemorating the 95th anniversary of the founding of the Chinese Communist Party], 人民日报 [*People's Daily*], July 1, 2016, http://cpc.people.com.cn/n1/2016/0702/c64093-28517655.html.

15. Xi Jinping, "Improve Our Ability to Participate in Global Governance," from a speech to a group study session of the CCP Politburo, September 27, 2016, in Xi Jinping, *The Governance of China II* (Beijing: Foreign Languages Press, 2017), pp. 487–490.

16. Quoted in Xi Jinping, "Secure a Decisive Victory in Building a Moderately Prosperous Society in All Respects and Strive for the Great Success of Socialism with Chinese Characteristics for a New Era," speech delivered to the 19th CCP National Congress, October 18, 2017, p. 9, http://www.xinhuanet.com/english/special/2017-11/03/c_13 6725942.htm; "Xi Urges Breaking New Ground in Major Country Diplomacy with Chinese Characteristics," *Xinhua*, June 24, 2018, http://xinhuanet.com/english/2018-06/24/c_137276269.htm.

17. Major General Jin Yinan quoted in Evan Osnos, "Making China Great Again," *The New Yorker*, January 8, 2018, https://www.newyorker.com/magazine/2018/01/08/making-china-great-again.

18. Kishore Mahbubani, "How China Could Win Over the Post-Coronavirus World and Leave the US Behind," *Market Watch*, April 14, 2020, https://www.marketwatch.com/story/how-china-could-win-over-the-post-coronavirus-world-and-leave-the-us-behind-2020-04-14; Sam Bresnick and Paul Haenle, "Amid Coronavirus Pandemic, China Seeks Larger Role on World Stage," Carnegie Endowment for International Peace, April 9, 2020, https://carnegieendowment.org/2020/04/09/amid-coronavirus-pandemic-china-seeks-larger-role-on-world-stage-pub-81515; Michael D. Swaine, "Chinese Crisis Decision Making: Managing the COVID-19 Pandemic Part Two: The International Dimension," *China Leadership Monitor*, no. 65, September 1, 2020, https://www.prcleader.org/swaine-1; Bates Gill, "China's Global Influence: Post-COVID Prospects for Soft Power," *Washington Quarterly* 43, no. 2 (2020): 97–115, doi: 10.1080/0163660X.2020.1771041.

19. For additional detail and analysis on the evolution of China's approach to global leadership under Xi Jinping, see, for example, Yi Edward Yang, "China's Strategic Narratives in Global Governance Reform under Xi Jinping," *Journal of Contemporary China* 30, no. 128 (2021): 299–313, doi: 10.1080/10670564.2020.1790904; Melanie Hart and Blaine Johnson, "Mapping China's Global Governance Ambitions," Center

for American Progress, February 28, 2019, https://www.americanprogress.org/iss
ues/security/reports/2019/02/28/466768/mapping-chinas-global-governance-
ambitions/; Liza Tobin, "Xi's Vision for Transforming Global Governance: A Strategic
Challenge for Washington and Its Allies," *Texas National Security Review* 2, no. 1
(2018), https://tnsr.org/2018/11/xis-vision-for-transforming-global-governance-a-
strategic-challenge-for-washington-and-its-allies/.

20. The classic work on the PRC's early years in the United Nations is Samuel S. Kim,
China, the United Nations, and World Order (Princeton, NJ: Princeton University
Press, 1979).

21. "China and the United Nations: Position Paper of the People's Republic of China
For the 74th Session of the United Nations General Assembly," Ministry of Foreign
Affairs of the People's Republic of China, September 18, 2019, https://www.fmprc.
gov.cn/mfa_eng/wjdt_665385/2649_665393/t1698812.shtml.

22. "Remarks by Amb. Zhang Jun at the Workshop on the 5th Anniversary of the United
Nations Peace and Development Fund," Permanent Mission of the People's Republic
of China to the UN, December 8, 2020, https://www.fmprc.gov.cn/ce/ceun/eng/
dbtxx/czdbzjds/zjdshd/t1838766.htm.

23. Rosemary Foot, *China, the UN, and Human Protection* (Oxford: Oxford University
Press, 2020), pp. 33–34; "China and the United Nations."

24. "Full Text of Xi's Statement at the General Debate of the 75th Session of the United
Nations General Assembly," *Xinhua,* September 23, 2020, http://www.xinhuanet.
com/english/2020-09/23/c_139388686.htm.

25. "Feature: Xi Jinping—A Champion of the UN Ethos," *Xinhua,* September 21, 2020,
http://www.xinhuanet.com/english/2020-09/21/c_139384099.htm.

26. Courtney J. Fung and Shing-hon Lam, "Staffing the United Nations: China's
Motivations and Prospects," *International Affairs* 97, no. 4 (2021): 1143–1163, doi.
org/10/1093/ia/iiab071.

27. The UN Human Rights Council (UNHRC) was established in 2006. Forty-seven
UN members are elected by the UN General Assembly to three-year terms. UNHRC
members are not eligible for immediate reelection after two consecutive terms. As a
result, China has not had a seat on the UNHRC only twice, in 2013 and 2020. "Which
Countries Have Been Members of the Human Rights Council?," United Nations
Dag Hammarskjöld Library, n.d., https://ask.un.org/faq/268839. On China and the
UNHRC and its predecessor organization, the UN Commission on Human Rights,
see Foot, *China, the UN, and Human Protection,* chapter 6.

28. For early assessments of PRC peacekeeping, see Bates Gill and Chin-hao Huang,
China's Expanding Role in Peacekeeping: Prospects and Policy Implications, SIPRI
Policy Paper 25 (Stockholm: Stockholm International Peace Research Institute,
November 2009), https://www.sipri.org/publications/2009/sipri-policy-papers/
chinas-expanding-role-peacekeeping-prospects-and-policy-implications. See also
Courtney J. Richardson, "A Responsible Power? China and the UN Peacekeeping
Regime," *International Peacekeeping* 18, no. 3 (2011): 286–297, doi: 10.1080/
13533312.2011.563082.

29. "Data," United Nations Peacekeeping, https://peacekeeping.un.org/en/data.

30. These were the UNPKOs in Western Sahara, Mali, Democratic Republic of the Congo, South Sudan, Sudan, Lebanon, Abyei (contested territory between Sudan and South Sudan), Cyprus, and the truce supervision operation in the Middle East. Data as of November 2021 and drawn from the United Nations Peacekeeping website, https:// peacekeeping.un.org/en.

31. Jerry Feltman, "China's Expanding Influence at the United Nations—and How the United States Should React," Brookings Institution, September 2020, https://www. brookings.edu/wp-content/uploads/2020/09/FP_20200914_china_united_nations_ feltman.pdf.

32. Feltman, "China's Expanding Influence," p. 2.

33. Ben Blanchard, "Taiwan Rejects China's Main Condition for WHO Participation," *Reuters,* May 15, 2020, https://www.reuters.com/article/us-health-coronavirus-tai wan-idUSKBN22R0HM; Jakob Wert, "ICAO Excludes Taiwan from Cooperation amid Coronavirus, Rejects Criticism," *International Flight Network,* January 28, 2020, https://www.ifn.news/posts/icao-excludes-taiwan-from-cooperation-amid-coro navirus-rejects-criticism/.

34. In comparing the UN's 2030 Sustainable Development Goals and the BRI, and echoing Beijing's rhetoric, Secretary-General António Guterres said that both initiatives can "create opportunities, global public good and win-win cooperation" and "deepen 'connectivity' across countries and regions: connectivity in infra-structure, trade, finance, policies and, perhaps most important of all, among peo-ples." António Guterres, "Remarks at the Opening of the Belt and Road Forum," Beijing, China, May 14, 2017, www.un.org/sg/en/content/sg/speeches/2017-05-14/ secretary- general's-belt-and-road-forum-remarks.

35. Maaike Okano-Heijmans and Frans-Paul van der Putten, "A United Nations with Chinese Characteristics?," Netherlands Institute of International Relations (Clingendael), December 2018, p. 14, https://www.clingendael.org/sites/default/files/ 2018-12/China_in_the_UN_1.pdf.

36. Anna Gross and Madhumita Murgia, "China Shows Its Dominance in Surveillance Technology," *Financial Times,* December 26, 2019, https://www.ft.com/cont ent/b34d8ff8-21b4-11ea-92da-f0c92e957a96; Robert C. O'Brien, "The Chinese Communist Party's Ideology and Global Ambitions," remarks delivered by National Security Advisor Robert C. O'Brien, Phoenix, Arizona, June 24, 2020, https://china. usc.edu/robert-o'brien-chinese-communist-party's-ideology-and-global-ambiti ons-june-24-2020.

37. The 2017 resolution is at "Resolution Adopted by the Human Rights Council on 22 June 2017," UN Human Rights Council, 35th Session, July 7, 2017, https://docume nts-dds-ny.un.org/doc/UNDOC/GEN/G17/184/81/PDF/G1718481.pdf.   See also "China's Party Paper Trumpets U.N. Rights Resolution as Combating West's Monopoly," *Reuters,* June 24, 2017, https://www.reuters.com/article/us-china-rights- un-idUSKBN19F0A8; "China on Behalf of 139 Countries Calls for Full Realization of Right to Development at UN," *Xinhua,* September 14, 2019, http://www.xinhuanet. com/english/2019-09/14/c_138390990.htm.

38. Catherine Putz, "2020 Edition: Which Countries Are for or against China's Xinjiang Policies," *The Diplomat,* October 9, 2020, https://thediplomat.com/2020/10/2020-edition-which-countries-are-for-or-against-chinas-xinjiang-policies/;   Natasha Kassam and Darren Lim, "How China Is Remaking the World in Its Vision," *The Conversation,* February 22, 2021, https://theconversation.com/how-china-is-remaking-the-world-in-its-vision-155377.

39. Eleanor Albert, "China Appointed to Influential UN Human Rights Council Panel," *The Diplomat,* April 8, 2020, https://thediplomat.com/2020/04/china-appointed-to-influential-un-human-rights-council-panel/.

40. Andréa Worden details the range of motivations and tactics driving PRC activity within the UNHCR in her "China at the UN Human Rights Council: Conjuring a 'Community of Shared Future for Humankind'?," in Nadège Rolland, ed., *An Emerging China-Centric Order: China's Vision for a New World Order in Practice,* NBR Special Report no. 87 (Washington, D.C.: National Bureau of Asian Research, August 2020), pp. 33–48, https://www.nbr.org/publication/an-emerging-china-centric-order-introduction/.

41. On China's evolving approach to UN intervention and use of force, especially in the 21st century, see Courtney J. Fung, *China and Intervention at the UN Security Council: Reconciling Status* (New York: Oxford University Press, 2019). See also Songying Fang, Xiaojun Li, and Fanglu Sun, "China's Evolving Motivations and Goals in UN Peacekeeping Participation," *International Journal* 73, no. 3 (2018): pp. 464–473, doi: 10.1177/0020702018795898.

42. "A Quick Guide to SCO and Its Military Cooperation," *CGTN,* June 5, 2018, http://english.scio.gov.cn/infographics/2018-06/05/content_51673238.htm. On "Peace Mission–2018," see Daniel Urchick, "What We Learned from Peace Mission 2018," *Small Wars Journal,* October 3, 2018, https://smallwarsjournal.com/jrnl/art/what-we-learned-peace-mission-2018.

43. The official English-language version of the SCO website is at http://eng.sectsco.org.

44. Data from the AIIB website, https://www.aiib.org/en/.

45. "亚投行：机遇与责任的复合体" [AIIB: Complex mix of opportunities and responsibilities], 新华 [*Xinhua*], May 5, 2015, http://www.xinhuanet.com/politics/2015-05/05/c_127766680.htm.

46. "Voting Powers," World Bank, March 1, 2021, https://www.worldbank.org/en/about/leadership/votingpowers.

47. Hai Yang, "The Asian Infrastructure Investment Bank and Status-Seeking: China's Foray into Global Economic Governance," *Chinese Political Science Review* 1 (2016): 754–778.

48. Background on BRICS appears at "History of BRICS," BRICS Information Portal, https://infobrics.org/page/history-of-brics. Details on the NDB are at its website: https://www.ndb.int/about-us/essence/history/.

49. Calculated from "Projects," New Development Bank, https://www.ndb.int/projects/list-of-all-projects/.

50. "The Beleaguered BRICS Can Be Proud of Their Bank," *The Economist*, September 29, 2019, https://www.economist.com/finance-and-economics/2018/09/29/the-bele aguered-brics-can-be-proud-of-their-bank.

51. "China's Twelve Measures for Promoting Friendly Cooperation with Central and Eastern European Countries," Cooperation between China and Central and Eastern European Countries, January 26, 2015, http://www.china-ceec.org/eng/zdogjhz_1/t1410595.htm.

52. Justyna Szczudlik, "China-Led Multilateralism: The Case of the 17+1 Format," in Rolland, *An Emerging China-Centric Order*, pp. 49–67.

53. "Introduction of the Secretariat for Cooperation between China and Central and Eastern European Countries," Cooperation between China and Central and Eastern European Countries, November 20, 2013, http://www.china-ceec.org/eng/msc_1/mscjj/t1411097.htm.

54. Andreea Brînză, "The '17 + 1' Mechanism: Caught between China and the United States," *China Quarterly of International Strategic Studies* 5, no. 2 (2019): 213–231, doi: 10.1142/S237774001950009X.

55. Stuart Lau, "China's Eastern Europe Strategy Gets the Cold Shoulder," *Politico*, February 9, 2021, https://www.politico.eu/article/china-xi-jinping-eastern-europe-trade-agriculture-strategy-gets-the-cold-shoulder/; Stuart Lau, "Lithuania Pulls Out of China's '17+1' Bloc in Eastern Europe," *Politico*, May 21, 2021, https://www.polit ico.eu/article/lithuania-pulls-out-china-17-1-bloc-eastern-central-europe-foreign-minister-gabrielius-landsbergis/.

56. "Summary of Probable SARS Cases with Onset of Illness from 1 November 2002 to 31 July 2003," World Health Organization, July 24, 2015, https://www.who.int/publicati ons/m/item/summary-of-probable-sars-cases-with-onset-of-illness-from-1-novem ber-2002-to-31-july-2003; "Still a Tough Battle to Win Fight against HIV," *China Daily*, November 29, 2018, http://www.chinadaily.com.cn/a/201811/29/WS5bffe9a5a 310eff30328be38.html.

57. *China's International Development Cooperation in the New Era* (Beijing: State Council Information Office, January 2021), http://www.xinhuanet.com/english/2021-01/10/c_139655400.htm.

58. Jacob Kushner, "China Is Leading the Next Step in Fighting Malaria in Africa," *The Atlantic*, July 4, 2019, https://www.theatlantic.com/international/archive/2019/07/china-tackles-malaria-kenya/592414/.

59. Ted Alcorn, "New Orientation for China's Health Assistance to Africa," *The Lancet* 386, no. 10011 (2015): 2379–2380, doi: 10.1016/S0140-6736(15)01232-5; Yanzhong Huang, "China's Response to the 2014 Ebola Outbreak in West Africa," *Global Challenges* 1, no. 2 (2017), doi: 10.1002/gch2.201600001.

60. Data on WHO contributions from "Contributors," World Health Organization, updated to fourth quarter 2020, http://open.who.int/2020-21/contributors/cont ributor. Figures are rounded. Note that a comparatively small proportion of WHO contributions are sourced from the assessed contributions of member states (12 percent in 2020). The remainder comes from a range of voluntary contributions from governments and nongovernment sources.

61. "Full Text: Speech by President Xi Jinping at Opening of 73rd World Health Assembly," *Xinhua*, May 18, 2020, http://www.xinhuanet.com/english/2020-05/18/c_139067018.htm.

62. "China Exported More Than 220 Billion Masks in 2020: Government," *Agence France Presse*, January 29, 2021, https://www.barrons.com/news/china-exported-more-than-220-billion-masks-in-2020-government-01611903004; Emma Newburger, "China Is Donating 1,000 Ventilators to Help New York in Coronavirus Fight," *CNBC*, April 4, 2020, https://www.cnbc.com/2020/04/04/china-is-donating-1000-ventilators-to-help-new-york-in-coronavirus-fight.html.

63. "China Pledges 300,000 Vaccine Doses for UN Peacekeepers," *Agence France Presse*, March 15, 2021, https://www.france24.com/en/live-news/20210315-china-pledges-300-000-vaccine-doses-for-un-peacekeepers.

64. Kurt M. Campbell and Rush Doshi, "The Coronavirus Could Reshape Global Order: China Is Maneuvering for International Leadership as the United States Falters," *Foreign Affairs*, March 18, 2020, https://www.foreignaffairs.com/articles/china/2020-03-18/coronavirus-could-reshape-global-order; Stephen M. Walt, "The Death of American Competence," *Foreign Policy*, March 23, 2020, https://foreignpolicy.com/2020/03/23/death-american-competence-reputation-coronavirus/.

65. Suisheng Zhao, "Rhetoric and Reality of China's Global Leadership in the Context of COVID-19: Implications for the US-Led World Order and Liberal Globalization," *Journal of Contemporary China* 30, no. 128 (2020): 233–248, doi: 10.1080/10670564.2020.1790900.

66. 杨洁篪 [Yang Jiechi], "积极营造良好外部环境（学习贯彻党的十九届五中全会精神）" [Actively build a favorable external environment (study and implement the spirit of the Fifth Plenary Session of the 19th CCP Central Committee)], 人民日报 [*People's Daily*], November 30, 2020, http://paper.people.com.cn/rmrb/html/2020-11/30/nw.D110000renmrb_20201130_1-06.htm?mc_cid=a7a519ea3d&mc_eid=f7f4a56338.

67. Jeff Nesbit, "China Finances Most Coal Plants Built Today—It's a Climate Problem and Why US-China Talks Are Essential," *The Conversation*, May 24, 2021, https://theconversation.com/china-finances-most-coal-plants-built-today-its-a-climate-problem-and-why-us-china-talks-are-essential-161332.

68. Lisa Williams, *China's Climate Change Policies: Actors and Drivers*, Lowy Institute for International Policy (July 2014), p. 6.

69. Sarah O'Meara, "China's Plan to Cut Coal and Boost Green Growth," *Nature*, August 26, 2020, https://www.nature.com/articles/d41586-020-02464-5.

70. Isabel Hilton and Oliver Kerr, "The Paris Agreement: China's 'New Normal' Role in International Climate Negotiations," *Climate Policy* 17, no. 1 (2017): 48–58, doi: 10.1080/14693062.2016.1228521.

71. "Full Text of Xi's Statement at the General Debate of the 75th Session of the United Nations General Assembly," *Xinhua*, September 23, 2020, http://www.xinhuanet.com/english/2020-09/23/c_139388686.htm. On carbon neutrality pledges, see Omri Wallach, "Race to Net Zero: Carbon Neutral Goals by Country," Visual Capitalist,

June 8, 2021, https://www.visualcapitalist.com/race-to-net-zero-carbon-neutral-goals-by-country/.

72. Azi Paybarah, "China Says It Won't Build New Coal Plants Abroad. What Does That Mean?," *New York Times,* September 22, 2021, https://www.nytimes.com/2021/09/22/world/asia/china-coal.html; Joe Lo, "President Xi Declares End to Chinese Support for New Coal Power Abroad," *Climate Home News,* September 21, 2021, https://www.climatechangenews.com/2021/09/21/president-xi-declares-end-chinese-support-new-coal-power-abroad/.

73. "China Dominates the Lithium-Ion Battery Supply Chain, but Europe Is on the Rise," BloombergNEF, September 16, 2020, https://about.bnef.com/blog/china-dominates-the-lithium-ion-battery-supply-chain-but-europe-is-on-the-rise/.

74. "China's PV Exports Could See Drop of 9% in 2020," *Global Times,* July 23, 2020, https://www.globaltimes.cn/content/1195371.shtml.

75. See, for example, Elsa B. Kania, *In Military-Civil Fusion, China Is Learning Lessons from the United States and Starting to Innovate,* The Strategy Bridge, August 27, 2019, https://thestrategybridge.org/the-bridge/2019/8/27/in-military-civil-fusion-china-is-learning-lessons-from-the-united-states-and-starting-to-innovate.

76. "Full translation: China's 'New-Generation Artificial Intelligence Development Plan' (2017)," Center for a New American Security Cybersecurity Initiative, August 1, 2017, https://www.newamerica.org/cybersecurity-initiative/digichina/blog/full-translation-chinas-new-generation-artificial-intelligence-development-plan-2017/.

77. Yujie Xue, "China Tops the World in AI Patent Filings, Surpassing the US for the First Time," *South China Morning Post,* November 26, 2020, https://www.scmp.com/tech/innovation/article/3111510/china-tops-world-ai-patent-filings-surpassing-us-first-time; Neil Savage, "The Race to the Top among the World's Leaders in Artificial Intelligence," *Nature,* December 9, 2020, https://www.nature.com/articles/d41586-020-03409-8.

78. Toru Tsunashima, "China Rises as World's Data Superpower as Internet Fractures," *Nikkei Asia,* November 24, 2020, https://asia.nikkei.com/Politics/International-relations/China-rises-as-world-s-data-superpower-as-internet-fractures; Ishan Sharma, "China's Catch-22 and the Fate of the World Wide Web," Responsible Statecraft, November 1, 2020, https://responsiblestatecraft.org/2020/11/01/chinas-catch-22-and-the-fate-of-the-world-wide-web/.

79. Eric Schmidt et al., *Final Report,* National Security Commission on Artificial Intelligence (March 2021), p. 25, https://www.nscai.gov/wp-content/uploads/2021/03/Full-Report-Digital-1.pdf; see also Graham Allison and Eric Schmidt, *Is China Beating the U.S. to AI Supremacy?,* Belfer Center for Science and International Affairs (August 2020), https://www.belfercenter.org/publication/china-beating-us-ai-supremacy.

80. Jinghan Zeng, "China's Artificial Intelligence Innovation: A Top-Down National Command Approach?," *Global Policy* (2021), doi: 10.1111/1758-5899.12914.

81. "IDC Forecasts Improved Growth for Global AI Market in 2021," International Data Corporation, February 23, 2021, https://www.idc.com/getdoc.jsp?containerId=prUS47482321.

82. Karen Kwon, "China Reaches New Milestone in Space-Based Quantum Communications," *Scientific American,* June 25, 2020, https://www.scientificameri can.com/article/china-reaches-new-milestone-in-space-based-quantum-communi cations/.

83. Zhang Zhihao, "Beijing-Shanghai Quantum Link a 'New Era,'" *China Daily,* September 30, 2017, https://usa.chinadaily.com.cn/china/2017-09/30/content_3 2669867.htm; Stephen Chen, "China Building the World's Biggest Quantum Research Facility," *South China Morning Post,* September 11, 2017, https://www.scmp.com/ news/china/society/article/2110563/china-building-worlds-biggest-quantum-resea rch-facility.

84. Rintaro Hosokawa, "China Beats US in Patent Filings for Second Straight Year," *Nikkei Asia,* March 3, 2021, https://asia.nikkei.com/Business/Technology/China-beats-US-in-patent-filings-for-second-straight-year.

85. "Triadic Patent Families," Organisation for Economic Co-operation and Development, accessed on February 6, 2022, https://data.oecd.org/rd/triadic-patent-families.htm.

86. Data in this paragraph also drawn from Soumitra Dutta, Bruno Lanvin, and Sacha Wunsch-Vincent, eds., *Global Innovation Index 2020: Who Will Finance Innovation?* (Geneva: World Intellectual Property Organization, 2020), https://www.wipo.int/ edocs/pubdocs/en/wipo_pub_gii_2020.pdf.

87. Valentina Pop, Sha Hua, and Daniel Michaels, "From Lightbulbs to 5G, China Battles West for Control of Vital Technology Standards," *Wall Street Journal,* February 7, 2021, https://www.wsj.com/articles/from-lightbulbs-to-5g-china-battles-west-for-control-of-vital-technology-standards-11612722698.

88. For example, "国家标准化体系建设发展规划 (2016–2020)" [National Standardization Construction and Development Plan (2016–2020)], 国务院办公厅 [Office of the State Council], no. 89, December 17, 2015, http://www.gov.cn/zhengce/ content/2015-12/30/content_10523.htm; "2020 年全国标准化工作要点" [Main points of national standardization work in 2020], 国家标准化管理委员会 [National Standardization Administration], no. 8, March 10, 2020, http://www.gov.cn/zhengce/ zhengceku/2020-03/24/5494968/files/cb56eedbcacf41bd98aa286511214ff0.pdf.

89. See a Chinese assessment of China Standards 2035 at "'中国标准2035'呼之欲 出,这才是中美科技竞争的关键" ["China Standards 2035" about to come out, this is the real key to China-U.S. technology competition], 智谷趋势 [ZG Trends], September 26, 2020, https://mp.weixin.qq.com/s/U07bu0YL7J0NQSGf732xgg?fbc lid = IwAR239LpawuFVM0mJAgf74ducrk3SaNiLvQHhvU9WxcIaIWLfF8kN cBZbkBE (English translation: Jeffrey Ding, "ChinAI #124: China Standards 2035— Coming Soon," *ChinaAI Newsletter,* December 21, 2020, https://chinai.substack. com/p/chinai-124-china-standards-2035-coming).

90. Adam Segal, "China's Vision for Cyber Sovereignty and the Global Governance of Cyberspace," in Rolland, *An Emerging China-Centric Order,* pp. 85–100. See also Maya Wang, "China's Techno-Authoritarianism Has Gone Global," *Foreign Affairs,* April 8, 2021, https://www.foreignaffairs.com/articles/china/2021-04-08/chinas-tec hno-authoritarianism-has-gone-global.

91. Xi, "Secure a Decisive Victory," p. 9.
92. Fu Ying, "在讲好中国故事中提升话语权" [Enhancing narrative power while telling China's story well], *People's Daily,* April 4, 2020, http://paper.people.com.cn/rmrb/html/2020-04/02/nw.D110000renmrb_20200402_1-09.htm; "Exclusive: Internal Chinese Report Warns Beijing Faces a Tiananmen-Like Global Backlash over Virus," *Reuters,* May 4, 2020, https://www.reuters.com/article/us-health-coronavirus-china-sentiment-ex/exclusive-internal-chinese-report-warns-beijing-faces-tiananmen-like-global-backlash-over-virus-idUSKBN22G19C. See also an essay by Zi Zhongyun, former director of the Institute of American Studies at the Chinese Academy of Social Sciences, translated by Geremie R. Barmé as "An Old Anxiety in a New Era: 1900 and 2020," China Heritage, April 23, 2020, http://chinaheritage.net/journal/1900-2020-an-old-anxiety-in-a-new-era/.

Chapter 7

1. Xi Jinping, "Enhance China's Cultural Soft Power," speech at the 12th group study session of the Political Bureau of the 18th CCP Central Committee, December 30, 2013, in Xi Jinping, *The Governance of China* (Beijing: Foreign Languages Press, 2014), n.p.
2. The Five Principles appear in "Agreement between the Republic of India and the People's Republic of China on Trade and Intercourse between the Tibet Region of China and India," Peking, China, April 29, 1954, https://digitalarchive.wilsoncenter.org/document/121558. The Bandung Conference of 1955 issued a declaration that included the Five Principles: "Final Communiqué of the Asian-African Conference of Bandung (24 April 1955)," https://www.cvce.eu/en/obj/final_communique_of_the_asian_african_conference_of_bandung_24_april_1955-en-676237bd-72f7-471f-949a-88b6ae513585.html.
3. Julia Lovell, *Maoism: A Global History* (New York: Alfred A. Knopf, 2019), especially chapters 4 through 8.
4. Jude D. Blanchette, *China's New Red Guards: The Return of Radicalism and the Rebirth of Mao Zedong* (New York: Oxford University Press, 2019); see also Lovell, *Maoism,* chapter 12.
5. See "Build Towards a Harmonious World of Lasting Peace and Common Prosperity," Statement by H.E. Hu Jintao, president of the People's Republic of China, at the United Nations Summit, New York, September 15, 2005, https://www.un.org/webcast/summit2005/statements15/china050915eng.pdf, and Zheng Bijian, "China's 'Peaceful Rise' to Great-Power Status," *Foreign Affairs* 84, no. 5 (2005): 18–24, https://www.foreignaffairs.com/articles/asia/2005-09-01/chinas-peaceful-rise-great-power-status; *China's Peaceful Development Road* (Beijing: Information Office of the State Council, December 2005), https://www.chinadaily.com.cn/english/doc/2005-12/22/content_505678.htm.
6. For a discussion of these concepts and the decision-making behind them, see Bonnie S. Glaser and Evan S. Medeiros, "The Changing Ecology of Foreign Policy-Making in

China: The Ascension and Demise of the Theory of 'Peaceful Rise,'" *China Quarterly,* no. 190 (2007): 291–310, doi: 10.1017/S0305741007001208.

7. Shaun Breslin, "China's Global Cultural Interactions," in David Shambaugh, ed., *China & The World* (New York: Oxford University Press, 2020), pp. 137–155.

8. "Xi Jinping's 19 August Speech Revealed? (Translation)," China Copyright and Media, November 12, 2013, https://chinacopyrightandmedia.wordpress.com/2013/11/12/xi-jinpings-19-august-speech-revealed-translation/. The Chinese-language version is available at "网传习近平8-19讲话全文" [Full text of Xi Jinping's 8-19 speech on the web], China Digital Times, November 4, 2013, https://chinadigitaltimes.net/chinese/321001.html.

9. "Xi Jinping's 19 August Speech Revealed? (Translation)."

10. "Full Text of Xi Jinping's 8-19 Speech on the Web" (author's translation).

11. See, for example, Xi Jinping, "Enhance China's Cultural Soft Power"; "Xi Calls for Better Fulfilling Missions of Publicity Work," *Xinhua,* August 22, 2018, http://www.xinhuanet.com/english/2018-08/22/c_137410956.htm; Cai Mingzhao, "提高 新闻舆论传播力,引导力,影响力,公信力" [Improve the power of news in communication, guidance, influence, and credibility], *Qiushi,* September 16, 2018, http://www.qstheory.cn/dukan/qs/2018-09/16/c_1123429161.htm. The author of the latter article was at the time the head of *Xinhua,* the Party's news agency.

12. Nadège Rolland, *China's Vision for a New World Order* (Washington, D.C.: National Bureau of Asian Research, 2020), p. 9.

13. Andrew Scobell et al., *China's Grand Strategy: Trends, Trajectories, and Long-Term Competition* (Santa Monica, CA: RAND, 2020), pp. 24–25.

14. Drawn from Xi Jinping, "Secure a Decisive Victory in Building a Moderately Prosperous Society in All Respects and Strive for the Great Success of Socialism with Chinese Characteristics for a New Era," speech delivered at the 19th CCP National Congress, October 18, 2017, section I, https://www.chinadaily.com.cn/china/19thcpcnationalcongress/2017-11/04/content_34115212.htm.

15. This term is also translated as "international discourse power." For a more in-depth analysis of the concept as it is discussed in China, see Rolland, *China's Vision for a New World Order,* especially pp. 7–13, and Johan Van de Ven, "Searching for China's International Discourse Power," China Trends by Institut Montaigne, August 2020, https://www.institutmontaigne.org/documents/china-trends/china-trends-6-EN-web.pdf. The following paragraph draws in part from this work.

16. 张忠军 [Zhang Zhongjun], "增强中国国际话语权的思考" [Thoughts on strengthening China's international narrative power], 国际视野 [*Theoretical Horizon*] (April 2014): 56–59.

17. The other two—the Central Organization Department and the Central Discipline Inspection Commission—are primarily focused inward on Party-related matters of personnel administration and member misconduct, respectively.

18. Breslin, "China's Global Cultural Interactions"; Rolland, *China's Vision for a New World Order; Hearing on the Long Arm of China: Exporting Authoritarianism with Chinese Characteristics,* before the Congressional-Executive Commission on China, 115th Congress, December 13, 2017, https://www.cecc.gov/events/heari

ngs/thelong-arm-of-china-exporting-authoritarianism-with-chinese-characterist ics; Anne-Marie Brady, *Magic Weapons: China's Political Influence Activities under Xi Jinping* (Washington, D.C.: Woodrow Wilson Center, September 18, 2017), https://www.wilsoncenter.org/article/magic-weapons-chinas-political-influence-activities-under-xi-jinping; Bates Gill and Linda Jakobson, *China Matters: Getting It Right for Australia* (Melbourne: Black Inc. / Latrobe University Press, 2017), chapter 4.

19. The following discussion on the three departments draws in part from Bates Gill, "The Party and External Relations," in Jacques deLisle and Guobin Yang, eds., *The Party Leads All: The Evolving Role of the Chinese Communist Party* (Washington, D.C.: Brookings Institution Press, 2022), chapter 14.

20. The ILD uses "International Department" as its official name in English. "International Liaison Department" is an accurate translation of the organization's name from the Chinese.

21. On the ILD's history and role through the mid-2000s, see David Shambaugh, "China's 'Quiet Diplomacy': The International Department of the Chinese Communist Party," *China: An International Journal* 5, no. 1 (March 2007): 26–54, doi: 10.1353/ chn.2007.0004.

22. Shambaugh, "China's 'Quiet Diplomacy,'" 31, 42.

23. The initial figures are from the website of the ILD, "Department Profile," https://www. idcpc.org.cn/english/Profile/profile/index.html. However, these figures appear to be somewhat dated and based on information from 2007. The more recent figures from 2002 to 2017 are meticulously documented and analyzed in Christine Hackenesch and Julia Bader, "The Struggle for Minds and Influence: The Chinese Communist Party's Global Outreach," *International Studies Quarterly* (2020): 1–11, doi: 10.1093/ isq/sqaa028.

24. Hackenesch and Bader, "The Struggle for Minds and Influence," 3.

25. Niel Thomas, "Proselytizing Power: The Party Wants the World to Learn from Its Experiences," MacroPolo, January 22, 2020, https://macropolo.org/international-liai son-department-ccp/.

26. Xi Jinping, "Working Together to Build a Better World," keynote address at the CCP in Dialogue with World Political Parties High-Level Meeting, December 1, 2017, http://www.bjreview.com/CHINA_INSIGHT/Special_Edition/201802/t20180212_ 800117836.html.

27. "Special Issue: The CPC in Dialogue with the World 2016," *China Insight*, October 19, 2016, https://www.idcpc.org.cn/english/chinainsight/201611/P02016112855375 7953157.pdf.

28. "中国共产党与世界政党高层对话会北京倡议" [Chinese Communist Party in Dialogue with World Political Parties High-Level Meeting Beijing Initiative], *Xinhua*, December 3, 2017, http://www.xinhuanet.com/world/2017-12/03/c_1122050 731.htm.

29. "Agenda of the CPC in Dialogue with World Political Parties High-Level Meeting," *NewsGD.com*, May 26, 2018, http://www.newsgd.com/news/2018-05/26/content_18 2022941.htm; "CPC to Dialogue with Political Parties in Africa," *China Daily*, July

14, 2018, http://www.chinadaily.com.cn/a/201807/14/WS5b49d12ba310796df4df6 782.html.

30. "First Dialogue on Exchanges and Mutual Learning among Civilizations Held in Beijing," International Department, Central Committee of the CPC, November 28, 2019, https://www.idcpc.org.cn/english/news/201912/t20191208_102119.html.

31. For details of the ILD's international activities, see https://www.idcpc.gov.cn (in Chinese) and https://www.idcpc.gov.cn/english/ (in English).

32. Hakenesch and Bader, "Struggle for Minds and Influence," 2.

33. Quoted from a list of formal ILD functions in Wang Fuchun, 外事管理学概论 [Introduction to foreign affairs administration] (Beijing: Beijing University Press, 2003), as translated by Shambaugh, "Quiet Diplomacy," 30–31.

34. Hakenesch and Bader, "Struggle for Minds and Influence," 2; see also David Shullman, ed., *A World Safe for the Party: China's Authoritarian Influence and the Democratic Response* (Washington, D.C.: International Republican Institute, 2021).

35. "The Extraordinary Meeting of Dialogue between CPC and Political Parties of Arab Countries Convenes," ILD, June 22, 2020, https://www.idcpc.gov.cn/english/news/202006/t20200630_139188.html.

36. "中国共产党与世界政党高层对话会北京倡议" [The Chinese Communist Party in Dialogue with World Political Parties High-Level Meeting Beijing Initiative] (in Chinese; translated to English by the ILD), December 3, 2017, https://language.chinadaily.com.cn/a/201712/04/WS5b20d2b9a31001b8257214af.html.

37. 中共中央对外联络部 [Central International Liaison Department], "深入学习习近平总书记对党的对外工作的重要思想,努力在党的对外工作中树立新的台阶情况" [In-depth study of General Secretary Xi Jinping's important thoughts on the Party's external work, strive to establish a new level in the Party's external work], 求是 [*Seeking Truth*], October 15, 2017, http://www.qstheory.cn/dukan/qs/2017-10/15/c_1121801004.htm.

38. James To, "Beijing's Policies for Managing Han and Ethnic-Minority Chinese Communities Abroad," *Journal of Current Chinese Affairs* 41, no. 4 (2012): 183–221, quotation on 186.

39. Xi quoted in "专设统战工作领导小组中央 '大统战' 思维升级" [Dedicated united front work leading small group: Upgraded thinking for the CCP's "Grand United Front"], 人民日报 [*People's Daily*], July 31, 2015, http://cpc.people.com.cn/xuexi/n/2015/0731/c385474-27391395.html (author's translation). In using this term, Xi is hearkening back to Mao Zedong, who famously said that united front work was one of three "magic weapons" that helped him win the Chinese Civil War (the other two were the Party itself and the CCP's Red Army).

40. On the background, mission, and activities of united front work, particularly domestically, see Gerry Groot, *Managing Transitions: The Chinese Communist Party, United Front Work, Corporatism, and Hegemony* (Abingdon: Routledge, 2004).

41. On united front work abroad, see Clive Hamilton and Marieke Ohlberg, *Hidden Hand: Exposing How the Chinese Communist Party Is Reshaping the World* (Melbourne: Hardie Grant Books, 2020), especially chapter 7; Alex Joske, *The Party Speaks for You: Foreign Interference and the Chinese Communist Party's United Front*

System, Australian Strategic Policy Institute Report no. 32 (2020), https://www.aspi. org.au/report/party-speaks-you; Alexander Bowe, *China's Overseas United Front Work: Background and Implications for the United States* (Washington, D.C.: U.S.-China Economic and Security Review Commission, August 2017), https://www.uscc. gov/research/chinas-overseas-united-front-work-background-and-implications-united-states; and Brady, *Magic Weapons*. On united front work targeting overseas Chinese, see James Jiann Hua To, *Qiaowu: Extra-Territorial Practices for the Overseas Chinese* (Leiden: Brill, 2015).

42. Gerry Groot, "The Expansion of the United Front under Xi Jinping," *China Story Yearbook 2015* (Canberra: Australia National University Press, 2016), 167–177; Peter Mattis and Alex Joske, "The Third Magic Weapon: Reforming China's United Front," *War on the Rocks,* June 24, 2019, https://warontherocks.com/2019/06/the-third-magic-weapon-reforming-chinas-united-front/.

43. Gerry Groot, "The CCP's Grand United Front Abroad," *Sinopsis,* September 24, 2019, 1. See also Alex Joske, "The Central United Front Work Leading Small Group: Institutionalising United Front Work," *Sinopsis,* July 23, 2019, 2, 4.

44. For more details on these measures, see Alex Joske, "Reorganizing the United Front Work Department: New Structures for a New Era of Diaspora and Religious Affairs Work," *China Brief* 19, no. 9 (2019), https://jamestown.org/program/reorganizing-the-united-front-work-department-new-structures-for-a-new-era-of-diaspora-and-religious-affairs-work/; Groot, "The CCP's Grand United Front abroad."

45. Joske, *The Party Speaks for You,* 10.

46. On the establishment and role of the United Front Work Leading Small Group, see Joske, "The Central United Front Work Leading Small Group."

47. "中共中央印发 '中国共产党统一战线工作条例（试行）'" [Central Committee of Chinese Communist Party issues "Regulations on Chinese Communist Party United Front Work (Trial)"], 新华社 [*Xinhua*], September 22, 2015, http://www.gov. cn/zhengce/2015-09/22/content_2937054.htm. On the impact of the regulations in strengthening united front work in China, see Ray Wang and Gerry Groot, "Who Represents? Xi Jinping's Grand United Front Work, Legitimation, Participation, and Consultative Democracy," *Journal of Contemporary China* 27, no. 122 (2018): 569–583, especially 578–579, doi: 10.1080/10670564.2018.1433573.

48. Bowe, *China's Overseas United Front Work,* 5.

49. A sampling of the research on expanding CCP united front work abroad would include Joske, *The Party Speaks for You*; Hamilton and Ohlberg, *Hidden Hand*; Bowe, *China's Overseas United Front Work*; Groot, "The Expansion of the United Front under Xi Jinping"; Groot, "The CCP's Grand United Front Abroad"; Brady, *Magic Weapons*; Thorsten Benner et al., *Authoritarian Advance: Responding to China's Growing Influence in Europe* (Berlin: Global Public Policy Institute, February 2018), https://www.merics.org/en/publications/authoritarian-advance.

50. "Regulations on Chinese Communist Party United Front Work."

51. John Dotson, "The United Front Work Department Goes Global: The Worldwide Expansion of the Council for the Promotion of the Peaceful Reunification of China," *China Brief* 19, no. 9 (2019), https://jamestown.org/program/the-uni

ted-front-work-department-goes-global-the-worldwide-expansion-of-the-council-for-the-promotion-of-the-peaceful-reunification-of-china/.

52. Kynge, "Inside China's Secret 'Magic Weapon.'"

53. Taksahi Suzuki, "China's United Front Work in the Xi Jinping Era—Institutional Developments and Activities," *Journal of Contemporary East Asian Studies* 8, no. 1 (2019): 83–98, doi: 10.1080.24761028.2019.1627714.

54. See, for example, Anne-Marie Brady, "On the Correct Use of Terms for Understanding 'United Front Work,'" *China Brief* 19, no. 9 (2019), https://jamestown. org/program/on-the-correct-use-of-terms-for-understanding-united-front-work/; Suzuki, "China's United Front Work," 93–94; Groot, "The CCP's Grand United Front abroad," 8.

55. On how the UFWD is gaining greater influence over PRC policy toward ethnic minorities, see Taotao Zhao and James Leibold, "Ethnic Governance under Xi Jinping: The Centrality of the United Front Work Department & Its Implications," *Journal of Contemporary China* 29, no. 124 (2019): 487–502, doi: 10.1080/ 10670564.2019.1677359.

56. From the China News Service website, http://www.ecns.cn (in English) and http:// www.chinanews.com (in Chinese).

57. Joske, *The Party Speaks for You,* appendix 2.

58. Xi's visit is covered in Zhuang Pinghui, "China's Top Party Mouthpieces Pledge 'Absolute Loyalty' as President Makes Rare Visits to Newsrooms," *South China Morning Post,* February 19, 2016, https://www.scmp.com/news/china/policies-politics/article/1914136/chinas-top-party-mouthpieces-pledge-absolute-loyalty; "Xi Jinping Asks for 'Absolute Loyalty' from Chinese State Media," *The Guardian,* February 20, 2016, https://www.theguardian.com/world/2016/feb/19/xi-jinping-tours-chinas-top-state-media-outlets-to-boost-loyalty. See also Philip Wen, "China's Propaganda Arms Push Soft Power in Australian Media Deals," *Sydney Morning Herald,* May 31, 2016, http://www.smh.com.au/business/mediaand-marketing/chi nas-propaganda-arms-push-soft-power-in-australian-media-deals-20160531-gp7 yz6.html.

59. David Shambaugh, "China's Propaganda System: Institutions, Processes, and Efficacy," *China Journal,* no. 57 (2007): 25–58, quotation on 26 (emphasis in original), doi: 10.1086/tcj.57.20066240.

60. Recognizing the negative connotation of "propaganda" outside of China, the Propaganda Department has since the early 2000s used "Publicity Department" as its official name in English. "Propaganda Department" is an accurate translation from the Chinese.

61. On the globalization of PRC media, see Sarah Cook, *China's Global Media Footprint: Democratic Responses to Expanding Authoritarian Influence,* National Endowment for Democracy, February 2021, https://www.ned.org/wp-content/uplo ads/2021/02/Chinas-Global-Media-Footprint-Democratic-Responses-to-Expand ing-Authoritarian-Influence-Cook-Feb-2021.pdf; Sarah Cook, *Beijing's Global Megaphone: The Expansion of Chinese Communist Party Media Influence since 2017,* Freedom House Special Report, 2020, https://freedomhouse.org/report/special-rep

ort/2020/beijings-global-megaphone; Daya Kishan Thussu, Hugo de Burgh, and Anbin Shi, eds., *China's Media Go Global* (Abingdon: Routledge, 2018).

62. These data are drawn from the Xinhua website (in Chinese), http://www.news.cn, and "新华社简介" [Introduction to Xinhua News Agency], http://203.192.6.89/xhs/zwfs.htm; the CRI website (in English),http://chinaplus.cri.cn; the *China Daily* website (in English), "About Us,"http://www.chinadaily.com.cn/e/static_e/about; and the CGTN website (in English), "About Us,"https://www.cgtn.com/about-us.

63. Mareike Ohlberg, "Propaganda beyond the Great Firewall: Chinese Party-State Media on Facebook, Twitter, and YouTube," Mercator Institute for China Studies, December 5, 2019, https://www.merics.org/en/china-mapping/propaganda-beyond-the-great-firewall. See also Lily Kuo, "China's Envoys Try Out Trump-Style Twitter Diplomacy," *The Guardian*, July 17, 2019, https://www.theguardian.com/world/2019/jul/17/truth-hurts-chinasenvoys-experiment-with-trump-style-twitter-diplomacy.

64. Sina Weibo has 462 million active monthly users. WeChat has over 1 billion active monthly users. See "Weibo," China Internet Watch, https://www.chinainternetwatch.com/tag/weibo/, and "WeChat (Weixin) User Statistics, Trends, and Insights," China Internet Watch, https://www.chinainternetwatch.com/tag/wechat/. Survey research by Wanning Sun and Haiqing Yu found that more than 60 percent of Mandarin speakers in Australia turned to their WeChat subscription accounts as their primary source of news and information. Wanning Sun, "How Australian Mandarin Speakers Get Their News," *The Conversation*, November 22, 2018, https://theconversation.com/how-australias-mandarin-speakers-get-their-news-106917.

65. Information on Twitter accounts drawn from email correspondence and data exchange with Bret Schafer, Alliance for Securing Democracy, German Marshall Fund of the United States, Washington, D.C., April 2020, and "Hamilton Monitored Accounts on Twitter," Alliance for Securing Democracy, German Marshall Fund of the United States, Washington, D.C., https://securingdemocracy.gmfus.org/hamilton-monitored-accounts-on-twitter/#china (accessed August 11, 2020).

66. Jeff Kao and Mia Shuang Li, "How China Built a Twitter Propaganda Machine Then Let It Loose on Coronavirus," *ProPublica*, March 26, 2020, https://www.propublica.org/article/how-china-built-a-twitter-propaganda-machine-then-let-it-loose-on-coronavirus; Tom Uren, Elise Thomas, and Jacob Wallis, *Tweeting through the Great Firewall: Preliminary Analysis of PRC-Linked Information Operations against the Hong Kong Protests* (Canberra: Australian Strategic Policy Institute, 2019), https://www.aspi.org.au/report/tweetingthrough-great-firewall.

67. Cook, *China's Global Media Footprint*, p. 2.

68. 左凤荣 and 刘勇 [Zuo Fengrong and Liu Yong], "发达国家怎样谋求国际话语权" [How developed countries obtain international narrative power], 北京日报 [*Beijing Daily*], February 29, 2020, http://www.cssn.cn/zm/zm_hwsc/202002/t20200229_5094770.shtml.

69. For an official interpretation of Xi Jinping Diplomatic Thought by the PRC foreign minister, see Wang Yi, "Study and Implement Xi Jinping Thought on Diplomacy Conscientiously and Break New Ground in Major-Country Diplomacy with Chinese

Characteristics," Ministry of Foreign Affairs of the People's Republic of China, July 20, 2020, https://www.fmprc.gov.cn/mfa_eng/zxxx_662805/t1799305.shtml.

70. Xi Jinping, "Transition to Innovation-Driven Growth," speech delivered to members of the Chinese Academy of Science and Chinese Academy of Engineering, June 9, 2014, in Xi, *Governance of China*, n.p. Xi voiced a similar message in a March 2013 address to People's Liberation Army delegates to the National People's Congress. See Daniel Tobin, *How Xi Jinping's "New Era" Should Have Ended U.S. Debate on Beijing's Ambitions*, Center for Strategic and International Studies (May 2020), p. 17 n. 77, https://www.csis.org/analysis/how-xi-jinpings-new-era-should-have-ended-us-deb ate-beijings-ambitions.

71. Xi Jinping, "Secure a Decisive Victory in Building a Moderately Prosperous Society in All Respects and Strive for the Great Success of Socialism with Chinese Characteristics for a New Era," speech delivered to the 19th CCP National Congress, October 18, 2017, pp. 21–22, http://www.xinhuanet.com/english/download/Xi_Jinp ing's_report_at_19th_CPC_National_Congress.pdf; Xi Jinping, "Follow the Trend of the Times and Promote Global Peace and Development," speech at the Moscow State Institute of International Relations, March 23, 2013, in Xi, *Governance of China*, n.p.

72. Xi, "Secure a Decisive Victory," 52–53.

73. Xi, "Secure a Decisive Victory," 53.

74. Yang Jiechi, "Study and Implement General Secretary Xi Jinping's Thought on Diplomacy in a Deep-Going Way and Keep Writing New Chapters of Major-Country Diplomacy with Distinctive Chinese Features," Ministry of Foreign Affairs of the People's Republic of China, July 17, 2017, https://www.fmprc.gov.cn/mfa_eng/wjdt _665385/zyjh_665391/t1478497.shtml. At the time of this speech, Yang was China's senior-most diplomat as a member of the Politburo and director of the CCP Central Foreign Affairs Leading Group.

75. Xi Jinping, "Let the Torch of Multilateralism Light Up Humanity's Way Forward," speech to the World Economic Forum, Davos, Switzerland, January 25, 2021, https:// www.fmprc.gov.cn/mfa_eng/zxxx_662805/t1848323.shtml.

76. On China's long-standing efforts to rein in human rights within the international governance system, see Rana Siu Inboden, *China and the International Human Rights Regime: 1982–2017* (Cambridge: Cambridge University Press, 2021).

77. "中华人民共和国和俄罗斯联邦外交部长关于当前全球治理若干问题的联合声明" [Joint statement between the foreign ministers of the People's Republic of China and the Russian Federation on several issues of contemporary global governance], 人民日报 [*People's Daily*], March 24, 2021, http://cpc.people.com.cn/n1/ 2021/0324/c64387-32058894.html. An English-language summary of the foreign ministers' meeting is at "Wang Yi Holds Talks with Russian Foreign Minister Sergey Lavrov," Ministry of Foreign Affairs of the People's Republic of China, March 23, 2021, https://www.fmprc.gov.cn/mfa_eng/zxxx_662805/t1863858.shtml.

78. On the national and international implications of China's online restrictions, see Harriet Moynihan and Champa Patel, *Restrictions on Online Freedom of Expression in China*, Chatham House Research Paper, March 2021, https://www.chathamhouse.

org/sites/default/files/2021-03/2021-03-17-restrictions-online-freedom-expression-china-moynihan-patel.pdf.

79. *International Strategy of Cooperation on Cyberspace*, Ministry of Foreign Affairs of the People's Republic of China, March 1, 2017, http://www.xinhuanet.com/english/china/2017-03/01/c_136094371.htm.

80. The English translation "China solution" is used in "Speech by H.E. Xi Jinping, President of the People's Republic of China at the Körber Foundation," Berlin, Germany, March 28, 2014, https://www.fmprc.gov.cn/mfa_eng/wjdt_665385/zyjh_665391/t1148640.shtml, and in Xi Jinping, "Stay True to Our Original Aspiration and Continue Marching Forward," speech to commemorate the 95th anniversary of the CCP, July 1, 2016, in Xi Jinping, *The Governance of China II* (Beijing: Foreign Languages Press, 2018), p. 17. The English translation "input" is in Yang, "Study and Implement General Secretary Xi Jinping's Thought on Diplomacy." The English translation "approach" is in Xi, "Secure a Decisive Victory," p. 9.

81. Xi, "Secure a Decisive Victory," p. 9.

82. For example, Xi, "Secure a Decisive Victory," p. 52.

83. Lutgard Lams, "Examining Strategic Narratives in Chinese Official Discourse under Xi Jinping," *Journal of Chinese Political Science* 23 (2018): 387–411, quote on p. 387, doi: 10.1007/s11366-018-9529-8.

84. For a discussion of how Beijing aims to promote certain values and norms to benefit the interests of the developing world—including China—over those of the developed world, see Timothy R. Heath, "China Prepares for an International Order after U.S. Leadership," *Lawfare*, August 1, 2018, https://www.lawfareblog.com/china-prepares-international-order-after-us-leadership.

85. Jessica Chen Weiss, "A World Safe for Autocracy?: China's Rise and the Future of Global Politics," *Foreign Affairs* 98, no. 4 (2019), https://www.foreignaffairs.com/articles/china/2019-06-11/world-safe-autocracy.

86. Robert C. O'Brien, "The Chinese Communist Party's Ideology and Global Ambitions," remarks delivered in Phoenix, Arizona, June 24, 2020, https://trumpwhitehouse.archives.gov/briefings-statements/chinese-communist-partys-ideology-global-ambitions/.

87. Joseph S. Nye Jr., *Soft Power: The Means to Success in World Politics* (New York: PublicAffairs, 2004), chapter 1; quotation from p. x.

Chapter 8

1. "习近平在中央党校（国家行政学院）中青年干部培训班开班式上发表重要讲话" [Xi Jinping delivers an important speech at the opening ceremony of a training session for middle-aged and young cadres at the Central Party School (Chinese Academy of Governance)], 新华社 [*Xinhua*], September 3, 2019, http://www.gov.cn/xinwen/2019-09/03/content_5426920.htm.

2. Xi Jinping, "Stay True to Our Original Aspiration and Continue Marching Forward," from a speech at a ceremony marking the 95th anniversary of the Chinese Communist Party, July 1, 2016, in *Xi Jinping: The Governance of China II* (Beijing: Foreign Languages Press, 2017), p. 36.

3. 王卫星 [Wang Weixing], "中国模式越来越具有影响力吸引力竞争力" [The China model wields more and more influence, attraction, and competitiveness], 人民政协报 [People's Political Consultative Conference], April 15, 2021, http://cppcc.china.com.cn/2021-04/15/content_77408025.htm.

4. William Zheng, "China's Officials Play Up 'Rise of the East, Decline of the West,'" *South China Morning Post,* March 9, 2021, https://www.scmp.com/news/china/diplomacy/article/3124752/chinas-officials-play-rise-east-decline-west.

5. Quoted in Chris Buckley, "'The East Is Rising': Xi Maps Out China's Post-Covid Ascent," *New York Times,* March 3, 2021, https://www.nytimes.com/2021/03/03/world/asia/xi-china-congress.html. These words appear to be attributed to Xi in authoritative accounts of his speech to the Fifth Plenum of the 19th Central Committee of the CCP in October 2020. See 董青 [Dong Qing], "在对外开放办学中贯彻全球治理观" [In opening the [Party] school to the outside world, have a global governance perspective], 学习时报 [*Study Times*], October 18, 2020, p. 3, http://152.136.34.60/html/2020-11/18/nw.D110000xxsb_20201118_2-A3.htm. For an in-depth analysis of PRC views on American decline, see Michael Swaine, "Chinese Views of U.S. Decline," *China Leadership Monitor* 69 (2021), https://www.prcleader.org/swaine-2.

6. "How It Happened: Transcript of the US-China Opening Remarks in Alaska," *NikkeiAsia,* March 19, 2021, https://asia.nikkei.com/Politics/International-relations/US-China-tensions/How-it-happened-Transcript-of-the-US-China-opening-remarks-in-Alaska.

7. "China's Xi Says Country Facing Period of 'Concentrated Risks,'" *Reuters,* September 3, 2019, https://www.reuters.com/article/us-china-politics-idUSKCN1VO11L. For the official PRC summation of this speech, see "Xi Jinping Delivers an Important Speech."

8. "Full Text: Speech by Xi Jinping at a Ceremony Marking the Centenary of the CPC," *Xinhua,* July 1, 2021, http://www.xinhuanet.com/english/special/2021-07/01/c_1310038244.htm.

9. "Global Indicators Database," Pew Research Center, updated March 2020, https://www.pewresearch.org/global/database/indicator/69; Julie Ray, "Image of U.S. Leadership Now Poorer Than China's," *Gallup,* February 28, 2019, https://news.gallup.com/poll/247037/image-leadership-poorer-china.aspx.

10. Jonathan McClory, *The Soft Power 30: A Global Ranking of Soft Power 2019* (London: Portland Communications, 2019), 38, 40, https://softpower30.com/wp-content/uploads/2019/10/The-Soft-Power-30-Report-2019-1.pdf.

11. Laura Silver, Kat Devlin, and Christine Huang, "Unfavorable Views of China Reach Historic Highs in Many Countries," Pew Research Center, October 6, 2020, https://www.pewresearch.org/global/2020/10/06/unfavorable-views-of-china-reach-historic-highs-in-many-countries/. Surveys conducted in Australia, Belgium, Canada,

Denmark, France, Germany, Italy, Japan, the Netherlands, South Korea, Spain, Sweden, the United Kingdom, and the United States.

12. Laura Silver, Kat Devlin and Christine Huang, "Most Americans Support Tough Stance Toward China on Human Rights, Economic Issues," Pew Research Center, March 4, 2021, https://www.pewresearch.org/global/2021/03/04/most-americans-support-tough-stance-toward-china-on-human-rights-economic-issues/.

13. "China," Gallup, n.d., https://news.gallup.com/poll/1627/china.aspx.

14. For an outstanding compendium of expert views on the difficulties in U.S.-China relations, see Jacques deLisle and Avery Goldstein, eds., *After Engagement: Dilemmas in U.S.-China Security Relations* (Washington, D.C.: Brookings Institution Press, 2021).

15. Malcolm Cook, "China's Polling Problems," Institute for Southeast Asian Studies, January 21, 2020, https://www.iseas.edu.sg/media/commentaries/chinas-polling-problems-by-malcolm-cook/; Natasha Kassam, *Lowy Institute Poll 2020,* Lowy Institute, June 2020, https://poll.lowyinstitute.org/files/lowyinsitutepoll-2020.pdf; Laura Silver, Kat Devlin, and Christine Huang, "Attitudes toward China," Pew Research Center, December 5, 2019, https://www.pewresearch.org/global/2019/12/05/attitudes-toward-china-2019/.

16. Sharon Seah et al., *The State of Southeast Asia: 2021* (Singapore: Institute for Southeast Asian Studies, 2021).

17. "习近平在中共中央政治局第三十次集体学习时强调　加强和改进国际传播工作 展示真实立体全面的中国" [At the 30th collective study session of the CCP Central Committee Politburo, Xi Jinping emphasized strengthening and improving international communication work to show a true, multifaceted, and comprehensive China], 新华社 [*Xinhua*], June 1, 2021, http://www.xinhuanet.com/politics/leaders/2021-06/01/c_1127517461.htm.

18. 杨洁篪 [Yang Jiechi], "在习近平总书记外交思想指引下不断开创对外工作新局面" [Under the guidance of General Secretary Xi Jinping's Thought on Diplomacy, continuously initiate a new phase in foreign affairs work], 中华人民共和国外交部 [Ministry of Foreign Affairs of the People's Republic of China], January 14, 2017, https://www.fmprc.gov.cn/web/zyxw/t1430589.shtml.

19. Jessica Chen Weiss, "China's Self-Defeating Nationalism: Brazen Diplomacy and Rhetorical Bluster Undercut Beijing's Influence," *Foreign Affairs,* July 16, 2020, https://www.foreignaffairs.com/articles/china/2020-07-16/chinas-self-defeating-nationalism.

20. Peter Gries, "Nationalism, Social Influences, and Chinese Foreign Policy," in David Shambaugh, ed., *China & the World* (New York: Oxford University Press, 2020), chapter 4.

21. See, for example, the essay by Huang Xianghuai (黄相怀), a senior researcher at the CCP Central Party School, titled "重视和加强党的意识形态工作" [Emphasizing and strengthening the Party's ideological work] and translated by Jude Blanchette, Center for Strategic and International Studies, August 13, 2020, https://www.csis.org/analysis/strengthening-ccps-ideological-work.

22. Gries, "Nationalism, Social Influences, and Chinese Foreign Policy," 65.

23. The challenge of "status signaling" to multiple domestic and foreign audiences in PRC foreign policy is a core insight in Xiaoyu Pu, *Rebranding China: Contested Status Signaling in the Changing Global Order* (Stanford, CA: Stanford University Press, 2019), especially chap. 3.

24. Luke Patey, *How China Loses: The Pushback against Chinese Global Ambitions* (New York: Oxford University Press, 2021); Richard McGregor, *Xi Jinping: The Backlash* (Melbourne: Penguin Books, 2019).

25. Michael R. Pompeo, "Communist China and the Free World's Future," remarks delivered at the Richard Nixon Presidential Library, Yorba Linda, California, July 23, 2020, https://2017-2021.state.gov/communist-china-and-the-free-worlds-future-2/index.html.

26. "Letter from Under Secretary Keith Krach to the Governing Boards of American Universities," U.S. Department of State, August 18, 2020, https://2017-2021.state.gov/letter-from-under-secretary-keith-krach-to-the-governing-boards-of-american-universities/index.html; Michael R. Pompeo and Betsy DeVos, "Joint Letter to State Commissioners of Education," United States Department of State, October 9, 2020, https://2017-2021.state.gov/joint-letter-to-state-commissioners-of-education/index.html.

27. "Clarity around Hanban Name Change," Confucius Institute U.S. Center, accessed March 15, 2021, www.ciuscenter.org/clarity-around-name-change.

28. Robert C. O'Brien, ed., *Trump on China: Putting America First: A Collection of Speeches Laying Out the Most Significant United States Foreign Policy Shift in a Generation* (Washington, D.C.: The White House, 2020), p. 2, https://trumpwhitehouse.archives.gov/wp-content/uploads/2020/11/Trump-on-China-Putting-America-First.pdf.

29. "Statement," Inter-Parliamentary Alliance on China, accessed February 7, 2022, https://ipac.global/statement/.

30. Steve Tsang, "Party-State Realism: A Framework for Understanding China's Approach to Foreign Policy," *Journal of Contemporary China* 29, no. 122 (2020): 304–318, quote on 305, doi: 10.1080/10670564.2019.1637562.

31. Tsang, "Party-State Realism," 310–316.

32. "U.S.-Japan Joint Leaders' Statement."

33. "Quad Leaders' Joint Statement: 'The Spirit of the Quad,'" The White House, March 12, 2021, https://www.whitehouse.gov/briefing-room/statements-releases/2021/03/12/quad-leaders-joint-statement-the-spirit-of-the-quad/; "Joint Statement from Quad Leaders," The White House, September 24, 2021, https://www.whitehouse.gov/briefing-room/statements-releases/2021/09/24/joint-statement-from-quad-leaders/. See also "Fact Sheet: Quad Leaders' Summit," The White House, September 24, 2021, https://www.whitehouse.gov/briefing-room/statements-releases/2021/09/24/fact-sheet-quad-leaders-summit/.

34. Alan Robles, "Philippines Won't Move an Inch on South China Sea, Duterte Tells Beijing," *South China Morning Post,* May 14, 2021, https://www.scmp.com/week-asia/politics/article/3133559/philippines-wont-move-inch-south-china-sea-duterte-tells-beijing; Bonnie S. Glaser and Gregory Poling, "China's Power Grab in the

South China Sea," *Foreign Affairs*, August 20, 2021, https://www.foreignaffairs.com/articles/china/2021-08-20/chinas-power-grab-south-china-sea.

35. Michael Crowley, "Biden Backs Taiwan, but Some Call for a Clearer Warning to China," *New York Times*, April 8, 2021, https://www.nytimes.com/2021/04/08/us/politics/biden-china-taiwan.html.

36. Lolita C. Baldor, "Sharp Jump in US Navy Transits to Counter China under Trump," *Associated Press*, March 16, 2021, https://apnews.com/article/politics-beijing-south-china-sea-china-taiwan-6e8129431137ef822344677092285dbd; "China Protests Latest US Navy Passage through Taiwan Strait," *Associated Press*, May 19, 2021, https://apnews.com/article/asia-pacific-china-taiwan-c663d4d0929398ff55086bcba 9ff9117.

37. Joel Wuthnow, "China's Inopportune Pandemic Assertiveness," *The Diplomat*, June 10, 2020, https://thediplomat.com/2020/06/chinas-inopportune-pandemic-assert iveness/.

38. Patey, *How China Loses*.

39. The Biden administration formally declared in March 2021 that "genocide and crimes against humanity occurred [in 2020] against the predominantly Muslim Uyghurs and other ethnic and religious minority groups in Xinjiang." See "2020 Country Reports on Human Rights Practices: China (Includes Hong Kong, Macau, and Tibet)," U.S. Department of State, March 30, 2021, https://www.state.gov/reports/2020-country-reports-on-human-rights-practicies/china/.

40. "China Announces More Tit-for-Tat Sanctions on U.S., Canadian Citizens over Xinjiang Criticism," *Radio Free Europe / Radio Liberty*, March 28, 2021, https://www.rferl.org/a/china-xinijang-tit-for-tat-sanctions-us-canadian-citizens/31173 466.html; Robin Emmott, "EU, China Impose Tit-for-Tat Sanctions over Xinjiang Abuses," *Reuters*, March 22, 2021, https://www.reuters.com/article/us-eu-china-sanctions-idUSKBN2BE1AI.

41. Catherine Putz, "2020 Edition: Which Countries Are for or against China's Xinjiang Policies?," *The Diplomat*, October 9, 2020, https://thediplomat.com/2020/10/2020-edition-which-countries-are-for-or-against-chinas-xinjiang-policies/. But see Jeffrey D. Sachs and William Schabas, "The Xinjiang Genocide Allegations Are Unjustified," *Project Syndicate*, April 20, 2021, https://www.project-syndicate.org/commentary/biden-should-withdraw-unjustified-xinjiang-genocide-allegation-by-jeffrey-d-sachs-and-william-schabas-2021-04.

42. "China: UN Experts Deeply Concerned by Alleged Detention, Forced Labour of Uyghurs," Office of the High Commissioner, United Nations Human Rights Council, March 29, 2021, https://www.ohchr.org/EN/NewsEvents/Pages/DisplayNews. aspx?NewsID=26957&LangID=E.

43. Lijian Zhao (@zlj517) (PRC Ministry of Foreign Affairs spokesperson), Twitter, October 30, 2019, https://twitter.com/zlj517/status/1189180972811472898.

44. "Trump Signs Tibetan Policy and Support Act into Law, Prompting Warnings from Beijing," *Radio Free Asia*, December 28, 2020, https://www.rfa.org/english/news/tibet/law-12282020181154.html.

45. The following data are drawn from "Changes in the Unification-Independence Stances of Taiwanese as Tracked in Surveys by Election Study Center, NCCU (1992-2020.12)," Election Study Center, National Chengchi University, January 25, 2021, https://esc.nccu.edu.tw/PageDoc/Detail?fid=7801&id=6963.

46. Hsu Szu-chien, *A Political Profile of Taiwan's Youth: Democratic Support, Natural Independence, and Commitment to Defense* (Washington, D.C.: Global Taiwan Institute, 2018), http://www.tfd.org.tw/export/sites/tfd/files/download/democracy_in_Taiwan_20180323_rev_Hsu3_04032018-1.pdf.

47. "2020 TFD Survey on Taiwanese View of Democratic Values and Governance," Taiwan Foundation for Democracy, October 16, 2020, http://www.tfd.org.tw/export/sites/tfd/files/news/pressRelease/Press_Release_2020_TFD_Survey_on_Taiwanese_View_of_Democratic_Values_and_Governance.pdf.

48. "Highlights of Xi's Speech at Taiwan Message Anniversary Event," *China Daily*, January 2, 2019, http://www.chinadaily.com.cn/a/201901/02/WS5c2c1ad2a310d91214052069_1.html.

49. "GDP, PPP (Current International $)—China, United States," World Bank, https://data.worldbank.org/indicator/NY.GDP.MKTP.PP.CD?end = 2019&locations = CN-US&start = 2008; Larry Elliott, "China to Overtake US as World's Biggest Economy by 2028, Report Predicts," *The Guardian*, December 26, 2020, https://www.theguardian.com/world/2020/dec/26/china-to-overtake-us-as-worlds-biggest-economy-by-2028-report-predicts.

50. Sui-Lee Wee, "China's 'Long-Term Time Bomb': Falling Births Stunt Population Growth," *New York Times*, May 10, 2021, https://www.nytimes.com/2021/05/10/china-census-births-fall.html.

51. Scott Rozelle and Natalie Hell, *Invisible China: How the Urban-Rural Divide Threatens China's Rise* (Chicago: University of Chicago Press, 2020).

52. *People's Republic of China: 2020 Article IV Consultation*, International Monetary Fund, December 2, 2020, https://www.imf.org/en/Publications/CR/Issues/2021/01/06/Peoples-Republic-of-China-2020-Article-IV-Consultation-Press-Release-Staff-Report-and-49992.

53. Min Ye, *The Belt Road and Beyond: State-Mobilized Globalization in China: 1998–2018* (New York: Cambridge University Press, 2020), chapter 8.

54. Mathieu Duchâtel, *The Weak Links in China's Drive for Semiconductors*, Institut Montaigne Policy Paper, January 2021, p. 7. See also Zhang Dan and Shen Weiduo, "China's Semiconductor IP Sector Accelerates Drive for Self-Reliance: Money Pours In, but Top Professional Talent Is Still Lacking: Analysts," *Global Times*, May 19, 2021, https://www.globaltimes.cn/page/202105/1223949.shtml.

55. Nicholas R. Lardy, *The State Strikes Back: The End of Economic Reform in China?* (Washington, D.C.: Peterson Institute of International Economics, 2019), chapter 5.

56. Jennifer Hillman and David Sacks, *China's Belt and Road: Implications for the United States*, Independent Task Force Report no. 79 (New York: Council on Foreign Relations, 2021), https://www.cfr.org/report/chinas-belt-and-road-implications-for-the-united-states/.

57. Daniel R. Russel and Blake H. Berger, *Weaponizing the Belt and Road Initiative* (New York: Asia Society, 2020), https://asiasociety.org/policy-institute/weaponiz ing-belt-and-road-initiative; Nadège Rolland, *China's Eurasian Century?: Political and Strategic Implications of the Belt and Road Initiative* (Washington, D.C.: National Bureau of Asian Research, 2017).

58. Ravi Prasad, "EU Ambassadors Condemn China's Belt and Road Initiative," *The Diplomat,* April 21, 2018, https://thediplomat.com/2018/04/eu-ambassadors-cond emn-chinas-belt-and-road-initiative/.

59. Kevin Acker, Deborah Brautigam, and Yufan Huang, *Debt Relief with Chinese Characteristics,* China Africa Research Initiative Policy Brief no. 46 (2020); Agatha Kratz, Allen Feng, and Logan Wright, *New Data on the "Debt Trap" Question,* The Rhodium Group, April 29, 2019, https://rhg.com/research/new-data-on-the-debt-trap-question/; Deborah Brautigam, "Misdiagnosing the Chinese Infrastructure Push," *The American Interest,* April 4, 2019, https://www.the-american-interest.com/2019/04/04/misdiagnosing-the-chinese-infrastructure-push/; Lee Jones and Shahar Hameiri, "Debunking the Myth of 'Debt-Trap Diplomacy,'" Chatham House, August 19, 2020, https://www.chathamhouse.org/2020/08/debunking-myth-debt-trap-diplomacy.

60. John Hurley, Scott Morris, and Gailyn Portelance, *Examining the Debt Implications of the Belt and Road Initiative from a Policy Perspective,* Center for Global Development Policy Paper 121, March 2018, https://www.cgdev.org/sites/default/files/examining-debt-implications-belt-and-road-initiative-policy-perspective.pdf; Luca Bandiera and Vasileios Tsiropoulos, *A Framework to Assess Debt Sustainability and Fiscal Risks under the Belt and Road Initiative,* World Bank Group Policy Research Working Paper 8891, June 2019, http://documents1.worldbank.org/curated/en/723671560782662 349/pdf/A-Framework-to-Assess-Debt-Sustainability-and-Fiscal-Risks-under-the-Belt-and-Road-Initiative.pdf.

61. Scott Morris, "A Reckoning for China's Opaque Overseas Lending," Center for Global Development, April 7, 2020, https://www.cgdev.org/blog/reckoning-chinas-opaque-overseas-lending.

62. Joshua Kurlantzick, "China's Digital Silk Road Initiative: A Boon for Developing Countries or a Danger to Freedom?," *The Diplomat,* December 17, 2020, https://thed iplomat.com/2020/12/chinas-digital-silk-road-initiative-a-boon-for-developing-countries-or-a-danger-to-freedom/.

63. "Carbis Bay G7 Summit Communiqué," The White House, June 13, 2021, https://www.whitehouse.gov/briefing-room/statements-releases/2021/06/13/carbis-bay-g7-summit-communique/.

64. Min Ye, "Adapting or Atrophying?: China's Belt and Road after the Covid-19 Pandemic," *Asia Policy* 16, no. 1 (2021): 65–95, doi: 10.1353/asp.2021.0004.

65. Philip Blenkinsop, "EU-China Deal Grinds into Reverse after Tit-for-Tat Sanctions," *Reuters,* March 24, 2021, https://www.reuters.com/article/us-eu-china-trade-idUSKBN2BF276.

66. Ryan Haas, "How China Is Responding to Escalating Strategic Competition with the U.S.," *China Leadership Monitor,* March 1, 2021, https://www.prcleader.org/hass.

67. Michael Beckley, *Unrivaled: Why America Will Remain the World's Sole Superpower* (Ithaca, NY: Cornell University Press, 2018), especially chapter 3.

68. James Reilly has shown in his research a range of cases where and why PRC economic leverage has succeeded or fallen short. See, for example, James Reilly, *Orchestration: China's Economic Statecraft across Asia and Europe* (New York: Oxford University Press, 2021), especially chapters 3 to 6; James Reilly, "China's Economic Statecraft in Europe," *Asia Europe Journal* 15, no. 2 (2017): 173–185, doi: 10.1007/s10308-017-0473-6.

69. *National Security Strategy of the United States* (Washington: The White House, 2017), p. 25, https://trumpwhitehouse.archives.gov/wp-content/uploads/2017/12/NSS-Final-12-18-2017-0905.pdf.

70. *Summary of the 2018 National Defense Strategy of the United States of America* (Washington, D.C.: Department of Defense, 2018), p. 2, https://dod.defense.gov/Portals/1/Documents/pubs/2018-National-Defense-Strategy-Summary.pdf.

71. On the actions taken by the Trump administration in 2020, see Bethany Allen-Ebrahimian, "Special Report: Trump's U.S.-China Transformation," *Axios,* January 19, 2021, https://www.axios.com/trump-china-policy-special-report-154fa5c2-469d-4238-8d72-f0641abc0dfa.html. On the "whole-of-government" approach, see O'Brien, *Trump on China.*

72. David E. Sanger, "Biden Expands Trump-Era Ban on Investment in Chinese Firms Linked to Military," *New York Times,* June 3, 2021, https://www.nytimes.com/live/2021/06/03/us/biden-news-today#biden-china-surveillance-order.

73. The quotation and a description of the bill are in "Chairman Menendez Announces Bipartisan Comprehensive China Legislation," United States Senate Committee on Foreign Relations, April 8, 2021, https://www.foreign.senate.gov/press/chair/release/chairman-menendez-announces-bipartisan-comprehensive-china-legislation.

74. On U.S. actions toward PRC telecommunications firms, see "Remarks of FCC Chairman Ajit Pai to the Center for Strategic and International Studies," Federal Communications Commission, January 5, 2021, https://docs.fcc.gov/public/attachments/DOC-369080A1.pdf.

75. "Timeline: U.S. Arms Sales to Taiwan in 2020 Total $5 billion amid China Tensions," *Reuters,* December 8, 2020, https://www.reuters.com/article/us-taiwan-security-usa-timeline-idUSKBN28I0BF; Melissa Conley Tyler, "Biden Wins Over Taiwan," *East Asia Forum,* June 29, 2021, https://www.eastasiaforum.org/2021/06/29/biden-wins-over-taiwan/.

76. Amy F. Woolf, *Conventional Prompt Global Strike and Long-Range Ballistic Missiles: Background and Issues,* Congressional Research Service, December 16, 2020, https://crsreports.congress.gov/product/pdf/R/R41464.

77. "Statement of Admiral Philip S. Davidson, U.S. Navy Commander, U.S. Indo-Pacific Command, before the Senate Armed Services Committee on U.S. Indo-Pacific Command Posture," U.S. Senate Armed Services Committee, March 9, 2021, https://www.armed-services.senate.gov/imo/media/doc/Davidson_03-09-21.pdf; Aaron Mehta, "Davidson Defends $27B Price Tag for Pacific Fund," *Defense News,* March 4,

2021, https://www.defensenews.com/pentagon/2021/03/05/indopacom-head-defe nds-pacific-fund-pricetag/.

78. Tsuruoka Michito, "Making Sense of Europe's Military Engagement in Asia," *The Diplomat,* March 23, 2021, https://thediplomat.com/2021/03/making-sense-of-euro pes-military-engagement-in-asia/; Dzirhan Mahadzir, "U.S. Begins Joint Exercise in Japan with French and Australian Navies," *USNI News,* May 13, 2021, https://news. usni.org/2021/05/13/u-s-begins-joint-exercise-in-japan-with-french-and-austral ian-navies.

79. "Joint Leaders Statement on AUKUS," The White House, September 15, 2021, https:// www.whitehouse.gov/briefing-room/statements-releases/2021/09/15/joint-leaders- statement-on-aukus/.

80. Scott L. Kastner and Margaret M. Pearson, "Exploring the Parameters of China's Economic Influence," *Studies in Comparative International Development* 56, no. 1 (2021): 1–27, doi: 10.1007/s12116-021009318-9.

81. 时殷弘, "美国及其他主要国家对华政策与未来世界格局," Pangoal Think Tank, November 17, 2020, https://mp.weixin.qq.com/s/EzZKIq-_2_qqUafee9QRwg, trans- lated by David Ownby as "The U.S. and Other Major Countries' Policies toward China and the Future World Configuration," Reading the China Dream, December 2020, https://www.readingthechinadream.com/shi-yinhong-future-world-config uration.html.

82. Xiaoyu Pu and Chengli Wang discuss the debate in China on these issues in "Rethinking China's Rise: Chinese Scholars Debate Strategic Overreach," *International Affairs* 94, no. 5 (2018): 1019–1035, doi: 10.1093/ia/iiy140. See also 时殷弘 [Shi Yinhong], "关于中国对外战略优化和战略审慎问题的思考" [Reflections on issues of strategic advancement and strategic prudence in China's foreign policy], 太平洋学报 [*Pacific Journal*] 23, no. 6 (2015): 1–5, doi: 10.14015/ j.ckni.1004-8049.2015.06.001; "Exclusive: Internal Chinese Report Warns Beijing Faces a Tiananmen-Like Global Backlash over Virus," *Reuters,* May 4, 2020, https:// www.reuters.com/article/us-health-coronavirus-china-sentiment-ex/exclusive-inter nal-chinese-report-warns-beijing-faces-tiananmen-like-global-backlash-over- virus-idUSKBN22G19C; Fu Ying, "在讲好中国故事中提升话语权" [Enhancing narrative power while telling China's story well], *People's Daily,* April 4, 2020, http:// paper.people.com.cn/rmrb/html/2020-04/02/nw.D110000renmrb_20200402_ 1-09.htm.

83. Emma Farge and Stephanie Nebehay, "Singaporean Defeats Chinese Candidate to Head U.N. Patent Office," *Reuters,* March 4, 2020, https://www.reuters.com/article/ us-un-election-wipo-idUSKBN20R17F.

84. Mary Hui, "China's Election to the UN Human Rights Council Revealed Its Shaky Global Status," *Quartz,* October 15, 2020, https://qz.com/1917295/china-elected-to- un-rights-council-but-with-lowest-support-ever/.

85. Colum Lynch, "U.S. State Department Appoints Envoy to Counter Chinese Influence at the U.N.," *Foreign Policy,* January 22, 2020, https://foreignpolicy.com/2020/01/22/ us-state-department-appoints-envoy-counter-chinese-influence-un-trump/.

86. "Senate Confirmation Hearing: Opening Statement Ambassador Linda Thomas-Greenfield," United States Senate Committee on Foreign Relations, January 27, 2021, https://www.foreign.senate.gov/hearings/nominations-012721; Edith M. Lederer, "Biden's Pick for UN Post Calls China a 'Strategic Adversary,'" *Associated Press,* January 28, 2021, https://apnews.com/article/joe-biden-biden-cabinet-linda-thomas-greenfield-diplomacy-china-ec8d520ff1a416b36603dba4e91507e2.

87. 何银 [He Yin], "联合国维和事务与中国维和话语权建设" [United Nations peacekeeping affairs and building China's peacekeeping narrative power], 世界经济与政治 [*World Economics and Politics*], no. 11 (2016): 40–61.

88. Richard Gowan, "China's Pragmatic Approach to Peacekeeping," Brookings Institution, September 14, 2020, https://www.brookings.edu/articles/chinas-pragmatic-approach-to-un-peacekeeping/.

89. "China Secured Bumper Trade Results with CEE Countries in 2020," *CGTN,* February 10, 2021, http://www.china-ceec.org/eng/zdogjhz_1/t1853326.htm. See also Reilly, *Orchestration*, chapter 4.

90. On these critiques and the mixed success of 17 + 1, see Ivana Karásková, Alžběta Bajerová, and Tamás Matura, *Images of China in the Czech and Hungarian Parliaments* (Prague: Association for International Affairs, March 2019), http://www.amo.cz/wp-content/uploads/2019/03/AMO_Images-of-China-in-the-Czech-and-Hungarian-Parliaments.pdf; John Varano, "China's 17 + 1 Initiative Stalls amid Security Concerns and Broken Promises," *The Strategist,* October 22, 2020, https://www.aspistrategist.org.au/chinas-171-initiative-stalls-amid-security-concerns-and-broken-promises/; Justyna Szczudlik, "China-Led Multilateralism: The Case of the 17+1 Format," in Nadège Rolland, ed., *An Emerging China-Centric Order: China's Vision for a New World Order in Practice*, Special Report no. 87 (Washington, DC: National Bureau of Asian Research, 2020), pp. 49–67.

91. Andreea Brînză, "How China's 17+1 Became a Zombie Mechanism," *The Diplomat,* February 10, 2021, https://thediplomat.com/2021/02/how-chinas-171-became-a-zombie-mechanism/. See also Stuart Lau, "China's Eastern Europe Strategy Gets the Cold Shoulder," *Politico,* February 9, 2021, https://www.politico.eu/article/china-xi-jinping-eastern-europe-trade-agriculture-strategy-gets-the-cold-shoulder/.

92. "Lithuania Mulls Leaving China's 17+1 Forum, Expanding Links with Taiwan," *LRT,* March 2, 2021, https://www.lrt.lt/en/news-in-english/19/1356107/lithuania-mulls-leaving-china-s-17plus1-forum-expanding-links-with-taiwan; Stuart Lau, "Lithuania Pulls Out of China's '17+1' Bloc in Eastern Europe," *Politico,* May 21, 2021, https://www.politico.eu/article/lithuania-pulls-out-china-17-1-bloc-eastern-central-europe-foreign-minister-gabrielius-landsbergis/.

93. Lucy Fisher, "Downing Street Plans New 5G Club of Democracies," *The Times,* May 29, 2020, https://www.thetimes.co.uk/article/downing-street-plans-new-5g-club-of-democracies-bfnd5wj57.

94. "习近平首提'两个引导'有深意" [The profound meaning of Xi Jinping's first mention of the "Two Guidances"], 人民网 [*People's Net*], February 20, 2017, http://politics.people.com.cn/n1/2017/0220/c1001-29094518.html.

95. "Designation of Additional PRC Propaganda Outlets as Foreign Missions," United States Department of State, October 21, 2020, https://2017-2021.state.gov/desi gnation-of-additional-prc-propaganda-outlets-as-foreign-missions/index.html; "Ofcom Revokes CGTN's Licence to Broadcast in the UK," United Kingdom Office of Communications, February 4, 2021, https://www.ofcom.org.uk/about-ofcom/lat est/media/media-releases/2021/ofcom-revokes-cgtn-licence-to-broadcast-in-uk.

96. Bates Gill, "China's Global Influence: Post-COVID Prospects for Soft Power," *The Washington Quarterly* 43, no. 2 (2020): 97–115, doi: 10.1080/0163660X.2020.1771041; Bates Gill and Yanzhong Huang, "Sources and Limits of Chinese 'Soft Power,'" *Survival* 48, no. 2 (2006): 17–36, doi: 10.1080/00396330600765377.

97. Peter Martin, *China's Civilian Army: The Making of Wolf Warrior Diplomacy* (New York: Oxford University Press, 2021), pp. 8–9.

98. See, for example, the extensive country case studies in Ties Dams, Xiaoxue Martin, and Vera Kranenburg, eds., *China's Soft Power in Europe: Falling on Hard Times* (The Hague: Netherlands Institute of International Relations, 2021), https://www.clin gendael.org/publication/chinas-soft-power-europe-falling-hard-times.

99. "West Feels Challenged by China's New 'Wolf Warrior' Diplomacy," *Global Times*, April 16, 2020, https://www.globaltimes.cn/content/1185776.shtml. On the role and motivations of China's diplomats, see Martin, *China's Civilian Army.*

100. On these developments see, for example, Jessica Brandt and Bret Schafer, "How China's 'Wolf Warrior' Diplomats Use and Abuse Twitter," Brookings Institution, October 28, 2020, https://www.brookings.edu/techstream/how-chinas-wolf-warr ior-diplomats-use-and-abuse-twitter/; Patrick Wintour, "France Summons Chinese Envoy after Coronavirus 'Slur,'" *The Guardian*, April 16, 2020, https://www.theg uardian.com/world/2020/apr/15/france-summons-chinese-envoy-after-coronavi rus-slur; Wisc. S. Res. 7, 2019–2020 Legislature, March 26, 2020, https://docs.legis. wisconsin.gov/ 2019/related/proposals/sr7.

101. Josep Borrell, "The Coronavirus Pandemic and the New World It Is Creating," European Union External Action Service, March 23, 2020, https://eeas.europa.eu/ headquarters/ headquarters-homepage/76379/coronavirus-pandemic-and-new-world-it-creating_en.

102. Patrick Wintour and Tobi Thomas, "China Loses Trust Internationally over Coronavirus Handling," *The Guardian*, October 28, 2020, https://www.theguard ian.com/world/2020/oct/27/china-loses-trust-internationally-over-coronavirus-handling.

103. See, for example, the work of Nadège Rolland, *China's Vision for a New World Order*, NBR Special Report no. 83 (Washington, D.C.: National Bureau of Asian Research, January 2020), https://www.nbr.org/wp-content/uploads/pdfs/publications/sr83_ chinasvision_jan2020.pdf; Daniel Tobin, *How Xi Jinping's "New Era" Should Have Ended U.S. Debate on Beijing's Ambitions,* Center for Strategic and International Studies, May 2020, https://www.csis.org/analysis/how-xi-jinpings-new-era-sho uld-have-ended-us-debate-beijings-ambitions; Nadège Rolland, "A World Order Modeled by China," testimony before the U.S.-China Economic and Security Review Commission hearing on the "China Model," March 13, 2020, https://www.

uscc.gov/sites/default/files/2020-10/March_13_Hearing_and_April_27_Roundt able_Transcript.pdf.

104. Liza Tobin, "Xi's Vision for Transforming Global Governance: A Strategic Challenge for Washington and Its Allies," *Texas National Security Review* 2, no. 1 (2018): 154–166, quotation on 157, doi: 10.26153/tsw/863.

105. Policy Planning Staff, Office of the Secretary of State, *The Elements of the China Challenge* (Washington, D.C.: U.S. Department of State, November 2020), p. 7, https://www.state.gov/wp-content/uploads/2020/11/20-02832-Elements-of-China-Challenge-508.pdf.

106. Robert J. Hanlon, "Thinking about the Asian Infrastructure Investment Bank: Can a China-Led Development Bank Improve Sustainability in Asia?," *Asia & the Pacific Policy Studies* 4, no. 3 (2017): 541–554, doi: 10.1002/app5.186.

107. Avery Goldstein, "China's Grand Strategy under Xi Jinping: Reassurance, Reform, and Resistance," *International Security* 45, no. 1 (2020): 164–201, doi: 10.1162/isec_a_00383. See also Natasha Kassam and Darren Lim, "Future Shock: How to Prepare for a China-Led World," *Australian Foreign Affairs*, no. 11 (2021), https://www.austr alianforeignaffairs.com/articles/extract/2021/05/future-shock.

108. Scott L. Kastner, Margaret M. Pearson, and Chad Rector, *China's Strategic Multilateralism: Investing in Global Governance* (Cambridge: Cambridge University Press, 2019).

109. Alastair Iain Johnston, "China in a World of Orders: Rethinking Compliance and Challenge in Beijing's International Relations," *International Security* 44, no. 2 (2019): 9–60, doi: 10.1162/ISEC_a_00360. See also Suisheng Zhao, "A Revisionist Stakeholder: China and the Post–World War II World Order," *Journal of Contemporary China* 27, no. 113 (2018): 643–658, doi: 10.1080/10670564.2018.1458029.

Conclusion

1. "习近平在中央党校（国家行政学院）中青年干部培训班开班式上发表重要讲话" [Xi Jinping delivers an important speech at the opening ceremony of a training session for middle-aged and young cadres at the Central Party School (Chinese Academy of Governance)], 新华社 [*Xinhua*], September 1, 2021, http://www.gov.cn/xinwen/2021-09/01/content_5634746.htm.

2. Richard McGregor and Jude Blanchette, "After Xi: Future Scenarios for Leadership Succession in Post–Xi Jinping China," Lowy Institute, April 22, 2021, https://www.lowyinstitute.org/publications/after-xi; Geremie R. Barmé, "Peak Xi Jinping?," *ChinaFile*, September 4, 2018, https://www.chinafile.com/reporting-opinion/viewpoint/peak-xi-jinping.

3. Adrian Zenz, "China's Domestic Security Spending: An Analysis of Available Data," *China Brief* 18, no. 4 (2018), https://jamestown.org/program/chinas-domestic-security-spending-analysis-available-data/.

4. Chris Buckley, "'The East Is Rising': Xi Maps Out China's Post-Covid Ascent," *New York Times,* March 3, 2021, https://www.nytimes.com/2021/03/03/world/asia/xi-china-congress.html; see also 黄相怀 [Huang Xianghuai], "重视和加强党的意识形态工作" [Emphasizing and strengthening the Party's ideological work], translated by Jude Blanchette, Center for Strategic and International Studies, August 13, 2020, https://www.csis.org/analysis/strengthening-ccps-ideological-work.

5. Kinling Lo and Kristin Huang, "Xi Jinping Says 'Time and Momentum on China's Side' as He Sets Out Communist Party Vision," *South China Morning Post,* January 12, 2021, https://www.scmp.com/news/china/politics/article/3117314/xi-jinping-says-time-and-momentum-chinas-side-he-sets-out.

6. 袁鹏 [Yuan Peng], "世界'百年未有之大变局'之我见" [My view on the world's "great changes not seen in a century], 现代国际关系 [*Contemporary International Relations*], no. 1 (2020). For other senior-level views of the "great changes," see "百年未有之大变局:重识中国与世界的关键" [Profound changes not seen in a century: The key to understanding China and the world], 探索与争鸣 [*Exploration and Free Views*] 1, no. 1 (2019): 4–31; "从大历史视野看百年未有之大变局" [Looking at the profound changes not seen in a century from a grand historical perspective], Central Commission for Discipline Inspection, May 14, 2020, http://www.ccdi.gov.cn/lswh/lilun/202005/t20200514_217207.html; and 袁鹏 [Yuan Peng], "新冠疫情与百年变局" [The new coronavirus epidemic and the once-in-a-century transformation], *Aisixiang,* June 17, 2020, available in English at Yuan Peng, "Corona Virus Pandemic," Reading the China Dream, accessed February 7, 2022, introduction and translation by David Ownby, https://www.readingthechinadream.com/yuan-peng-coronavirus-pandemic.html.

7. "习近平在中央党校 (国家行政学院) 中青年干部培训班开班式上发表重要讲话" [Xi Jinping delivers an important speech at the opening ceremony of a training session for middle-aged and young cadres at the Central Party School (Chinese Academy of Governance)], 新华社 [*Xinhua*], September 3, 2019, http://www.gov.cn/xinwen/2019-09/03/content_5426920.htm.

8. Bates Gill, "Bounded Engagement: Charting a New Era in Australia-China Relations," *Australian Financial Review,* March 14, 2019, https://www.afr.com/world/asia/bounded-engagement-charting-a-new-era-in-australiachina-relations-20190312-h1c9vf.

9. Steven Ward characterizes this phase in China's rise as one of "distributive dissatisfaction" and not radical revisionism in his *Status and the Challenge of Rising Powers* (Cambridge: Cambridge University Press, 2017), especially chapter 7.

Index